A Glorious Disaster

For God's sake, let us sit upon the ground
And tell sad stories of the death of kings.

—From *Richard II* by William Shakespeare

A Glorious Disaster

The first and final victory

In what Jerusalem's Muslim defenders took to be a prelude to surrender, monks and soldiers of the bedraggled First Crusade process around the city's forbidding walls with prayers and hymns, their enemies jeering at them from the walls. The following day, though vastly outnumbered, they took the city, the first and only crusade to gain its objective.

Details from the illustration
by Tom Lovell,
page 12,13

A.D. 1100 to 1300

The Crusades: blood, valor, iniquity, reason, faith

The Christians

THEIR FIRST TWO THOUSAND YEARS

Seventh Volume

CHRISTIAN HISTORY PROJECT
An Activity of SEARCH
The Society to Explore And Record Christian History

THE EDITOR:

Ted Byfield has been a journalist for sixty-two years and was a western Canadian news magazine publisher more than twenty-five. In 1973 he founded the *Alberta Report* news magazine and in 1988 *British Columbia Report*. A columnist for many years with Canada's *Sun* newspapers and sometime contributor to the *National Post* and *Globe and Mail* newspapers, he was a winner of the National Newspaper Award for spot news reporting while serving as a reporter for the *Winnipeg Free Press* in the 1950s. He was also one of the founders of the St. John's Anglican schools for boys, where he developed a new method of teaching history. In the 1990s he became editor of *Alberta in the Twentieth Century*, a twelve-volume history of his province of Alberta. He is the visionary behind the Christian History Project and served as general editor of the first six volumes. When the Project became insolvent in 2005, he formed SEARCH—the Society to Explore And Record Christian History—which has undertaken to publish volumes 7 through 12. Byfield is president of SEARCH and continues as general editor of the series.

THE COVER:

The cover illustration, by Glenn Harrington of Pipersville, PA, shows the dubbing of a young recruit into the Knights Templar, who with the Knights Hospitaller formed the backbone of the crusader armies in the Middle East. He is younger than crusaders are usually portrayed, intended to reflect the truth that it is young men, then and now, who do most of the fighting in most of the wars. Harrington had to reflect in the face the resolve, the faith, and the quiet fear that all sensible men feel as they prepare for battle. Harrington's paintings have been featured in such publications as *American Arts Quarterly*, *American Art Collector*, and *International Artists Magazine*. He has had numerous solo exhibitions in New York and Japan and has provided the covers for more than five hundred books.

SEARCH CANADA:

The Society to Explore And Record Christian History is incorporated under the Alberta Societies Act. It has been registered as a charity by the Canada Revenue Agency.

Directors:

Ted Byfield, Edmonton, Alberta, President
Douglas G. Bell, CA, Edmonton, Treasurer
Richard McCallum, Edmonton
Allen Schmidt, Chase, British Columbia

SEARCH USA:

The Society to Explore And Record Christian History is incorporated under the Societies Act of the Commonwealth of Virginia. The Society has been recognized by the Internal Revenue Service as a 501(c)(3) tax exempt organization, donations to which are tax deductible.

Directors:

Jaan Holt, Alexandria, VA, Chairman
Ted Byfield, Edmonton, AB, Canada, President
Christopher Gerrard, Rockville, MD, Treasurer
Douglas G. Bell, CA, Edmonton
George Kurian, Yorktown Heights, NY
Richard McCallum, Edmonton
Joe Slay, Richmond, VA
General Manager: Keith T. Bennett

The Glorious Disaster, A.D. 1100 to 1300, The Crusades: blood, valor, iniquity, reason, faith
being Volume 7 of the series: The Christians: Their First Two Thousand Years

Writers: Ross Amy, Virginia Byfield, Vincent Carroll, Ric Dolphin, Steve Hopkins, Jared Tkachuk, Joe Woodard
Illustrators: Stephen Fritz, Greg Harlin, Glenn Harrinton, Rob Wood,
Director of Research: Jared Tkachuk
Design Director: Dean Pickup
Art Researcher: Peter Henderson
Indexer: Louise Henein

Academic advisers: David J. Goa, director of the Chester Ronning Centre for the Study of Religion and Public Life, University of Alberta, Edmonton; Fr. James Hanrahan, former superior general of the Basilian Fathers and fellow of the Pontifical Institute of Mediaeval Studies; Dr. Nigel Hiscock, retired principal lecturer in architecture at the Department of Architecture of Oxford Brookes University; Fr. Brian Hubka, priest of the Roman Catholic Diocese of Calgary, Alberta; Dr. Dennis Martin, professor of historical theology, Loyola University, Chicago; John Moscatiello, a graduate cum laude from New York University; Dr. Eugene Teselle, emeritus professor of Church history and theology, Vanderbilt University, Nashville.

Research Readers: Greg Amerongen, Ross Amy, Clare Bennett, P. A. Colwell, Ross Cleary, Ben Coughlin, Francis Fast, Joseph Friesen, Louise Henein, Rick Hiebert, Micha Kennedy, Nicole Moeller, Dianne Penner, Robert Saunders, Jennifer Sawyer, Alita Voss, Jim Wainwright, Kathy Woodard, Tom Woodard

Style Control: Pro-Noun Editorial Services

Proofreaders: P. A. Colwell, Final-Eyes Communications

©The Society to Explore And Record Christian History.
203, 10441 178 Street, Edmonton AB, Canada T5S 1R5
Chairman and President Ted Byfield

Library and Archives Canada Cataloguing in Publication

    A glorious disaster : A.D. 1100 to 1300 : the Crusades : blood, valor,
iniquity, reason, faith / editor, Ted Byfield.

(The Christians : their first two thousand years ; 7)
Includes bibliographical references and index.
ISBN 978-0-9689873-7-7

    1. Church history--Middle Ages, 600-1500. 2. Crusades. 3. Christianity
and other religions--Islam--History--To 1500.
4. Islam--Relations--Christianity--History--To 1500.
I. Byfield, Ted II. Society to Explore and Record Christian History
III. Series: Christians : their first two thousand years 7

D157.G56 2008   270.4   C2008-904660-9
PRINTED IN CANADA BY FRIESENS CORPORATION

CONTENTS

ILLUSTRATIONS

The publisher, the Society to Explore and Record Christian History (SEARCH), is deeply indebted to the work of Paul Gustave Doré (1832-1883), some of which is published in this volume. The wood and steel engravings of the French illustrator graced hundreds of books in France and England. They covered both historical and geographic subjects as well many great works of fiction in both languages. His illustrations, while appreciated by a worldwide audience, were sometimes criticized as too "literal." He "gives us sketches in which the commonest, vulgarest external features are set down," complained the *Westminster Review*. Doré was, in short, ahead of his time, as his imaginary reenactment of events in the Crusades, many carried in this volume, amply evidence.

FOREWORD

The striking aspect of this volume is its focus on violence and war. Three chapters center on the Crusades and a fourth on the Mongol invasions. The latter, in terms of violence and mindless destruction, were far worse than all the Crusades put together. Nevertheless, most of the wars in the volume were instigated by Christian leaders, fought as Christian endeavors, and consequently dominated the Christian story in the twelfth and thirteenth centuries.

In considering the Crusades, two indisputable facts should be noted. First, they were not an attack; they were a counterattack. They are often presented as an unprovoked assault by avaricious Christians against the tranquil and irenic Muslim civilization in the Middle East. This is far from the truth. All the lands the Christians sought to conquer had been seized from them by Muslim armies that burst out of Arabia in the seventh and eighth centuries, as detailed in volume 5, *The Sword of Islam*. The Muslims occupied Spain, and then in the following three centuries, they ruled southern France for a time, Sicily, Greece, and southern Italy, and three times attacked Rome. It seemed obvious to the Christians that unless this aggression was stopped at its source, sooner or later Europe too would become Muslim.

Second, the Crusades did not work. As both a military endeavor and a religious one, they failed miserably and left eastern Europe wide open to the next Muslim attack, which came over the following three centuries. From this whole experience, the Christians could conclude that while they must resist Islamic aggression by force, they could not hope to overcome Islam itself in that way. If Christ is to conquer, it must be by love, not by violence.

Paradoxically, the same violent centuries also witnessed an astonishing outburst of Christian creativity. Throughout western Europe there appeared cathedrals and churches whose soaring height and staggering beauty have awed humanity ever since. This phenomenon, Gothic architecture, we have covered more in image than in words.

Meanwhile, a second conflict, which many would hold more pivotal to Christendom than the clash with Islam, raged in western Europe. It concerned the ultimate power to make the law. Should that power reside with what we would now call the secular authority, represented then by the emperor? Or should it reside with religious authority, represented in western Europe by the pope? Three chapters describe this ferocious dispute.

Is it relevant today? It most assuredly is. For the point at issue is the making of the law, and the problem, then and now, is that every law rests on or expresses some moral principle. So whose principles should the law embody? Behind all our "cultural" conflicts lies that essential question. Sooner or later it must be answered, and the answer will not be easily found.

Finally, one chapter centers on the remarkable Thomas Aquinas and his perceptive analysis of the relation between reason and faith. Here we see the first appearance of a generally neglected question. Why is it that the whole scientific revolution, which has transformed the world, arose exclusively in countries with Christian foundations? In the story of Thomas we get the beginning of the answer.

But this volume, like all its predecessors, is not a book about issues. It's about the people who made the issues and fought them. And in the Christian view, that is surely how it should be. Issues come and go. People live forever.

Ted Byfield

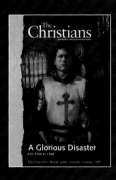

OUR THANKS GO OUT TO THE PEOPLE WHOSE FINANCIAL GIFTS TO SEARCH MADE THE PRODUCTION OF THIS VOLUME POSSIBLE

PATRONS OF THE PROJECT

L.R. Cable, Edmonton   John Hokanson, Edmonton   Jack Klemke, Edmonton
Sandy Mactaggart, Edmonton   Stanley A. Milner, Edmonton
Ray Nelson, Lloydminster, AB

THE TWELVE APOSTLES OF VOLUME 7

When Volume 7 was ready for the printer and all the expenses were paid, we were still $145,000 short — $82,000 to print the book and another $63,000 to mail it. So we urgently sought twelve people to donate $12,000 each to SEARCH. Here are the twelve who came forward:

Charles Allard, Edmonton   Richard Bird, Calgary   William L. Britton, Calgary
Margo S. Cable, Edmonton   Don Graves, Calgary   James K. Gray, Calgary
Dan Klemke, Edmonton   Masha Krupp, Ottawa   Herman Leusink, Edmonton
Hugh MacKinnon, Toronto   Ed Sardachuk, Calgary   Al Stober, Kelowna, BC

414 OTHER NORTH AMERICANS WHOSE GIFTS SAW THE VOLUME FINISHED

A-D

Marilyn Abel, Manassas VA; Harry Aldinger, Tuscaloosa AL; Rebecca Allf, Cincinnati OH; Robert Anderson, Duluth MN; William Anderson, Anderson IN; Katherine Asleson, Moline IL; Eckehart Augustiny, Gibsons BC; Larry Austin, Grosse Pointe Farms MI; Virginia Austin, Flankin NH; David Austring, Newmarket ON; Leslie Avila, Germantown TN; Paul & Arlene Bailey, Rocky Mountain House AB; Suzanne Balensifer Warrenton OR; Kenneth & Sherry Bannister, Edmonton; Rosie Barnes, Killeen TX; Gary & Cynthia Bartz, West Caldwell NH; Raymond Bates, Washougal WA; Wallace Bays, Wasilla AK; Muriel Beatty, Kingston ON; Dennis Becker, Aurora IL; Anthony Bell, Stow OH; Myfanwy Bently Taylor, Toronto; Isabelle Berg, Marshfield WI; Katherine Billesberger, Edmonton; Jeffery Bird, St. Louis Park MN; Trevor Birkholz, Fresno CA; Loren Blanchard, McMinnville OR; Sam Bledsoe, Topeka KS; Leda Boland, Vienna VA; David & Christine Boliver, Greenfield NS; Etna Bonertz, Drayton Valley AB; Helen Bosch, Abbotsford, BC; Dorothy Bright, Lemoore CA; Geoffrey & Philippa Broadhurst, Irvington NY; William Bronson, Great Falls MT; Timothy & Catherine Brush, Edinburg TX; Andrew & Mary Burghardt, Dundas ON; Mamie Burton, Fairfax VA; Vivian Butler, Aurora IL; Monti Byrd, Bellville TX; Sylvia Byrnes, Los Lunas NM; Barbara Campbell, Longmont CO; Don W. Calvert, Slave Lake AB; Robin Carpentier, Maryville TN; Clarence & Femmie Cazemier, Red Deer AB; James Christensen, Calgary; Judith Clark, Hoonah AK; Ross & Sally Cleary, Ottawa ON; Marie-Luise Cleaver, Vancouver WA; Patrick Clock, Kalama WA; Graham Cochenet, Loveland CO; Gerald Cole, Stettler AB; Robert Coleman, Everett WA; Stewart & Corinne Collin, Foremost AB; Charles Conrad, Spartanburg SC; Gwen Converse, Winter Haven FL; Tim Copeland, Bradford VT; Daniel Couch, Roseburg OR; Richard Coulter, Grabill IN; Barbara Crouse, Lebanon OH; John Crowell, Solvang CA; Marcia Crumley, Uniontown OH; Cynthia Curtis, Imperial MO; James da Silva, Norfolk VA; Russell Dart, Odon IN; Maurice De Putter, Richmond BC; Mark & Mary Deboer, Burlington ON; Richard DeFibaugh, Crozet VA; Helen Demario, Port Republic NJ; Craig & Olga d'Entremont, Edmonton; Jack & Marj Derochie, Claresholm AB; Descent of the Holy Spirit Ukrainian Orthodox Church, Regina SK; Doris Dewitt, Orlando FL; William Disch III, Georgetown TX; James Dixon, Orchard Park NY; Mark & Adele Dolan, Hudson WI; Stephen Dolson, Harker Heights TX; Mary Frances Doucedame, Newbury Park CA; Don Dowdeswell, Pennant Station SK; Fred Downing, Saint Paul MN; Richard & Susan Dubetz, Smoky Lake AB; Tim & Renee Dugan, Portland OR; John & Gisela Dyck, Brooks AB; Edward Dzielenski, Longmeadow MA

E-I

The Edmonton Sun, Edmonton; Cynthia Edson, Huntington Beach CA; Jerome Emerson, Dover DE; Susan Endo, Wai'anae HI; Hugo & Faye Engler, St. Albert AB; Elizabeth Epp, Surrey BC; Terry Epp, St. Albert AB; Andrew Erskine, Scotland AB; Caryl Evjen, Hampton MN; Willie Falk, Niverville MB; William Faulkner, Cape Coral FL; Greg & Lydia Fedor, Edmonton; Billie Ferguson, North Pole AK; Eileen Finlay, Edmonton; John Gerald Fischer, Jr., Inver Grove MN; Mark Fischer, Mokelumne Hill CA; Bill Flitcraft, Monroeville, NJ; Noral Ford, Livonia MI; Sandra Forslund, Spencer IA; Katherine Frankos, Raleigh NC; Carol Fraser, Calgary; Debra Friedli, Ada MI; Gloria Frieje, Glendale AZ; Donna Gallier, Alabaster AL; Evelyn Garrett, Somerset KY; Herman Gartner, Lloydminster SK; Eleanor Gasparik, Toronto ON; Margaret Gennaro, Canoga Park CA; Justin George, Edmonton; Rosemary Gerig, Auburn IN; Dianne Giffen, Federal Dam MN; Peggy Glover, Mount Pleasant SC; Sharon & Mike Good, Hudson OH; LuAnn Gorichanaz, Mukwonago WI; W. D. (Bill) Grace, Edmonton; Gary Lee Graves, Asheville NC; Barbi Gravdahl, Pequot Lakes MN; Melinda Gray, Lorain OH; Stephen Grenat, West Lafayette IN; David Groseth, Pasadena CA; Margaret Hailey, Pennsburg PA; Frank & Eva Haley, Edmonton; Monika Halwass, Calgary; Paul Hamlin, Leroy MN; James & Patrice Hammar, Saint Paul MN; Ron Hammersley, Germantown MD; William Harding, Lexington SC; Linda Hardy, Edmonton; George C. Harper, Nashville TN; Norman Harper, Fayetteville PA; Jakob Heckert, Ann Arbor MI; Ralph Hedlin, Calgary; Lisa Heilman, Oregon City OR; Henry Heinen, Picture Butte AB; Susan Helder, Volga SD; Robert Henderson, Apopka FL; John Herman, Colville WA; Adrian Herren, Gulf Shores AL; Jim & Marcia Hibbert, Calgary; Michael Hickey, Crystal Lake IL; Donald Highland, Fairless Hills PA; Sandra Hill, Flint TX; Colleen Hillery, Placentia CA; Gary Hinkle, Bremen IN; Peter Hinterkopf, Waynesboro PA; Ernest Hodges, Edmonton; Elaine Hogan, Curtice OH; Shirley Hogue, Winnipeg; John Holcombe III, Phoenix AZ; Cory & Nora Holden, Finland MN; Anthony & Frederica Holochwost, Lake Almanor CA; Barbara Holt, Vlg. of Lakewood IL; Jaan & Helen Holt, Alexandria VA; Paul & Ameda Hooley, West Liberty OH; Earle & Terry Hoover, Milwaukee OR; Natalia Hosker, Edmonton; Elaine Houger, Creston WA; Rev. Brian Hubka, Calgary; Rev. Harold Hunt, Maple Ridge BC; Kenneth Hutchinson, Calgary; Dudley Inggs, Saint Helena CA

J-M

Richard Jahn, Jr., Signal Mountain TN; Wallace & Pamela Jans, Medicine Hat AB; Allen Janzen, Castlegar BC; Timothy Jenkins, Warrenton VA; Alexei Jernov, Edmonton; Tammy Johnson, Plant City FL; Guy Johnston, Victoria BC; Steven Kachell, Tomah WI; Robert Kalbach, Farmington NY; Ed Kalish, Brewer ME; Dr. Ted Kasper, Edmonton; Olga Keaschuk, Edmonton; Patrick Kennedy, Troy OH; George Keys, Tobyhanna PA; Nagui Khouzam, Winter Garden FL; Donald Kiehl, Bothwell WA; Jonathan Kincaid, Lansing KS; Ryan & Ann Kingma, Oak Harbor WA; Thomas Knott, Baltimore MD; Mary Ann Koerschner, Iron Mountain MI; Peter Kogler, Seattle WA; Eric Kolkman, Ardrossan AB; Peter Kooiman, Red Deer AB; Phyllis Kopen, Edmonton; Barry Kossowan, Edmonton; Tom Krajecki, Aurora IL; Ronald Kratz, Nazareth PA; Walter Kunze, Jr., Arlington Heights IL; Anna Kuzmenko, Edmonton; Cheryl Kuziw, Sherwood Park AB; Pierre & Mary Labelle, Cochrane AB; Oakley Lambert, Columbus MS; Dorothy Lane, Athabasca AB; William Laprise, Elk Grove Village IL; Clara Larrivee, Moose Jaw SK; Tresa Latham, Orting WA; John Lawrence, Calgary; Valerie Mee Lee, Honolulu HI; Anthony Leenheer, Edmonton; Harry Lehman, Chambersburg PA; Charles Lester, Tallahassee FL; Michel Levasseur, Winnipeg; Cary Levjen, Hampton MN; Walter Lint, Winnipeg, MB; Joe Livernois, Prunedale CA; Betty Lloyd, Snellville GA;

Louise Lobdell, Carbon AB; Joseph Lorenz, San Leandro CA; Mark Losey, Champion AB; Dale Lunty, Edmonton; Terrence Lysak, Edmonton; Don Macdonald, Three Hills AB; William Mackay, Brentwood TN; Roger Mackin, Moose Jaw SK; John Maclean, Calgary; Patricia Maczko, Edmonton; Marcia Magnus, Alpine CA; Juanita Mahieu, Davenport IA; Yuri Makarov, Edmonton; Nina Malioujenets, Edmonton; Emmanuel Malterre, Calgary; James Martens, Wetaskiwin AB; Joseph Martens, Havelock ON; Doug & Peggy Matheson, Edmonton; Sharon Mayo, Arlington TX; Richard & Lorna McCallum, Edmonton; Neil McCaskill, Burnaby BC; Michael McClelland, Pleasanton CA; James McDermott, Fayetteville NC; David McGaffey, Auburn WA; Elizabeth McGeachy, Campbell River BC; Lydia McIntosh, Belden MS; Annie McIntyre, Langley BC; Audrey McKay, Blackfalds AB; Jim McKee, Woodville ON; Roger McKinstry, Ryan IA; Leonard Meador, Lynchburg VA; Thomas & Beverly Mercer, Langley BC; Milford Miller, Boise ID; Carol Milner, Spruce Grove AB; Charmaine Milner, Edmonton; Pauline Miyaluchi, Grand Lake CO; Mark Moesker, Wyoming ON; Celestine Montgomery, Edmonton; Charles C. Moore, Nashville TN; Phillip Moore, Mechanicsville VA; Dr. Fawzy & Cory Morcos, Edmonton; Allan & Lettie Morse, Ottawa ON; Sandra Moulton, Melfort SK; Sandra Mulcahy, Arlington TX

N-S

Robert & Barb Nagy, Mistatim SK; Julie Neumen, Albuquerque NM; Dr. Philip G. Ney, Victoria BC; Erland Nord, Edmonton; Esther S. Ondrack, Spruce Grove AB; Our Lady & St. Michael Anglican Catholic Church, Edmonton; John & Trudy Paetkau, Edmonton; Ed & Judy Palm, Drumheller AB; Helena Palynchuk, Hamilton, ON; Glenn C. Parker, Oakhurst CA; David Penner, Mission BC; Carol Pennings, East Lansing MI; Carol Perkins, Rainbow City AL; Helmut Peters, Calgary; Keith Peters, Kerrobert SK; Howard Pettengill, Jr., Indialantic FL; Melanie Phelps, Masaryktown FL; Joshua Phillpotts, Edmonton; Fred & Marilyn Pilon, Richmond Hill ON; Gregory Priatko, Eagle WI; Vanni Prichard, Barrow AK; Sophonia Rainey, Orango Park FL; Raise Inc., Edmonton; Rev. Gary & Cynthia Reynolds, Noblesville IN; Margaretta Rice, Victoria BC; JoAnn Rinke, Eastpointe MI; Sue Roat, Havana IL; Richard Robarts, Windsor ON; David Robbins, Alhambra CA; R. Terrance Rodgers, Glenn E. Rogers, Corpus Christi TX; Charleson WV; Patricia Rooke, Victoria BC; John Rosevear, Knowlton QC; Michael Roshko, Edmonton; David Rousseau, Haverhill MA; Nathan Rousu, Edmonton; Clay Rowe, Gadsen AL; William Rowland, San Diego CA; Carl Rusnell, Edmonton; Randy & Suzie Sage, Republic WA; Wesley Sandberg, Smithers BC; Ben & Dorcas Sawatzky, Spruce Grove AB; William Saxon, Guyton GA; Richard

Schalich, Mesa WA; Dan Schmidt, Aurora IL; Garry Schmidt, Bakersfield CA; Ted & Frieda Schmidt, Kelowna BC; Axel Schoeber, Victoria BC; Gary Schwab, Dousman WI; Alan Scott, Sugar Land TX; Seedsowers, Jacksonville FL; David & Barbara Sellick, Edmonton; Craig Sever, Gardnerville NV; Simon Sevgian, Scarborough ON; Arnold Sexe, Worthington MN; Regina Shanklin, Bloomfield NJ; Regina Sheafer, Cincinnati OH; Dr. David & Mary Skelton, Edmonton; Isak Skorohodov, Salem OR; John Sloan, Devon, AB; Gordon Small, Waynesville NC; Rod & Alma Small, Edmonton; Elmer Smith, Kelowna BC; Gordon & Alice Smith, Hayes VA; John Smith, Cameron Park CA; LaRosha & Cassie Smith, Alexandra VA; Walter Smith, Shreveport LA; Irwin Smutz, La Grande OR; Walter Sobole, Las Vegas NV; Joan St. Denis, Ladysmith BC; St Luke's Parish, Maple Ridge BC; John & Donna Stadt, Thetis Island BC; Chris Stafford, Calgary; Sarah Steffer, North Collins NY; Lynn Stegman, Red Deer AB; Donald Stevenson, Veno Beach FL; Alice Stewart, Lower Burrell PA; James Stolee, Edmonton; Lief & Elizabeth, Stolee, Edmonton; William Stubbs, Elkton MD; Doreen Sullivan, Edmonton; Sandra Louise Sully, Cary NC; David Sundheimer, Phoenix AZ; Randal Suttles, Franklin IN; Audrey Swinton, Edmonton; Gabrielle Szczerba, Troy MI

T-Z

Bill & Grace Tanasichuk, Edmonton; Bill; Teichroew, Carberry MB; Ben & Betty Thacker, Calgary; Henry Thalheimer, Kelowna BC; Cathy Thompson, Creston BC; William Thompson, Winston-Salem NC; Mary Thornton, Linden AB; Valerie Timm, Sauk Rapids MN; Lois Toedter, Bloomington MN; Peter & Elsie Toews, Olds AB; Raymond Toews, Glaslyn SK; Fran Towse, Edmonton; David Trice, Canaan IN; Jelle & Henrietta Tuininga, Lethbridge AB; Leslie Tulloch, Sault Ste. Marie ON; Gordon Unger, St. Albert AB; Peter & Rita Van Belle, Abbotsford BC; Hendrikus & Dianne Van Dalfsen, Leduc AB; John & Lucie Van De Laak, Linden AB; Harry Van Gurp, Belmont ON; Willy Van Randen, Jean Van Wieringen, Picture Butte AB; Surrey BC; Arie Van Wingerden, Sunnyside WA; Oliver Vandagriff, Ormond Beach FL; John & Teena Vant Land, Lethbridge AB; Dan Varnell, College Place WA; Melvin Veldhuizen, Loveland CO; Peter & Barbara Verhesen, Trochu AB; Hans Visser, Taber AB; Hank Vissers, Qualicum Beach, BC; Una Vogel, Leduc AB; Anthony Vogrincic, Edmonton; Ronald Vorpahl, Random Lake WI; Fred & Henny Vreken, Jordan ON; Frances Vuletich, Upper Sandusky OH; Lynda Wakelin, Regina SK; Eldora Warkentin, San Luis Obispo CA; Reginald

Watson, Sundre AB; Steve & Jayne Weatherbe, Victoria BC; Ted & Margaret Weaver, Okotoks AB; Alfred Weimann, Sherwood Park AB; Tom Wex, Omro WI; Ed & Mary Wiebe, Kelowna BC; Erwin Wiebe, Niverville MB; Vic Wiebe, Airdrie AB; Frank & Nancy Wiens, Selkirk MB; Allan Wierschke, Blackduck MN; John Wiggins, Grays Lake IL; William Williams, West Chicago IL; Jennifer Wilson, Roseville CA; Robert & Rosalie Wilson, Brooks AB; Fred Wisniecoski, Mt. Prospect IL; Dr. Paul Wittmer, Canton CT; Clint & Joy Wood, Denver CO; Charles Wootten, Matoaca VA; Gregg Wren, San Antonio TX; Elyssa Wright, Roanoke VA; Scott Wycherley, Townsend WI; Joyce Young, Vancouver BC; Sheila Ypma, Taber AB; Lois Zadler, Edmonton; David Zamudic, San Jacinto CA; Ingrid ZaZulak, St. Albert AB; Tim Zerface, Apple Valley MN; Philip Zodhiates, Waynesboro VA

No record of address: V. Francis; S Gardiner; Jeffrey Idep; Merideth Setty; Robert Tyrrell; Christine Van Boom

Finally SEARCH thanks all those hundreds of other supporters who by ordering extra copies of Volume 1 enabled us to convert some of our huge inventory into cash, all of which went into this volume's production.

In this nineteenth-century Gustave Doré lithograph, Peter the Hermit, standing in front of Pope Urban II, fires up a crowd in Clermont, France, with stories of Muslim atrocities to Christian pilgrims in the Holy Land. Though these two men probably didn't appear in public together as shown here, the artist is conveying how men were inspired to undertake an unprecedented challenge. The pope preached, "A barbarous people, estranged from God, has invaded the lands of the Christians," assuring those who took up the cross "imperishable glory."

CHAPTER 1

Centuries under attack, Europe's Christians finally strike back at Islam

Tens of thousands answer the pope's call for war, and after a grim fight through the Muslim lands, they take Jerusalem, then besmirch their victory

As the sun rose on that historic July 8 of the Christian year 1099, incredulous Muslims looking down from Jerusalem's forty-foot walls burst into hoots of scornful laughter. Some began derisively flaunting homemade crosses while others hurled down garbage. Below them, armor-clad Christian knights and soldiers, led by black-robed priests, were trudging along in procession, barefoot and singing hymns. This bedraggled contingent of twelve thousand men had besieged the Holy City for a full month, but now—starving, mad with thirst, sickened by the stench of dead and rotting oxen and horses, and outnumbered five to one by the city's sixty thousand well-fed defenders—they apparently had given up.

This sorry parade, the jeering crowds on the walls concluded, was clearly a procession of defeated penitents. The vaunted Christian resolve to reclaim the Muslim heartland for Jesus Christ had turned into a humiliating, costly, and catastrophic flop.

The Muslim jubilation was premature, however. After thirty-four months and two thousand arduous miles on the road, these battle-hardened soldiers and clergy had spent the past three days fasting and in prayer. Now they were about to launch one last do-or-die assault on Jerusalem's formidable defenses.

Their war with Islam went back much further than thirty-four months. Four long centuries had passed since conquering Muslim armies seized Christian Jerusalem and the whole Christian Middle East west of the Euphrates as well as Christian Egypt, Christian North Africa, and, finally, Christian Spain. Moreover,

1. Urban's speech quoted here has been taken from portions of four different chronicles. Each was written by an author who claimed to have heard the pope preach at Clermont but wrote his version years later. In his written correspondence during the months after his sermon, Urban repeatedly reiterated all of these themes.

for three of these intervening centuries, Christians had been defending Europe itself against recurring Islamic aggression. Sicily, southern Italy, and southern France had all experienced Muslim occupation; even Rome had been attacked three times. At length, therefore, Christians had taken the offensive in what they saw as a valiant and inescapable mission. If Islam were not destroyed at its source, they reasoned, one of its inevitably renewed attacks would ultimately succeed, and all Christendom would fall.

This Christian resolve carried with it an abiding problem, of course. Jesus had warned the apostle Peter that he who takes the sword will perish by the sword (Matthew 26:52). If Christianity as a whole took the sword, would Christianity therefore perish by it? That was one of the questions their blood-drenched journey to Jerusalem and the two-hundred-year endeavor that would follow from it were about to answer.

If any such qualms had been on the mind of Pope Urban II three years earlier, however, he didn't mention them when he addressed the dozen cardinals and archbishops, eighty bishops, and ninety abbots he had summoned to a historic church council in the town of Clermont, midway between Paris and the Pyrenees. Among other pressing things, the council was to deal with evidence of renewed problems in the East. Christian pilgrims to Jerusalem were increasingly being attacked. More serious still, Alexius I Comnenus, the Byzantine emperor, was begging for soldiers because the Muslim Seljuk Turks were threatening Constantinople, Christendom's last bastion in the East. To meet these ominous threats, Urban had formed a plan, and on November 27, 1095, some five hundred people gathered in a field near Clermont to hear him disclose it.

The scene would prove memorable. The French-born Urban, a tall, handsome, black-bearded man, courteous in manner and eloquent of speech, was known for

As the Muslims jeered from the walls of Jerusalem, the ragged, half-starved Christians trudged around the city singing hymns, looking the very picture of penitent defeat, their vaunted reconquest of the Holy Land evidently a complete failure. Two days later the fate of this motley group would be determined by history.

smooth diplomatic skill and unusual breadth of vision. He had been summoned from the monastery at Cluny to become cardinal-bishop of Ostia, then papal legate in France, and finally pope. Though stern and firm, he was also viewed as a collegial fellow who avoided controversy. This made the sermon he now delivered, which some historians deem one of the most influential speeches ever made anywhere, all the more astonishing.

Wearing a white robe and a black woolen vestment adorned with small crosses, Pope Urban addressed the throng from a stage beneath a glittering gold canopy. Around the stage clustered red-robed cardinals, purple-robed bishops, and a host of monks clad in either black or white. Beyond them, a restless crowd of barons and bourgeois, laymen and pilgrims, was suddenly still as the pope began to preach in vernacular Romance, the common language of the region.

"From the borders of Jerusalem and the city of Constantinople ominous tidings have gone forth . . ." he declared. "A barbarous people, estranged from God, has invaded the lands of the Christians. . . . These invaders are Turks and Arabs. . . . The empire of Constantinople is mutilated. . . . Until now this empire has been our rampart." He described the horrors perpetrated upon local Christians ("torturing and binding them, filling them with arrows . . . ravishing women") and pilgrims ("their bowels were cut open with a sword") and desecration of churches ("befouling altars with the filth out of their bodies"). The Muslims were "laying waste to the kingdom of God."[1]

Tall, handsome, and eloquent, Pope Urban II was arguably the most effective advocate of the whole crusading era. Both women and men wept as they heard him. This Renaissance statue of him stands at Clermont-Ferrand, in the Auvergne region of France, where he preached the First Crusade.

It was time, he declared, for Christendom to respond. The courageous knights of Europe must cease their petty, murderous private squabbles and begin to save their souls by restoring Jerusalem and the Holy Sepulchre to Christendom. "Come forward to the defense of Christ," he implored. Women wept, then men too, and gradually a murmur crescendoed into a mighty roar: "*Deus le vult! Deus le vult!*" ("God wills it!") Men drew and waved their swords. Urban raised his arms to still the tumult. "Let it be your battle cry when you go against the enemy: 'God wills it!' . . . And whosoever shall make his vow to go shall wear the sign of the cross on his head or breast." And he promised absolution and remission of sins to any who died en route or in battle.

As Urban finished, one bishop pushed forward and knelt before him, offering himself as spiritual guide to the mission; he had been a pilgrim, he said, and he knew what such a project would involve. This was Adhemar of Monteil, destined to become known as the army's most indispensable man. A trickle of barons followed him, then other senior clergy, then knights, freemen, and peasants. In the following weeks, all over Europe that trickle turned into a deluge. Word of the pope's appeal

Godfrey of Bouillon was of a family traditionally at odds with the papacy. Such, however, was the intensity of the crusade fever inspired by Pope Urban II that Godfrey, shown here in equestrian statuary at Brussels, would become one of the most enthusiastic generals, commanding the two hundred thousand soldiers who embarked for Jerusalem.

echoed and reechoed from the Pyrenees to Venice, on the Adriatic, from Sicily through Normandy to Scotland, across the Rhine and north to Sweden. It resonated from churches and public squares into castles and cottages. In a world where almost none but the wealthy traveled more than a few score miles from home in a lifetime, hundreds of thousands would embark on journeys ranging from fifteen hundred to more than two thousand miles—knights riding horses but most men walking.

The church's vast infrastructure was thrown behind the movement. Couriers rode from abbey to abbey while from monasteries monks reached out to freemen and peasants. The heralds wore crosses of red cloth and explained that anyone taking part would be granted indulgence from all penance for three years. The eloquent Urban labored tirelessly, moving from a Christmas sermon at Limoges to Poitiers in the Loire Valley, on through southern France, then over the Alps into Lombardy and eventually back to the Rhineland. More pledges came in from key nobles: Count Hugh of Vermandois, brother of the excommunicate king of France, Philip; Count Stephen of Blois, whose son would become king of England; more remarkable still, men like Godfrey of Bouillon, whose family had been traditional foes of the papacy. Europe had never seen anything like it. Within a year nearly two hundred thousand individuals of every social stripe would uproot their lives to embark on perilous journeys into the unknown.

A day after Pope Urban's rousing speech at Clermont, Count Raymond of Toulouse, the battle-scarred commander of thousands of soldiers and the most powerful noble in what would one day become southern France, took up the cross. Raymond, shown here in this nineteenth-century painting by Merry-Joseph Blondel, remained unhappy at the pope's refusal to make him supreme commander of the crusade.

Why did they do it? For most, rich and poor, it required notable sacrifice. For example, Duke Robert of Normandy, eldest son of William the Conqueror, mortgaged his entire duchy to raise money for horses, armor, provisions, and weapons for himself and his vassals. For a few land-poor knights like Bohemond of Taranto and Baldwin of Boulogne, eager to acquire an estate, it might mean material gain. But to every one of them it offered a share in the noblest cause they could imagine and an unparalleled adventure. Besides—and this was no small matter—there was the papal promise. For three years they need not fear the judgment of God. Their sins would be forgiven. This was not, in fact, what Urban had promised, but it is plainly the way many men took it.[2]

Urban's reasons were likewise various. The persecution of Christian pilgrims was well established, and his concern for the Eastern Empire was certainly genuine. After conquering Armenia, the Muslim Seljuk Turks had trounced the Byzantines at Manzikert in 1071 (see volume 6, pages 276–278), had taken Antioch in 1085, and now occupied Nicea, a few short hours by ship from Constantinople. But while Alexius wanted "soldiers," he had never envisaged the avalanche that was about to descend upon him. However, as Urban well knew, the greatest benefit for the church was this: the crusade, as it came to be called, would unite a Christendom torn by feudal strife, and it would be Rome and the papacy that did the uniting.

2. At the Council of Clermont Urban had granted the same full remission from the canonical penalties of sin that was gained by pilgrims to Jerusalem. Its propaganda force would probably have remained limited if persons had adhered to the Clermont decree, whereby the armed pilgrimage was merely a commutation for the penitential exercises imposed by the church. "However," notes Hubert Jedin in his *History of the Church*, "the preaching of the crusade, now getting under way and increasingly eluding the supervision of the Church, probably disregarded the moderate decree of the council and held out to the crusaders the prospect of a 'plenary indulgence,' that is, the remission of all penalties for sin that were to be expected from God either in this life or the next, and in this connection there may well have been mention occasionally of forgiveness of sins in quite a crude way."

The mad march
of the little people

After the smelly spellbinder Peter the Hermit calls for a common man's crusade,
uncontrollable hordes loot their way across Europe to a death far short of Jerusalem

In appearance he was decidedly uncharismatic. A short, swarthy man with a long, homely face rather like a mule's, he favored a filthy cape and was invariably barefoot. He also smelled. Nevertheless, he was the most powerful recruiter of the First Crusade, one of its many problems, and possibly its worst embarrassment.

Peter the Hermit, they called him. An itinerant monk born somewhere near Amiens, in France, the fiery evangelist ate neither bread nor meat, but he did eat fish and drink wine. Most significantly, he was an impassioned and riveting preacher who believed that Christians must at all costs rescue the Holy Land. "Whatever he said or did," wrote contemporary Guibert of Nogent, "it seemed like something half-divine." And wherever he went, men and women left their homes to follow him.

Astride his donkey, Peter galvanized much of northern Europe in what became known as the Peasants' Crusade, a collective term for five large bands of enthusiasts who left separately from Germany in the late spring and early summer of 1096. Each intended to march to Jerusalem by way of Constantinople. Some made it. Most perished and were never heard of again.

Initially, recruiting for the Crusades did not go well in Germany. The feud between Holy Roman Emperor Henry IV and the papacy (volume 6, chapter 3) kept high-ranking German nobles from forming a regional army like those in France and southern Italy. As a consequence, leadership and organization splintered among lesser nobles and clergy. Knights did take part, along with many prosperous middle-class freeholders and townsmen. But the German contribution consisted principally of arms-bearing peasants beyond the control of the pope, the barons, the clergy, the knights, or anybody else. Apart, that is, from Peter, who, while he could certainly inspire, could not control anything.

Peter began drawing crowds and followers in the central French province of Berry in December 1095. His appeal was apocalyptic, populist, and visionary, in contrast to the more theological message of Pope Urban and his bishops, who talked church authority and penance. Peter promised forgiveness. Many of the poorest believed he would lead them to the New Jerusalem and an earthly paradise of milk and honey.

Over three months he gathered more disciples in the countryside of Orleanais, Champagne, and Lorraine and then Aachen and the cities around the Meuse River. In mid-April he reached Cologne, a wealthy center where he hoped to attract more nobles. There his French followers, who had been traipsing along with him, grew impatient. Several thousand set out immediately on the road to Hungary under one of the few baronial devotees, Walter-sans-Avoir of Boissy. A few days later Peter followed Walter with more than fifteen thousand. Although incidents of stealing food, misunderstandings of local customs, absence of authority and discipline, and general unruliness led to bloodshed in Hungary and Bulgaria, by August both groups had arrived in Constantinople.

After these forces departed, three other armies coalesced in Germany. These inaugurated their crusades by attacking the Jews—inspired by Peter's assertions of Christian superiority and his emphasis on the need to avenge Christ Crucified, and in spite of the efforts of the bishops in many cities to prevent the slaughter. Most notorious were the Rhinelanders and Swabians under Emich of Leiningen, who began their massacres at Speyer, presided over more pogroms at Worms and Mainz (where they were joined by recruits from Lorraine, England, and France), and then killed more Jews in Cologne, Trier, and Metz. Unlike the other forces, these included five German and French counts and their knights.

A second army of Saxons and Bohemians under a priest named Volkmar conducted pogroms in Magdeburg, Wesel, and Prague. In northern Germany a fifth army formed under a Rhineland priest named Gottschalk. These massacred Jews in Bavaria at Regensburg. All contended that because the Jews had a hand in crucifying Christ, they were as pernicious as the Seljuk Turks who now held Jerusalem. They also complained that Jews were charging unfair interest on loans to crusaders.

None of these three armies made it to Constantinople because none could pay for food and the Hungarians would not tolerate their pillaging. Volkmar's notoriously unruly force was the first to enter Hungary but was massacred at Nitra (now in Slovakia), the first city it reached. Gottschalk's group arrived next, similarly ill behaved and violently abusive in pillaging. The Hungarians slaughtered them at Stuhlweissenburg. Finally, Emich's army with its five counts found Wieselburg's gates locked against them at the Hungarian border. They set up a siege, but when the Hungarians counterattacked, the entire contingent ingloriously fled.

Meanwhile, the mobs led by Peter and Walter accomplished little more. Although Byzantine Emperor Alexius I greeted them with courtesy and

In this nineteenth-century painting by Eugenio Lucas Velazquez, a train of peasant crusaders snakes its way through the European countryside, where they took their frustration out on the Jews. Hungarians, exasperated by their pillaging, drove many back home, and few actually made it much past Constantinople, where an ill-advised attack on the Turks results in their death or enslavement.

gave them food, he kept the horde safely outside Constantinople, then hurriedly ferried them across the Bosporus to Helenopolis, just thirty miles from the Turkish capital of Nicea. There they were to await the professional armies of the First Crusade.

But as food supplies dwindled, quarreling began. The Germans and Italians broke away under an Italian named Rainald, the French under Geoffrey Burel. The two factions vied in raiding the countryside, killing, among others, local Christians. Finally, while Peter was back in Constantinople seeking further material assistance, the Rainald and Burel sides taunted each other into a disastrous decision: together they would attack the Turks.

Vastly outnumbered and with only five hundred mounted warriors, the whole throng was ambushed. Many thousands were slaughtered or taken into slavery. Some three thousand took refuge in an abandoned castle until rescued by Byzantine soldiers. Thus ended the Peasants' Crusade, victim of inexperience, ill discipline, and hopelessly inadequate provisioning.

Some few survivors joined the armies of the First Crusade coming up behind them. Fewer still eventually made it to Jerusalem. One of the latter was Peter himself. While he played an insignificant role in the fighting, his fiery speech is credited with rousing the starving crusaders to take Antioch, and he is said to have led the penitential procession around Jerusalem prior to its capture. Albert of Aix records that he died in 1131 as prior of a Church of the Holy Sepulchre that he had founded in France. ∎

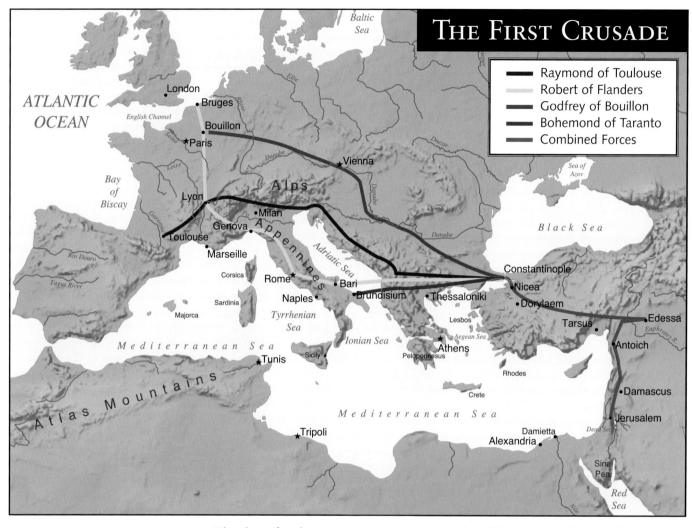

Raymond of Toulouse
Robert of Flanders
Godfrey of Bouillon
Bohemond of Taranto
Combined Forces

The day after his sermon couriers arrived at Clermont with magnificent news: Count Raymond of Toulouse would take up the cross. The most powerful noble in southeastern France and one of the wealthiest in western Europe, he commanded hundreds of knights and thousands of soldiers. At fifty-three, he was blind in one eye and scarred from his many battles with the Muslims in Spain. He wore a clipped gray beard and carried his short frame with rigid military bearing. Impulsive and quick to anger, he was vain and arrogant, and lacked what a later generation would call charisma. He was also a notorious womanizer and had twice been excommunicated by the reforming Pope Gregory VII. But he was, nonetheless, considered a devout Christian and was a close friend of both Pope Urban and Bishop Adhemar.

Raymond's decision conferred, as he knew it would, great credibility on the project. He donated his most valuable possessions to the Abbey of St. Gilles and made a large donation to Bishop Adhemar's cathedral, indeed giving away more than any other man to join, and he assumed that Urban would name him commander. When Urban did not (in fact, he refused to name anyone), Raymond was angry and bitterly disappointed. Further and greater disappointments would follow.

The army consisted of four contingents, each from a different homeland, under its own command and departing independently between August and October 1096 to rendezvous at Constantinople. Those from the farthest north, from Flanders and the lower Rhine Valley, marched overland via Germany and

3. Although his physical appearance and battlefield heroics in Jerusalem turned Godfrey into a mythic figure following the First Crusade, he would eventually be eclipsed in significance by his younger brother Baldwin, who created the first crusader county of Edessa and became the first king of Jerusalem.

4. Remarkably, despite his antagonistic history and dubious credentials, Bohemond would emerge as the most significant leader of the crusade for most of its duration and would play a key role in its eventual success. There is a strong case that the expedition would never have reached Jerusalem without his superb tactical fighting skills.

Hungary under the command of the tall, handsome, husky, golden-bearded Godfrey of Bouillon, age thirty-five, who had financed the enterprise honorably by selling two large estates and pledging his castle to a bishop, and dishonorably by blackmailing Jews with threats of persecution.[3]

The northern French contingent set out from Paris under the joint command of Duke Robert of Normandy, brother of England's King William II; Count Stephen of Blois; and Count Robert II of Flanders. Mightily moved by Urban's preaching, Duke Robert, at age forty, would contribute both his charm and his indolent interest. Wealthy Stephen of Blois reputedly did not in fact want to go at all. He had joined, it was said, because his wife, Adela, daughter of William the Conqueror, had shamed him into it. More admirably, Robert of Flanders was following the example of his father, who had once made the dangerous journey to Jerusalem as a pilgrim. Meanwhile, the southern French assembled under Raymond in Provence. With them was Bishop Adhemar, designated as Urban's legate. This third contingent also included a notorious mob of rowdy Spaniards. Crossing through the Alpine passes, they gained northern Italy and Dalmatia, which put them on the old Roman road to Constantinople—all of which was cheaper than hiring ships.

The fourth contingent was an afterthought. A host of Normans from southern Italy under the leadership of Bohemond of Taranto took up the cross after the army of northern France and his Norman cousins passed by on their way to Constantinople by sea. Bohemond called a meeting where he dramatically tore off his rich scarlet cloak and ripped the cloth into pieces to make crosses. His vassals quickly followed his lead. Brilliant, brave, crafty, opportunistic, and ruthless, the towering Bohemond was at once the crusade's greatest asset and worst liability. His past was unpropitious. He had acquired a small duchy by rebelling against his half-brother and then had launched an attack on Byzantine possessions along the Adriatic. Though it failed, he was dreaded and despised by the Byzantines, whose cause he now offered to champion. The mere mention of his name, wrote the emperor Alexius's daughter, "occasioned panic" in Constantinople.[4]

The crusaders began arriving in that fabled city as early as 1096. Nothing in Europe had prepared them for its size and splendor. It teemed with more than a half million people, against thirty thousand in Paris. Its skyline silhouetted a stunning mélange of Greek, Roman, and eastern architecture, and to awestruck crusaders it delivered one overwhelming impression: wealth. They thoroughly alarmed the emperor. He had already diverted away from the city a brawling mob of some twenty thousand German peasants who had hastened pell-mell to answer Urban's call (see sidebar, pages 16–17). He was not about to allow through his gates these thousands of armed westerners either. His objective was to get the four armies beyond Constantinople, not into it.

Alexius was a small man with oiled black hair and beard, his dark brows arching over large brown eyes, and nothing in his manner of monarchy endeared him to the muscular soldiery of the West. He seemed to them effete, with his luxurious purple mantle worn over a gold tunic and his velvet cap covered in diamonds and rubies. Most comfortable on his

The Byzantine emperor Alexius, shown here in a contemporary drawing, was a much stronger and more effective leader than his effete dress and manner suggested to the crusaders. Before helping them cross the Bosporus Strait into Asia, he required an oath from each western leader that guaranteed they would return any reconquered territory in Syria to the Byzantine Empire. They didn't.

Godfrey of Bouillon and his brother Baldwin stand by the mast as their troops cross the Bosporus in this nineteenth-century painting by Emile Signol. Godfrey would distinguish himself in the capture of Jerusalem and become its first ruler, much to the chagrin of rival commander Raymond of Toulouse. Baldwin succeeded Godfrey the following year, becoming chief architect of the feudal organization in the conquered Christian territory known as Outremer.

throne or a horse, he was poker faced and studiously polite, loved to impress friends and enemies alike with displays of wealth, and flattered and bribed shamelessly, all the while milking his empire through high taxes and, so it was said, also stealing from the church. He had seized power only five years earlier in a bloodless coup and now blunted persistent threats of rebellion and assassination by conferring an array of empty titles that placed potential plotters under his watchful eye at the imperial court.

Improbable as it might seem to western sensibilities, however, this popinjay paladin was a formidable commander. Alexius had decisively thwarted Bohemond on his western frontier, after all, and was holding the Turks in check on the east. He was confident that the Eastern Church would remain secure as long as the remaining Byzantine Empire survived, but to regain all the territory lost to Islam, he would need more troops; hence his appeal to Urban. Beyond that, he did not believe Christians needed to control Jerusalem. Further, if the four armies descending upon him took Syria, he wanted it restored to the Byzantine Empire, not to the West. To guarantee this, he required an oath of loyalty from the crusade leaders.

First to arrive was the Flanders–Rhine Valley contingent, a vast array of armor-clad chivalry with massed lances who celebrated Christmas of 1096 encamped outside the city walls. No, said Godfrey, he would not swear allegiance to Alexius, because he had already sworn it to the western emperor, who, he said, took precedence. Alexius insisted. Armed skirmishes followed, verging on open war. With the army of the redoubtable Bohemond also approaching, Alexius offered Godfrey a deal: free transit across the Bosporus for his troops plus supplies of food if he would take the oath. Grudgingly, Godfrey complied, and a veritable landslide of gifts from the emperor descended upon him as he crossed into Asia.

By now it was March 1097. Oaths presented no problems for Bohemond, who appeared in early April and crossed immediately, proposing that Alexius name him supreme commander. The emperor refused but placated him, too, with money and gifts. Raymond, reaching Constantinople later that month, initially refused to take Alexius's oath—God was now his only suzerain, he claimed—but compromised with a vow not to "allow harm" to the emperor. The northern French, having wintered in Italy, arrived last. Their leaders took the oath and crossed the Bosporus to catch up with the rest. The Christian army now numbered over one hundred thousand, though more than half were noncombatants. Almost immediately the crusade's most besetting problem emerged: intense rivalry between the short, gray-bearded Raymond and the tall, powerful Bohemond. For the moment it was agreed that decisions would be made by the leaders in council.

The enemy, the Muslim Turks, were not far away. Nicea, the Seljuk capital where more than seven centuries earlier the Christian faith was first defined in a

Almost immediately the crusade's most besetting problem emerged: rivalry between its two leaders, Bohemond and the aging Raymond. Gray bearded or not, Raymond was first to distinguish himself.

creed by an ecumenical council, lay a scant four days' march from Constantinople. It stood at the end of a lake, its massive walls rising from the water and describing a four-mile circuit on the landward side. Alexius had emphasized, and all had agreed, that this must be their first objective, though the emperor's contribution to the effort was limited to a few siege machines and a general. The contingents positioned themselves at four points along the landward walls.

Raymond was the first to distinguish himself. The Seljuk sultan had taken his army from the city to fight rival Muslims elsewhere, possibly assuming that these latest arrivals would resemble the peasants' brigade that he had casually liquidated the previous year. Alerted to the siege, his cavalrymen swept in from the south, met Raymond's Provençals head-on before the city gates, and were quickly beaten back when Bishop Adhemar's force attacked their right flank. While the other three armies occupied themselves with the walls, the Provençals repelled wave after wave. Finally, the sultan, recognizing that man for man his troops were no match for these people, left his capital to its fate.

The elated crusaders hacked the heads off dead Turkish cavalrymen and hurled them over the walls as an edifying message to the defenders, but the garrison, amply supplied via the lake, knew it could hold out indefinitely. Then a small flotilla of boats arrived, courtesy of Alexius, and was transported overland to the crusaders. Nicea was thereupon sealed, and the crusaders prepared for an assault and a promising haul of loot the following day. They needn't have bothered.

Daylight disclosed new flags flying over the city: the flags of the Byzantine Empire. Alexius's envoys, with some Byzantine troops, had stolen into the city during the night and negotiated a surrender; the defenders now marched out under Byzantine escort. Alexius somewhat assuaged the rage of the westerners by bestowing gifts all round, including silks, valuable horses, and heaps of gold and jewels from the sultan's treasury. Even so, though Nicea was again Christian, relations with the emperor Alexius had not been improved.

From Nicea the crusaders headed east in two groups, one led by Raymond and the other by Bohemond. The latter, always impatient, got his troops ready first. Soon miles ahead, they encamped that night on a plain surrounded by low hills near the village of Doryleum. At dawn the sultan's shrieking Turks came swooping over one of those hills to encircle them in a wild, howling attack.

Bohemond responded instantly. Ordering noncombatants into the camp's center, where there were springs, he told women to keep carrying water to a front line that he assembled in a circle around them. He also dispatched a messenger back to Raymond for help, then ordered his knights to dismount and had his

What might well have been a major disaster for the crusaders turned into a landmark victory, one that destroyed the Turkish sultan's authority and burnished Bohemond's reputation as a general.

soldiers pack tight together in a solid defensive formation. For the next five baking hours, they were attacked by wave after wave of mounted Turkish archers releasing showers of arrows from their horn bows, then wheeling back for another onslaught.

Finally, about noon Bohemond's allies thundered in with Godfrey and Hugh of Vermandois in the lead and Raymond close behind. The reinforcements surprised and confused the Turks, slowing them down, and then, just as the crusaders began to gain, Bishop Adhemar rode in from farther west at the head of still more Provençal knights. This sight panicked the Turks and sent then fleeing eastward. What might well have been a major disaster for the crusaders turned into a landmark victory, one made all the sweeter because the Seljuks abandoned considerable treasure along with their tents. Moreover, news of the rout at Doryleum destroyed the sultan's authority and burnished Bohemond's reputation as a field general. But his impatient decision to divide the army further fueled his antagonism with Raymond.

Through the heat of August 1097 the armies proceeded slowly across the arid high plains of Anatolia, where the Seljuks pillaged towns and destroyed food supplies ahead of them. Hundreds of Christians died of thirst, as did horses, donkeys, oxen, and even camels. By late summer the weary expedition reached a region called Pisidia, north of the Mediterranean, where water and food were relatively plentiful and they were welcomed by the largely Armenian Christian population.

The next objective was Antioch, five hundred miles southeast. But on the direct overland route were two narrow mountain passes that Muslims could easily blockade:

Nicea, the Seljuk Turk capital, was the first Muslim city attacked. While the crusaders laid siege to the landward walls, however, Emperor Alexius's troops came in by ship from the adjoining lake, as shown in this National Geographic illustration. Unbeknownst to the crusaders, they negotiated a surrender with the Turks and raised the Byzantine banners over the city the next day. This embarrassment to the crusading forces was only slightly lessened by the gifts lavished on them by Alexius.

5. The leaders did dispatch two fiery young nobles and their knights along the shorter Cilician route to establish contact with sympathetic Armenians: Baldwin of Boulogne, who was Godfrey's younger brother, and Tancred of Hauteville, Bohemond's cousin. In attempting to take over two local communities, they clashed, and a few knights on both sides were killed in a bloody brawl. Although the pair established strategically useful garrisons northeast of Syria, their display of raw ambition dismayed the less self-interested in the crusader camp.

the Cilician Gates, north of Tarsus, and the Belen Gates, near Antioch. So the council agreed to turn northeast and travel twice as far through the region of Cappadocia, which would require two extra months on the road, with a mounting toll of human and animal life in the dry, rugged terrain.[5] But at last the crusaders—hungry, dispirited, many in rags—reached the Orontes River. There they beheld Antioch, an intimidating sight. Behind eight miles of stone walls that rose sixty feet from the marshy ground, the city climbed fifteen hundred feet up a mountainside to a fortress at the summit. Five heavily guarded gates allowed entrance from the western plain, with a sixth at the mountaintop citadel.[6]

In Antioch the apostle Peter had served as bishop and had established one of the first Christian dioceses. Here, in fact, the very word *Christian* had come into being (Acts 11:26), and the population still comprised many Greek, Armenian, and Syrian Christians along with Arab and Turkish Muslims and Jews. Alexius wanted Antioch back in his empire for both strategic and economic reasons. The crusaders also wanted it, if only because it provided the Turks with a stranglehold

The intense heat beat down upon the crusaders as they crossed the Anatolian plain, and many died from dehydration. This National Geographic *painting conveys something of this, one of the many ordeals endured by the Christian army. In their three-year trek to Jerusalem, disease and starvation claimed more lives than fighting.*

on the overland pilgrimage route to Jerusalem. But by now their numbers had been reduced to forty thousand and their fighting strength to five thousand knights and six thousand infantry. Moreover, there was no wood to make siege engines, food was running low, and lightning attacks by mounted Turkish archers were taking a continual toll.

In mid-November thirteen Genoese ships carrying food and reinforcements arrived at the port of St. Simeon, twenty miles away. Equally comforting, the sly Bohemond lured marauding Muslim archers into an ambush, then wiped them out. But by late December the westerners were starving again, now in cold rain and snow, and there was worse to come. Bohemond and Robert of Flanders led four hundred knights to forage the countryside for food and supplies, and encountered a Muslim reinforcement contingent from Damascus twenty times their strength. Bohemond managed to fight them to a stalemate. Back at Antioch, however, Raymond had been lured by the Muslim garrison into a reckless chase and then forced into a chaotic retreat in which he lost thirty men. Even more humiliating, Bishop Adhemar's flag, which depicted the Blessed Virgin Mary, was captured and was thereafter waved from the walls with jeers and ridicule. When Bohemond returned, victorious but with no food, morale plummeted. By January 1098 crusaders were chewing on skins of rotted animals and eating manure for the grain seeds.

All this misfortune must undoubtedly be due to sexual sin, Bishop Adhemar insisted, whereupon all women, wives included, were banished from the camp. But nothing improved. Desertions mounted, and by early February, when a Muslim relief force of twelve thousand was spotted approaching the city, the end seemed at hand. But Bohemond produced a daring plan. Rather than await their attack, he contended, he and Robert of Flanders should lead a thousand mounted knights (using every remaining horse) to strike first while the rest stayed by the wall. Even Muslim accounts affirm that Bohemond was outnumbered twelve to one, but he chose his battleground with great ingenuity—a narrow strip between a river and a hill—thus preventing encirclement. Once the enemy vanguard was in that narrow ground, eight hundred Christian knights charged headlong into them, and as they reeled back, down from the hill thundered Bohemond and the other two hundred. The bewildered Turks suffered heavy losses; the survivors fled.[7] Once more the crusade had been saved, and a month later Bohemond captured a Muslim supply train trying to get into the city.

6. The emperor Justinian had erected Antioch's impressive walls in 560, but, ravaged by earthquakes and plague, the city was subsequently sacked by the Persians. Reconquered by the Byzantines in 969, it had become a linchpin of Empire defense for more than a century until the Seljuks took it in 1085 through betrayal from within.

7. An admiring contemporary who was there wrote: "Bohemond . . . charged the Turkish forces like a lion which has been starving [and] comes roaring out of its cave thirsting for the blood of cattle. . . . His attack was so fierce that the points of his banner were flying right over the heads of the Turks. Seeing Bohemond's banner carried ahead so honorably, our men in a body charged the Turks, who were amazed and took flight." In fact, Bohemond had gambled the entire crusade on his ability to break the massed Turkish ranks with a perfectly timed charge. He chased the Turks for miles, suffered few casualties, and captured many horses.

Be it the 11th century or the 21st, Christian warriors face a dilemma

Prior to the Crusades a massive peace movement produced a Christian code of rules for battle, but in the war against Islam it was rarely applied

In 2005 Petty Officer First Class Marcus Luttrell, heading a four-man party of U.S. Navy SEALs sent in secret to kill or capture a notorious terrorist leader in Afghanistan, was closing in on the village where the man was believed hiding. Suddenly three goat-herders appeared. What was Luttrell to do? Let the three go free and risk their tipping off the terrorist nest? Or shoot the three on the spot?

The trio, two men and a boy, denied frantically that there were any terrorists in the village. Luttrell believed them. One of his three comrades did not; the other two were uncertain. So Luttrell had to decide. In his military soul, he said, he knew they must be shot. "But my trouble is, I have another soul. My Christian soul. And it was crowding in on me. Something kept whispering in the back of my mind, it would be wrong."

So he set the goat-herders free, and they promptly tipped off the terrorists. One hundred and forty of them attacked Luttrell's party, killing his three companions and sixteen more Americans sent to rescue them. Luttrell was held hostage and eventually released, bitterly condemning himself for "the stupidest, most southern-fried, lame-brained decision I ever made."

But in sparing the lives of the goat-herders and thereby (as it turned out) dooming his own men, did Luttrell do what Jesus would have done in like circumstances? Did Luttrell's "Christian soul" truly reflect God's will?

Jesus is often portrayed as a pacifist, but this is not altogether supported by what he said and did. True, he observed that those who take the sword will perish by it, but this could be a statement of probable fact, not necessarily of admonition. In almost every instance in the New Testament where a Roman centurion is mentioned, he appears in a favorable light. Paul's portrayal of the Christian virtues in one of his letters is composed entirely of military metaphors: "the breastplate of righteousness . . . the shield of faith . . . the helmet of salvation . . . the sword of the Spirit" (Ephesians 6:13–17). If these weapons of war were instantly repulsive to early Christians, why would Paul have used them at all?

Finally, the commandment sometimes cited as "Thou shalt not kill" does not properly translate the Greek and Hebrew from which it is derived. Both languages have different words for "kill" and "murder," and in each case the latter word is used.

The dilemma in which Luttrell found himself, however, is in no sense new to Christians, who have been trying for two thousand years to resolve the moral issue raised by war. In the Christian Eastern Empire, whose army held the Muslims at bay for more than seven centuries, soldiers who killed a man in battle were denied communion for three years, though, ironically, they were often sent off to war with prayers and holy water.

In the West the issue became serious in the tenth century, a lawless time when monarchies had broken down and warring feudal armies spread destruction and chaos. The church decided to act. Church councils began to institute a process that by the middle of the eleventh century would be called the "Peace of God" (*Pax Dei*). Specific rules of engagement were enacted, first under threat of retaliatory action by the powerful relatives of a local bishop, later by the dire threat of excommunication, which meant that all oaths of fealty and debts to the excommunicated were cancelled.

Initially the Peace of God prohibited three crimes: theft of church property, assaults on clerics, and theft of cattle from peasants. But through the eleventh century the scope became much more comprehensive until a vast "peace movement" was under way. Large outdoor peace assemblies became common. Miraculous cures were said to occur, communal penances were undertaken, and the declaration of a Peace was believed to ward off natural disasters such as famine, disease, and flood. Bishops and monks brought relics to help spiritually persuade nobles and knights to take oaths to observe the Peace.

In 1038 an early version of a peacekeeping force appeared when Archbishop Aimon of Bourges created a "peace militia" to enforce the Peace of God. Comprising clergy and peasants, it went from castle to castle importuning the nobles to swear the Oath of the Peace. Unhappily, like many exuberant religious campaigns, it got out of hand. According to one chronicle, the militia set fire to the castle at Beneciacum, near Vienne, in France, and fourteen hundred of its occupants perished.

An adjunct to the Peace of God known as the "Truce of God" sought to impose on knights civilizing codes of conduct: no fighting between Thursday and Sunday (the days of Christ's Passion and Resurrection), during Lent or Advent, or on holy days. Out of the Truce came a canon (i.e., a law) passed by a church council at Narbonne in 1054: "No Christian should kill another Christian, since whoever kills a Christian doubtless sheds the blood of Christ."

Did these controls work? Undoubtedly they did restrain violence throughout western Europe, but they could apply only to war between Christians. In the Crusades and in the long war in Spain, where the enemy was Muslim, they had no application, though they were sometimes observed anyway and by both sides.

The moral principles behind the Peace of God

Petty Office First Class Marcus Luttrell, third from right, is pictured in Afghanistan in 2005 with a group of U.S. Navy SEALs. Nineteen men died as a result of Lutrell's eminently Christian decision to spare the lives of three goat-herders. The goat-herders reported the soldiers' presence to the Taliban enemy, who wiped out Luttrell's comrades and the entire team sent to rescue them. For Christians in arms, such a dilemma raises an eternal question: what would Jesus have done?

descend into the twenty-first century in such things as the U.S. military's rules of engagement, to which Luttrell adhered and which specifically prohibit attack on unarmed civilians. But in his book Luttrell understandably pleads, "They're not *their* rules. They're *our* rules, the rules of the western countries, the civilized side of the world. And every terrorist knows how to manipulate them in their own favor."

Out of the Truce of God grew the twelfth-century ideal of the chivalric knight, which, it might well be argued, Luttrell has personified in the twenty-first century. By the time Pope Urban II preached the First Crusade in 1095, the knight was not only prohibited from spilling Christian blood; he was enjoined to become valorous, protective of the poor, truthful, a keeper of the peace at home, and a defender of Christendom against its enemies, which included, of course, the infidel.

But since some crusaders thought they had the

church's assurance that by "taking the cross," they were absolved from all sins anyway, why should they bother with the stern moral restrictions of the Truce of God, whether fighting infidels or other Christians? This was not the response the church expected to these indulgences, but as many incidents in the Crusades evidence, it was frequently the one that occurred.

The Christian Luttrell, nearly a thousand years later, is left with a dilemma. If in cold blood he had shot and killed the two men and the boy, he would have had to live with it for the rest of his life. Since he didn't, he brought on the deaths of his companions and had to live with that instead. But he can take consolation from the fact that hundreds of thousands of Christians fighting in wars over two thousand years have faced precisely the same dilemma, and all can hold fast to the single hope that Christ in his boundless mercy will understand. ■

Bohemond of Taranto was able to break the siege of Antioch by bribing a Muslim guard to help the crusaders raise a ladder to scale the walls, as shown in this lithograph by Gustave Doré. Once he and his men were inside the walls, they opened the gates and the city was swiftly taken. But the erstwhile besiegers soon found themselves besieged by a counterattacking Muslim force.

Raymond of Toulouse, having recovered from an illness, now formally proposed that he become sole commander, but Bohemond was working on yet another stratagem. Having secretly persuaded Emperor Alexius's legate to return to Constantinople with an urgent plea for help, he proclaimed that the legate had deserted them. This obviously signified that no help could be expected from the Byzantines, Bohemond contended, clearly voiding any oaths made to the emperor. Therefore, he himself should be given responsibility for taking Antioch and, when he succeeded, should be made its lord. The others vehemently refused, but then came truly terrifying news. Kerbogha, the notorious Turkish *atabeg* (governor) of Mosul, was approaching with an army of nearly forty thousand. On May 29 the panic-stricken crusade council adopted Bohemond's proposal after all, with only one negative vote. An oath was an oath, Raymond insisted.

There followed one of history's more notable swindles. A handpicked body of men stealthily joined Bohemond outside Antioch's Bridge Gate on the night of June 1, and about two o'clock in the morning, someone lowered down the wall a rope, to which Bohemond's men attached a strong oxhide ladder. Up it they swarmed as soon as it was hauled back; they quickly killed the nearby watchmen, jumped down, and opened the Bridge Gate. Christian troops poured through, then raced up the hill to the Citadel Gate, where Godfrey was waiting with another powerful force. The explanation soon emerged: the Greek-speaking Bohemond had subverted an Armenian Muslim inside the city, a man who had a grudge against its Turkish governor.

As the waiting troops raced in with trumpet blasts and shouts of "*Deus le vult!*" the city awoke in confusion amid a cacophony of terrified screams. At dawn Bohemond ordered his red banner raised above the walls near the citadel, and a full-scale massacre ensued. By day's end the streets were strewn with corpses. The Muslim garrison had achieved one success, however, by securing the citadel before Godfrey could break in. Meanwhile, Raymond had taken advantage of his Bridge Gate position to raise his blue banner over several nearby buildings, thus establishing his own claim.

The battle for Antioch was far from over, however. Next day Kerbogha's men laid siege to it, and soon the Christians found themselves starving again, inside the city instead of outside it. Moreover, they clearly did not have nearly enough men to defend its walls. The atabeg managed to make contact with the citadel garrison. Morale dissolved. Some Christians took refuge in buildings where they hoped to escape the inevitable vengeance of Kerbogha, who now had much to avenge. Bohemond and Bishop Adhemar set the buildings afire to force them out.

But in all the strange annals of the First Crusade, what now ensued was strangest of all. A pilgrim sought audience with Raymond and Adhemar to inform them that buried beneath Antioch's Basilica of St. Peter they would find the spear that pierced Christ's side on Good Friday, perhaps brought there by St. Peter himself. Whoever carried it, this man insisted, would be invincible. Although even Adhemar was skeptical, a search was carried out that produced a steel shard. This information was duly conveyed by special emissary to Kerbogha along with a demand that he either withdraw his troops immediately or, to avoid unnecessary bloodshed, choose a single man or group to confront a similar number of Christian knights. Since the Turks outnumbered the Christians about seven to one, the atabeg countered by demanding the surrender forthwith of the Christian army, reduced at this point to some two hundred horses.

This Gustave Doré depiction of the Christians fighting off the Muslim counterattack at the Citadel Gate in Antioch gives a sense of the desperate nature of siege warfare during the Middle Ages. In this clash the Christians successfully fought off the attackers.

So after confession of sins and a three-day fast, the Christian foot soldiers marched out the gates to face the enormous Muslim host while Bohemond and his remaining knights waited by the gates behind them. He noticed, however, that Kerbogha's force was assembled in separate groups with wide gaps between them and that the foot soldiers were advancing on a group that was bounded on three sides by the river, so it could not be reinforced quickly. Meanwhile, a black flag hoisted over the citadel warned Kerbogha that his enemies were coming out to attack him.

Kerbogha pondered. Should he advance to meet them immediately, or should he wait and let them join battle on his own ground? He decided to wait, the accounts say, because he was deeply absorbed in a chess game. Then he abruptly changed his mind

and advanced with his main force toward the gate. The delay was about to cost him everything he had, save only his life.

The crusader infantry, battling such daunting numbers, fought so fiercely that some of the Turks began to panic; when Bohemond's knights galloped in, they turned and ran. Seeing this, others followed, thus crashing into Kerbogha's main force, coming up behind them and shattering his line of advance. The remaining Turkish contingents, thrown into complete disarray, joined what was becoming a rout, sweeping Kerbogha himself along with them. It was a stunning defeat. As the crusaders overran and plundered Kerbogha's camp, Antioch's citadel garrison also surrendered. Raymond's troops, bearing the Holy Lance, contended afterward that the mere sight of it had paralyzed the Turkish commander. In truth, the crusaders had actually killed only a small fraction of the Muslim army. What they utterly destroyed, however, was the atabeg's reputation. He was finished.

News of the great crusader victory struck terror into Muslims all the way to Jerusalem, but the Christians were now stalled in Antioch. Bohemond declared himself its ruler and decided to stay. Raymond said he would not leave while the oath to Alexius was being violated. Papal legate Adhemar, concerned for East-West church relations, insisted that the city be given to the Byzantines, but within weeks he died of typhoid. The council wrote asking Urban to take command. The pope declined.

Below: The Tower of David citadel embedded in the walls of Jerusalem stood formidable and defiant as the Christians approached the city, a seemingly impregnable obstacle to their army, now down to twelve thousand troops—less than a tenth of its original size. The Christians solved the problem by attacking at a less formidable point in the walls. Above: The fortress as it stands today.

Meanwhile, the wealthy Raymond tried bribing the vassals of other leaders to support him. It didn't work. He declared that the apostle Andrew, Peter's brother, had made him custodian of the Holy Lance. This didn't work either. At length Raymond moved his Provençal knights southward, disrupting Bohemond's supply line into Antioch, and built towers to besiege the town of Marrat. Bohemond followed; he took control of Raymond's towers, and the town fell in a bloody battle.

This victory soon turned very sour indeed. By December Raymond had bribed enough of Bohemond's supporters to back him to gain control of Marrat. He began knocking down mosques and declared the town Christian, but the Turks cut off his supply lines, and the starving poor of Marrat were reduced to digging up Muslim dead and eating the rotted corpses. Disgusted local Christians broke into open rebellion. Raymond thereupon gave up Marrat, tacitly yielded Antioch as well to Bohemond, and announced that he himself would now lead the way to

The prophet of the Holy Lance proclaimed that in order to purge the crusader army of sinful soldiers, two of every five men must die. He consented to trial by fire to prove it. The burns killed him.

Jerusalem. He set out in early January 1099, walking barefoot and calling for God's mercy at the head of a religious procession.

Now events became increasingly bizarre. Raymond had gambled that Godfrey and Robert of Flanders would immediately follow him. They didn't, but in any case his five thousand troops encountered no resistance at first. Then, for reasons never explained, he diverted his force to lay siege to an insignificant town called Arqa. It refused to yield; Raymond refused to leave. After three pointless months Godfrey and Robert joined him, bringing the total Christian strength to more than ten thousand. So did the prophet of the Holy Lance, now proclaiming a new vision. Christ had told him, he insisted, that the crusader army must be purged of sinful soldiers, so two out of every five men must be executed immediately. When the outraged crusaders challenged the man, he volunteered to undergo trial by fire. Holy Lance in hand, he walked through blazing olive branches. The burns killed him.

Most of Raymond's "bought" vassals now deserted him, but when a message arrived from Constantinople protesting Bohemond's seizure of Antioch and promising troops within three weeks for an attack on Jerusalem, Raymond nevertheless demanded to be made sole leader. The council rejected this plea, however, and on May 16 what was left of the First Crusade departed from Arqa for Jerusalem, two hundred miles ahead. Bypassing major centers like Acre and Beirut, they arrived unopposed at the magnificent Holy City on June 7 and from the plain to the northwest beheld a breathtaking view. Its looming stone walls, laid out originally by the Roman emperor Hadrian, stood four stories high and ran three miles around an irregular perimeter. To the east, south, and southwest, rugged, dry hills and deep ravines made approach difficult. A small outside rampart enclosed the main wall, which had five gates. On the city's western edge rose two tall buildings, a citadel called the Tower of David and another fortress, the Quadrangle Tower. The governor, Iftikhar al-Dawla, who had taken Jerusalem from the Turks three months earlier, commanded a garrison of Sudanese and Arab troops.

At this crisis point in the whole endeavor, past quarrels were forgotten. Even Bohemond's cousin Tancred of Hauteville and Raymond, who had been feuding, put aside their animosities, publicly vowing together that they would fight on the same side for the cross.

This painting by Francesco Hayez, entitled Crusaders Thirsting near Jerusalem, *is a highly romanticized nineteenth-century interpretation of the scene outside the walls of Jerusalem when a priest speaks of a vision calling for the crusaders to fast and walk barefoot around the city in atonement for their sins. The fasting meant little change for the Christians since most were already near starvation and parched for water. The enemy had poisoned the wells and destroyed all the nearby pastures.*

After three years the crusaders were finally there, but they also were desperate. There was little food, and the governor had poisoned the wells and destroyed the pastures for miles around. They had too few troops to blockade the city. Their four contingents, such as they were, nevertheless took up positions at various points around the walls. After using ladders in attempting one assault, which brought heavy casualties and no success, they took to scouring the bare hills for wood, food, and water.

On June 17, however, six ships from Genoa and England landed at the port of Jaffa with food, armaments, ropes, and craftsmen. The crusaders cannibalized two ships for their timber and found more wood in Samaria to construct battering rams and two siege towers fitted with wheels. Even so, after two more weeks in oppressive daytime heat, morale sank. Then a priest announced a vision in which Adhemar called on all of them to seek forgiveness by fasting and walking barefoot around Jerusalem. With spirits renewed, the crusaders enthusiastically complied, and thus the Muslims beheld them at dawn on July 8.[8]

But meanwhile the crusader council had also formulated a two-pronged assault strategy, to be led by Raymond on the southwest and Godfrey to the northeast. In full view of the enemy, they built two thirty-foot siege castles while Jerusalem's defenders heavily fortified the adjacent city walls. As night fell on July 10, Godfrey's castle was standing near the Quadrangle Tower, but in the

darkness his troops took it apart and carried the pieces a half mile. By dawn they had reassembled it where the walls were not reinforced at all. The appalled defenders saw it—too late— only at first light.

A massive battering ram initiated the attack by breaching Jerusalem's small outer wall. By nightfall the Flanders and Rhine men and northern French had broken through and pushed their siege castle, filled with soldiers, close to the inner wall. Raymond had made little progress because massed Muslims, led by the governor himself, poured down rocks and fire. Godfrey's attack fared better. From his siege castle's topmost chamber, he noted with satisfaction that the tough hide covering was resisting the flames. Unhappily for the defenders, the same was not true of the wooden substructure of their city wall. When it caught fire, Godfrey and his men poured out of their siege castle and rapidly fashioned a makeshift bridge to reach the top of the wall and drop scaling ladders. More crusaders followed while others gained the gates and threw them open. The defense collapsed in chaos. Some ran for cover to the Dome of the Rock and the Mosque of al-Aqsa, but crusaders were there before them. The governor took refuge in the Tower of David but later turned it over to Raymond in exchange for his life.

When the wooden top of Jerusalem's wall caught fire, Godfrey of Bouillon made a bridge to reach the ramparts. This nineteenth-century lithograph by Gustave Doré shows Godfrey leading his troops from the bridge into the city and the ensuing carnage.

But the next twenty-four hours converted what could have been a magnificent Christian victory into a historic disgrace that Christians would spend the next ten centuries ruing, apologizing for, and trying desperately to fathom. Insane with their victory, the crusaders ran through the streets and into houses and mosques, killing people regardless of age or sex, the massacre continuing through the night until bodies littered the streets. Jews hiding in a synagogue were burned alive there, on the grounds that they had aided the Muslims. No one knows the number slaughtered.

Why had it happened? The human tendency commonly called "mob violence" sweeps people into conduct that would revolt them as individuals. Oppressed

Following their slaughter of Jerusalem's inhabitants, the victorious crusaders gather in the reclaimed Church of the Holy Sepulchre to beg forgiveness from God, as shown in this National Geographic *illustration. In the twenty-four hours following the taking of the city, the crusaders indulged in an orgy of slaughter, killing virtually everyone regardless of age or sex, until the streets were littered with bodies. The inglorious slaughter had the effect of besmirching an amazing victory.*

populations, suddenly liberated, may be especially given to such conduct, as were the Jews themselves when Zoroastrian Persia took Christian Jerusalem in 614 (volume 5, pages 136–137). Conquering armies, when discipline has been lost, are also prone to it. Nearly a century and a half after the fall of Jerusalem, Mongol warriors, sweeping into both Islamic and Christian territories, would acquire the worst reputation in the medieval world for wholesale slaughter. Next evening, filled with deep remorse, the Christians prayed for forgiveness. But the stain remained and became a rallying point for Islam.

While nearly all the crusaders returned to their homelands in Europe, some remained and continued fighting. Raymond died at the siege of Tripoli in 1105. Bohemond was captured by the Muslims in 1100 and spent three years in a Muslim jail but was ransomed and then again beaten by them. Then he raised a great army in Europe to attack not Islam but Alexius, who also thoroughly defeated him. He died in 1111 as a vassal of Alexius and a broken man. Godfrey was made Advocate of the Holy Sepulchre in 1099, having refused the title "king." He died the next year—by Muslim accounts, of a poisoned arrow at the siege of Acre but according to Christian records at Jerusalem, in great agony after eating a poisoned apple. Pope Urban, who had started it all, died just weeks before word reached Rome of the crusade's success.

These Christian conquests barely dented the vast domains of Islam. Christian states—the county of Edessa, the principality of Antioch, the county of Tripoli, and, most notably, the kingdom of Jerusalem, known collectively as *Outremer* ("Beyond the Sea")—were rapidly established. Though their governance was interminably in dispute, they lasted virtually unchallenged by Islam for nearly half a century. Then the tide would begin to turn. ∎

The fighting monks of Outremer

Feared and hated by the Muslims, the Hospitallers and Templars fast became the standing Christian army of the Holy Land but bitter rivals of one another

When a Cistercian abbot proposed founding a monastery in the Holy Land after the Crusaders had captured Jerusalem, the twelfth-century church reformer Bernard of Clairvaux scoffed aloud. "The necessities there," he declared, "are fighting knights, not singing and wailing monks."

Bernard, a devout monk himself, was keenly aware of the harsh realities in Outremer, where any Christian life was at risk beyond the walls of a fortified castle. But suppose, he mused, you could combine in one man the spiritual purity of a monk with the valor and skill of a knight? Such a warrior-monk was what the Holy Land really needed.

Thus, in 1129 Bernard persuaded the pope to recognize a new type of order: armed monks. They were to be called the Poor Knights of Christ and the Temple of Solomon, the last a reference to their residence in Jerusalem's Al Aqsa Mosque, believed located above the site of Solomon's Temple.

A tiny band at first, known as "the Templars," they fulfilled the vision of the French knight Hugh de Payns. They had begun ten years earlier under the Benedictine Rule, dedicated to the protection of pilgrims on the roads leading to Jerusalem. But soon the desperate shortage of professional soldiers spurred them to become an autonomous order reporting directly to the pope. Founder Hugh scoured Europe for donations and for recruits, who would don the order's distinctive white mantle with a large red cross.

Meanwhile, another group of monks devoted to the care of pilgrims had already been at work for about ten years in the Holy Land. This was the Order of St. John of the Hospital, another subset that adhered to the Benedictine life.[1] Founded by a veteran of the First Crusade known to history only as "Brother Gerard," they ran a hospice for pilgrims and traders at Jerusalem that by 1113 could accommodate two thousand people. When their founder died seven years later, he was described in his epitaph as "the most humble man in the East and the servant of the poor."

By 1113 the Hospitallers, as they became known, also gained papal recognition as an independent order dedicated to assisting the poor and sick. But what pilgrims needed as much as a hospital was physical protection. So under a new leader, Raymond du Puy, they added soldiering to their hospital services. Their knights wore a white cross on a mantle of red or black.

The Templars and Hospitallers became popular charities and bitter rivals as both expanded rapidly and grew rich throughout the twelfth century. At their height the Templars had fifteen to twenty thousand members, about ten percent of them fighting knights. The Hospitallers, with some eight thousand knights and scores of general members, became even larger and richer.

Both acquired a reputation for extraordinary courage and fighting skills. They were widely admired throughout

This painting of Hugh de Payns, founder of the Order of the Knights Templar, is from the Chateaux de Versailles et de Trianon, Versailles, France, and was commissioned in 1841. The painting is by Henri Charles Lehmann.

1. The order was named after St. John the Evangelist, although for many years historians mistakenly believed that it had originally been connected to St. John the Almsgiver, a seventh-century patriarch of Alexandria said to have devoted all his church's revenues to the relief of suffering and poverty.

Right: The Templars' traditional role of guarding pilgrims is depicted in this nineteenth-century English engraving. The exhilaration of the pilgrim's first view of the Holy City is seen in the person prostrating himself in the center of the picture. Inset: The Templar emblem showed two knights riding one horse to emphasize their poverty. It later became a source of scorn when the Templars were running the biggest bank in Europe.

The Hospitallers' fortress of Kerak des Chevaliers was regarded as the strongest fortress in Outremer. It still stands in its entirety, forty miles west of the Syrian city of Homs, near the border of Lebanon.

Christendom and feared and hated by the Muslims. Initially their members were esteemed for pursuing an ascetic lifestyle that included vows of poverty, chastity, and obedience to the Rule of Benedict augmented by their own customs. The Templars slept fully dressed in dormitories lighted round the clock (both to remain ever prepared for battle and to discourage homosexual liaisons). Each order was headed by a grand master. Templar soldiers included knights, who were of noble birth, and sergeants, who were not. The Hospitallers made no such distinctions in social class.

Gradually, however, resentment and suspicion began to surround the orders, particularly after a papal bull in 1139 exempted them from taxes. Both orders set up businesses across Europe that ranged from banking to millworks to shipping companies. They bought and managed vineyards, were active in mining, constructed churches and castles, ran import and export businesses, and had their own fleets of ships.

The Templars acquired more than six thousand manors and estates that employed thousands of lay workers as well as monks. Such activity was common to most monasteries, though the spectacular scale of the Templar operations attracted particular attention. In fact, many Templars who had volunteered to fight for the Holy Land never left Europe. Within Outremer the Hospitallers held seven great fortresses, including mighty Kerak des Chevaliers in Tripoli, and another forty fortified towers and one hundred and forty estates, while at their peak the Templars had nearly forty fortresses, with the strongest at Acre, on the Mediterranean coast west of the Sea of Galilee.

But the secrecy surrounding their operations raised questions about their true purposes and their use of the resources given them to secure the Holy Land. This suspicion focused more on the Templars than on the Hospitallers because the latter never did abandon their compassionate role. They maintained their hospice and hospital in Jerusalem, erected similar pilgrim facilities in Europe's port cities, and distributed alms daily to the poor. The Templars displayed few humanitarian concerns and scant generosity. However, they did make pilgrimage safer and easier by inventing checks so that travelers could avoid carrying large sums of money. In trade they also developed a close relationship with Muslim merchants, which angered crusader allies.

None of these diversions, however, was allowed to eclipse their military role. Together they formed, in effect, the only standing army in the Holy Land and became crucial in almost every military campaign. At Montgiscard in 1177, for example, an ambush by five hundred Templars routed Saladin's army of twenty-six thousand and saved Jerusalem from imminent capture.

But the rivalry of the two became a deepening problem. In one Egyptian campaign led by the king of Jerusalem, the Templars refused to aid the Hospitallers, who consequently lost two hundred and ninety-seven of three hundred knights in battle. When Jerusalem negotiated a treaty with the Assassins, the Templars scuttled the deal by killing a Muslim envoy so that they would not lose the annual tribute the Assassins were paying them.

Christians in the Holy Land slowly fractured into two competing factions. The Hospitallers, combined with second- and third-generation Outremer barons, tended to cooperate with surrounding non-Christian neighbors and were opposed to military risks. The Templars, allied with newly arrived European nobles and adventurers, leaned toward more aggressive tactics. Their rashness eventually led to disaster. At a crucial moment the Templars prevailed on a weak king of Jerusalem to make a move that proved fatal to Christian Jerusalem (see chapter 3).

The two orders maintained the crusaders' toehold in Outremer through to the late thirteenth century. Driven out, they both reestablished headquarters on Cyprus. By then, however, jealousy of their wealth and power had grown irrepressible, bringing the Templars to a sad end (see sidebar, page 224). But the Hospitallers survived to conduct on the island of Malta in the year 1565 one of the most spectacular and heroic victories the Christians would ever record against Islam. That story will be told in volume 9. ■

The fraternity displayed in this illustration of a Hospitaller (right) helping a Templar remove an arrow from his chest most likely exists more in the mind of the twentieth-century Anglo-Swiss artist Gerry Embleton than it did in real life. Historically the Templars and Hospitallers were bitter rivals who on occasion even refused to help each other against their common enemies.

Light streams through windows under the vaulted ceiling of St-Denis, bringing to the worshipper the luxurious sense of purity that Abbot Suger intended. The abbot, inspired by the writing of Dionysius the Pseudo-Areopagite, saw light as a vehicle of God's grace.

CHAPTER 2

To let there be light, the builders composed symphonies in stone

The visionaries of Gothic married technology to faith, and across western Europe there arose soaring structures that move men toward God

A s anyone could plainly see, a clash between Bernard, the caustic but internationally revered abbot of Clairvaux, and this man Suger (pronounced *Soo-jay*), the newly appointed Benedictine abbot of St-Denis (pronounced *San-Denee*), was inevitable. Each had a firm concept of what constituted a fit environment for the worship of God that appeared diametrically at odds with the equally firm concept of the other. Both were men of decision and action, both were very powerful, both knew they were dead right, and both seemed to agree on almost nothing.

Moreover, they came from sharply different backgrounds. Bernard, a member of one of the great noble families of Burgundy, had chosen a monastic life of poverty, chastity, and obedience—and unquestionably lived it. (His story is told in the next chapter.) Nobody seemed to know for sure where Suger came from. By one account he was the son of a poor knight, by another the child of peasant parents, and by yet another the illegitimate son of a former abbot of St-Denis. But by 1122 he had risen to the peak of power in France, was destined to serve as a regent and rule the country brilliantly when King Louis VII went to the Crusades, and had now been named head of the Abbey of St-Denis, shrine of the patron saint of France, where the kings were buried, indeed the visible link between the French royal household and Almighty God.[1]

As things turned out, both men would leave an imprint on western Europe from that time forward, Bernard through the Cistercian order that he brought to spiritual ascendancy in the twelfth century and would still be active at the end of the second millennium, and Suger, not as a great ruler but as a renowned architectural visionary.

1. The patron saint of France, St-Denis (Dennis in English, Dionysius in Greek), is recorded in a sixth-century history as one of seven bishops sent in the middle of the third century to convert Gaul, where he became bishop of Paris and was martyred. Various miracles are attributed to his martyrdom (see volume 3, page 27). In 626 his remains were translated to the royal tombs that King Dagobert established at St-Denis.

Bernard of Clairvaux (left) seems to look on askance as Louis VI (right) presides over the consecration of Suger as abbot of St-Denis in this seventeenth-century painting by Justus van Egmont. Bernard's view of the appropriate environment for Christian worship seemed at such odds with Suger's that a clash appeared inevitable. Yet somehow each persuaded the other, and they became fast friends.

It was no surprise to Suger why Louis had named him to St-Denis. However august its pedigree, the place was, frankly, a wreck. Suger himself cataloged its physical condition: gaping fissures in the walls, damaged columns "threatening ruin," valuable ivories left to "molder away," furnishings falling to pieces, finances in chaos with obligations to princely benefactors unfulfilled, revenues being illicitly handed over to favored laymen, tenants on the abbey's extensive farms being mercilessly oppressed by nearby squires and barons.

As to the abbey's spiritual condition, that was becoming similarly dilapidated. Before Suger's appointment Bernard had already deplored St-Denis as a monument of monastic sloth, an "obscenity" cast on the French crown, a "workshop of Vulcan . . . a synagogue of Satan," the monks wallowing in indolent ease. These problems Suger addressed immediately. He restored "holy order" to the monastery, he writes, "in a peaceable fashion without disturbance of the brethren." Bernard had had something far more ferocious in mind that would have disturbed the brethren a great deal, but he never pushed this on Suger. Rather, he congratulated him for the improvements made and let it go. Why did he back off? There seems only one explanation: Bernard had asked Suger to intervene with the king regarding an individual with whom Bernard was having problems. The individual was promptly fired. Although Bernard would remain a critic of opulence, he thereafter found no fault at all with the Abbey of St-Denis.

Now, this was very odd. Bernard's Cistercians were building their abbeys in a style as austere as the life they led. There must be neither towers nor porches, said Bernard, nor polished stones nor costly carvings and paintings, and certainly no gold near the altar. St-Denis, though run down, had never evidenced such austerity, and Suger had had a love affair with the place ever since his boyhood. At nine or ten he had been turned over to the monastery by his parents, designated to become a "black monk" of the Benedictine tradition. He found himself being educated along with the future King Louis VI of France, with whom he formed a lifelong friendship, as he later would also do with the king's son Louis VII.

Hence his rocketing rise in the service of the French crown. Now at age forty or forty-one he would continue to serve the kings of France as abbot of St-Denis. For Suger, St-Denis was the spiritual center of the monarchy, a proper place of pil-grimage. If the glory of the monarchy was to be reflected in St-Denis, it must become the most beautiful, luxurious, and instantly captivating place of worship in the entire West.

St-Denis was the burial place of French kings from the fifth to the nineteenth century.

He had acquired some definite ideas on how to do this, having been inspired by the descriptions of Justinian's church Hagia Sophia (pronounced *Eye-ya So-fee-ya*, Holy Wisdom), in Constantinople, and the biblical description of Solomon's Temple. He had observed the new Norman churches, where the crossed ribs of the roof carried its weight not to the walls but to columns that conveyed it directly to the ground. He had carefully inspected the new monasteries and churches being built by the Benedictines in Burgundy, where stained glass had been in use for many years, though the windows were never large because that would weaken the walls. More than anything else, however, it was not the building but the writings ascribed in those days to St-Denis himself, patron saint of France, that had enthralled Suger.

He would have heard that there were, indeed, three men named Denis who had been conflated by French tradition—meaning, in this case, legend—into one. There was the aforementioned third-century bishop and martyr, about whom almost nothing is known. There was the Dionysius (the Greek name for Dennis) listed as a convert of St. Paul (Acts 17:34) following Paul's sermon on the hill called the Areopagus in Athens, about whom nothing more is known. Finally, there was the man known as Dionysius the Pseudo-Areopagite, probably a fifth-century Syrian monk, about whom a great deal is known. This Denis left voluminous records of his theology, a blend of Christianity with Platonic philosophy, all

Light filters through the stained glass of St-Denis' high windows. The Benedictines in Burgundy had long used stained glass, but their windows must of necessity be small because the roof weight of their churches was supported by heavy, thick walls. Not so with the new Gothic style, whose piers and vaulted roofs bore the weight to the ground, making possible much bigger windows and far greater breadths of stained glass.

of which was firmly ascribed to St-Denis, the third-century martyr and France's patron saint, and avidly devoured from boyhood onward by Suger.[2]

To this Denis, commonly called "the Pseudo-Areopagite," the chief element through which God discloses himself to men is light. But he gave the word a much broader meaning than mere physical energy, borrowing from Plato the perception of light as the ultimate reality. In the material world it makes biological nature possible. But it also acts through and illuminates our intellect so that we can perceive what is true, good, and beautiful. He identifies this with the "light" portrayed in the opening verses of St. John's Gospel: "In him [i.e., in Christ] was life, and the life is the light of men," and "the light shineth in the darkness and the darkness did not overcome it."

Since the contemplation of the material leads the mind to the spiritual, this justified Suger's encrusting his great rood (cross), chalices, and Gospel covers with gemstones, and it was one of his principal answers to Bernard's asceticism. Suger reasoned that every segment of a great church should be pervaded by light, and not just daylight or sunlight but light in all shades and colors as it filtered through the stained glass of expansive windows that depicted the figures and events of the Christian faith and its biblical background, with the light from the higher windows drawing the eye upward to the vaulted roofs and the soul upward to God.

But how could this be made possible? The walls of big churches had to be thick and sturdy to bear the weight of the roof. Putting many windows in them would represent a fatal weakness. That was why the old Romanesque churches were of necessity dark and candlelit. Yet the Romanesque buildings were not without their own charm and beauty. The style had spread through Europe in the late tenth century and the eleventh, with its message of sheer massiveness—sturdy piers, large towers, thick walls, and decorative arcading. Because of its round arches, it appeared to be a return to Roman architecture, though much simplified, hence the term "Romanesque."

It came at a time of unprecedented church growth across Europe, and many Romanesque churches—such as Santa Maria in Cosmedin in Rome, the Baptistery

2. The clever, insightful, and ostentatious theologian Peter Abelard, a monk at St-Denis before Suger's time, proclaimed the St-Denis tradition to be pure legend. He thereupon was driven from the monastery by the enraged monks and threatened with a charge of treason. He was absolved of this but not of other things. His story appears on page 188.

in Florence, and San Zeno Maggiore in Verona—would survive to the end of the second Christian millennium. In England nearly all the twenty-seven cathedrals that went back to early Christian times were begun in the Romanesque period, as in Spain was the famous Santiago de Compostela. In Germany the Rhine and its tributaries were dotted with Romanesque abbeys, and Romanesque churches appeared in Tunisia, Serbia, Hungary, Sicily, Scotland, and Scandinavia.

But with the twelfth century, men like Suger and others in the Paris area realized that the Normans had solved the weight problem with their cross-ribbed vaulted roofs borne by piers. However, the Normans had not yet grasped the full potential of their discovery. Neither had they realized that the round "barrel arches" of their Romanesque churches could be brought to a point at the top, enabling them to carry and disperse a far greater load.

Suger's mental visions soon began appearing as a physical reality. His ideas found their way into the new choir at St-Denis—that part of a church, later called the chancel, that included the "sanctuary"

The western face of St-Denis Basilica retains one of the twin towers with which Suger adorned the original building. The nineteenth-century restoration architect Eugene Violett-le-Duc ordered the other demolished as hopelessly disintegrated. Only its lower portions remain.

around the main altar. It was completed in an amazing three years, and no one had seen anything quite like it before. The historian Otto von Simson (*The Gothic Cathedral*) calls it "one of the epoch-making buildings in the history of architecture." The entire sanctuary "is pervaded by a wonderful and continuous light." It was the first church where the facade at the approach to the building was specifically designed "to evoke the idea that the sanctuary is the gate of heaven." Next came the nave, the main body of the church that accommodates the worshippers. This was a major job that would not be completed until after Suger's death in 1151.

But he worked on it tirelessly. Though his responsibilities to the king remained heavy, his heart was unquestionably centered on the new St-Denis. A small, unimposing man of short and spare body, he was nevertheless a hands-on manager. When his workmen complained that he was calling for roof beams larger than anything local trees could provide, he spent a sleepless night, then personally searched the nearby forests until he found what he wanted. The work plainly thrilled him, but it was preeminently a spiritual endeavor. On one occasion, writes his twentieth-century biographer Erwin Panofsky (*Abbot Suger on the Abbey Church of St-Denis*), when he noticed newly made arches tottering dangerously in midair as they were hoisted into position, his solution was a quick "prayer to the holy martyrs." That saved the day and the arches.

Suger supervises the masons at work on St-Denis. When his plans called for timbers of a size that the workmen said were unavailable, Suger himself searched the forests around Paris and found them. The seventeenth-century painting is by Justus van Egmont.

Though he could certainly inspire men, Suger was far from universally beloved. He was "enormously vain," writes Panofsky, reveled in and boasted about his connections at court, and brazenly recorded his name at thirteen places in the new St-Denis. Nevertheless, infatuated though he was with the gold and jewels that glittered in his church, the tiny cell where he slept, not much bigger than a large cupboard, astonished other monks. In his personal life "he puts us all to shame," said Peter the Venerable, abbot of Cluny.

However vain, he also developed close personal friendships, one in particular. That was Bernard, who through Suger's stream of letters to him came to accept that for people who were not monks, beauty is essential to inspire the worship of God. But the influence worked both ways. From Bernard's new Cistercian abbeys Suger discovered and adopted the beauty manifested in simple geometric patterns and symmetry, a beauty that also found its way into the new St-Denis.

On his deathbed Suger pleaded for "one last visit" by Bernard. Bernard had to tell his "dearest and most intimate friend" that he could not come, and he prayed for the dying man's blessing. If, as Jesus had said, one can identify his servants because they love one another (John 13:35), here, surely, was a case in point.

But could Suger be called the "Father of Gothic," the role mid-twentieth-century historians assigned to him? No, writes Lindy Grant in a more recent biography (*Abbot Suger of St-Denis*). "Suger's position as patron of a seminal building is unassailable. But assessments as to his real involvement range right across the spectrum from those who have seen Suger as the creator of Gothic to those who see his own contribution as little more than paymaster. The truth, as we might expect, lies somewhere between the two." Without doubt, Gothic was far bigger than Suger and far bigger than France.

Even so, two other of Suger's friends would begin adopting his revolutionary architectural ideas and spreading them throughout the immediate area of Paris, known as the Ile-de-France. Thence they would reach all France and most of western Europe. This first became apparent in the new cathedral at Sens, where Suger's longtime colleague the volatile Archbishop Henry, swayed by the preaching of Bernard, had abandoned his courtly life and worldly ways and had proclaimed himself "converted" to Christlike austerity. He modeled his own new church on that of St-Denis, and Sens became the first of the new cathedrals.[3]

3. Archbishop Henry had other problems. He became so strident in his condemnations of courtly decadence and extravagance that Louis VI lost all patience with him, and even Suger couldn't restrain the monarchial wrath. But Henry roared on undaunted until his own clergy couldn't stand him either and Bernard himself had to admonish him for lacking charity.

Not far away, another Suger colleague, the bishop of Chartres Geoffrey
of Leves, who reputedly helped bring
about the "conversion" of Archbishop
Henry, was in personality nothing like
his convert. Gentle and learned, he
brought the works of the School of
Chartres in theology, philosophy, and
literature to such international renown
that they reached across Europe and
even, it was said, into Islam. Geoffrey,
too, was among the first to discern the
power of Suger's vision and worked it
into the new facade and western tower
then under way at Chartres.

There were other more substantial
emulators. In the eleven years before
Suger died, construction began on two
new cathedrals, at Noyon and Senlis in
Picardy, followed in four years by a
third at Laon. Then Louis VII, deeming
it essential that Paris have such a cathedral of its own, began the project in
1163. Thus, Notre Dame of Paris came
into being. Tours was started seven
years later, and four years after that an
architect named William, a layman who

*Suger is wrapped in a shroud for his
burial. From his deathbed he had
called for Bernard to pay him one
last visit. Unable to come, Bernard
bid him a comrade's farewell and
asked for his prayers. This
sixteenth-century painting is by
Charles Erard the Elder.*

had worked on Henry's project at Sens, was commissioned by Canterbury, the
archepiscopal center in southern England, to rebuild Christ Church Cathedral,
which had been destroyed by fire. The Gothic vision had crossed the Channel.

Fire also accounted for what is almost universally regarded as the greatest architectural triumph of the whole movement, in particular for the technical innovation
it initiated. On the night of June 10, 1194, a blaze broke out in Chartres that
destroyed most of the town and most of the cathedral. More serious still, it was
assumed to have destroyed the relic that made Chartres one of the most sacred sites
in all Christendom. For here, it was generally and fervently believed, was preserved
the very tunic that the Virgin had worn when she gave birth to Jesus. Without the
tunic and without the cathedral, it was thought, Chartres as a city was doomed.

How boundless therefore was the joy of the faithful when amidst the ruins the
tunic was found and declared authentic. This could mean only one thing: Blessed
Mary herself had seen a purpose in the fire. Clearly, she wanted a new cathedral
of the new visionary design. Thus it was decided that Notre Dame of Chartres
must be Europe's most beautiful church. Although the costs would be astronomical, far greater than any other public project in the Middle Ages, everyone would
contribute to it. In 1194 the great work was begun, with money streaming in
from all over France and beyond.[4]

The builders faced a daunting task. Expectations were soaring, not only those

4. A young English scholar returning home from France chanced to
hear a sermon extolling the Chartres
project and was inspired to donate
to the cathedral his sole possession
of any value, a golden necklace
intended for the young lady he
loved. England was then at war with
France, but the young man's gesture
so moved King Richard I (the
Lionheart) that he authorized
fundraisers for Chartres to canvass
all England under royal protection.

The soaring towers and delicate carving of Chartres Cathedral make it the most notable of all the Gothic structures in France. More than 150 of its 186 stained glass windows date from the thirteenth century. When it was built, the nave, at 118 feet, was the highest in Christendom. Its two towers today rise 344 and 371 feet above the ground. Toward those towers a group of student pilgrims make their way after a week in the French countryside.

of the people, but also (in the view of just about everybody) of the Virgin Mary herself, who, to the medieval mind, was there, an invisible but living presence, watching the work as it progressed. What would *she* think if they failed? They did not fail, however, proving equal to this challenge by a masterstroke of architectural ingenuity. By the crossed ribs in the vaulted roofs, they had been able to channel the weight of the roof to slender columns that took it to the ground. But as their churches rose higher, the thrust on the columns was not only downward but also outward. Too much height and the columns would buckle, collapsing the whole structure. The solution became known as the "flying buttress," an arch-shaped stone support that transferred the outward thrust from the exterior of the building to a freestanding pier conveying it to the ground. (But where the idea originated for the flying buttress has remained a matter of historical debate. Some ask if it was really at Chartres. Something like the flying buttress had appeared earlier at Notre Dame in Paris and also in Reims.)

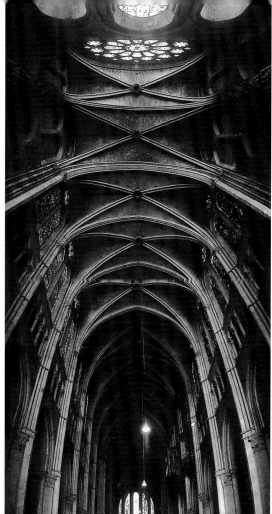

Whatever its origins, the result at Chartres was a phenomenon that still enthralls, raising ceilings to truly impressive heights. When Chartres was finished, one could stand on the floor of the nave and look upward to the roof vaults 121 feet above—the height of a modern ten-story building. Cologne, started in the following century, would top that with a nave 142 feet high, equaling a thirteen-story building.

But at Beauvais, in Picardy, the builders finally went too far. The vaulted roof of its new cathedral, begun in 1220, boasted a ceiling 159 feet above the floor, the highest church in Christendom, and at about eight in the evening of November 29, 1284, it came crashing down. There is no record of injuries, but Beauvais never recovered from the disaster. It would remain to this day a cathedral with only choir and transepts.[5] Beauvais sought to compensate for its loss by building a great tower 291 feet high and topped by a spire that took it to 438—equivalent to a forty-story building—at the point where the transepts meet the choir. On April 30, 1573, the whole thing collapsed into a heap of rubble just twenty minutes after the Great Procession for the morning Mass had left the church. Two people, still in the building, were injured. The tower was never replaced.

Before the end of the twelfth century, fascination with the new church architecture was engulfing western Europe, and cathedrals exploiting the new methods were under construction in fourteen French and English cities. Soon they began to appear elsewhere as well: in Spain, Germany, Flanders (Belgium), Holland, Portugal, and Italy. Between 1050 and 1350, writes the historian Jean Gimpel (*The Cathedral Builders*), eighty cathedrals, five hundred large churches, and more than ten thousand parish churches would be erected in Europe. In the year 1220 alone, work started on new cathedrals at Amiens, Toul, Metz, Beauvais, Salisbury, and York.

By the end of the Middle Ages there would be one church or chapel for every two hundred people in western Europe. Norwich, Lincoln, and York, cities of five to ten thousand, boasted fifty, forty-nine, and forty-one churches, respectively. Some of these edifices were enormous, such as the cathedral at Amiens, which

Left: *The flying buttresses of Chartres Cathedral solved the problem that Gothic design gravely intensified. As the piers took the roof weight to the ground, the stress was not only downward but also outward. The piers threatened to buckle. To bear this force, the builders designed exterior buttresses that in effect transformed a lateral thrust into a downward one.* Right: *A panoramic view of the interior of Chartres, looking up the nave toward the main altar.*

5. One possible cause of the Beauvais collapse in 1284 was a feud between young king Louis IX (St. Louis) and the bishop of Beauvais, which for several years cut off royal funding for the cathedral project. In the course of this conflict nobles supporting the bishop attempted to kidnap the king, and the bishop accused the king's mother, the devout Blanche of Castile, of being pregnant by a papal legate. Furious, Blanche appeared before a church council, where she stripped off her clothes to demonstrate conclusively by her flat stomach that she definitely was not pregnant by anybody. The dispute was eventually settled in the king's favor, but the funding cutoff may have compromised materials used in the cathedral construction. A more probable explanation is that the choir piers settled differently, destabilizing the roof vaults.

could accommodate, by one account, nearly ten thousand worshippers. Not until the twentieth century would the world see another such building boom.

That each cathedral town should have one of these spectacular buildings was altogether understandable, especially since the cathedral was far more than a place of worship. Its nave was the municipality's central place of assembly, where trade was talked, deals made, politics discussed, marriages negotiated, and gossip exchanged. There were no chairs or pews; people from all strata of society mixed and strolled about, intent upon worship, business, or socializing.[6] They sometimes brought their pets with them: dogs, cats, falcons. They ate in the nave, and some slept in the crypt (i.e., basement). City councils often met there, as did business and trade guilds. But the cathedral's choir and sanctuary, where the *cathedra* (chair) of the bishop was located, and where Mass was celebrated and the daily offices observed, was separated from all this rabble by a "chancel screen," intended to protect the clergy from the noise of everyday affairs and the common people. (And "also the smell," notes one memoir).

So construction of one of these mammoths was a momentous undertaking. Direction of the work early moved away from bishops and abbots and was taken up by professional architects or master builders, who developed into a well-paid professional caste. Monks still worked as laborers, but bishops and abbots set forth what they wanted in the new building and the professionals provided it. Wooden lodges were built to house the "free" masons, who moved from project to project. Among these, says Gimpel, eventually arose the Masonic movement.

The Cathedral of St. Pierre in Beauvais, France. Here the builders went too far. With the new cathedral, begun in 1220, they produced a ceiling 159 feet above the floor. One evening in 1284 it came crashing down. Beauvais sought to compensate for its loss by building a great tower 291 feet high and topped by a spire that took it to 438—equivalent to a forty-story building—at the point where the transepts meet the choir. In 1573 the whole thing collapsed into a heap of rubble.

Building a cathedral was more than a job of work, however; it was preeminently a communal endeavor. The church itself provided much of the financing, but money also poured in from kings, barons, knights, merchants, and wealthy widows. Accounts also survive of "cart pilgrimages," where lords and ladies trudged along rocky roads or through knee-deep mud, pushing or hauling carts full of stones, building supplies, or food to the jobsite.

Thus they could enter into the thrill of the project, shared by both spectators and workmen, and well captured by author Ken Follett in his best-selling historical novel *The Pillars of the Earth*. He describes "the irresistible attraction of building a cathedral—the absorbing complexity of the organization, the intellectual challenge of the calculations, the sheer size of the walls, the breathtaking beauty and grandeur of the finished building." Dorothy L. Sayers in her excellent play on the construction of Canterbury puts the same sentiment into the mouth of its architect, William of Sens: "We all have our dreams . . . Churches we shall never live to see. Arch shouldering arch, shaft, vault and keystone, window and arcading higher, and wider and lighter, lifting roof, tower, spire into the vault of heaven—columns slender as lily-stalks—walls only a framework for the traceries—living fountains of stone" (*The Zeal of Thy House*, Part II).

Although such churches continued to appear right to the dawn of the sixteenth century—and two, Washington National Cathedral and St. John the Divine in New York, even in the twentieth (see pages 60–61)—much of the passion and creativity went out of the movement early in the 1300s. Thereafter, writes Gimpel, practically no progress was made in construction technique. Most historians attribute the decline to the Hundred Years' War, which in the fourteenth and fifteenth centuries crippled France, seedbed of the whole phenomenon. In the Renaissance that followed, the entire movement was vehemently denounced as barbaric by artists and architects like Raphael Sanzio and Georgio Vasari. It was truly "Gothic," they sneered, a product of the wild tribes who had destroyed the cherished civilization of Greece and Rome. The derisive term stuck. The fact that some seven hundred years had separated the vision of Suger from the brutal onslaught of the Ostrogoths and Visigoths did not subdue the scorn.

The three following centuries continued to frown on the great cathedrals. In 1568 Sainte-Croix (Holy Cross) of Orleans was destroyed, a victim of the Protestant-Catholic wars, although it was rebuilt within forty years. St. Lambert of Liege was not so fortunate. It was destroyed and permanently lost in the French Revolution, when statuary and artwork were vandalized in many cathedrals and hundreds of ancient monasteries were demolished.[7]

In the nineteenth century there came a dramatic turn, however, when the whole Gothic phenomenon was reappraised and discovered to be astonishingly beautiful. The connotation of the word was now reversed. No longer a term of contempt, it came to signify the majestic, the awesome, and the aesthetically powerful. This gave rise to new Gothic, or "neo-Gothic," which inspired tens of thousands of churches, both Protestant and Catholic, throughout much of the Christian world, all modestly imitating some outward aspects of the originals. Ironically, however, some of the great cathedrals now fared ill at the hands of their would-be friends, whose determination to "restore" them became efforts to "improve" them—often with what many view as deplorable results.

6. Seating was not provided in western churches until the thirteenth century; worshippers either stood or knelt throughout the service. By the end of the century, benches began appearing along the walls for use by the infirm, giving rise to the expression "Let the weak go to the wall." E. L. Cross's *Oxford Dictionary of the Christian Church* (revised 1983) speculates that the word "pew" probably derives from the Latin *podium*, a platform raised above floor level. Pews did not become common in western churches until the eighteenth century and were never adopted in the East, where ecclesiastical seating remains sparse in many Orthodox churches to this day.

7. "Eighteenth-century Christians simply could not believe that medieval works permitted a dignified glorification of God," writes Gimpel. "Gothic taste, as it was then called, merited only the sledgehammer and ax of demolition." Typical of many was the fate of St-Denis, where vast "improvements" were made to the central portal: the statue of St-Denis was destroyed along with the statuary of the kings and queens of the Old Testament, the royal tombs of France on the side aisles were denounced as "hideous," and an Italian contractor was hired to whitewash the entire interior of the building.

But then the modernist movement of the early twentieth century brought on yet another wave of anti-Gothic revulsion. Once again, Gothic was portrayed as an unedifying vestige of the crude, prerationalist delusions of an antiquated Christian culture. Such delusion, it was decreed, must now yield architecturally to the austere higher purity of the straight line, the right angle, and the fluorescent tube. Not everyone was enthused. To some, this turned out to mean living in houses that looked like boxes, sending children to schools that looked like warehouses, and attending churches that looked like experimental union halls. A reaction ultimately set in.

That reaction is generally known as postmodernism, and as the second Christian millennium closed, it was producing some opinions and theories that many postmodernists may have found disturbing, if not downright alarming. Some few art historians actually appeared to be looking back on those eight-hundred-year-old houses of worship as a possible source of insight. Could it perhaps be, they were asking, that the creators of the seemingly imperishable Gothic knew something that modern man never knew or has forgotten?

Mary Carruthers's book *The Craft of Thought: Meditation, Rhetoric and the Making of Images, 400–1200* shows how medieval techniques of rhetoric enabled monks to memorize holy scripture by mentally filing verses away in rooms of imagined monasteries. Qualities became associated with them, such as happiness with the cloister garden, and visions of architecture could lead to actual construction; such was famously the case with Cluny Abbey. It was a process that carried over into their own abbeys, in which holy imagery and relics in altars became prompts for commemoration.

Even the number of altars could be symbolic, as demonstrated in Nigel Hiscock's book *The Symbol at Your Door: Number and Geometry in Religious Architecture of the Greek and Latin Middle Ages.* Because it was believed that God, as the Divine Architect, had created order in the universe "by measure and number and weight," the liberal arts taught how the divine order could be comprehended, and this gave importance and meaning to number and geometry. For instance, it is no coincidence that baptisteries and fonts are usually eight-sided, since the number eight signifies salvation. Similarly, in the geometric tracery of church windows, trefoils can signify the Holy Trinity, quatrefoils the four Gospels, and cinquefoils the five books of Moses.

As the desire for meaning gathers pace, many will look up at the distant vaults of Winchester Cathedral in Britain, or the two great towers of the Elizabeth Church in Marburg, Germany,[8] or St. Michael's Cathedral in Brussels, or Chartres, or Cologne, or St. Eulalia's in Barcelona and find themselves captivated by the overwhelming grandeur all around them and above them. Such works as these occur when faith combines with reason to produce power and beauty, and thereby bring into being a whole new world. In the oncoming era, such a transformation was about to occur to thirteenth-century Christianity, and these great churches were but the first instance of it. ■

8. During the Reformation of the sixteenth century, the Gothic cathedrals in England were expropriated by the crown and were administered by the Anglican Church, while in France nearly all the historic cathedrals are now state owned. In other countries most have remained in the possession of the Roman Catholic Church. One exception was St. Elizabeth's in Marburg, Germany, long the principal city of Hesse. In 1233 this Gothic structure, which houses the shrine to St. Elizabeth of Hungary (see page 123), became the religious center of the Teutonic Knights. For many years after the Reformation, both Protestant and Catholic services were held in it.

WORKING WITH POWER UPON THE SOULS OF MEN . . .

Look then upon this Cathedral Church of Christ:
Imagined by men's minds,
Built by the labor of men's hands,
Working with power upon the souls of men;
Symbol of the Everlasting Trinity,
The visible temple of God.
As you would honor Christ, so honor His Church;
Nor suffer this temple of His body to know decay.

From *The Zeal of Thy House* by Dorothy L. Sayers

*The nave of the Cathedral Church
of Christ, Canterbury, England*

A paradox of history

That the same bellicose Christians who launched the Crusades should produce the greatest flowering of Christian creativity yet seen poses an unexplained mystery

To Heinrich Heine, the nineteenth-century German romantic poet, the Gothic cathedrals were built by men filled with conviction. "We moderns," he writes in a letter to his friend August Lewald, "have opinions, but it requires something more than an opinion to build a Gothic cathedral." In 1160 Maurice de Sully, certainly a man of conviction and bishop of Paris, decreed that the old Romanesque church that had existed upon this site since the sixth century was not befitting of Paris's new role as "the parish church of the kings of Europe." Therefore he ordered the old church demolished along with the houses around it to make room for the first western cathedral built on such a monumental scale. Legend portrays him sketching the original plan in the dirt outside of the old church. De Sully was also the cathedral's original benefactor, directing most of his modest fortune towards its construction. But he never saw the completed cathedral. He died in 1196, more than half a century before the work was done. Similarly deep convictions launched the Crusades; in fact the Third Crusade set forth from the very steps of Notre Dame of Paris.

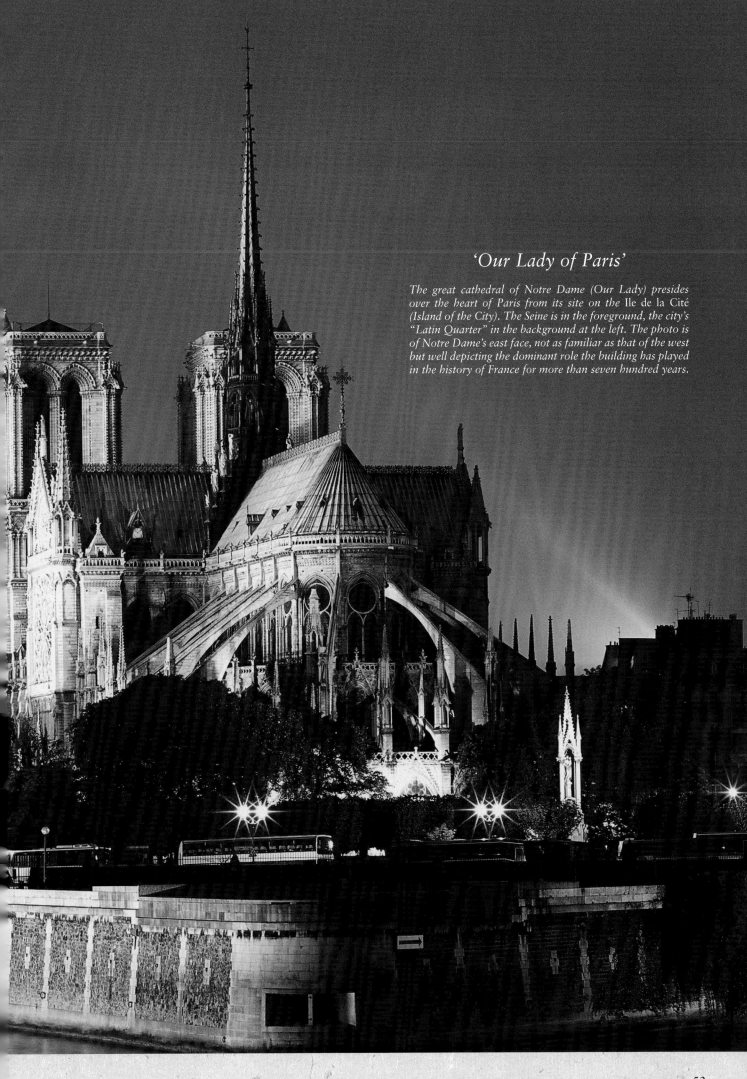

'Our Lady of Paris'

The great cathedral of Notre Dame (Our Lady) presides over the heart of Paris from its site on the Ile de la Cité (Island of the City). The Seine is in the foreground, the city's "Latin Quarter" in the background at the left. The photo is of Notre Dame's east face, not as familiar as that of the west but well depicting the dominant role the building has played in the history of France for more than seven hundred years.

Cologne: after 400 years, resurrection

Long left derelict by the contempt of the Renaissance Gothic suddenly revived

A testament to the enduring faith of the German people, Cologne Cathedral took over six hundred years to reach completion. Begun in 1248, the work initially proceeded at a steady pace, with the choir finished seventy-four years after the cornerstone was laid.

But then the work began to slow down, and by 1473, with all things medieval falling under the disfavor of the Renaissance, work was stopped altogether. One tower was completed, the other topped by a crane that was to become the landmark of Cologne for the next four hundred years.

Not until a new enthusiasm for the Middle Ages arose in the nineteenth century did work begin again. Construction was spurred by the discovery of the original plans and by the zeal of Cologne's Central Cathedral Building Society, formed in 1842 to finish the job and maintain the building. The primary benefactor was the emperor William I, who provided one third of the approximately one billion dollars (in twenty-first century money) required for completion. The rest came from the people of Germany. In 1880, with a national day of celebration and great festivities, the job was declared done. By the twenty-first century the building society had about ten thousand members and a board of forty. It raises through membership fees, bequests, and the revenues of a lottery the $3.5 million required annually for staff and upkeep.

Highlighted by floodlights at dusk, the Cologne Cathedral of St. Peter and St. Mary stands near the Hohenzollern Bridge over the Rhine River. Around 1248 Archbishop Conrad von Hochstaden ordered work on the new Gothic cathedral to begin, based on the design of a master builder named Gerhard. The specific purpose of the cathedral was to showcase the magnificent gold reliquary of the "three magi," brought from Constantinople. Above: Looking east to the high choir, the central nave is illuminated by a vast expanse of stained glass. This tremendous height and very open wall system was made possible by an engineering advancement that used a series of compound piers around a core pier that was egg shaped in cross section. Immediate left: To the left of the main entrance stands a stone sculpture of St. John the Baptist. He points to the symbol of the Lamb of God, reflecting the biblical account (John 1:29).

Canterbury: murder and miracles

What provided a setting for Chaucer's 'Tales' would become Anglicanism's mother church

The cathedral immortalized by Chaucer's *Canterbury Tales* in the fourteenth century functions in the twenty-first as the "mother church" of the Anglican Communion. However, Chaucer would not have known Canterbury Cathedral in that role, since there was no such thing then as the Anglican communion. Rather, he would have known it as the successor to the church built by the missionary Augustine in the sixth century, who brought Roman Christianity to England, which was Celtic Christian.

More particularly, Chaucer would have known Canterbury as the site of countless miracles wrought in the name of St. Thomas Becket, murdered before Canterbury's altar two hundred years before Chaucer's time (see pages 96–97). Here, too, would come King Henry II, founder of the Plantagenet dynasty and often cited as England's greatest king, to do penance for Becket's murder. In fact, the shrine erected to Becket, known as the Trinity Chapel, has been a pilgrimage site since it was built in 1220.

The stairs leading into the chapel are so worn they appear hollowed like a saucer from the feet and knees of people climbing in penitence to visit his shrine. The first miracles attributed to Becket are portrayed in the stained glass of Trinity Chapel.

Opposite page: *The Great Western Window of Canterbury Cathedral, which contains the oldest known piece of stained glass in Britain, an image of Adam dating from the late twelfth century, visible in the middle of the bottom row. Above it are images made in the fifteenth century of eight English kings.* Above top: *The cathedral seen from the west, showing the two western towers, built in perpendicular Gothic, and the* center tower, Bell Harry, built in 1498. Above left: *The cathedral from the air showing the full range of its architecture from the Norman to the Gothic.* Above right: *Dean Wooton, first dean of Canterbury, appointed after the dissolution of the monasteries in the fifteenth century. Wooton served under four sovereigns, surviving the fierce Protestant-Catholic struggle to die in 1567, during the reign of Queen Elizabeth I.*

Lincoln: fated start, fine finish

Despite a fire and an earthquake, William the Conqueror's vision is finally fulfilled

Lincoln, the largest diocese in England, was without a cathedral for centuries under the Saxon kings until the Normans arrived and William the Conqueror erected a Romanesque structure to meet the pressing need. Fortune, however, did not favor Lincoln. The cathedral lasted about half a century, until the roof caught fire and destroyed much of the building.

At this time Gothic architecture was gaining wide acceptance, and it was decided to replace the old roof with a vaulted one to prevent future fires. Reversals, however, continued. Forty years later an earthquake hit Lincoln, and much of the cathedral collapsed, leaving only the western face.

Thus, in the year 1192 the revered Bishop St. Hugh, whose tomb lies with the present cathedral, began rebuilding it in gothic style, with only the western front and towers retained from the earlier constructions. Once completed, this thirteenth-century structure has proved indestructible and still stands to this day.

The nave of Lincoln Cathedral (above right) was built during the first half of the thirteenth century in the early English Gothic style, using pointed arches, ribbed vaulting, and flying buttresses to make possible larger windows. The buttresses are visible in the imposing view of the cathedral from the southeast (below). The cathedral's twin towers look down on the city of Lincoln (above). The city's walls may be seen in the distance.

Milan: the captivity of Mark Twain

The great bard of the Mississippi confesses himself wholly smitten by a cathedral

Mark Twain perhaps best described the rapture that embraces people when they first see the *Duomo* (cathedral) of Milan. "What a wonder it is! So grand, so solemn, so vast!" he wrote, "and yet so delicate, so airy, so graceful! A very world of solid weight, and yet it seems ... a delusion of frostwork that might vanish with a breath! ... They say that the Cathedral of Milan is second only to St. Peter's at Rome. I cannot understand how it can be second to anything made by human hands." Undeniably, in terms of height it is second only to the uncompleted Beauvais. However, it can be argued that it is superior to Beauvais in the fact that it is still standing and completed. (Beauvais' great tower collapsed.)

Above: *The intricacies of the great pinnacle of the Duomo (Cathedral) of Milan, known as the Tiburio, manifest the Italian Gothic style. It dates back to the fifteenth century.* Below: *The upper part of the facade was completed early in the nineteenth century. Note the typically Gothic windows.* Right: *The summer sun sets over the cathedral spires.* Across the bottom: *The north face of the cathedral in the winter fog of Milan.*

Washington: Gothic crosses the sea

Though the National Cathedral was founded by Congress, its funding is wholly private

The Gothic phenomenon is not limited to Europe. In fact, the cathedral that graces these pages is located in Washington D.C. and it was put there by an act of the United States Congress. Envisioned by President Benjamin Harrison as a non-denominational house of national prayer he signed the charter in 1893, Congress approved and the project began.

However, this was not a new idea. As early as 1793 Pierre l'Enfant, when designing the first street plan for Washington created space for a "great church for national purposes." Unfortunately, the land he set aside was eventually used to house the National Portrait Gallery. Therefore a new plot of land would be required for Washington's new great church.

The site eventually chosen, Mount Saint Alban, dominates the American capital, the central spire of the cathedral being the highest point in the city. Construction began on the cathedral in 1907 with the foundation stone laid by President Theodore Roosevelt. The first services began only five years later in the Bethlehem Chapel, now located in the crypt. These services have been held daily ever since.

Astonishingly, the cathedral has had no public funding during any period of its history. Its construction was financed in its entirety by private donations. These funds are collected and administered by the National Cathedral Association. Members of the association were told that if they were to seek public funding, it would be denied under the First Amendment's establishment clause.

Left: *The two towers of Washington National Cathedral look down on Connecticut Avenue, the left for St. Peter and the right for St. Paul, whose names the cathedral bears. Inside the door on the right, Attilio Piccirilli's statue of George Washington greets visitors. Designed by Lee Lauerie, it was dedicated in 1947, two years after Piccirilli's death.*

Above: *The view from the center of the Great Crossing, looking westward down the nave.* Right: *The high altar, viewed from the east through the Great Choir.*

The cathedral, highest point on the Washington skyline, viewed at dusk from the east.

King Louis VII of France took the cross from Pope Eugene III in March of 1146 prior to embarking on the Second Crusade. In this nineteenth-century oil painting by Jean Baptiste Mauzaisse, Bernard of Clairvaux stands on the pope's left; Queen Eleanor of Aquitaine kneels on the right.

CHAPTER 3

The resurgence of Islam and an incendiary monk fuel a second crusade

As Edessa's fall imperils the new Christian kingdoms, Bernard of Clairvaux reawakens an apathetic Europe, but a disaster at Damascus collapses the whole effort

Edessa had fallen. There was no denying it. The rumors were true. Mighty Islam had recovered strength, and the great Christian citadel near the banks of the Euphrates, 150 miles inland from the Mediterranean, had gone down before it. Now the whole precarious Christian recovery of the East was plainly at risk. All Europe was said to be shocked.

But was it? Was anyone even interested? While the news was filtering west midway through 1145, the papacy was embroiled in political turmoil with the kings of Sicily, France, and Germany. In November that year Eugene III was elected pope and immediately issued a formal crusade, which many took to mean that crusaders would be forgiven all their sins and guaranteed admission to heaven, though this was not what the church had promised.[1] However, their property would be protected and loan interest forgiven. But his call had fallen flat. Even when King Louis VII of France made a Christmas appeal to rouse his vassals, they remained distinctly unenthused. Help for the imperiled Christians of Outremer looked hopeless.

Could anyone, anywhere, somehow bring Christendom alive to the danger? There was perhaps one man, though whether he would agree was another matter. He was almost everywhere revered but was preeminently a man of peace and prayer. In desperation Louis appealed directly to this powerful personality, the abbot of Clairvaux known to history as St. Bernard.

It was Bernard who had been primarily responsible for the astounding rise of the Cistercians, known from their undyed habits as the "white monks," the reformed

1. The Council of Clermont, at which the First Crusade had been launched, granted an indulgence from the penances imposed by the church for specific sins, penances normally made in this world, not the next. As for those who undertook a crusade for personal gain, the council became even more definitive. It decreed: "Whoever, out of pure devotion, and not for purpose of gaining honor or money, shall go to Jerusalem to liberate the Church of God, let the journey be counted in lieu of all penance." This was far from the kind of blanket, or "plenary," indulgence that many came to believe had been conferred.

Louis VII, portrayed here in a nineteenth-century lithograph by Jacques Etienne Pannier, commanded the foremost of five armies that undertook the Second Crusade. He blamed the Byzantines for the damage inflicted on his army by the Turks in Anatolia and later planned an attack on Constantinople.

2. The moment of commitment for Conrad of Hohenstaufen came during Abbot Bernard's sermon, when the monk stared fixedly at him and demanded, as though asking on behalf of Christ himself, "Man, what ought I to have done for you that I have not done?"

monastic order that had already mushroomed under his inspiration from two small, poor monasteries to more than 170. He plainly preferred a life of prayer and meditation but had repeatedly been summoned back to the world as a power broker and moral compass in papal politics, had served or would serve as an adviser to five popes, and had once courageously rescued the papacy from open schism. Frail, gray-haired, and renowned for his captivating sermons, he was far more highly regarded than Eugene, who had been his pupil. No, he told Louis, such a call must come from the pope himself.

Bernard did not conceal his reluctance to back a second mass expedition to recover Christian lands in the East. Quite apart from his personal asceticism, he considered the heresies of Europe more important than (as he saw them) the ravings of an Arab cult, no matter how militarily successful. But as a monk he was sworn to obedience. When the pope's appeal affirmed that of Louis, Bernard complied. On March 31, 1146, at Vezelay, with pale King Louis and vivacious Queen Eleanor of Aquitaine next to him, the abbot preached his first sermon for what would become known as the Second Crusade. Face aglow, voice impassioned, he marveled at this extraordinary opportunity for redemption from sin. And in a scene reminiscent of Clermont fifty years before, the resultant clamor for crosses, led by the royal couple themselves, prompted him to fling off his habit so that pieces could be torn from it to supply them. "Receive the sign of the cross," he told each person who came forward, "and thou shalt likewise obtain the indulgence of all thou hast confessed with a contrite heart."

Thereafter he threw all his gifts of word, voice, faith, and physical strength into the recruiting campaign. Dying in this cause, he declared, was the best thing that could happen to a man: "You should rejoice and give thanks if you go to join the Lord. . . . This age is like no other that has gone before; a new abundance of divine mercy comes down from heaven. . . . Look at the skill God is using to save you. Consider the depths of his love and be astonished, you sinners. He creates a need . . . while he desires to help you in your necessity. This is a plan not made by man, but coming from heaven and proceeding from the heart of divine love."

Preaching in both Latin and French through Burgundy, Lorraine, and Flanders, Bernard sparked a fire that swept across Europe. In the Rhineland, where the message was delivered by others and morphed into a wave of anti-Semitism, the abbot himself hastened to stem such "perversion." He also traveled in Switzerland and twice preached at the court of the German king Conrad III in Frankfurt. There, to the surprise of the entire continent, his fiery Christmas sermon about Judgment Day prompted Conrad to join with Louis. Thus Europe's two most powerful rulers were committed.[2]

Meanwhile, the enthusiasm kept spreading. King Alfonso VII of Castile persuaded Eugene to extend the crusade into Spain by offering special indulgences to the Genoese and southern French. More dubious was the support the pope and Bernard agreed to give German Saxons, who sought indulgences for a territorial war against neighboring Slavic Wend pagans.

Thus the vision widened. In another letter Eugene authorized indulgences for crusaders on all three fronts—the East, Spain, and Germany—as part of one vast enterprise. In the East five armies would eventually converge: those under Louis, Conrad, Amadeus of Savoy, and Alfonso Jordan of Toulouse and an Anglo-Flemish force, which stopped on its way eastward to liberate Lisbon from the Muslims. In the northeast the Saxons, Danes, Brandenburgers, and Poles would attack the Wends. In Spain the French and Genoese would wage four campaigns against the Muslim Moors.

Precedents were set. Louis became the first monarch to levy a crusade tax. Conrad repaired roads and bridges in foreign lands as he marched through Hungary rather than risk involvement with his enemy Roger of Sicily by taking the sea route. Louis followed a few weeks behind him to allow local food supplies to be replenished.

Their combined force was perhaps stronger than that of the First Crusade, but its task was much more formidable. The First Crusaders, having taken Antioch and Jerusalem in 1099, had only then realized that they had no plan to govern them. Ominously, the vast majority of crusaders returned home that September, leaving a mere three hundred knights and two thousand infantry to hold Jerusalem. The Christians subsequently moved inland two hundred miles, then took a six-hundred-mile strip along the Mediterranean coast with only two ports and several fortress cities. To the east lay mighty Persia, much of central Asia, India, and Indonesia

After some initial hesitation Bernard of Clairvaux threw himself wholeheartedly into recruiting for the crusade. He is seen here preaching to Louis VII at Vezelay, exhorting the king and his subjects to take up the cross. This 1840 oil on canvas is by Emile Signol.

3. Edessa, originally called Osrhoene and renamed in 303 BC for the former capital of Macedonia, had been the site of a Christian council in 197. Many martyrs had suffered there, and priests from Edessa had evangelized eastern Mesopotamia and Persia. One of the largest of the crusader states, Edessa was small in population: ten thousand inhabitants in the city, and the rest of the county almost empty except for a few fortresses. The inhabitants were mostly Assyrian, Jacobite, and Armenian Orthodox Christians, with some Greek Orthodox and some Muslims. Although the number of Latins was minimal, Edessa had a Roman Catholic archbishop.

4. King Baldwin's empathy with the local inhabitants had notably unscrupulous, not to say unchristian, aspects. After securing her dowry, he repudiated his Armenian wife in order to marry a wealthy Sicilian widow, whom he also divorced shortly after running through her dowry as well. His motives in being adopted by a childless Armenian prince also fell under deep suspicion, to say the least. Having promised to protect his new "father," Baldwin seemingly allowed him to be murdered by a mob, then took over his title and possessions.

Although often short on manpower, the crusaders were known for building strong fortifications. The castle on Coral Island (also known as Pharaoh's Island), at the northernmost reach of the Gulf of Aqaba, one of the two "fingers" at the northern end of the Red Sea, was built by the Byzantines to protect pilgrims traveling between Jerusalem and St. Catherine's Monastery, at the base of Mount Sinai. It was strengthened by the crusaders, then captured by Saladin in 1182.

and to the south Egypt and North Africa, all under Muslim rule. The Christian presence in Outremer was, in other words, highly tenuous.

It was also highly fractious. Their most powerful religious ally, the Byzantine emperor Alexius I, had withdrawn his support for them after they arbitrarily took possession of former Byzantine territory. The rulers of Jerusalem, Antioch, and Edessa, all largely self-appointed, endlessly quarreled while Rome ignored them. Godfrey of Bouillon, Jerusalem's leading liberator, had died of typhoid within a year. His brother Baldwin, although the most competent among the city's would-be rulers, was nevertheless a somewhat unsavory candidate. He had disgraced himself in the First Crusade by initiating a blood-soaked brawl in which fellow Christian knights had killed one another. Later, with some hundred renegade knights, he abandoned the Crusade altogether and took Edessa, helped greatly by the resident Armenian Christians, who had long smarted under Muslim rule.[3]

For the next eighteen years Baldwin almost single-handedly established a functioning government in Outremer. A just but ferocious ruler, he handily suppressed local Muslim uprisings, rewarded friends, and had enemies publicly tortured before execution. He negotiated deals with European sea captains, swapping trading rights for arms and supplies. He exploited Muslim rivalries while himself embracing local customs, wearing a turban (with a cross) and white burnoose embroidered in gold, for example. He married an Armenian woman for her dowry and encouraged his vassals to do likewise. Gradually he made himself liege lord of the Christians and was crowned Baldwin I, King of Jerusalem, on Christmas Day, 1100.[4]

By the time he died in 1118, it all looked so permanent: a new, viable kingdom linked to Europe by sea with a physical infrastructure and revenue systems to support and defend it. The two orders of fighting monks, the Knights Templar and the Hospitallers, provided a much-respected standing army (see sidebar page 35), and a workable treaty with Damascus had secured the northern frontier. Two powerful kings followed Baldwin I: his cousin Baldwin II (1118–1131) and the latter's son-in-law Fulk V of Anjou (1131–1143). But Fulk's premature death in a freak hunting accident ended those golden years.

In actuality, however, history would record that the downfall of Outremer had already begun sixteen years earlier. In 1127 the Muslim sultan in Baghdad had chosen as governor of Mosul, on the Tigris 250 miles northwest of Baghdad, a squat figure with piercing black eyes that glared from beneath his turban. His sadistic and savage ferocity frightened both followers and foes. He crucified his own troops if they marched out of line; one man reputedly had been so terrified at the mere sight of him that he fell dead on the spot.

This governor's name was 'imad al-Din Zengi ibn Aq Sonqur, and he was a Seljuk Turk with ambitions to take over Syria. Since his first opponents were Muslim, he

kept the peace, even sought treaties, with Baldwin II while he subdued them. Once when his army accidentally tangled with Christian troops, he had trapped King Fulk in a castle but then, astonishingly, freed him in exchange for the castle and a sumptuous robe.

Nevertheless, a clash with the Christians was inevitable. Whatever else his motives, Zengi knew that faithful Muslims were under a perpetual obligation of jihad, which meant (along with other, more spiritual interpretations) taking arms against unbelievers. In an Islamic world where all authority derives from religion, embracing jihad had always offered non-Arabs a way to elevate their social status. As the champions of orthodoxy they could enhance their political profile. By 1144, with his Muslim rivals crushed, the time to tackle the Christians had come, and the obvious and most vulnerable target was Edessa.

Moreover, the city had been ripe for the taking. Its latest governor, Count Joscelin of Courtenay, had been weak, dissolute, negligent, and at bitter odds with his immediate overlord, Raymond of Antioch. Zengi had correctly suspected that Raymond would not aid his vassal. Preaching jihad, he had marshaled Turkomans and Kurds from the upper Tigris region to swell his army. Then in

This nineteenth-century engraving from the Bibliothèque des Croisades by Gustave Doré depicts the death of Baldwin I, king of Jerusalem and Edessa, from an old hunting wound aggravated in battle. A just but ferocious ruler, Baldwin maintained a strong Christian presence in Outremer.

late November 1144 he had duped Joscelin and most of his troops into leaving Edessa by attacking one of Joscelin's allies elsewhere. Once the count and his army had departed, Zengi laid siege to the city and undermined a wall, causing it to collapse. On Christmas Eve the Muslims had poured in to slaughter thousands of Christians while Joscelin awaited reinforcements from Jerusalem that arrived too late.[5] In Baghdad the caliph had conferred on Zengi the title "Ornament of Islam, the Auxiliary Commander of the Faithful, the Divinely Aided King."

Although it had taken nearly three years, the magnitude of this news had finally roused the West to action. Curiously, despite their lengthy preparations neither Louis nor Conrad had communicated with Christians in Outremer. Apparently, they expected to march directly from Constantinople to Edessa and easily retake it without assistance. Indeed, both the French and the Germans treated the crusade rather like a family holiday. Following the example of Eleanor, many spouses, children, chambermaids, and household staffs accompanied the knights, as did mammoth trains of trunks and luggage.

5. Many Christians were trampled to death—by each other—when the Muslims broke through the walls of Edessa in 1144. Running to the citadel for protection, they found its gates locked by order of the Latin archbishop Hugh II, who had been placed in charge (supported by the Armenian bishop John and Jacobite bishop Basil). The archbishop apparently feared that the crowd would create confusion within.

Conrad and his multitude arrived outside Constantinople early in September 1147. The young Byzantine emperor, Manuel Comnenus, like his grandfather Alexius before him, did not want to deal with more than one foreign army at a time. After Conrad swore an oath not to harm Byzantine interests, Manuel (who was married to Conrad's sister-in-law) convinced him to accept transportation across the Bosporus rather than await Louis. However, he could not persuade Conrad to have pilgrims and noncombatants sail directly to Jerusalem instead of traveling with the overland expedition. Conrad gathered provisions at Nicea, in Asia Minor, and immediately started his unwieldy entourage moving. Unfortunately, the lumbering group was so large and so slow that it rapidly used up supplies. In October, near the ruins of the ancient city of Doryleum, about one hundred miles southeast of Constantinople, the Germans met disaster. Routed by Turks in an ambush, the few survivors were harassed all the way back to Nicea, whence most headed for home. The experience left Conrad's second in command, young Frederick Barbarossa, firmly resolved that there must be another crusade and it must not be run like this one (see chapter 4).

King Louis and his queen had meanwhile encountered a chilly reception in Constantinople. The French were deeply mistrusted by Manuel, not only because of their close ties to his Italian Norman enemies but because Eleanor's uncle Raymond was now

Above: A representation of the young Byzantine emperor Manuel Comnenus and his wife, Maria of Antioch. Constantinople was less than welcoming to the crusaders. The emperor had a treaty with the Turks that prevented the crusaders from proceeding by land. Below: The entrance to the citadel at Aleppo, the formidable fortress two hundred miles northeast of Damascus that would take the Muslim hero Saladin eight years to conquer.

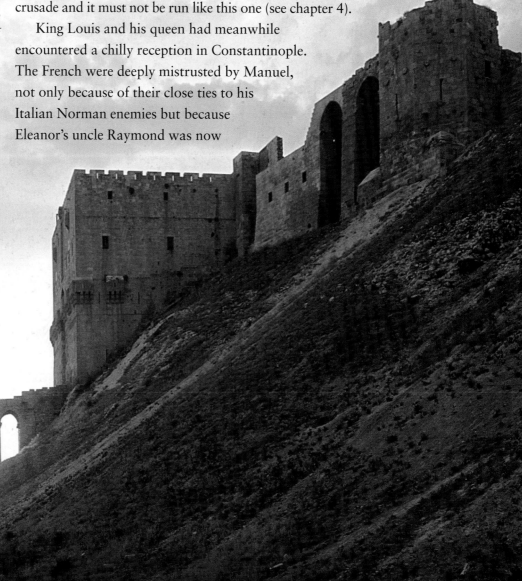

prince of formerly Byzantine Antioch. For his part, Louis was infuriated to discover that Manuel had made a treaty with the Turkish sultan who controlled the territory his crusaders must cross. At length, however, he reluctantly mollified Manuel by taking an oath of homage to the Byzantine, and his army was thereupon ferried to Asia Minor—though, like Conrad, he disregarded Manuel's advice to have his noncombatants travel by ship around Asia Minor to the Mediterranean.

At Nicea Louis was joined by the remnant of Conrad's army and learned of the Germans' debacle. Rather than head directly overland as planned, he decided to take a longer route along the coastline, in part to ensure adequate provisions. At Ephesus, however, Conrad became ill, so he returned to Constantinople (where Manuel served as his personal physician). Meanwhile, as their food supplies dwindled, the French ignored warnings that the Turks were massing against them. Turning southeast, they marched inland on a more direct route, apparently relying on the goodwill of Manuel within his empire. But the local populace and garrisons provided neither food nor military assistance, and the Turks repeatedly attacked. By January 1148 people and animals were facing starvation. Toward the end of the month the Turks inflicted enormous casualties at Antalya, on modern Turkey's southwest Mediterranean coast, making conspicuous use of a nearby Byzantine fortress obviously assisting the enemy.

This and other incidents have persuaded most historians that Manuel so feared and distrusted the French that he deliberately plotted their destruction. With the expedition now back on the coast, for example, he promised a fleet to take it to Antioch but provided only enough ships for the royal party and a few knights. The rest of the army and the pilgrims, deserted by their king, were left to continue overland; barely half ultimately made it to Outremer.

Louis and Eleanor, meanwhile, reached Antioch's port of St. Simeon in late March to find that Conrad had already arrived. The whole purpose of their undertaking was

Louis' army was under constant attack by the Turks as they traveled through the Byzantine Empire, receiving no help from the emperor Manuel. In this Gustave Doré lithograph in the Bibliothèque des Croisades they are shown being ambushed in a gorge with rocks and arrows raining down upon them.

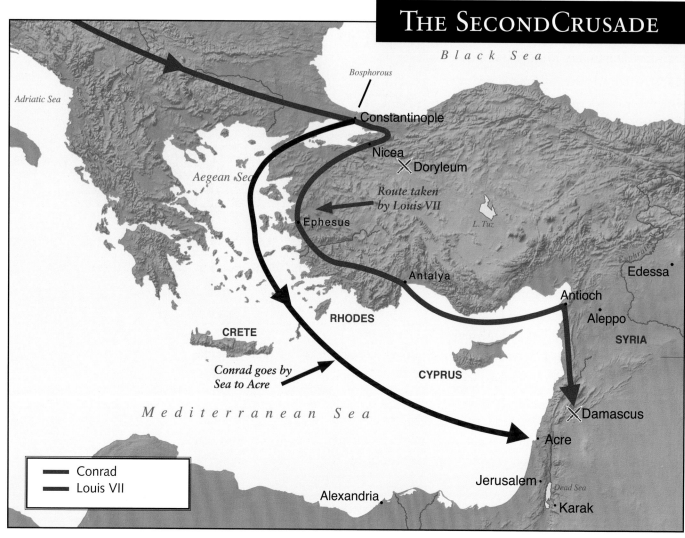

Black Sea

Bosphorous

Adriatic Sea

Constantinople

Nicea

✕ Doryleum

Aegean Sea

*Route taken
by Louis VII*

Ephesus

L. Tuz

Euphrates

Antalya

Edessa

Antioch

RHODES

Aleppo

CRETE

SYRIA

*Conrad goes by
Sea to Acre*

CYPRUS

✕ Damascus

Mediterranean Sea

Acre

Jerusalem

Dead Sea

Alexandria

Karak

— Conrad
— Louis VII

now in dispute, the destruction of their armies in Asia Minor having ended any chance of regaining Edessa. Louis proposed that they merely proceed to Jerusalem as pilgrims. Then came another problem, something he did not need: embarrassingly public displays of affection between his wife, the insatiable Eleanor, and her uncle Raymond—her past paramour (when she was fifteen), it was said. When Louis opposed Uncle Raymond's proposal to attack Aleppo, Eleanor loudly supported her uncle. Eventually the king ordered her confined under guard outside the city.

Meanwhile, a war council held at Acre in June decided that the crusaders could still strike a resounding blow for Christendom by seizing Damascus, the chief city in Syria, about halfway between Antioch and Jerusalem. In fact, this could have effectively hindered the passage of any Muslim army along the coast and would have significantly strengthened the Christian military position. But local Christian leaders from Outremer had their doubts. Damascus, though Muslim, had faithfully observed its treaty obligations and protected the Christian kingdom's northern flank.[6] Why attack it? Moreover, who would govern it if the attack succeeded? Nobody knew.

The attack nevertheless proceeded in July, with the western Christians assembling their largest force yet. Under the joint command of Louis, Conrad, and the teenaged King Baldwin III of Jerusalem, they attacked Damascus from the west, basing their army in suburban orchards with abundant supplies of food, water, and wood. They rapidly drove back the defenders and occupied most of the area needed for a long siege.

6. Christians and Muslims regularly struck pragmatic military alliances with one another that could pit them against their coreligionists. In one battle between rival Turks, for example, the emir Jawali was aided by crusaders Baldwin of Le Bourg and Joscelin of Courtenay. They fought fellow Christian Tancred of Taranto, who was supporting the Seljuk sultan of Aleppo.

But then came an extraordinary decision. Apparently panicked at the approach of a Turkish army, they abandoned their camps and moved to the eastern side of the city, where allegedly weaker walls would provide them with a faster entry. But they could not break through. Moreover, there was no water and little food anywhere nearby, and the Muslims had immediately retaken the area the crusaders had vacated. They had placed themselves in a position from which they could only withdraw.

In this illustration from a medieval manuscript, Chronique d'Ernoul et de Bernard le Trésorier, *produced in the fifteenth century, the crusader armies are shown at the walls of Damascus during the ill-fated siege of 1148, whose failure collapsed the Second Crusade. Visible are the standards (left to right) of Baldwin III of Jerusalem, Louis VII of France, and Conrad III of Germany.*

So the assault failed. Five days after the arrival of its armies at Damascus, the Second Crusade in the East was over—just like that. Recriminations followed, featuring accusations of Damascene bribery and betrayal on the part of Outremer's barons and knights, including the Templars. The bitterest accusations were made by the French against the Byzantines for sabotaging the original plan, and those sores were rubbed open when Louis' royal party, returning home by sea, was attacked by Manuel's navy because it was sailing aboard Roger of Sicily's ships. The king narrowly escaped capture, and the vessel carrying Queen Eleanor was briefly detained. Upon landing in Sicily, Louis and Roger mapped out a campaign against the Byzantines, but nothing came of it.[7] Meanwhile, many blamed Eleanor for the expedition's failure. Her fling at Antioch led eventually to a marital annulment.

While the reconquest of Spain did prove largely successful (see pages 170–175), crusaders on the third front against the Slavic Wends produced unimpressive results. One major siege, at Dobin, ended inconclusively with a peace treaty in which the Wends agreed to renounce idolatry. Another, at Demmin, was unsuccessful, while a third, at Stettin, was abandoned when attackers discovered that the place was already Christian.

Across Europe disappointment in the failed Second Crusade ran deep. The effect on church morale was devastating. Most judgmental were two German commentators, the anonymous "Wurzburg annalist" and one Gerhoh of Reichersberg, who said the entire enterprise had been the work of the devil and a revolt against God's righteous punishment, inspired by "pseudo-prophets, sons of Belial and witnesses of the Anti-Christ, who by stupid words misled Christians." On the other hand, the Cistercian bishop Otto of Freising, half-brother of Emperor Conrad, took a more dispassionate view. Attributing the outcome to the mysterious but always benevolent ways of God, he observed that nonetheless, "it was good for the salvation of many souls."

Bernard was held most responsible and was said to be devastated by the outcome. He had simply done what the pope asked him to, he pleaded, and the failure was undoubtedly due to the impurity of the leadership. But the depth of his disappointment

7. Returning to France from the Second Crusade, an embittered King Louis did some campaigning for another crusade—this time against Byzantium. Pope Eugene was only lukewarm in his support, but many churchmen were enthusiastic, including even Bernard of Clairvaux. Like Louis and Roger of Sicily, they blamed the failure of the Second Crusade mainly on the "treachery" of Manuel Comnenus. Conrad III refused to assist them, however, which killed the idea.

is difficult to discern in the highly disciplined tone of his written comments. In any case, his role in the Second Crusade did not significantly affect his reputation. He would continue to be revered for spiritual insight, and upon full reflection he wrote *De Consideratione*, one of the finest expositions in Christian literature of resignation to the will of God: "How can human beings be so rash as to pass judgment on something they are not in the least able to understand? ... It is true the hearts of mortal men are made in this way: we forget when we need it what we know when we do not need it. . . . The promises of God never prejudice the justice of God."

Bernard would die just four years after the forlorn return of the crusaders, mercifully spared knowledge of the later consequences of the mission that he had so fervently preached. For as the Christian armies slunk away westward, with them went the lingering myth that heavily armored crusaders in large numbers would always prove invincible. This conviction alone had helped sustain Outremer. Now the Muslim world knew that the Christians' presence was by no means permanent. They could be driven out.

Though the fearsome Zengi had been the first to discover this, he did not live to see the failure of the Second Crusade; he was murdered during drunken slumber by

The twelfth century's liveliest lady

Mother of two kings, wife of two kings, and imprisoned by both for plotting against them, eligible heiress Eleanor of Aquitaine scandalized Europe for most of her 82 years

In her time Eleanor of Aquitaine was called many things. To her youngest son, England's King John, she was "an unhappy and shameless woman." To Gervase, the monk-recorder of Canterbury, she was "an exceedingly shrewd and clever woman . . . but unstable and flighty." To late twentieth century feminists she was a valiant "gender warrior." Beyond all argument, however, she was the wife of two kings and the mother of two, and certainly one of the most influential women in medieval Europe.

Born in 1122 and raised in Aquitaine's hedonistic ducal palace at Poitiers, Eleanor was a pampered, headstrong, learned, and very beautiful auburn-haired girl. When her father, Duke William X, died young with no male heir, he left the duchies of Aquitaine and Gascony and the county of Poitou to the fifteen-year-old Eleanor, with France's King Louis VI as her guardian. Louis, by a marital treaty, wed her to his son, the future Louis VII, in order to secure her vast territory, stretching from the Loire to the Pyrenees, for the French crown. Neither the treaty nor the marriage worked. The marriage lasted fifteen years and produced only daughters. The melancholy Louis rarely visited her bed. But many others did, including, by one account, her forty-seven-year-old uncle Raymond, prince of Antioch, with whom the royal couple stayed during the ill-fated Second Crusade (see accompanying chapter).

Eleanor's role in the crusade is noteworthy. One chronicle records that she arrived in Outremer with a troop of female crusaders in an Amazonian couture of white tunics slit up the side to reveal knee-high red leather boots turned with an orange lining. Eleanor, as the leader, had a royal crest on her arm and a plume in her hat. The spectacle, observes the chronicler, much distracted the troops.

At one point when the ladies insisted that the crusaders camp in a charming green valley surrounded by treed hills, a Muslim army descended on Louis' forces. The French fought them off but lost seven thousand men. By then the conviction was growing among the troops that Eleanor's presence had doomed the Second Crusade. An enraged Louis had Eleanor confined to her quarters. He then brought her against her will back to France. Their marriage survived two more years but then was annulled.

She now contrived to marry the youthful, lustful, brazen, redheaded Henry of Anjou, aged nineteen, who would become Henry II, one of England's greatest ever monarchs, and establish the Plantagenet line of English kings. Eleanor was about thirty (her birth date is uncertain), and over the next thirteen years she produced for Henry five sons and three daughters. Two sons, Richard and John, would become kings of England.

But her marriage to Henry was to prove even more tumultuous than her first had been. While Henry consolidated his hold on England and much of France, masterminded the institution of English common law, and developed an effective bureaucracy to unite the a disgruntled eunuch slave. He was succeeded by his son **Nur al-Din Abu al-Qasim Mahmud**. Nur al-Din of Aleppo inherited his father's militant Sunni Muslim zeal if not his vindictiveness. Accompanied by Palestinian émigré jihadist poets, who called for the reconquest of their homeland "until you see Jesus fleeing from Jerusalem," Nur al-Din pushed into the Christian territories. But first he must suppress Damascus, which blocked his path south and whose residents feared his grip even more than they disliked the Christians. In 1154 he took the city by assault.

The Christian kingdom of Jerusalem was the next logical objective, but here he faced the formidable Angevin family, who had ambitions of their own. The youthful Baldwin III had first had to overcome the rivalry of his own mother, Melisende, who thwarted his assumption of power until, after winning civil a war with her, he banished her from the kingdom. He then married into the Byzantine royal household, and to strengthen the Christian position on the Mediterranean coast, he installed the Templars in Gaza and captured the port of Ascalon, near the Egyptian border. When Baldwin III died childless, his brother Amalric was crowned king.

Amalric invaded Egypt, where the Fatimid regime had disintegrated and the country had descended into complete anarchy. He found himself confronting not only the

country, he also developed liaisons with an assortment of tarts and mistresses, eventually driving an infuriated Eleanor back to Aquitaine. There she provided a charter to an abbey for nuns at Fontevrault, fashioned her Poitiers court into a center for troubadours and the celebration of courtly love, raised and schooled her favorite son, Richard, and plotted against Henry with all her sons to divorce Aquitaine from the English crown.

Learning of this betrayal, Henry confined Eleanor in various English castles for sixteen years. Yet their marriage, while certainly beset by argument, quarrels, and even war, was not altogether unhappy. Eleanor herself described it as much happier than her union with Louis. The couple often spent Christmas together, providing a plot for the delightful 1968 film *The Lion in Winter*, winner of three Academy Awards, with Katharine Hepburn playing Eleanor and Peter O'Toole Henry. It portrays that species of dysfunctional marriage where the couple cannot live together and cannot live apart either.

Henry died in 1189 at age fifty-six. Eleanor would outlive him by fifteen years. She threw herself into the production of a splendid coronation for Richard at Westminster, and she remained a behind-the-scenes instigator and fixer for her son. She arranged his strategic marriage to Berengaria of Navarre, she kept an eye

This still from Anthony Harvey's 1968 movie The Lion in Winter *features Katharine Hepburn as the aging Eleanor of Aquitaine and Peter O'Toole as the old lion Henry II. In the film, as in history, it was the case of a couple who could live neither together nor apart.*

on England while he was crusading, she arranged for the lavish ransom paid to free Richard from imprisonment in Austria, and she organized his funeral after he was killed by an arrow in a skirmish in France in 1199.

On April 1, 1204, as her husband's once vast territory was being lost to Philip of France by John, Eleanor, observes a monastic chronicler, "passed from the world as a candle in the sconce goeth out when the wind striketh it." She was eighty-two. Her body was interred in the crypt at the abbey at Fontevrault in a fine tomb between those of Henry II and Richard I, her second royal mate and her first royal son. ∎

Egyptians but rival invaders, namely the army of Nur al-Din, which had bypassed Jerusalem and was intent on bringing heretical Fatimid Egypt into the fold of orthodox Sunni Islam. For the next five years Egypt's two invaders fought it out inconclusively until Nur al-Din's Egyptian commander died. He then had to appoint a new vizier, and thus appeared upon the stage of history the great pivotal figure of the Crusades. His name was Salah al-Din Yusuf ibn Ayyub—known in the West as Saladin.

A nephew of the former commander, Saladin had served with unobtrusive competence as his uncle's chief lieutenant, but at age thirty-two he was not viewed as a promising soldier. In fact, his reluctance to fight had brought upon him the contempt of many in the military, who were also unimpressed by what they saw as his scrawny physique and meek demeanor. However, his father was a Kurdish mercenary who had served as governor of Damascus, and he was known in Nur al-Din's circle for intelligence, religious zeal, and courtly propriety. Women thought him dark, handsome, and charming, and in his youth, Saladin later confessed, he had enjoyed both them and wine with abandon.

Until, that is, he discovered the power of the Qur'an, after which he became known for ascetic simplicity, drank only water, ate mainly fruit, lived in a small house near a mosque and a library, and always slept on a simple roll-up mattress. Serious and contemplative by nature, he had been unenthusiastic about his uncle's military mission but nonetheless had taken an active fighting role, commanding the vanguard in the successful invasion of Fatimid Cairo. Whatever his martial disinclinations, the new vizier, erect and dignified, looked very much the military leader in his coarse black woolen coat trimmed with gold thread, black fez wrapped in a white turban, and scimitar at his side, with his mounted and yellow-cloaked Mamluk bodyguards always preceding him, beating kettledrums to signal his approach.

His piety reinforced his instinct for iron discipline. When Sudanese guards were suspected of disloyalty, he massacred them. When rioters rampaged in Cairo, he hanged them. When the habitually unruly Bedouin Arabs defied him, he declared open war on them. On Nur al-Din's orders, he changed the Egyptian state liturgy from Fatimid to Sunni, requiring prayers for the caliph in Baghdad. His was, in short, a very effective regime—altogether too effective for Nur al-Din, who, with reason, began to fear him. Twice, for instance, he had called on Saladin for military aid and none had arrived. But then, while preparing to attack him in Egypt, Nur al-Din died of a heart attack, leaving a ten-year-old heir. Turmoil soon reigned in Damascus. Saladin, while professing great admiration for the late Nur al-Din, marched north, brutally took over all Syria and Mesopotamia, and proclaimed himself sultan of a vast territory that surrounded Christian Outremer.

Outremer's vulnerability was by now obvious in other respects. Amalric I had died two months after Nur al-Din and was succeeded by his son, Baldwin IV,

The Muslim leader known in the West as Saladin (Salah al-Din Yusuf ibn Ayyub) is portrayed in a painting by an unknown European artist (circa 1600–1800). Proclaimed sultan of Syria and Egypt in 1174, Saladin would do more to confound Christian aspirations in Outremer than any other Muslim. Not only was he a commander of extraordinary skill, he also proved a chivalrous opponent, respected by his adversaries.

thirteen years old and suffering from leprosy. The kingdom was torn by interfamily feuding. "Old-resident" Christians wrangled with newcomers, who considered their predecessors degenerately self-absorbed, given to perfumed extravagances, and hopelessly quarrelsome and corrupt. Military reinforcement from the West dwindled. Between 1148 and 1183, seven papal communiqués calling for a new crusade had produced no armies. Christian knights totaled only about twelve hundred throughout Outremer, and these were mainly Templars and Hospitallers, now bitter rivals, refusing to associate with one another and both growing rich on the boundless bequests of admirers. Throughout the feeble eleven-year reign of the disabled Baldwin IV and his two successors, battles raged over the control of the monarchy. By 1187 Guy of Lusignan, who had married into the Baldwins but was widely despised as a cowardly and self-seeking parvenu, reigned as king.

Saladin was altogether aware of these deep Christian disabilities, but in preliminary clashes he encountered unexpected resistance. Christian forces prevailed against him in a number of horrific battles, the most dramatic of them in 1177 at Montgisard, near Ascalon, when Saladin was moving in for the kill on Jerusalem. Outremer's leper king, then sixteen, rose from his sickbed to rally his vastly outnumbered knights against the Muslim army. Saladin, overconfident and uncharacteristically undisciplined, met near disaster, barely escaping with his life thanks to a fast camel and his faithful Mamluk guard.[8] So he patiently dickered with the Christians instead, making and renewing treaties with them at Jerusalem, Tripoli, and Antioch while he strengthened his position, which was not easy. It took him three more years to claim Mosul and eight to gain control of Aleppo, about two hundred miles northeast of Damascus, during which he again escaped murder by the Assassins (see sidebar, pages 76–77).

Still, his most humiliating problem, if not his most serious, was his repeated failure to take the stronghold castle of al-Kerak. From behind eighty-foot walls, it overlooked the south end of the Dead Sea on the main caravan route between northern Arabia and Cairo. Its master was a renegade Christian, Reynald of Chatillon, who was as much an irritant to the government at Jerusalem as he was to Saladin. The man's daring defied reason. When he built five galleys in the desert, transported them 130 miles to the Red Sea, then led a series of pirate raids down the Arabian coast, this prompted a rebuke to Saladin from the Baghdad caliphate for failing to protect pilgrims.

8. When he learned of Saladin's approach, the stricken King Baldwin had ridden to Ascalon leading a force of five hundred men, with the bishop of Bethlehem bearing the true cross. There he was trapped by Saladin, who then marched on toward Jerusalem assuming he would meet no further opposition. But with the aid of Templars from Gaza, the king broke out of Ascalon. They rode up the coast and ambushed Saladin in a ravine, thus thwarting his attack on Jerusalem.

This painting of the Battle of Ascalon in 1177 by C. P. Larivière in the Versailles Museum depicts one of Saladin's few defeats. The Christians are on the left, the Muslims on the right. Saladin was thwarted here by the sixteen-year-old Baldwin IV of Jerusalem, known as the Leper King. Saladin escaped with his life thanks to his Mamluk guard and a swift camel.

History's hardwired hit men

The Assassin cult, motivated by hashish and visions of heavenly virgins, became the killers of choice for both Muslims and Christians who needed a reliable exterminator

In 1175 the great sultan Saladin set out to subdue the dissident Islamic sects of Syria—and one sect in particular, known as the *Hashshashin*. Three dagger-wielding servants of the cult suddenly appeared among his bodyguards. All three were killed immediately, but the close call unnerved Saladin and gave him nightmares. Though he increased his guards, within a year the sect again infiltrated his camp, this time wounding him so badly that only the chain mail under his turban saved him.

That persuaded him. He agreed to stop all his attacks on the *Hashshashin* if they promised not to kill him. They concurred and complied. But the incident was instructive. It meant that one of the most powerful rulers in the world had surrendered to a terrorist society.

During the previous eighty years the *Hashshashin* had established their reputation as the most determined hit men ever known, and their name, pronounced in the West "Assassin," gave every western language a word for political murder. But in the case of Saladin, the Assassins were content to stop short of actually killing him because his fear was enough. It had removed his threat to their ultimate goal: revolution.

The Assassins' signature was selective high-profile murder, but like all terrorists, their broad aim was societal change. They attracted Shi'ite Muslims frustrated by the domination of the Seljuk Turks, who were Sunnis. Led by a grand master who claimed divine inspiration, they saw themselves as paving the way for a yet-to-be-revealed successor to Muhammad, called the "hidden imam."

Following the motto "Believe nothing and dare all," the Assassins became a critical third force in the Christian-Muslim struggle. Their selective murders helped the Christians establish some of the crusader states. By Saladin's rise in the 1160s, the Assassins had already liquidated some seventy-five heavily guarded Islamic officials, mainly sultans, viziers, and military commanders, always by dagger, often as a public spectacle in broad daylight.

The unquestioning obedience and fanatical devotion of the disciple to the leader made these grandstand executions possible, with each executioner assured a martyr's reward in paradise. Stories abound of the unswerving submission to the sect's founder, Hassan ibn al-Sabah. In one, for example, an emissary arrives at Hassan's mountain fortress to demand that he take a vow of fealty to the reigning sultan. Turning to a white-robed disciple, Hassan commands, "Kill yourself." Instantly the man plunges a dagger into his own heart. Then Hassan points to a guard high on the castle wall. "Jump!" he orders, and the man leaps to his death. "That's my answer to your master," he tells the emissary, and as a postscript, the sultan is shortly stabbed to death.

Hassan had begun as a servant of the Seljuk sultan but quarreled with the sultan's vizier and military commander and was arrested and exiled. By then he had become disenchanted with fellow Ismaili Shi'ites in Cairo. All of Islam's previous luminaries were irrelevant to "true religion," he decided, which was wholly a matter of "feeling," not externals.

He became an itinerant missionary, discovered his astounding ability to influence people, both men and women, of all ages—like the frightened sailors so amazed at his serenity on a storm-tossed ship that they joined his cult, or the disaffected Shi'ite Muslims southwest of the Caspian Sea, where he spent years recruiting followers with visions of a new and better Islam. Estimates of his following run from forty to seventy thousand. Joseph von Hammer-Purgstall, in his history of the sect, puts it at forty thousand in the 1090s, with only a very few pledged to commit murder. These, known as the *fedayeen* (faithful), were given a foretaste of their eternal happiness with opium and hashish in a garden where beautiful young women beckoned their lust. (The Arabic word *hashshashin* means "consumer of hashish," although there are other interpretations.)

In 1190 Hassan commandeered a mighty fortress called Alamut (Eagle's Nest) on a six-hundred-foot cliff in a remote mountain valley southwest of the Caspian and never left it. As his following grew, the Assassins captured over one hundred other castles, many of which, like Alamut, included the indispensable garden of paradise.

The sect's record of political murder began with the Seljuk vizier who had caused Hassan's exile, then went on to include the sultan himself. A long list of designated victims followed. The Seljuks launched four major sieges against Alamut, one of three years' duration, but all failed. By the time Hassan died in 1124, the sect was established as a terrorist state without boundaries. The process for choosing successive grand masters was murky, but dedication to the mission of wreaking divine disruption never changed.

Between 1106 and 1174 crusaders and Assassins repeatedly struck alliances against their mutual enemy, the Seljuks. The Christians suppressed any qualms over partnering with known murderers, while the Assassins believed their eventual (though largely undefined) version of Islam would trump all rival powers, including Christendom. Cooperative efforts with Christians diminished after an alliance was made between Syrian Assassins and the Kurdish Saladin. But by 1228 the emperor Frederick II was again negotiating with them, and in 1230 the Hospitallers allied with them against Christian Prince Bohemond IV of Antioch (whose subsequent complaint prompted the pope to demand an end to alliances with these people). Nevertheless, in 1250 the French king Louis IX tried to make a deal, and for years both the Templars and Hospitallers collected tribute from the sect.

This nineteenth-century lithograph by Gustave Doré envisions the attempted assassination of England's King John. The Muslim sect of the Hashshashin was so feared that Christians and Muslims alike made treaties with them to protect their leaders from certain death. The "Assassins," as they were known in English, gave virtually every western language a word for political murder.

After Hassan, the most notorious Assassin leader was Sinan, Syrian chief from 1162 to 1192, who was feared even by kings in Europe as "the Old Man of the Mountain." Renowned as a clairvoyant, astrologer, alchemist, and healer, he compared himself to Jesus. No one ever saw him eat or drink. He was a figure of legend, half-truth, and perpetual propaganda. One story tells how he used psychokinesis to prevent people from being crushed by rocks, another how he telepathically immobilized Saladin's attackers until his troops could escape.

It was said that he needed no bodyguards, traveled perpetually from fort to fort to keep the cult close-knit and alert, and insisted on traditional Islamic morality and ritual. He was also a ruthless and a skilled trickster. It was told how he amazed disciples by conversing about paradise with the severed head of an alleged martyr. The man was in fact standing below the floor with his head protruding through it. After his audience left, as a reward for a convincing performance, Sinan drew his scimitar and decapitated the actor. For more than a decade he promoted alliance with the crusaders because his fighting energies were aimed at hostile Shi'ites and Sunnis, but eventually he deemed Saladin's goodwill more useful and switched sides.

Sinan engaged in a brief war with the Alamut-based Assassins after their grand master mutinied against the sect's religious conventions, announcing that all of the traditional prayers they had been saying, all the rituals and moral strictures they had observed were useless. Instead, the faithful were instructed to demonstrate their contempt for these pathetic traditions and respect for the grand master's divinely inspired inner feelings by following him into a life of debauchery, filled with promiscuity, orgies, and drunkenness.

Both Hassan II, who launched this bizarre regime, and his son Muhammad II, who continued it, were murdered. Their successors changed course and returned the order to standard Shi'ite practice in 1210. The Assassins were effectively destroyed in Persia when the Mongols took Alamut and the rest of the region's strongholds in 1258 (see chapter 9). They disappeared in Syria after the Fatimid sultan Baibars drove out the Mongols, then captured all the Syrian strongholds in the early 1270s. By one account, they still exist but under different names in Yemen, India, and Iran. ■

When in violation of a truce he pillaged a treasure-laden caravan, slaughtering its guards and taking Saladin's own sister prisoner, this brought rebukes from Jerusalem and Damascus. He sneered at both. Three times Saladin laid siege to al-Kerak but couldn't take it. The Christians didn't even try.

However, as Saladin moved once again against Jerusalem, he saw that Reynald could serve a purpose. Thus, in May 1187 he amassed a great army near the Sea of Galilee. Then, under the terms of a treaty with the feckless King Guy at Jerusalem, he "requested permission" from the Christians to bring seven thousand soldiers peacefully through their territory to avenge Reynald's caravan attack. The Christian commander on the spot, the heroic Raymond of Tripoli, knew he could not possibly stop them, so he sent a warning to Jerusalem that this was no punitive mission but an all-out offensive. Hearing this, 120 Hospitallers launched what amounted to a suicide mission against the Muslim army and were wiped out. But full-scale war was now on. Withdrawing, Saladin built up his army to thirty thousand, including twelve thousand cavalry. In July he struck, surrounding the Christian fortress at Tiberias, on the west shore of the Sea of Galilee, and trapping the residents, one of

The smoke blew westward into the valley as the desperate, exhausted, and thirsty Christians struggled uphill toward the Sea of Galilee on the very slope where Jesus had preached the Sermon on the Mount.

them Raymond's wife. His main force now occupied a high ridge between two pointed peaks known as the Horns of Hattin, near the Galilee shore.

Filled with mutual mistrust and barely on speaking terms, the Christians had gathered in late June at the fortress of La Safouri, a few miles east of Acre on the Mediterranean. By emptying garrisons everywhere, they had managed to assemble the largest Christian army in Outremer history, some twenty thousand soldiers, although only twelve hundred were knights. One contingent was led by the mutinous Reynald from al-Kerak, another by King Guy closely guarding the true cross, which he did not want to leave behind in defenseless Jerusalem. But what now? Should they march east and confront Saladin at Hattin? No, said Raymond, they should withdraw to the security of the coastal fortress and let Saladin besiege them rather than march fifteen miles through parched, nearly waterless valleys under a blazing sun. With thirty thousand men to feed, he contended, Saladin would soon have to withdraw; then they could attack his exiting rearguard. But Reynald argued for immediate attack, and after much vacillation Guy sided with Reynald.[9]

Marching out July 3, the Christian forces arrived at a well-watered campsite early in the afternoon where, again rejecting Raymond's advice, King Guy insisted they press on. Along the bare hilltops the Muslims were now visible all around. As soon as the crusaders passed, they swept down from behind, cutting them off from any water supply. Leading the vanguard with the Hospitallers, Raymond tried to hurry the army to another site with water, but a mile from the Horns of Hattin their path was blocked by thousands of Muslim troops.

9. Raymond's argument initially seemed to have persuaded Guy, but Gerard, the grand master of the Temple, cornered the king privately after the council broke up at midnight. He told Guy that Raymond was a traitor and a coward who could not be trusted. Only marching to Tiberias, Gerard contended, would provide the Templars with the chance they deserved to have their revenge on the infidel Saladin.

With the Christians now effectively waterless, at dusk Saladin set fire to the dry grass of the valley, filling the air with smoke. All through a sleepless night his archers shot the knights' horses; dawn came, and still he did not attack. In the high heat of late morning, when he set a remaining field ablaze, the smoke blew westward into the valley as the desperately exhausted and thirsty Christians struggled uphill toward the Sea of Galilee. They were climbing the far side of the very slope where Jesus had preached the Sermon on the Mount. King Guy's thirsty soldiers joined the weak assault, refusing to stay behind with him, true cross or no true cross, but none could break through the Muslim line.

Now the Muslim cavalry fell upon the rearguard Templars and pushed them back toward the center, where, ineffectually and inexplicably, King Guy had erected tents for defense. A few knights, Raymond among them, were allowed to escape, but nearly all the Christians were butchered where they stood. At the end of the day, Guy's red tent fell as the Muslims seized the true cross along with the king himself, Reynald, and the master of the Templars. Presented to the sultan at his pavilion as the sun set, they all were treated with courtesy, but only Guy, as a fellow monarch, was spared. Saladin personally sliced off Reynald's arm with his sword; then, in a show of contempt, he ordered slaves to cut off his head. He had Muslim scholars and holy men execute every Hospitaller and Templar (except the master of the Templars, whom he saved as a future bargaining chip). The rest of the prisoners were sold as slaves. The true cross was stuck upside down on a spear and carried to Damascus.

With the Christian army destroyed, Saladin spent the rest of the summer seizing one Christian stronghold after another. In September he laid siege to Jerusalem, which he took on October 2. Then, to the surprise of the inhabitants and the everlasting luster of his reputation, he spared all its Christian inhabitants. The disintegration of the crusader states, signaled in Edessa and accelerated by the humiliating failure of the Second Crusade, was now complete. Jerusalem was lost. The heroic legacy of the First Crusaders and the early Outremer kings was left in utter ruin. On October 29, 1187, Pope Gregory VIII issued "Audita Tremendi." It was the eighth papal letter since 1148 to call for a crusade—and the first that would bring a response. ■

The great turning point in the history of the Crusades was the Battle of the Horns of Hattin, wherein Saladin's forces virtually eradicated the Christian army. The Christian hold on the Holy Land was irrevocably broken, and many major Christian defeats followed, chief among them the fall of Jerusalem. This Gustave Doré engraving depicts the aftermath of the battle.

Saladin's 1187 siege and attack on Jerusalem is reenacted in the 2005 film Kingdom of Heaven, by director Ridley Scott. The capture of the city was the highlight of Saladin's campaign against the Christians and established his reputation as a Muslim hero second only to Muhammad. To the grateful surprise of Jerusalem's Christian inhabitants and to the luster of his reputation, Saladin spared most of the vanquished, even providing passage for the widows and families of the slain defenders to the remaining Christian forts on the Mediterranean. Saladin's Muslim successors would show no such mercy.

More powerful than pope or prince

Loved and feared, advocate and agitator, irritant and pacifier, visionary and vigilante, Bernard of Clairvaux dominated Christendom but never lost his anguished humility

There is but one opinion held by all the faithful shepherds among us. Namely that justice is vanishing in the Church, that the power of the keys is gone, that episcopal authority is altogether turning rotten, while not a bishop is able to avenge the wrongs done to God, nor is allowed to punish any misdeeds whatever, not even in his own diocese. And the cause of this they put down to you and the Roman court.

The author of this denunciation of papal incompetence and corruption was neither a sixteenth-century Protestant reformer nor a thirteenth-century skeptical emperor warring, as usual, with the bishop of Rome. He was, in fact, a twelfth-century monk who, although he yearned for tranquil communion with God in the cloister, was dragged away from that refuge times without number to serve five popes, to become the storm center of a dozen or more major controversies, and to go to his grave recognized as the most spiritually powerful figure of his era.

Such was Bernard of Clairvaux, the man chiefly responsible for the explosive growth of the Cistercian order and for the reform movement of Benedictine monasticism that swept western Europe in the twelfth century, bringing into being about 340 new monasteries, as many as 163 of them founded by Bernard himself. They represented a tough renewal of the monastic ideal, in notable contrast to the far less demanding Cluniac Benedictines, who two centuries earlier had themselves wrought a similarly radical reform (see volume 6, chapter 1).

But Bernard's undoubted skills as a mediator, arbitrator, visionary, cheerleader, agitator, irritant, and vigilante on behalf of popes (whom he helped to elect and

Twenty-first-century Cistercian monks walk through the mist past a life-size cross on their way to morning Mass. Dressed in the white robes that Cistercians have worn for nine hundred years, the monks follow the same rule practiced by their great exemplar, St. Bernard of Clairvaux. In 1940 there were eighty-two monasteries of strict-order Cistercians, known as Trappists. Their number had grown to 169 by the year 2000.

also freely castigated, as in the excerpt above) saw him repeatedly called from his beloved monastery at Clairvaux and plunged into theological and ecclesiastical controversy. One such summons led to the worst miscall of his life. At the behest of Pope Eugene III, himself a Cistercian, he preached the disastrous Second Crusade (see chapter 3) and had to live thereafter with its onerous consequences.

That such an incendiary personality drew respect is understandable; he solved major problems and enhanced thousands of lives. Unlike Francis of Assisi or the sainted King Louis IX of France, however, his image in the historical record is hardly endearing. Adulatory contemporary accounts, for example, insistently emphasize his "piety"—a word that both then and now can carry a strong odor of self-righteousness. Yet Bernard of Clairvaux had nothing of the pharisee, his admirers insist. Acutely conscious of his faults, he easily laughed at himself and before he died squarely faced the central ambiguity of his life. As he wrote to a friend,

It is time for me to remember myself. May my monstrous life, my bitter conscience, move you to pity. I am a sort of modern chimera, neither cleric nor layman. I have kept the habit of a monk, but I have long ago abandoned the life. I do not wish to tell you what I dare say you have heard from others: what I am doing, what are my purposes, through what dangers I pass in the world, or rather down what precipices I am hurled.

He may indeed have thought himself a sinful failure, this man who yearned from childhood to seek and serve God as a monk. His father was a crusader knight. His equally devout mother, the austere Aleth of Montbard, dressed her six sons as monks and fed them and their only sister on a hermit's diet. But Aleth always considered Bernard special. While pregnant with him, recounts Abbot William of Thierry, his friend and first biographer,

she dreamed that she carried in her womb a barking dog. Do not be alarmed, she was counseled, for this "dog" would become the guardian of the Lord's house, barking at enemies of the faith and licking its master's wounds "clean of all that may poison them."[1]

This prophecy he would certainly fulfill. Aleth died in 1103, when Bernard was thirteen, but her influence continued. The boy was meticulously educated and is recorded as heroically surviving his youthful combats with carnality. In one instance young Bernard reportedly resisted sexual sin by plunging himself up to the neck in cold water; in another he summarily evicted from his bed a predatory married woman. At twenty-one he arrived at the abbey of Cîteaux to join a faltering circle of thirteen monastic reformers there, the beginning of the Cistercian order. But he did not come alone. With him were some thirty other eager young recruits, early evidence of his powers of persuasion. They included some of his brothers, all five of whom would eventually join along with, finally, their father. Their sister would become a nun.

The Cistercians had been founded fourteen years earlier by a Cluniac abbot "appalled by the laxity into which the Order of Cluny had fallen," says the *Catholic Encyclopedia*. They saw themselves as a corrective to the dominant Benedictines, known from their dress as the "black monks," many of whose scores of monasteries were directed by Cluny (see volume 6, chapter 1). Though they still nominally followed the sixth-century rule of St. Benedict—"stability, obedience, and conversion of life"—things had definitely slackened, in the view of the Cistercians. "I chose Cîteaux in preference to Cluny," wrote Bernard, "because I was conscious that my weak character needed strong medicine."

For the early Cistercians, who from their white habits became known as the "white monks," pleasure was not minimal; it was totally denied. Food was

BERNARD ON THE BEST WAY TO FIND GOD:

It is not necessary for you to cross the seas, nor to pierce the clouds, nor to climb mountains to meet your God. It is not a lengthy road that is set before you; you have only to enter into yourself to find him.

1. The extraordinary combination of strength and gentleness that typifies the magnificent mountain dog the St. Bernard sometimes causes it to be identified with the abbot of Clairvaux. But this breed, which appeared in the seventeenth century, took its name from a hospice in the St. Bernard Pass, in the Western Alps between Switzerland and Italy, that honored St. Bernard of Menthon, a Benedictine monk who predated Bernard of Clairvaux by a century and a half.

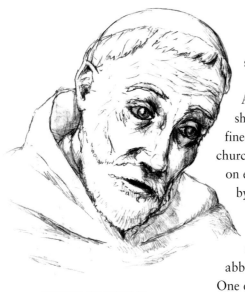

2. Several of Bernard's hymns later
appeared in Protestant hymnals. The
best known, translated as "O sacred
head, sore wounded," provided the
English words to one of the great
chorales of Bach's *St. Matthew
Passion*. Another of Bernard's
hymns, "*Jesu, Rex Admirabilis*,"
found its way into popular
Protestant worship in the translation
made by Edward Caswall in 1849,
an Anglican priest who had become
a Roman Catholic two years before:

*O Jesu, King most wonderful,
Thou Conqueror renowned,
Thou Sweetness most ineffable,
In Whom all joys are found!*

*O Jesu, Light of all below,
Thou Fount of life and fire,
Surpassing all the joys we know,
And all we can desire!*

*Thee may our tongues forever bless;
Thee may we love alone;
And ever in our lives express
The image of Thine own.*

sparse, plain, and unappetizing.
Manual labor was mandatory.
Architectural ornamentation was
shunned. Reading was largely confined to the Scriptures and the
church fathers. Citeaux, then verging
on early extinction, would be saved
by Bernard's early infusion of
recruits. Scores, hundreds, and
then thousands of men would
soon follow until Cistercian
abbeys dotted Europe.

One of the first such "missions" was
Clairvaux, founded in 1115 with Bernard
himself as its abbot. A rude habitation situated in a rugged and desolate gorge,
Clairvaux would become his lifelong base
and refuge. Here pilgrims could come to
hear his renowned sermons. Here also he
likely produced much of his written work
on the grace of God that would captivate
so many earnest seekers and composed
the hymns that so plainly radiate his
unabashed love for Jesus.[2]

It might actually be considered miraculous that Bernard even survived his first
years at Clairvaux, where he reportedly
embraced Cistercian privations with a
youthful zeal that nearly killed him. He
wore a hair shirt under his habit and for-
sook food and sleep until he became so ill
as to impair his health for life. His skin
took on a translucent pallor, and his
digestive system was so unsettled that, to
the distress of fellow monks, he would
suddenly vomit during liturgies. (A basin
had to be installed in the floor at his place
in the choir.) Finally a friendly bishop had
a small house built outside the monastery
boundaries, and there for a full year
Bernard was put on an improved diet
under the dictatorial eye of a physician
(though the physician, according to one
account, was a "quack").

Sick or not, Bernard was already
involved in the first of the imbroglios that
would absorb so much of his life. The
target was Cluny, whose lifestyle and
majestic monasteries he castigated with
typic-ally satirical invective:

Quite apart from the vast height of your
churches, their immoderate length, their
superfluous breadth, their costly polish-
ings, which attract the worshipper's
gaze and hinder his attention, let's let all
this pass. . . . We are supposed to be
monks who have left all the precious
and beautiful things of the world for
Christ's sake, who have counted but
dung the things fair to look at, or sooth-
ing to hear, sweet to smell, delightful to
taste, or pleasant to touch—in a word
all bodily delights. So pray tell me,
whose devotion do you aim to excite by
all these things?

This conflict worsened after Pope
Innocent II visited Clairvaux in 1131 and
was fed a pauper's meal of bread and fish,
then visited Cluny the next year and feasted like royalty. The impoverished should
not support the affluent, the pope decided, and cut off the traditional levy
Clairvaux was required to pay Cluny, per-
petuating the conflict for another twenty
years. It was eased, however, by Cluny's
abbot, the affable Peter the Venerable,
whose response to Bernard's acid observa-
tions could hardly have been milder:
"Candid and terrible friend," he began,
"what could quench my affection for
you?" Like so many of Bernard's targets,
Peter became his fast friend.

So did Innocent II, the man to whom
he addressed the castigation of the papacy
that leads this subchapter. "The Church,"
Bernard fumed, "is resplendent in her
walls, beggarly in her poor. She clothes her
stones in gold and leaves her sons in
rags." This sort of thing, along with his
moving sermons on the power of the grace
of God, would cause Protestants four centuries later to hail him as a forerunner of
the Protestant Reformation and Luther to
call him "the greatest of monks." Bernard
was actually the papacy's most outspoken
champion, and for centuries popes would
cite his essays on its necessity and obligations. But his praise was conditional: he
lauded what the papacy was supposed to
do, rarely what it was doing.

Similar ambiguity attended his passionate devotion to the Virgin Mary, a veneration that had long flourished in the Orthodox Church and had become increasingly evident in the West since the tenth century. Bernard was the first to call her "Our Lady," writes the historian Henri Daniel-Rops in his biography (*Bernard of Clairvaux*), and he advised his followers, "Do you want an advocate near Jesus? Turn to Mary. I will say it unhesitatingly. The Son will listen to his Mother and the Father to his Son. This is the sinners' ladder."

Yet when theologians began pressing to have the conception of Mary declared "immaculate," Bernard was opposed. If Mary was never subject to original sin, she would never have needed a redeemer, he reasoned. Yet Mary herself acknowledged her "Savior" in the *Magnificat* (Luke 1:47). The Immaculate Conception of Mary was not proclaimed as a dogma of the Catholic Church for another seven centuries.[3]

In 1127, renowned throughout Europe as a teacher and evangelist, Bernard received the kind of papal summons that would largely separate him from the monastic life for his remaining twenty-six years. He was asked to act as secretary for a church council at Troyes in 1128, and his report greatly irked the papal secretary, Cardinal Harmeric. "It is not fitting," the cardinal indignantly protested, "that noisy and troublemaking frogs should come out of their marshes to trouble the Holy See and the cardinals." Bernard's reply was such a skillful blend of deep respect and delicate sarcasm that it amused and delighted much of the college of cardinals, making him thereafter the favored designate for "sensitive" jobs.

These rapidly arrived, with three in 1130 alone. One was to lecture the archbishop of Sens and the bishop of Paris on episcopal responsibilities. Bernard's communiqué with the archbishop in this case was by no means subtle: "You are so despicable, so hard to deal with that I had resolved to do nothing more for you. You

Apart from stirring all Europe to take part in the Second Crusade, another of Bernard's contributions to the crusading movement was his composition of a rule for the Knights Templar, the soldier-monks much feared and hated by the Muslims, who with the Hospitaller order formed a standing army for Outremer. Bernard is shown above bestowing the rule on the master of the Templars. This nineteenth-century lithograph is in the Bibliothèque des Arts Décoratifs in Paris.

discourage your defenders in advance and create your own accusers. In all circumstances, you know no law but your own pleasure. Your every act is despotic. You never think of God nor do you fear him."

A far more climactic endeavor was to decide between two claimants to the papal throne. One had taken the title Anacletus II and was backed by money and an army. The other, Innocent II, was supported by most of the cardinals, most of France, and all of Germany, Spain, and England.

3. The dogma of the Immaculate Conception, referring to the conception of the Virgin Mary, not of Jesus, was proclaimed by Pope Pius IX in 1854. The Orthodox Church has never accepted it.

Innocent II, having been banished from Rome by Anacletus, took refuge in France. King Louis VI convened a national council of the French bishops at Etampes and with the consent of the bishops summoned Bernard there to judge between the rival popes. He decided in favor of Innocent II as the most "pious, disinterested and morally the most worthy" and because he had been chosen by "the sanest party."

This caused Innocent to be recognized by all the great Catholic powers. Bernard next reconciled Pisa and Genoa with the pope and attended the Council of Reims at the side of Innocent II, whose oracle he became. Anacletus, backed by his army, held Rome and clung to the papal office until he died eight years later. His chosen successor soon yielded to Innocent, however, after Bernard's eloquence swayed the people of Rome to Innocent's cause.

Battling for Innocent had meanwhile plunged Bernard into a whole series of new confrontations, the sharpest with Duke William of Aquitaine, father of the flamboyant Eleanor (see sidebar page 72) and a backer of Anacletus. First, wrote William of Thierry, Bernard spoke quietly to the duke, who agreed—but only in part. Then Bernard, "with eyes no longer meek and persuasive, but blazing and full of menace," warned his noble adversary that by flouting the church and most of the people of Aquitaine, he would face the judgment of Christ. "Do you dare despise him," thundered the monk, dwarfed beside the huge William, "as you have despised most of us and your people? Tell me! Do you dare?" whereupon the duke, a giant of a man, collapsed groaning. When he awoke, he capitulated entirely, and Bernard, in a voice remarkably changed, addressed him as a father would and urged him to keep his word.

In 1139 began the first of his two most celebrated battles, his victorious showdown with the brilliant Abelard (detailed on pages 188–189). The other was the heresy trial in 1148 of Bishop Gilbert of Poitiers, who was accused of teaching that God's nature never did become incarnate in Jesus Christ because the attributes of God could not take fleshly form. (Gilbert, in fact, denied the accusation, and teachings such as these were never found in his published works.) After hearing Bernard's refutation, he declared that he believed as Bernard believed and did not believe what he was accused of teaching. The church condemned the teaching ascribed to Gilbert but did not condemn Gilbert himself.

Something definitely not a victory began that same year, when Bernard so convincingly preached the Second Crusade, which sent thousands of young men to what proved to be pointless deaths. For this he shouldered all the blame, although most of it rightly belonged with the crusade's commanders. Bernard, writes John Richard Meyer in the *Encyclopaedia Britannica*, "was an idealist with the ascetic ideals of Citeaux grafted on those of his father's knightly tradition and his mother's piety, who read into the hearts of the crusaders—many of whom were bloodthirsty fanatics—his own integrity of motive."

Idealist he may have been, but he was also preeminently human. The death of his brother Gerard, his favorite, shook him to the core in grief. Reminded that grief was of the flesh, not the spirit, he brokenly replied,

> You tell me, "*Do not weep!*" My entrails have been torn from me and they tell me, "*Do not feel pain!*" I confess my suffering. "*It is very carnal,*" they tell me. It is human, I admit. But I also admit that I am a man. It is carnal, I well know, as I also know that I am carnal, given over to sin, condemned to die and subject to suffering. What do you expect? I am not insensitive to pain. I have a horror of death, for my own people and for myself. Gerard has left me. I suffer. I am wounded to death.

There, some might say, was Bernard of Clairvaux at his clearest and best. He himself died at his monastery on August 23, 1153, of the digestive disease that had plagued him so long. Pope Alexander III canonized him twenty-one years later, but controversy surrounded him after death as before it, and his reputation suffered, particularly in the eighteenth century's age of rationalism. This lofty comment from philosopher-poet Johann Christoph Friedrich von Schiller is typical:

> I have been absorbed by my study of St. Bernard these days, and am quite pleased by this acquaintance. It would be difficult to find another equally clever spiritual rogue in such an excellent position for playing such a dignified role. He was the oracle of his time and controlled his time, in spite of the fact, and especially because of the fact, that he remained aloof and let others stand in the important positions. Popes were his pupils and kings his creatures. He hated and oppressed as much as he could, and stimulated none but the greatest monkish stupidities. He himself was only a monk and possessed nothing but shrewdness and hypocrisy.

Perhaps the best response in Bernard's defense would be to cite the Cistercian order. In the twentieth century it would number five thousand monks and nuns, mostly the "strict observant" Cistercians known as Trappists, who would expand from 82 monasteries in 1940 to 127 in 1970 and 169 by the year 2000. Fully 850 years after Bernard's death (and some three hundred after Schiller's), all these dedicated men and women would still be drawn by the imperishable influence of the tempestuous abbot from Clairvaux. ∎

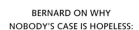

BERNARD ON WHY NOBODY'S CASE IS HOPELESS:

We have seen how every soul—even if burdened with sin, enmeshed in vice, ensnared by the allurements of pleasure, a captive in exile, imprisoned in the body, caught in the mud, fixed in mire, bound to its members, a slave to care, distracted by business, afflicted with sorrow, wandering and straying, filled with anxious foreboding and uneasy suspicions, a stranger in a hostile land—every soul, I say, standing thus under condemnation and without hope has the power to turn. Why should it not venture with confidence into the presence of him by whose image it sees itself honored and in whose likeness it knows itself made glorious?

Barbarossa's shadow lingers over the German nation from a mountain known as the Kyffhäuser, where in this imposing memorial the red-bearded Hohenstaufen warrior sleeps through the centuries. When the ravens fly away from the Kyffhäuser mountaintop, goes the legend, he will awaken and Germany shall rise to lead the world.

CHAPTER 4

Frederick I Barbarossa, medieval man of steel: from ruin came victory

The red-bearded emperor had his own rules, an iron fist, and a Grand Design that no papal ire nor civil insurrection nor excommunication could daunt; God was another matter

A bove the bountiful meadowlands of Thuringia's Golden Meadow Valley, where some thirty species of wild orchid are said to bloom in spring, looms a mystical mountain called the Kyffhauser. Above it the ravens swoop and circle, and within its limestone caverns, according to legend, an ancient warrior has slept for the past eight centuries. Seated at a stone table, his red beard slowly growing longer and longer, he awaits the day when a united and powerful Germany will rise again to spread justice and culture across the world. Then the ravens will fly away, and he will awake.

Moreover, on the mountain's peak the menacing copper figure of another warrior atop a great stone monument declares just how Germany must triumph. He is helmeted and armored and is mounted on a magnificent warhorse. This is Kaiser (emperor) William I, whose grandson and namesake would send German armies marching eastward and westward in 1914 to fulfill this dream. But Kaiser William II did not succeed in achieving these visions of glory, nor did another would-be German conqueror a quarter century later. Far from the ascendant grandeur they had anticipated, all that they accomplished by 1945 was the ruin of their country on a scale hitherto unimaginable.

The legendary sleeper in the caverns below (and who is also depicted on the monument) could have forewarned them of their folly. He, too, was a German kaiser: Emperor Frederick I, known as "Barbarossa" because of his red beard. He, too, had been a would-be conqueror. But in the very hour of his triumph, he saw his plans overturned by what he viewed as a stern and reproving God.

Kaiser William I's equestrian statue stands atop the Kyffhauser peak. Neither his grandson William II in 1914 nor another would-be German conqueror, Adolf Hitler, two decades later could fulfill the dream of an internationally ascendant Germany. Barbarossa failed too, but then he discovered the secret they never found.

1. The family name came from its principal castle, near the great Staufen Rock, east of Stuttgart. Frederick's mother, Judith, was a sister of Welf leader Henry the Proud, duke of Bavaria, and also of Welf VI, who ruled Tuscany. In Italy later on the Hohenstaufens (or Staufens) would be known as the Waiblingen—or Ghibelline as pronounced by the Italians—after their major homeland stronghold, while Italianate pronunciation would transform "Welf" to "Guelph," under which names the feud became endemic in Italy.

2. The papacy's claim for secular control of the Patrimony of St. Peter, or papal states, was supported by the so-called "Donation of Constantine," a document ostensibly dating from the fourth century in which the emperor gave the pope control over large territories, including North Africa, the Middle East, the Greek-speaking Balkans, Germany, France, and Spain. Though the Donation was generally accepted as legitimate through the Middle Ages, by the twelfth century the pope's actual temporal jurisdiction in Italy had shrunk to the area of the papal states. In the fifteenth the Donation would be revealed as part of a collection of documents known as the "False Decretals," created in the ninth century and almost all forgeries. This supposed gift to the papacy contributed to one of its most lasting problems.

After crossing the Alps and passing through hostile Lombardy, the young Barbarossa would have surveyed a Tuscan landscape much like the one seen below. Although Tuscany was also a German jurisdiction, it was controlled by the Hohenstaufens' archrivals, the Welfs.

The lesson that Barbarossa drew from this catastrophic reversal changed him to the soul, and he lived to become one of the most revered figures in European history.

Frederick Barbarossa was born in or about 1126, probably at Hohenstaufen Castle, east of Stuttgart—nowhere near Kyffhauser Mountain. Although little is recorded of his childhood, much can reasonably be deduced. Within and around Hohenstaufen's massive stone walls the growing youngster would have roamed from his mother's solarium to the kitchen and bakehouse, kennels and stables, battlements and keep, great hall and chapel. He would have been taught from his cradle the central fact of medieval life: that he was Christian and therefore a child of God, a servant of Christ, and an inheritor of the kingdom of heaven. This demanded a loyalty that all his life would haunt, direct, inhibit, infuriate, inspire, and baffle him—but would ultimately save him from his darkest enemy, the one within himself.

There were other essential loyalties, of course, of which the first was to his father, Duke Frederick II of Swabia, known as "Frederick the One-Eyed," whose title he would inherit, and to his father's family, the Hohenstaufens, and their allies. Also of primary importance, however, were his mother's people, his assorted uncles and cousins of the powerful Welf clan, whose frequent feuding with the Hohenstaufens often resulted in open warfare.[1]

As the young Frederick's understanding increased, he would have learned from his tutors something of the political geography of twelfth-century Europe. In France the descendants of Hugh Capet had ruled as hereditary kings for 165 years and would continue for another 640 through five successive dynasties, gradually asserting authority over France's twenty-five counties and the four great duchies of Normandy, Burgundy, Gascony, and Aquitaine. However, the dukes of Burgundy still sometimes called themselves kings, while the dukes of Normandy had by seaborne invasion established monarchies in England and Sicily, and had expanded their Sicilian kingdom northward over nearly half the Italian peninsula.

The rest of the peninsula, known as the kingdom of Italy, consisted of three often hostile regions: Lombardy, where some dozen largely independent cities competed both commercially and militarily; the Welf-run duchy of Tuscany, north of Rome; and the so-called Patrimony of St. Peter, or papal states, ostensibly (and, to a degree, actually) ruled by the pope on the basis of an ancient document later discovered to be a forgery.[2] Adding to Italy's fractious composition was the Greek-speaking Byzantine Empire to the east, still calling itself Roman fully eight centuries after Constantine founded it. Farther east the Slavic peoples were steadily being absorbed into either eastern or western Christianity. In Spain the Christians were halfway

CITIES OF LOMBARDY

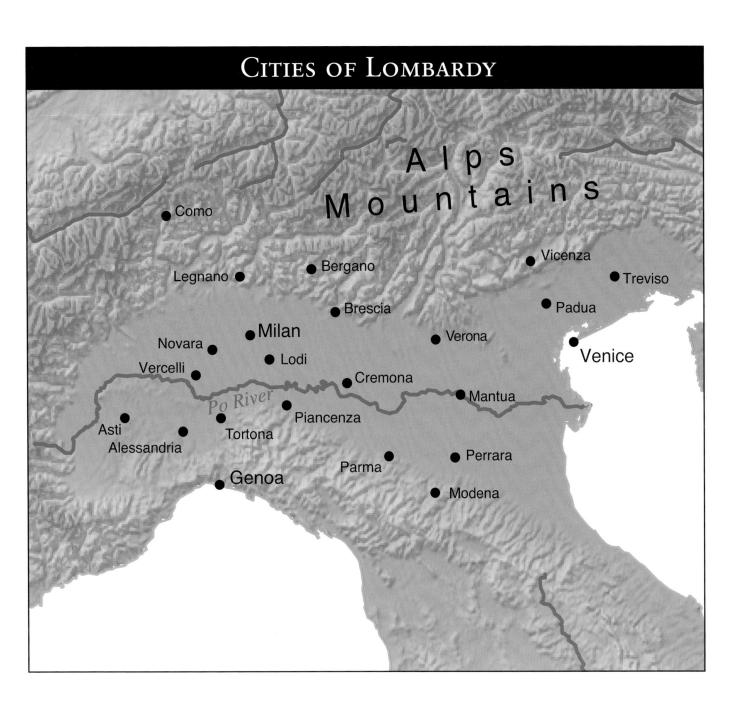

Alps Mountains

Como

Bergano

Vicenza

Treviso

Legnano

Brescia

Padua

Milan

Verona

Novara

Lodi

Venice

Vercelli

Cremona

Po River

Mantua

Piancenza

Asti

Tortona

Alessandria

Parma

Perrara

Genoa

Modena

This nineteenth-century oil painting by Giuseppe Sabatelli depicts a fight between the Hohenstaufens and the Welfs. Such internecine warfare was common in the Europe of Barbarossa's youth and childhood, and he took part in it himself while still a teenager. Since he was descended from both families, he aspired to put an end to it.

through their eight-hundred-year war to reclaim their country from Islam.

The boy would have been enthralled by stories and songs about heroic knights, especially those who a quarter century earlier had reclaimed Jerusalem for the Christians, defeating the infidel Muslims, who for five hundred years had tried to supplant Christianity and in much of the world, in fact, had. Joining such a crusade (a term not yet invented) was called "taking the cross." This was regarded as the highest duty of a man, and dying in such an enterprise was the noblest death. Frederick would never lose this conviction, says his biographer Peter Munz (*Frederick Barbarossa: A Study in Medieval Politics*), and one day he would fulfill it.

Closer to home, even a child could perceive another reality throughout the countryside, namely the price of interminable petty warfare among Germany's three-hundred-odd "noble" families: crops seized, burned, or trampled; castle, mansion, and hut destroyed by raiders; bridges and roads in ruin; marketing nearly impossible. In France, England, and Norman Italy, hereditary monarchies were beginning to provide a semblance of central authority. But jealously guarded tribal tradition required Germany's king to be elected by the country's chief nobles, indebting him to his supporters and guaranteeing political instability.

Such was the background of the boy's entire life. A year before Frederick's birth, when Emperor Henry V died, his own father had stood for election as king but had lost to the Welf-backed candidate, who became King Lothair III. Bitter and resentful, Duke Frederick and his younger brother, Conrad, launched a seven-year rebellion, which caused them at one point to be anathematized by the pope. By 1134, in immediate danger of losing their lands and titles, they had been forced to capitulate and acknowledge King Lothair. But when Lothair died in 1137, Conrad of Hohenstaufen was elected king despite fierce Welf opposition.

Inter-duchy warfare continued as usual, with the youthful Frederick Barbarossa soon playing a significant role. Contemporary accounts describe him as of medium height but strongly built, with blond hair, a reddish beard, piercing blue eyes, and thin lips habitually curved in a quizzical smile, and also as intelligent, energetic, and practical. In his late teens he led an invasion of Bavaria, capturing "a certain Count Conrad of Dachau" but chivalrously releasing him without ransom, then trounced a rebellious branch of the rival Zahringen clan in Swabia. Duke Frederick II, satisfied with his son's capability, left him in charge of the duchy and retired to a monastery.

But in 1147 came a major disruption from outside, when the famous and charismatic Abbot Bernard of Clairvaux began preaching the dire need for a second crusade. Edessa, eastern outpost of the Christian king-doms in the Levant, had fallen to the Muslims, who were now on the offensive. "If none stay their hand," Bernard warned, "the time is near when they will burst into the city of the living God, to overthrow the very workshop where our redemption was wrought, to pol-lute the holy places with the crimson blood of the lamb without spot." Twenty-one-year-old Frederick could not resist such an appeal. He arranged for Abbot Adam of Ebrach to deliver this message at a rally at Speyer, where he himself "took the cross" along with a throng of dukes, counts, and lesser nobility. King Conrad agreed to command them, apparently with some reluctance.

This powerful army set out eastward from Nuremberg that spring, and what followed would devas-tate the confidence of Christian Europe. As it proceeded through Hungary and then across Byzantine territory, it proved to be as much rabble as army. The crusaders fought with villagers and stole their goods. They fought with the Greek troops sent to escort them and with the French troops coming up behind them. They rioted, deserted, and rebelled. Finally, as they camped one night in a seemingly idyllic valley by a small river, a thunder-storm turned the stream into a raging torrent that drowned many. Frederick's men, camped on higher ground, were unharmed. Then King Conrad rejected the advice of the Greek emperor, namely to skirt Anatolia (future Turkey) by sea. He marched half his troops direct to Damascus instead, where they were massacred in a surprise attack by Turkish cavalry. "The leg-end of the invincible knights of the West, built up during the great adventure of the First Crusade," writes Steven Runciman in his *History of the Crusades*, "was utterly shattered."

Already shattered was the lifelong friendship between Frederick's father and his uncle Conrad. Frederick the One-Eyed, grief stricken and angry with his brother for permitting his son to take the cross, died that year. Thus, Barbarossa returned home as Duke Frederick III of Swabia and, judging from his subsequent conduct, with very specific conclusions of his own. He may already have resolved that to counter this disgrace, there must be a third crusade, although with all Europe so disheartened, this would be difficult. And it must be different in many respects. Every man, down to the last foot soldier, for example, must be a wholly committed Christian. Looting and pillaging must be unthinkable. So, too,

The young Barbarossa joined his uncle Conrad III, seen above in a medieval manuscript and a seal, in the Second Crusade, which was preached by Bernard of Clairvaux. The organization of the crusade was deeply flawed, and though Barbarossa fought bravely in it, the result was a disaster. He resolved that one day there must be another crusade that would avoid the errors of the Second.

must the seemingly inevitable persecution of Jews, which had marred both the First and the Second Crusades.

Swabia's new duke may even have decided by then that such an enterprise would require nothing less than genuine restoration of the imposing realm ruled in the ninth century by the great Charlemagne, even suggestive of that of the Roman caesars four centuries before that.[3] Therefore, the title of emperor, vacant since the death of Lothair III because Welf and papal opposition had denied it to Conrad, must be reclaimed and its Germanic prestige restored. Only thus could an army be assembled against which Islam would prove impotent. Ironically, the deplorable Second Crusade had actually enhanced Frederick's own reputation; he had acquitted himself with courage and distinction. Nor had it diminished his respect and love for King Conrad. Although almost everything his uncle attempted seemed to have failed, Frederick would be inclined to blame Germany's endemic internal warfare, not Conrad. The two remained close, and three years later Conrad, on his deathbed, entrusted to his nephew the regalia of the German monarchy, thus clearly indicating *his* choice of successor.

Duke Frederick III of Swabia was indeed a strong contender when the German nobility met at Frankfurt in March 1152 to elect their new king but not primarily because of Conrad's blessing. The major factor, historians surmise, was his significantly intertwined Hohenstaufen-Welf lineage, carrying the hope that as a compromise candidate he might somehow mitigate that weary conflict. The vote for him was almost unanimous—an unprecedented occurrence. Then each elector swore fealty to the new monarch, a crucially important ceremony in a society where all authority hung on the sanctity of a simple oath. To violate an oath and not repent of doing so was to consign yourself to eternal damnation. Hell was real, as was paradise, and to arrive at the latter and not the former was life's most dire challenge.[4]

With the oath-taking completed, the royal retinue voyaged down the Main and Rhine rivers to Cologne and thence by land to Aix-la-Chapelle (Aachen), with cheering and hopeful subjects—peasants and priests, tradesmen and soldiers—lining the riverbanks and roads. In Aachen, on the throne said to have been installed by order of Charlemagne himself, Frederick was crowned and anointed king of the Germans by Archbishop Arnold of Cologne: the first step toward fulfillment of his vision of a German-led Europe. Next, the pope must be persuaded to crown him emperor, first of the Hohenstaufens to hold that title.

The timing was propitious. The populace of Rome, under the sway of an extreme and very popular preacher named Arnold of Brescia (see sidebar, page 101), had driven Pope Eugene III from the city. The new Norman king of Sicily, ominously known as William the Bad, was simultaneously threatening him from the south. Frederick's proper course seemed self-evident—raise an army, invade Italy, rescue the pope, hang Arnold, defeat the Sicilian Normans, and graciously receive the imperial crown from the grateful pontiff—and the ecclesiastics among his counselors heartily agreed. The dukes, who must provide most of the army, did not. Peace and order in Germany must come first, they insisted. Reluctantly acquiescing, Frederick dispatched an ambassador to negotiate amicable relations with Pope Eugene, and set about establishing royal authority at home.

3. "Caesar" was the cognomen of Gaius Julius Caesar (102–44 BC), the great forerunner of the vast Roman Empire. As an auxiliary term for "emperor" (Latin *imperator*) it was maintained by the western emperors until their final defeat in the fifth century. The Frankish conqueror Charlemagne (AD 742–818) regarded his Carolingian Empire as the direct inheritor of that Latin civilization, and later Germanic rulers also claimed to be successors to the Roman caesars (German *kaiser*). The last "Deutscher Kaiser" to actually rule was Wilhelm II, from 1888 to 1918. Meanwhile, the Russian supreme title "tsar" (or "czar") was derived in more roundabout fashion through "tsesar," Old Church Slavonic for "caesar." Ivan III in the fifteenth century may have been the first to rule under this title; the last was Tsar Nicholas II, from 1894 to 1917.

4. "When a man takes an oath," the sixteenth-century martyr Thomas More tells his daughter in Robert Bolt's play *A Man for All Seasons*, "he's holding his own self in his hands. Like water. And if he opens his fingers, then he needn't hope to find himself again. Some men are capable of this, but I'd be loath to think your father one of them." Similarly, the courts in the western world have long viewed perjury as a very grave crime; unless a witness's testimony can be assumed true to the best of his knowledge, the whole judicial system becomes unworkable. In the teaching of Eastern Orthodox Christianity, the taking of an oath under any circumstances was until recently discouraged on biblical grounds, and no vows are taken in the wedding service of many Orthodox churches.

He proceeded to settle one stubborn territorial dispute after another, his chroniclers claim, often by arbitration. He tried to strengthen the monarchy by assembling a larger "royal domain," quietly attaching key estates whenever they lacked an obvious heir and administering them through officials unconnected to the hereditary dynasties. He strove to ensure the allegiance of the dukes by reinforcing their authority within their own territories at the expense of their feudal vassals, expecting them in return to furnish him money and troops when needed. Of particular importance was his younger Welf cousin the powerful and unpredictable Duke Henry the Lion of Saxony.

Equally important, however, was the support of Germany's bishops, who usually also served as temporal governors, collecting revenues and raising armies. Who was to appoint them, pope or king? And to which one must they chiefly answer? This knotty question had caused a deadly contest between Frederick's great-grandfather Emperor Henry IV and the fiery reforming Pope Gregory VII, known as Hildebrand (see volume 6, chapter 3). Ostensibly, the issue had been settled by the Concordat of Worms in 1122, under which a king invested a bishop with secular authority over his territory and the pope with the spiritual authority of his office. This required mutual agreement on the actual selection, however, something not always easy to achieve.

Frederick tested Pope Eugene's resolve early by appointing his own candidate to the strategic archdiocese of Magdeburg without papal consultation. Would the pope now bestow upon Frederick's man the *pallium*, which conferred papal approval and spiritual authority?[5] Well, no—at least, not yet. Frederick's nominee eventually received it, however, from Eugene's successor, Anastasius IV. A year after Frederick's coronation he and Eugene arrived at a concord called the Treaty of Constance, whereby Frederick agreed to suppress the rebellious Romans, rid the city of Arnold, and protect the pope against the Sicilians while Eugene promised to crown Frederick emperor and to excommunicate any subject who defied his imperial authority. Both swore to make no treaty with the Sicilian-Norman monarch, and Eugene, in a goodwill gesture, even retired several German bishops so that Frederick could replace them with his own choices. It was time for step two, King Frederick decided, namely a significant military sortie into Italy.

He seems to have seriously underestimated one factor, however, one that would plague him for the next two decades. As emperor he could also claim the title "king of Italy," with at least theoretical sovereignty over the north, including the chronically warring and increasingly wealthy cities of Lombardy. Milan in particular had assembled a mini-empire of allied municipalities that was often fiercely and bloodily opposed by other towns. In October 1154, when Frederick confidently led his small German army over the Brenner Pass (on the Italian-Austrian border), heading for Rome and his coronation as emperor, he seemingly expected to act as a benign and independent arbiter bringing peace to Lombardy. But such was not to be.

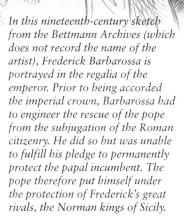

In this nineteenth-century sketch from the Bettmann Archives (which does not record the name of the artist), Frederick Barbarossa is portrayed in the regalia of the emperor. Prior to being accorded the imperial crown, Barbarossa had to engineer the rescue of the pope from the subjugation of the Roman citizenry. He did so but was unable to fulfill his pledge to permanently protect the papal incumbent. The pope therefore put himself under the protection of Frederick's great rivals, the Norman kings of Sicily.

5. Frederick's appointee was Bishop Wichmann of Naumburg-Zeitz, who as archbishop of Magdeburg would become an unfailing Frederick supporter. Reputedly a bon vivant, good ecclesiastical administrator, and skilled diplomat, he is described in the *Catholic Encyclopedia* as "more of a soldier than a bishop." The vital *pallium* is a liturgical garment made of wool and black silk. Worn around an archbishop's neck and shoulders, it symbolizes that the archbishop shares with other archbishops and the pope the responsibility of preserving the unity of the church.

Murder by miscall

England's Henry II thought his faithful servant Thomas Becket would help him control the church, but Becket answered to a higher authority and paid for it with his life

In the late afternoon of December 29, 1170, Archbishop Thomas Becket, aged fifty, lay bleeding on the stone floor of England's Canterbury Cathedral, hacked to death in the interests of his former companion King Henry II. It was the bitter end of a fast friendship.

Henry had become king of England sixteen years earlier, at twenty-one years of age, and was also feudal lord over about a quarter of the future France. Already a seasoned warrior, he devoted himself to sound governance for his vast domains. In England he introduced the concept of common law and would be hailed by some historians as the greatest king in English history. But Henry was a stern leader, intolerant of any dissidence—a man one followed and a man one feared.

Becket, the son of a London merchant, after an indifferent academic career, had joined the staff of Archbishop Theobald of Canterbury. Theobald was a shrewd man who recognized administrative talent and persuaded Henry to make Becket chancellor of England, and by all accounts he became the king's most faithful and effective servant. A superb administrator and a brilliant military commander, Becket helped establish law and order throughout England and also became the king's hunting companion, drinking companion, and partying companion. They were friends in every sense of the word.

Thus, as Henry schemed to limit the power of the church, it occurred to him that Thomas Becket would make an excellent archbishop of Canterbury. As occupant of the country's highest ecclesiastical office he could greatly advance the royal plans. To his amazement, however, Becket not only balked but predicted dire implications and a tragic outcome. "Our friendship," he warned, "will turn to bitter hatred." But the king insisted, and on June 3, 1162, Becket's consecration took place.

Although the appointment was highly popular, the new archbishop soon dismayed admirers by refusing, for example, to lavish money on such things as sumptuous entertainment. "I am not the man I was when I was chancellor," he warned. "Church funds are for the church and for the poor." Even more alarming, he became determined to extend the legal powers of the church, not the king. He was blunt about it: "I have gone from being a patron of play actors and a follower of hounds to a shepherd of souls." The astonished Henry began to suspect that he had installed an intractable man in a key position—and lost a friend.

Conflict mounted. To Henry, Becket was so consistently interfering in state matters that he wondered whether his archbishop was deliberately provoking him. Even Pope Alexander III, who had consistently supported Becket, cautioned him to be more submissive to his monarch. In 1164 the situation came to a crisis when Becket refused to ratify the Constitutions of Clarendon, which, as Becket saw it, were central to Henry's efforts to control the church. The king, Becket insisted, could legitimately claim no such authority for the state.

Henry summoned him to account for his refusal to sign, and Becket defied the summons. God and the pope were his only masters, he declared. To the king, politically frustrated and personally offended, this was a final and unconscionable outrage and Becket was a traitor. Hastily fleeing England, the archbishop began six years of self-imposed exile in France.

In the absence of his archbishop of Canterbury, Henry had his son crowned as his successor by the archbishop of York, the kingdom's second-highest ecclesiastical official. Becket, discerning this affront to his office, became bitter. He intensified his efforts to restrain the monarchy, seeking from the pope unlimited power to excommunicate the king. "The more potent and fierce the prince is," he argued, "the stronger the stick and the harder the chain needed to bind him and keep him in order."

Thus, on December 1, 1170, although fully aware of the peril involved, Becket left Flanders and returned to Canterbury. "I go to England," he said, "whether to peace or to destruction I know not." At a last meeting with Henry he prophesied his own doom: "My Lord, my heart tells me that I part from you as one whom you shall see no more in this life."

His next defiant move was to excommunicate the bishops who had crowned Henry's son. This news soon reached Henry in France, with one of the excommunicates indignantly informing him that Becket wanted "to tear the crown from the young king's head." Henry exploded in one of his famous rages. "What a pack of fools and cowards I have nourished in my house," he roared at his courtiers. "Not one of them will avenge me of this turbulent priest!"

Advisers urged caution, but it was too late. Four knights, taking this outburst at face value, had slipped quietly away and sailed for England. William de Tracy, Richard le Bret, Reginald FitzUrse, and Hugh de Morville were bound for Canterbury to confront a man they considered a dangerous traitor.

Becket, in his Christmas homily at Canterbury Cathedral, had hinted at his imminent death, and on Monday, December 28, while his enemies brooded twelve miles away at Saltwood Castle, he went to bed with foreboding. Next afternoon the four knights rode to Canterbury and confronted him, demanding that he absolve the excommunicated bishops. When Becket refused, the knights left—but only to arm themselves.

His terrified monks hustled him to safety in the cathedral, but he insisted the doors be left unbarred: "The Church of Christ is not to be made into a castle." Soon came the four knights, FitzUrse roaring, "Where is that traitor?" Becket, wearing his miter and holding his episcopal cross, stood on the steps leading

up to the high altar. "Here I am," he calmly replied, "not a traitor but a priest." Again he refused to absolve the bishops and, as the knights tried to drag him from the building, contemptuously called FitzUrse a "pimp." Finally, while he commended his soul to God, his killers cut him down. Within seconds he lay still in his blood-soaked vestments.

The murder of Thomas Becket traumatized England and the continent, some calling it the worst crime since Christ's own death. Pope Alexander III excommunicated his murderers and four years later would declare him a martyr. Accounts rapidly spread of miracles wrought over his bloody vestments. Soon his tomb became Europe's most famous, to be immortalized over two centuries later as the destination of the pilgrims in Chaucer's *Canterbury Tales*.

King Henry, informed by New Year's Day of his old friend's death, appeared utterly devastated. For three days he secluded himself and fasted while his court feared he might die of grief himself in the belief that his rash words made him as guilty as the actual assassins in the cathedral. Soon he began what a later generation would call damage control, however, writing letters to the pope to exonerate himself by questioning Becket's character. Yet he also made a pilgrimage to Becket's tomb, where he did public penance that included a scourging.

In 1172 Pope Alexander formally absolved King Henry of the murder of Thomas Becket, but the assassination permanently damaged him. Weakness was unacceptable in a medieval king. Rebellions flared in his realm; his sons fought over the succession; under papal pressure he had to repeal laws that displeased the church. Thus, the great King Henry II spent his last years fighting a rearguard action against the forces set in motion by his disastrous outburst. ■

Pope Eugene III, who reigned eight years, nearly all of them as a refugee driven from Rome by the hostile populace.

6. Frederick Barbarossa dealt with the coastal trading cities of Venice, Pisa, and Genoa in a very different fashion from the inland centers—almost as equals. His treaty with Venice in 1154, for example, made large concessions for little return. To Pisa, near the Ligurian coast, he later promised territorial concessions in southern Italy, and his approach to Genoa, also strategically located on the Ligurian Sea, was very circumspect. Always conscious of the prospect of invading Sicily, he knew that only the fleets of these maritime republics could provide him with the necessary sea power.

Initially all went well. He issued edicts strengthening the senior Italian nobility, as in Germany, and formally recognized the maritime republic of Venice.[6] But soon he found himself more deeply embroiled in Lombard politics than he had intended. First, for example, came delegates from Pavia, capital city of his "kingdom of Italy," beseeching him to compel the town of Tortona, an ally of Milan, to acknowledge certain Pavian claims, after which they would joyfully confer upon him the iron crown of the Italian monarchy. Tortona proving uninterested in Frederick's polite requests, he was compelled to attack it.

The town was quickly overcome and the townsfolk dispersed, but its guardian castle held firm. Days became weeks. Frederick's frustration grew. As a "persuader" he tried hanging prisoners in good view of the castle walls. Still no surrender. He poisoned the water supply. No surrender. Tortona's clergy begged him to lift the siege, pleading that the defenders were starving and sick. Absolutely not, he replied, and three weeks later hunger and disease at last forced the capitulation of the castle. Frederick let the garrison go, then looted the place. The Pavians, with an eye to the future, paid him handsomely to let them completely demolish Tortona's castle, and then with great festivity they crowned him king of Italy. But such experiences began to sour him on Italy, an attitude that was heartily reciprocated, and he was gaining a reputation for brutality—something he would never acquire in Germany.

In Rome, meanwhile, matters were deteriorating. In July 1153 Pope Eugene had died at Tivoli, in the papal states, after reigning eight years, nearly all them as a refugee. His successor, Anastasius IV, was friendly to Frederick but died after a mere seventeen months in office. And now came a radical change, notably the election of one Nicholas Breakspear as Pope Adrian IV at the relatively youthful age of fifty-four, the only Englishman ever so honored. No aristocrat—the new pope's father had been a lowly man (one account calls him a shoemaker)—Breakspear neither liked nor trusted Frederick Hohenstaufen. In his youth he had been rejected as a monastic postulant. He nevertheless persisted, studied in Paris, became abbot of a monastery, and later was a notably successful papal legate. The usual problems soon beset him as pope. "Thorny is the throne of St. Peter," he lamented, "and so full of the sharpest spikes is his mantle that it would lacerate the stoutest shoulders."

For whatever his doubts about Frederick, right now Pope Adrian urgently needed him. Even before the arrival of the incendiary Arnold, the Roman populace had reestablished the ancient Senate and declared their city a republic. Now a mob had beaten up one cardinal, leaving him for dead, and made the pope, in effect, a prisoner within the Leonine City. In 1154, by threatening to place all Rome under interdict (a serious threat since it would have barred the faithful from the approaching Easter services), Adrian had forced the Roman Senate to expel Arnold. Such serious rioting followed, however, that he had to withdraw to Viterbo, sixty-five miles north. He begged Frederick to hurry.

Even so, their first meeting, in June 1155, at Frederick's camp near Sutri nearly foundered on a crucial misunderstanding. It was customary for Frankish and, after them, German monarchs to honor a pope by leading his horse a short distance and

THE EMPIRE UNDER FREDERICK I BARBAROSSA

FRIESLAND

POMERANIA

SAXONY

LOWER LORRAINE

Aachen

THURINGIA

FRANCONIA

Frankfurt

BOHEMIA

UPPER LORRAINE

MORAVIA

BAVARIA

Vienna •

SWABIA

Graz •

A l p s

CARINTHIA

BURGUNDY

▲ Mont Blanc

LOMBARDY

Venice •

Milan

Genoa •

ROMAGNA

A p p e n n i n e s

TUSCANY

Corsica

Rome •

Adriatic Sea

Tyrrhenian Sea

Naples

Sardinia

KINGDOM OF SICILY

M e d i t e r r a n e a n   S e a

Sicily

I o n i a n   S e a

holding his stirrup while he dismounted. But Frederick had decided not to do so, possibly fearing that with the growth of feudal ideas it might be seen as acknowledging himself the pope's vassal. He did prostrate himself before Adrian, as was also customary, and kissed his feet—and was very upset when the offended pope did not in turn raise him up nor give him the kiss of peace. In earnest discussion, however, the German princes persuaded Frederick that he must follow precedent. But to make things right, they had to contrive a second papal arrival, so Frederick broke camp and departed. Pope Adrian joined him the next day, and this time Frederick held his stirrup—not as an act of feudal dependence, he insisted, but to honor St. Peter and St. Paul. With this matter settled, they all proceeded toward Rome.

Barbarossa's troops made camp in the Leonine City,[7] the rest of Rome being far too dangerous, but Frederick feared that hostile Romans might yet break through to St. Peter's Basilica and disrupt his coronation as emperor. Papal advisers proposed a stratagem. The populace would expect the ceremony to occur on Sunday, so why not hold it on Saturday instead? Thus, on the Friday evening

7. The Leonine City (Latin *Civitas Leona*) is a district on the west bank of the Tiber River in which are located St. Peter's Basilica and the Lateran Palace. An outlying suburb in the ninth century, it was badly damaged in a devastating attack by Muslims from North Africa. Three years later another such raid was frustrated chiefly by a violent storm that destroyed the Islamic fleet. The Leonine City is named in honor of Pope Leo IV, who restored its buildings and in 852 began the construction of a defensive wall forty feet high, punctuated by circular towers. Some of this wall still survives.

Pope Adrian IV, above, an Englishman who would prove a determined opponent to Barbarossa, briefly took him as an ally in his fight against Arnold of Brescia and the rebellious Roman population. A breach of protocol on Barbarossa's part soon showed the fragility of the alliance.

8. Cardinal Roland was pernicious, that is, in the eyes of Frederick Barbarossa. But the cardinal's strong influence in the papal curia was due not to his skill as a political manipulator but, rather, to his skill in canon law, the law of the church. As Master Roland Bandinelli he had taught canon law at the University of Bologna, where much recent work had been done in synthesizing into a comprehensive body of law the vast number of decisions made over the centuries by church councils, the decrees of popes, and the statements of noted authors. This greatly aided the popes in their conflicts with the emperors. But to Frederick, he was what a later generation would call "a smart lawyer," and he was on the wrong side. However, he was also a very holy man, and one day Frederick would discover this.

imperial troops cannily deployed around St. Peter's, pope and cardinals stole over early next morning, and Frederick's entourage rode up at eight o'clock. Kneeling before Adrian, he vowed to faithfully protect the pope and the Roman church. Then came a solemn procession and litany, after which Adrian anointed the prostrate king between his shoulders and on his right arm. Then, in the course of a Solemn Mass, he bestowed upon Frederick the sword, scepter, and crown of the empire. The German knights erupted in thunderous shouts of approval and then all prudently withdrew.

Before long, as word of this deception spread through Rome, furious citizens fought their way across St. Peter's Bridge into the Leonine City to loot and kill. By nightfall Frederick's soldiers had managed to beat them back, but the position remained precarious. Lacking provisions and seriously outnumbered, pope and emperor retreated next day to Tivoli, whence they were able to commandeer aid from neighboring small cities. Adrian said Mass on the Feast of the Apostles on June 29 and pronounced absolution for anyone guilty of killing Romans because, he declared, it was done in just vengeance in defense of the empire.

Now that Barbarossa was emperor, the German dukes considered their job done. They and their forces therefore left for home, and Frederick had little choice but to abandon the pope and do likewise at the head of his own relatively small contingent. Eighty miles north of Rome, needing supplies, he laid siege to Spoleto, trounced the overconfident citizen army that rashly emerged to give battle, then looted and burned the place. Next came Verona, 250 miles farther north, whose citizens, in one of history's daffier ventures, built a special bridge across the Adige River downstream from the town. They planned to release a great mass of logs to collapse it as the Germans were crossing, while attacking them from the rear. But the logs arrived late, after Frederick's men had crossed safely. Many Veronese soldiers were drowned instead, and Frederick hanged any who did make it across.

Not until October 1155, three months after fleeing Rome, did the new Emperor Frederick Barbarossa reach Augsburg, and hardly in triumph. Although he had gained the imperial crown, he had made powerful enemies, and the pope remained in acute danger. The following summer worse news arrived. Sicily's William the Bad, striking northward, had trapped Pope Adrian at Benevento, and Adrian had signed a treaty making the Sicilian Normans the papacy's new defenders. William had agreed to pay homage to the pope along with a substantial annual tribute that well might enable Adrian to satisfy Rome's rebellious citizenry.

Back in Germany, the emperor erupted in fury at the news of Adrian's "betrayal," but it compelled him to acknowledge the failure of his plan. The Sicilian Normans were stronger than ever, and their friend and virtual agent, the pernicious Cardinal Roland, clearly dominated the papal curia.[8] Far from rescuing Adrian, Frederick had left him a virtual refugee under Norman protection.

The revolutionary who ruled Rome

Arnold of Brescia wanted the church to give up its properties and adopt poverty, but the advance of Barbarossa ended his rule; he was hanged, unrepentant, then burned

His foes, who were numerous, describe him as fervently self-disciplined, intelligent, and biblically eloquent, yet fractious, vindictive, and malicious. But to Arnold of Brescia himself, he was pursuing an elemental truth. No longer, he charged, was the church the Body of Christ. Riddled with vice and focused on the secular rather than the spiritual, it had lost its way. The church must repent. In so doing, it must surrender its expansive lands, and the clergy must live in poverty as Christ's apostles had.

Some of these ideas were far from new, having been voiced again and again in the previous seven centuries. The church had usually tolerated, even encouraged, some of them. Indeed, many Christians over the years had tried to implement them. What chiefly made Arnold's version intolerable, however, was Arnold himself. To him, outright rebellion against established church authority not only was commendable, it was obligatory—even sacramental. Most alarming of all, in pursuit of these doctrines he managed at one point to take over the entire city of Rome and expel the pope.

Arnold was born around 1090 in Brescia, fifty miles east of Milan in the foothills of the Alps. According to one source, at twenty-five he briefly became a pupil of the controversial Peter Abelard (see sidebar, pages 188–189), some five years later was made a priest and an Augustinian monk, and eventually became an abbot. From this office he plotted against the local bishop, who, on returning one day to the city, found its gates locked against him.

Having thus incited the papacy's ire, Arnold chose this moment to reassociate himself with Abelard. The timing was bad. Abelard was at that moment facing his showdown with the redoubtable Bernard of Clairvaux before a council that would condemn his teaching. Arnold was consequently deposed as abbot, banished to a French monastery, and forbidden to communicate with his teacher, Abelard.

At this he abandoned the monastic life, set up a school, and began to do some teaching on his own, volubly denouncing to a like-minded band of followers the worldly church and the tyrannical Bernard. The school survived about a year before King Louis VII closed it and banished Arnold from France. He fled to Switzerland, where he lived in relative peace until his ever-restless soul led him back into battle.

He headed for Rome, whose rebellious populace had set up a commune and driven Pope Eugene III into French exile. Here was a heaven-sent opportunity to put his ideas into action. Though excommunicated, he became a member of the newly constituted Roman Senate and later the central figure of the city's rebellion.

Imperial politics, however, began to overtake the local situation. In one of the intermittent armistices between the emperor Frederick Barbarossa and the papacy, Frederick agreed to restore the new pope, Adrian IV, to Rome. This meant suppressing the rebellion and getting rid of Arnold, who was by now working on a plan to abolish the whole empire.

Adrian placed Rome under an interdict, denying its citizens all services of the church. That finished Arnold. As the populace capitulated, he fled but was captured and brought before Frederick, who had him hanged and his body burned. He died with a prayer on his lips, refusing the final rites of the church. ∎

To Arnold of Brescia, briefly the ruler of Rome, the church didn't need buildings and the clergy should live by begging. But when the pope placed Rome under an interdict, ending all church services, the Roman citizenry deposed Arnold and turned him over to Barbarossa's army. He was first hanged, then burned. In this sketch Arnold's body is cremated, and his remains are plucked from the fire for burial. The name of the artist has been lost.

As for orderly government in northern Italy, he had, if anything, worsened that situation while leaving more than one bloody memorial to ironfisted brutality. Was this what God intended for him?

Surely not. There must be another way. Had his plans been too grandiose—or not grandiose enough? From such musings, historian Peter Munz theorizes, Frederick's fertile imagination evolved a better idea, which Munz calls his "Great Design." He would develop Swabia, Burgundy, and northern Italy into a powerful *terra imperia*, an imperial territory dominating Europe's very center. Through German military power, Lombard financial power, and the spiritual power of a friendly papacy (Pope Adrian couldn't live forever), he would gradually and unobtrusively expand the terra imperia until he had restored Charlemagne's entire glorious realm. "God has committed to me the government of the Holy City and the world," he confided to his official biographer, Bishop Otto of Freising.[9]

Barbarossa also discovered a man he thought could make this happen: one Rainald of Dassel, whose vaulting ambition far exceeded the horizons of the lesser Saxon nobility into which he was born. Rainald, seeking greatness, had decided the church offered the surest route. He might not be overly given to piety, he reasoned, but this was the twelfth century, after all; the church was broadening. He rose quickly in the Hildesheim diocese, near Hanover, refused as too limiting an offer to become its bishop, and joined a local delegation to Pope Eugene in Italy. There Frederick met him, was mightily impressed, and before long made him chancellor of his empire.

Though a consummate opportunist, Rainald did not lack strong convictions. He believed deeply in the concept of an empire governed by a German prince with uninhibited power both secular and spiritual. The pope clearly must be subject to the emperor, he reasoned, in fact must be appointed by the emperor. Thus, an imperial decree would carry the authority of God himself, and any who resisted would be subject to God's punishment, with the emperor or his servants divinely appointed to administer it. How completely Barbarossa agreed with such views is unclear, but he conferred upon Rainald the chief responsibility to carry out his Great Design.

Within two years the emperor achieved three important preliminary steps. First, with a small but efficient army he whipped rebellious Poland into line. Second, he ingeniously settled the seemingly irreconcilable dispute between Duke Henry of Babenberg, in Bavaria, and Duke Henry the Lion of Saxony, who had long disputed jurisdiction over the duchy of Bavaria.[10] The third coup, and the most spectacular, was his marriage to the heiress of Burgundy, the sprawling territory that covered much of the future southwestern Germany, France, and parts of Switzerland. Beatrix of Burgundy was still a child, possibly about ten, when she and Frederick were married, and their first child was born eight years later. Their marriage was by all accounts unusually happy. Unlike most medieval wives, the strikingly attractive Beatrix accompanied her husband almost everywhere; she would even be at his side a decade later when all his ambitions were destroyed by what inescapably seemed an act of God himself.

With the German problems resolved, Frederick addressed himself once again to Lombardy, particularly Milan. Surely, the Milanese would now see that with just a little imperial supervision and the consequent cessation of their endless wars, everyone would grow much wealthier, including the imperial treasury, of course. But Milan, still zealously defending its independence, predictably refused

9. Bishop Otto of Freising (1110–1158) was another of Frederick's uncles. With his assistant, the monk Rahewin, he undertook at his nephew's request to write the *Gesta Fridorici I Imperatori*, the most thorough early chronicle of the first eight years of Frederick's reign. Otto had studied in Paris under the famous Peter Abelard (see pages 188–189) and later became a Cistercian monk and a recognized historian and theologian. Although hardly a disinterested observer, he provides a vivid picture from the royal perspective.

10. Henry the Lion (1129–1195), so named for his fighting prowess, was the son of the powerful Welf leader Henry the Proud, duke of Saxony and Bavaria. In 1138 Henry the Proud went to war against King Conrad III after Conrad bestowed Bavaria on his own half-brother, Henry of Babenberg, known as *Jasomirgott* ("so help me God") for his favorite oath. Henry the Proud died in 1139, but his son resumed the fight as soon as he was old enough, notwithstanding his mother's marriage to Henry Jasomirgott. Barbarossa's innovative solution in 1156 was to enlarge and split Bavaria and persuade Jasomirgott to turn over much of it to Henry the Lion. He received in return a newly created duchy composed of Bavaria's expanded eastern regions under an imperial charter granting him virtually complete power within it. Thus, both Henrys were satisfied, and thus was born Austria (Eastland), destined to become a Germanic nation of tremendous importance and cultural achievement.

the emperor any such role. War followed, and as Barbarossa's army advanced upon the city in June 1158, it was met by a pitiful demonstration. The town of Lodi had recently been razed by the Milanese. Its citizens—homeless, penniless, and set on vengeance—besought him to authorize the rebuilding of Lodi and also begged to share in the looting of Milan. Barbarossa gladly granted the first request but refused the second. Indeed, a month later, when starvation forced the Milanese to surrender, there was no looting. So lenient were the emperor's terms that they converted Milan from enemy to ally, and Frederick felt justified in declaring peace upon Lombardy. His Great Design appeared to be working.

But this was not to last. For one thing, he had misjudged Pope Adrian. The tough old Englishman, now nearly sixty, backed by the canny and equally intransigent Cardinal Roland, accurately assessed Barbarossa's determination to make the Christian church a virtual government department. So he fought back. Because Frederick had recruited Romans as reinforcements in the siege of Milan (making allies of the very people from whom he had "rescued" the pope), Adrian sent agents to foment further rebellion there. In November Barbarossa added fuel to that fire by calling an assembly of nobles and ecclesiastics at Roncaglia, outside the city of Piacenza. There he promulgated a series of decrees asserting wide imperial control over Lombardy and the papal states, covering everything from the appointment of dukes to the authorization of bake ovens and gristmills to the construction of bridges and control over taxes and excise duties. Of course, he emphasized, he did not really intend to exercise such domination—merely to declare it—but this, understandably, reassured no one.

Adrian, meanwhile, raised another issue. As a young man Frederick had married Adelaide of Vohburg.[11] The marriage was childless and had been annulled. Adrian now publicly questioned the validity of the annulment, thereby humiliating both emperor and empress. More serious yet was the case of the kidnapped cardinal.

11. In an earlier marriage, sometime before 1147, Barbarossa had wed Adelheid (Adelaide), daughter of Margrave Dieter II of Vohburg, possibly to ensure Vohburg's adherence to the Staufen cause. She was older than Frederick, was never crowned queen, and bore him no children. In 1153 Pope Eugene annulled the marriage on the grounds that his great-great-grandfather was a brother of her great-great-great-grandmother, putting them within six degrees of consanguinity. Although theoretically forbidden by the church, this was not unusual. Otherwise, as historian Munz comments, the aristocratic families of medieval Europe would have been hard put to contract "suitable" marriage alliances. Later Adelaide reportedly married a man below her in rank and had many children.

One of Frederick's major coups was his marriage to Beatrix, heiress of Burgundy, a sprawling territory that covered much of the future southwestern Germany, France, and parts of Switzerland. Their marriage—shown here in an eighteenth-century fresco—was not only strategically beneficial but proved an unusually harmonious partnership despite a more than twenty-year age difference. Though she looks older in the painting, Beatrix was actually around ten when they were married.

When the aged and much-respected archbishop of Lund (then part of Denmark), passing through Germany, was seized and held for ransom by brigands, Adrian asked the emperor to punish the kidnappers. Frederick did nothing.

Much worse trouble occurred when Cardinal Roland traveled to the imperial court at Besançon to deliver the pope's protest. The wording of Adrian's letter, as translated into German by Rainald, seemed to imply that the empire was a fief of Rome and Frederick the pope's vassal. "If we weren't in a church," the angry emperor shouted, "you would find how German steel bites!" Rainald's close associate Otto of Wittelsbach reportedly drew his sword to kill Cardinal Roland on the spot but was restrained by Frederick himself.

A further dispute erupted over the appointment of the bishop of Ravenna, and another over a feud between the cities of Brescia and Bergamo as to who should adjudicate between them, emperor or pope. And then there were "the notorious

The pope's letter implied that the empire was a mere papal fief. Naturally, Frederick was furious. 'If we weren't in a church,' he thundered, 'you would find how German steel bites!'

paintings" (as Rainald regarded them) in the Lateran Palace, which allegedly portrayed Barbarossa's predecessor, Emperor Lothair III, as a papal vassal. Despite imperial requests that they be removed, there they remained. Adrian's biographer Horace K. Mann calls this one "a childish quarrel."

Far from childish, however, was the rapidly deteriorating Lombard situation, which soon issued again in bloody slaughter. Rainald, pursuing imperial policy for "peace" in Lombardy, was energetically dismantling the fortifications of cities traditionally allied to Milan. When imperial troops began pulling down the defenses of Crema (an ally of Milan) while leaving undisturbed those of Cremona (an enemy of Milan) twenty-five miles away, Crema's citizenry violently resisted. Barbarossa laid siege, and a horror followed, with both sides hanging and dismembering captives in full view of their enemies. Crema soon surrendered, its twenty thousand citizens fled, and the place was thoroughly looted and then burned.

Next came riots in Milan, where the anti-imperial party, probably spurred on by Pope Adrian and Cardinal Roland, was regaining power. The angry populace drove out Rainald and his commissioners when they tried to restore order, then proceeded to besiege the imperial town of Trezzo, slaughter the entire garrison except for knights, who might be ransomed, and pillage the place. The angry emperor consequently put Milan under "the ban of the empire," meaning that it deserved complete destruction and its people should be enslaved. He called for reinforcements from Germany, and they arrived by the tens of thousands, bent on the destruction and pillage of Lombardy's richest metropolis.

Milan held out for nearly two years while atrocity followed atrocity. Finally, with their people starving and sick, its consuls offered to surrender to imperial authority provided that the city not be destroyed and that the populace be spared. Barbarossa wanted to accept. Rainald did not; he demanded unconditional surrender, and he got it. On March 1, 1160, Milan's consuls appeared before the emperor with their naked swords hung about their necks, swearing to obey his every command. On March 6 they returned with three hundred Milanese knights, who fell at his feet and begged for mercy. The unconditional surrender now proved a major error. Towns long dominated and exploited by Milan insisted on its total destruction, and with much of his army already dispersed homeward, Barbarossa had to agree. But Milan's looting and burning as a concession to its enemies clearly demonstrated that the emperor could not rule Lombardy, that he could be manipulated, which doomed his whole plan.

Chancellor Rainald was by now otherwise occupied. Six months earlier Pope Adrian IV had died at Anagni, about thirty miles southeast of Rome. In Rainald's view, it was time for the emperor to name Adrian's successor, and both he and Frederick knew just the man. Cardinal Octavian was a member of the powerful Monticelli family, whose tenth- and eleventh-century ancestors had regarded the papacy as their private possession. His family's Ghibelline (i.e., Hohenstaufen) connections extended through Bavaria and Saxony, and he shared bloodlines with the royal households of England, France, and Christian Spain. Furthermore, he headed the "imperial party" within the papal curia, in militant opposition to Cardinal Roland and the Sicilian Norman party. Thus, when the cardinals met in the chamber behind the main altar at St. Peter's to name the new pope, Octavian was viewed as Barbarossa's man. Rainald used money, threats, and anything else he could contrive to support him while the Sicilian Norman faction worked just as hard for Cardinal Roland.

After a three-day wrangle the vote was taken. Although Roland clearly won, both sides agreed to adjourn to the morrow, allowing time to reach a compromise and avoid schism. However, a truly bizarre scene followed. While Octavian's backers ate their dinner, Roland's supporters—arguing that their candidate, after all, had a majority—returned to St. Peter's and sought to place the papal mantle on his unwilling shoulders and declare him elected. Then Octavian's people suddenly appeared with an armed escort and a crowd of Roman citizens. In the resulting brawl, they, too, produced a papal mantle, placed it (upside down) upon Octavian, led him to the throne of St. Peter, and declared him Pope Victor IV, to the jubilant cheers of the crowd.

Milan, shown here in modern times, was ever an obstacle to Barbarossa's plans, taking the anti-imperial position and holding out for two years in a siege. Eventually Barbarossa had to allow Milan's enemies to raze almost every building in the city, including the cathedral. The new cathedral, shown in the center of this photo, went under construction in the late fourteenth century and would become the second-largest Gothic cathedral in the world after that of Seville.

Barbarossa, seen here in an equestrian statue in the town of Goslar, about thirty miles southeast of Hanover, had so much difficulty gaining control of the Italian states that he acquired a reputation for brutality unknown of him in his native Germany. Much of the savagery, however, was the work of Frederick's chief strategist and emissary, Rainald of Dassel, archbishop of Cologne.

Roland and his supporters fled to the Castel Sant'Angelo, where Roland accepted the reassurance that he had indeed been properly chosen by the cardinals. Spirited out of the castle, he took refuge in Campagna, sixty miles southeast of Naples, safely inside Sicilian Norman territory, where the ceremony of immantation was once more performed and he was crowned Pope Alexander III.[12] He took up residence at Anagni, where Adrian had died. Victor retreated to Segni, forty miles southeast of Rome, inside imperial territory. Each excommunicated the other.

Once more Barbarossa grew confident, having for the moment pounded Lombardy into submission and acquired his own pope. To make quite certain, however, he called a special church council to arbitrate the papal dispute, inviting only his own episcopal appointees. It, unsurprisingly, endorsed Pope Victor, who was also crowned again for good measure. But Frederick found it impossible to ignore Alexander, now far more formidable as pope than he had been as Cardinal Roland. Although destitute and militarily powerless, he was fearless and diplomatically brilliant, presenting a compelling figure for any devout Christian who did not consider wealth and power evidence of sincere faith. His response to the re-crowning of Victor was a thunderous declaration that the emperor had committed violence and fraud, was the "chief persecutor of the Church of God," and had shattered its unity. He was therefore excommunicate and any oath of fidelity to him invalid.

Barbarossa dismissed his excommunication as meaningless and was shocked that many bishops did not so regard it. Over the ensuing six years, he watched in wonder as one prelate after another declared for Alexander. The clergy of Rome rejected Victor, as did two great religious orders, the Cistercians and the Carthusians. A plot conceived by Rainald to trick King Louis VII of France into opting for Victor backfired when Louis discovered the stratagem. France and, later, England came in on the side of Alexander.

Wrathfully Frederick and Rainald arranged another council from the thinning ranks of acquiescent bishops and issued a declaration of imperial power that seriously alarmed most European monarchs. This Barbarossa, they concluded, was obviously menacing them all. Even his German bishops began to favor Alexander.

In 1163, in the midst of the conflict, Victor died. Rainald, fearful that Frederick might now reconcile with Alexander and thus end the schism, acted on his own authority to name a successor, who styled himself Pope Pascal III. By one account, Frederick sent orders forbidding Rainald to do any such thing, but they reportedly arrived too late; he was stuck with Pascal III, whose validity was everywhere questioned. So Rainald came up with a final and desperate expedient known as the Oath of Wurzburg. By imperial order all bishops of the church and princes of Germany, including Frederick himself, must swear never to recognize Alexander as pope. Few bishops took this oath, however, and some who did added provisos effectively negating it. Rainald himself backed out when it came to the point, fearful of losing his title of archbishop of Cologne if the wrong pope

Though destitute and militarily powerless, Pope Alexander was bold and diplomatically brilliant, presenting a compelling figure for any devout Christian who did not equate wealth and power with faith.

ever won. Frederick finally became exasperated with him. "You acted like a traitor and deceiver when you saddled me with a new pope," he stormed. "Now you refuse to go into the trap you are preparing for others."

The following year Chancellor Rainald did considerably redeem himself. By then the emperor believed that all his problems could be solved if only he could capture the pestilent Alexander. That intrepid gentleman had defiantly returned to Rome, where he was buying popularity with money provided by the Sicilian Norman king. Both Lombardy and Rome, having suffered several years under Rainald's onerous taxes and corrupt administration, were in open rebellion against the emperor. Therefore, in October 1166 Barbarossa once again led an army into Italy, this time with Rome as the goal. Bypassing Lombardy, he sent Rainald ahead to Rome with a thousand men, and at Tusculum the chancellor's small force sent some thirty thousand Roman troops fleeing across the Tiber. It was a sensational victory.

But still Alexander eluded them. As Frederick moved up to besiege the city, Alexander's little group barricaded itself in the Castel Sant'Angelo. Several days later when the imperial troops broke through and began looting, they found it deserted. Alexander was rumored to have escaped down the Tiber to the sea, disguised as a pilgrim. So Frederick enthroned Pascal III at St. Peter's and watched as the pope formally crowned Beatrix empress. His army was now in undisputed control of Rome and his own pope, in the Holy City. Furthermore, William I, the Norman king who had caused him so much grief, was dead. His heir was a ten-year-old boy, and civil war had broken out in Sicily. All Italy lay well within his grasp. What could stop him now?

The answer was not long in coming. Within a week it began to rain. Day after day it poured down. Flooded streets became veritable rivers. The city's ancient

Having succeeded in occupying Rome and appointing his own pope, and with his Norman Sicilian rivals subdued, Barbarossa now stood at the pinnacle of power in Europe. But suddenly everything changed. A malady broke out in his army, killing many of his senior officers, and he found himself forced to flee with his wife through hostile Lombardy and then the Alps to the safety of Germany. In this painting, commissioned by this series, a lone couple make their way on foot through the mountains, possessing little more than the clothes they wear. This swift plunge from worldly triumph to the desperation of a fugitive wrought a profound alteration in Barbarossa's character. To whom could he attribute such a swift downfall? As a religious man he reached the only possible conclusion.

sewage system failed. Food supplies were destroyed. Drinking water was polluted. Then came disease. Soldier after soldier failed to report for duty. Soon the army was in ruins. Word came that Rainald was sick, then that he was dead. Frederick himself became gravely ill and barely survived. The challenge now was to get out of the city and get home. With a small party the emperor and empress made their perilous way north through Lombardy. Twice they were held for ransom and escaped alone in disguise, much like Alexander had only weeks earlier. On March 16 they reached Basel, on the Rhine, with little more than the clothes they wore.

Then began in Frederick Barbarossa a profound transition that has baffled historians, who appear to ignore the obvious explanation. In mere days this man had fallen from the pinnacle of the world to a state of destitution and desperation. One question must have beset him: why had this happened? And given his beliefs, he can have arrived at only one answer, for however brutal, however cruel, however ruthless and crafty he had been, his Christian convictions had never wavered. Every campaign, every policy decision, indeed every day had begun and ended with prayer. So who could have destroyed him? Clearly, not the Lombards, not the

Sicilian Normans, not even his archenemy, Alexander III. None of them brought on that rain. Who, indeed, could have done it but God himself? He had made God his enemy. He had been following the wrong path. Something had to change.

But what could be the right path? Forgive your enemies, Jesus said, but how could he do that? Left unpunished, his enemies would instantly destroy him. Who takes the sword, Jesus said, perishes by the sword. Then, must evil triumph? Early Christians had died bravely under persecution by an empire. But he as a Christian had to *run* an empire. Could Jesus Christ enable him to do so? "I am the Way," Jesus said. But just what did that statement mean for an emperor? For some six years Frederick dithered, now seeming to follow his old master plan, now to reject it, now just to drift. But a new tendency gradually became apparent: rather than violently oppose the flow of events, he began more often to peaceably direct it. Yet there was one enemy he refused to stop hating, namely Alexander III. Love your enemies, said Jesus. Not this one, said Frederick.

This so-called pope seemed to take perverse pleasure in offending him, and his accumulating successes were as gall to Frederick's soul. No sooner had the emperor

The Battle of Legnano, depicted in this nineteenth-century painting by Amos Cassioli, saw Barbarossa and some fellow German princes assemble what seemed an invincible force against the Lombard cities. At the rear of the painting is a carroccio *(a sacred war chariot) ringed by trumpeters. A kneeling priest pleads with God to turn the tide against the oncoming Germans. The outcome provided an answer that ended the war.*

fled Rome, for example, than Alexander sponsored a coalition called the "Lombard League." For the first time in history Lombardy's sixteen biggest cities were in full accord, all swearing to support one another against any German invasion. More outrageous yet, the homeless citizens of Milan were busy building a brand-new city about fifty miles away, which they defiantly named Alessandria—after the pope, of course. Equally troubling, Frederick had belatedly discovered the chief reason he was so thoroughly hated in Lombardy: Rainald's administrators had purloined vast sums from the citizenry, looted their houses, blackmailed them, exacted forced labor, and, on occasion, raped their wives and daughters. Such was the record of Barbarossa's empire in Italy.

Nevertheless, he realized that he must somehow reassert his authority there or abdicate all pretence to imperial suzerainty, so there must be yet another invasion. But few of the German princes rallied round. It took Frederick more than five years to assemble an army, and when it set out for Italy in 1174, it consisted largely of mercenaries out for loot. Moreover, Frederick's customary tactic of allying himself with some Lombard cities against others no longer proved workable. Their oath to support the League held firm.

Still, his foremost target was the new city of Alessandria, which seemed an easy conquest because the city began by dickering with him for an imperial charter. When he laid siege to it, however, its citizens proved highly disciplined and mightily resolved. They held him off all winter. That spring when his troops successfully tunneled under the city walls, Frederick again compromised his faith by attacking through the tunnel on Good Friday, a violation of the Truce of God (see sidebar, pages 26–27). In any event, this strategy backfired. The defenders beat back the assailants, sealing off the tunnel and burying many of them alive, while those who had gained entry to the city fled in terror over the walls. The remaining mercenaries headed home, to cheers and jeers from the ramparts. It was a major defeat and humiliation for Barbarossa. He was still on the wrong path.

Worse was to come. Plainly shaken by the tenacity and efficiency of the Lombards, he began peace negotiations, which failed when league delegates insisted that Alexander participate. Frantically Barbarossa appealed again for help from Germany, and this time it came. Although Henry the Lion categorically refused, other German princes sent a thousand knights and as many foot soldiers. On the morning of May 29, 1176, when the imperial army met the Lombard force near the town of Legnano, about twenty miles northwest of Milan, Frederick's powerful mounted force crashed into the less experienced Lombard cavalry and sent them flying in retreat.

It only remained to cut down the Lombard foot soldiers. But then a curious spectacle confronted the Germans. In the midst of the Lombard infantry stood a kind of sacred wagon, called a *carroccio*, bearing Milanese flags assembled around an altar and a cross. Seven hundred citizens who called themselves the "Company of Death" formed a phalanx before it. Savagely the German cavalry attacked, but the defenders fought back ferociously against repeated assaults, unhorsing and slaying many. Finally, in a pause in the battle, the soldiers of the Company of Death dropped to their knees, made the sign of the cross, and offered their lives to Christ. Frederick's men may have scoffed, but it is doubtful that the emperor did. Could this be yet another sign? Was he still on the wrong path?

Suddenly trumpets blared from behind the imperial horsemen. The Lombard cavalry had re-formed and now smashed into the German rear, swiftly cutting its way right through to Barbarossa. His immediate guardsmen were killed; he himself, repeatedly slashed, was seen to fall, bleeding, from his horse. With the emperor down and surely dead, the Germans fled the field while the Lombards broke through and pillaged the imperial camp.

Some German knights escaped alive to bring the dreadful news to Empress Beatrix in Pavia, forty-five miles distant. So this, she must have thought, is how the story ends—but it was not. Several days later a small party of horsemen arrived at Pavia. Upright in their midst—bandaged, bloody, and bruised—rode her husband. Though the enemy had zealously searched the field for him or his body, he had somehow escaped. Now, amid the delirious rejoicing of his court, he had an urgent task still to perform. He sent emissaries to Anagni to acknowledge to the former Cardinal Roland that he was, indeed, Pope Alexander III and that in Pavia there was a beaten man who wanted to repent of his sins. Don't fall for this, Alexander's advisers warned; it has to be another of Frederick's tricks. But Alexander knew his man, and he knew this was no trick.

Thus, the following summer, on July 21, 1177, Emperor Frederick Barbarossa signed a document known as the Peace of Venice, whereby he repudiated both the Oath of Wurzburg and the arrogant Declaration

This monument in Legnano, Italy, created by Henri Butti in 1900, honors Alberto da Giussano, said to have been the leader of the "Company of Death," whose task it was to guard the sacred carroccio *with their lives during the Battle of Legnano. Their stubborn resolve proved the decisive factor in the Lombard victory.*

of Roncaglia, swore to respect the traditional rights of the Lombard cities, and proclaimed his empire at peace with both the Byzantine Empire and the Sicilian Normans. In a subsequent ceremony at St. Mark's Cathedral in Venice, he was formally received back into the church by Alexander, whose eyes, say the accounts, were streaming with tears. After Frederick led the pope's horse into the church, symbolizing his subservience to the papacy, Alexander conferred his blessing on the emperor while the people intoned an ancient hymn, the *"Te Deum,"* which concludes, *"In te, Dómine, sperávi. Non confúndar in ætérnum"* (Lord, in thee have I trusted. Let me never be confounded).

Frederick reigned another thirteen years, and it is a matter of record that from then on he never was "confounded." As he undoubtedly already suspected, Henry the Lion, who now more than matched the emperor himself in German lands and power, was about to mount a major challenge. Rather than respond with an army, however, in 1180 Frederick summoned Henry before a feudal court, then a relatively novel development, to answer to a charge of treason. When Henry stubbornly refused to appear, the court found him guilty of contumacy instead and deprived him of both Saxony and Bavaria.[13] Only then did Frederick assemble an imperial army against him, and in 1181 the Lion finally capitulated. He was deprived of almost all his lands and banished from Germany, to return only with the emperor's permission. Barbarossa was acquiring the legendary aura that would surround him for centuries to come.

The year 1184 stands as a pinnacle. In the seven years since his repentance many of Frederick's youthful ambitions had somehow been accomplished. He was now unchallenged as ruler of Germany. The Lombard cities were at peace among themselves and with the empire, whose ultimate authority they recognized while retaining their cherished independence. The long rivalry between the Hohenstaufens and Sicilian Normans had subsided. The pope had become his strong ally and supporter. His two eldest sons were ready to enter the knighthood.

Emperor Frederick and Empress Beatrix therefore decided to put on a magnificent festival at Mainz. A great wooden church was constructed for the ceremony; dignitaries flocked in from across the empire and beyond; chefs, minstrels, and poets prepared entertainment. But following the knighting ceremony, just as further festivities were getting under way, it began to rain and then to flood. The church collapsed, killing fifteen people. Ominously reminded of those dreadful days in Rome seventeen years earlier, Frederick abruptly canceled the rest of the event.

The following month saw another major diplomatic achievement, however. Pope Alexander, vindicating the stalwart claim of the bishops of Rome to be the *"Servus Servorum Dei"* (Servant of the Servants of God), had died, reportedly of exhaustion, three years earlier. His successor, Pope Lucius III, now arranged a marriage between Barbarossa's son Henry and Constance, aunt of the king of Sicily, who was believed impotent and likely to die without heirs. This marriage was in fact destined to unite the crowns of south and north Italy, and both Henry and his son after him would become emperors.

Even so, the great year ended sadly. In November 1184 Beatrix of Burgundy, the onetime child bride who had given Frederick six sons and two daughters and had accompanied him through most of the triumphs and disasters of his life, departed this world.[14] Some claimed that this was the greatest loss he would ever suffer.

13. "Contumacy" (from Latin *contumax*, insolent) signifies obstinate or contemptuous resistance to authority and early acquired the legal meaning of deliberate failure to appear in court to answer to a charge. In either mode, it fit the personality and history of Duke Henry the Lion. Married to Matilda, daughter of King Henry II of England, the Lion spent his years of exile at the courts of his father-in-law in Normandy and England, along with his entire family. In 1185, after three years, Barbarossa allowed him to return. But by 1189, after a further brief exile, the Lion was back making trouble in northern Germany for still another Henry: Barbarossa's son and successor, Emperor Henry VI.

14. Although eight children were born to Beatrix and Frederick, three did not survive childhood. Their first child, Beatrix, born in 1162 and betrothed in childhood to William II of Sicily, died at age twelve. Their first son, Duke Frederick V of Swabia, was born in 1164 and died in 1170. Daughter Agnes, betrothed to Emeric of Hungary, died in 1184 before they could be married. The other royal offspring were second son and Holy Roman Emperor Henry VI (1165–1197), third son Duke Frederick VI of Swabia (1167–1191), fourth son Count Otto of Burgundy (1170-1200), fifth son Duke Conrad II of Swabia and Rothenburg (1173–1196), and sixth son Phillip of Swabia (1177–1208), who reigned as king of Germany from 1198 to 1208. The last three all met violent deaths.

His defeat at Legnano persuaded Barbarossa that his enemy all along had been not the pope, nor the Milanese, nor the Welfs, nor the Sicilian Normans but God himself, against whom there could be no victory ever. On these grounds he returned as a penitent to the Christian fold and is received here by a weeping Pope Alexander III. In the remaining thirteen years of his reign he sought peace instead of conquest, becoming in the process a ruler beloved even by his former enemies. Paradoxically, by surrendering to defeat, he found the victory that had so long eluded him.

On his way to the Holy Land, leading what was the largest and most disciplined army that the West had yet sent to retake Jerusalem, Barbarossa unexpectedly died while crossing the Saleph River. His death—probably from a heart attack brought on by the icy water—is shown in this late-nineteenth-century painting by Hermann Vogel. Saladin, the Muslim general, said Barbarossa's death came as an answer to prayer.

The marriage of Henry and Constance was celebrated fourteen months later, with great pomp and ceremony, by clergy from Lombardy, Sicily, and Germany in the last sizeable church Frederick's troops had left standing in Milan. The city was rebuilding, the conflict that destroyed it assuredly over.

His sons now grown to manhood, Barbarossa's work seemed to be done—yet such was not yet the case. In the fall of 1187 came appalling news: Jerusalem had fallen to the Muslims. Papal envoys hastened to the imperial court and to the courts of England and France, seeking aid for the Holy City. Propaganda spread everywhere, one picture portraying a horse defecating in Jerusalem's Church of the Holy Sepulchre, another showing Arabs cruelly beating Christ. Such factors, however, may not have been what chiefly moved Frederick. To join a crusade, as everyone knew, could be a supreme act of penitence. Pondering his life, Barbarossa well knew how much he had to repent. And at nearly seventy he would also have known he was unlikely to return.

He therefore assembled what reputedly was the most highly trained and disciplined force ever to set out for Jerusalem, and also the largest: by one account, fifty thousand horsemen and one hundred thousand foot soldiers. Thieves, beggars, fraudsters, and prostitutes were forbidden to join. Crime against civilian populations was to be severely punished. Any lord accused of mistreating his men was to be tried by the clergy and executed if found guilty. Anyone discovered abusing a Jew would lose a hand and be sent home.

The massive contingent passed smoothly through Hungary but met setbacks in Byzantine territory, where Emperor Isaac Angelus, a weak-willed court sycophant who had gained the imperial throne by chance, mistrusted Barbarossa. Open warfare threatened before he finally agreed to transport the German army across the Dardanelles at Gallipoli. Thence, often parched for water and harassed by the Seljuk Turks, the army painfully crossed arid Anatolia and traversed the Taurus Mountains to the Cilician Plain, near Antioch.

And there, while fording the Saleph River in advance of his troops, Emperor Frederick Barbarossa perished, either by drowning or from a heart attack caused by the icy waters. With its hero-commander dead, discipline in his massive force collapsed. Some men deserted and went home; some units pushed south from Antioch and were quickly defeated; some moved south by sea and laid siege to Muslim-held Acre, on the Mediterranean coast, later joining the French and English forces. The great Muslim general Saladin, who reportedly had kept careful track of Frederick's approach—and dreaded it—gratefully attributed his death to Allah.

The emperor's body was carried into Antioch and buried, and there it remains, far from the circling ravens of Kyffhauser, where the legendary sleeper awaits the worldwide triumph of his people. Some might say that his people have triumphed already. With Japanese choirs diligently learning to sing Bach's *St. Matthew Passion* in its original language, with tens of thousands of children of every race and creed striving earnestly to master Brahms's Violin Concerto, when the poet Goethe has been translated into more than two hundred languages, and when mankind travels to the planets on technology born in such places as Saxony, Austria, Burgundy, Prussia, Bavaria, and Swabia, German culture is certainly leaving an imprint on mankind without the use of an army.

But others see Frederick as triumphant in a very different way. He was a man who, like political leaders before and after him, strove passionately to hold together his strong sense of obligation to rule and yet still to *be* ruled by God. In the end he managed to do both, and that is no mean accomplishment. ∎

In a cave underneath the Kyffhauser memorial lies this symbolic throne of Frederick Barbarossa. Upon the table sits a replica of his crown. But the real grave of Barbarossa is many hundreds of miles away, in Antioch, Syria, not far from the place of his death in the Third Crusade.

In this famous 1860 statue by Carlo Marochetti, Richard the Lionheart, sword in hand, stands guard outside the Houses of Parliament in Westminster. Early on, in wars fought for his father and against him, Richard established a well-deserved reputation as a superb military commander. Like his father, he was mercurial, given to snap decisions he would later regret. But war was his métier, and as a strategist, general, and leader of men he had no equal. His father's death made him king of England and duke of Normandy. Almost immediately he embarked on the Third Crusade.

CHAPTER 5

In valor and infamy the Crusades collapse into a tale of calamity

The lionhearted Richard reaches Jerusalem and folds, the sack of Constantinople fuels fury against the West, Acre falls, and Christian thousands are sold into slavery

For a thoroughly shocked and shaken Europe, the fall of Jerusalem in October of 1187 raised a difficult theological question. Why would a just God allow his people to lose their holiest city to the Muslims? The news of the city's dire peril may even have fatally shocked Urban III, pope for less than two years, whose death on hearing it left his amiable, frail, but energetic eighty-seven-year-old successor, Gregory VIII, to come up with an explanation. Gregory didn't or couldn't. All he could and did do was issue a desperate call for a third crusade. It would prove the biggest ever, and it would fail.

Saladin, Jerusalem's conqueror, had had a theological epiphany of a different sort. By sword and sagacity he had united Egypt, Damascus, and northern Syria, then, at age forty-eight, had fallen gravely ill and hovered near death. But, astonishingly, he had recovered, renewed his fervid piety, and decisively defeated the Christians. Now he reigned supreme in the Holy City—a recovery and victory he attributed wholly to Allah.

Saladin had crowned these accomplishments by strictly prohibiting the killing of any Christians, freeing those who could raise a ransom and some who couldn't, immediately releasing the widows of slain crusaders, sending civilians safe to the surviving Christian forts along the Mediterranean coast, and guaranteeing accessibility to the Holy Sepulchre for Christian pilgrims. All this was much in contrast to the slaughter the Christians had unleashed upon Jerusalem when they took the city a century earlier and to the savage vengeance Saladin's

Henry II, first Plantagenet king of England, was also duke of Normandy, of Aquitaine, and of Gascony; count of Anjou and of Nantes; lord of Ireland; and the richest monarch in Europe. In atonement for his role in the assassination of Thomas Becket, archbishop of Canterbury (see pages 96–97), he had been sending sizeable annual stipends to support Outremer. He now vowed to raise an army to fight there but would not live to make good on his promise. The illustration is from Cassell's 1902 History of England.

1. Muslim chroniclers wholly ratified the bishop's assessment. The Arab scribe 'imad al-Din, for example, described Christian women who remained under Muslim rule as "proud and scornful, foul-fleshed and sinful, ardent and inflamed, tinted and painted, desirable and appetizing, exquisite and graceful, seductive and bullying, with shapely buttocks and nasal voices." He summed them up as "broken down little fools" and gloatingly detailed their ravishment and debasement by Arab men into whose servitude they fell.

Muslim successors would inflict on Christians in the century that followed.

Meanwhile, Archbishop Josias of Tyre, who had brought the bad news to Europe in a ship somberly equipped with black-dyed sails, had a ready explanation for the calamity: God clearly had become exasperated with the sinful lives Christians were leading in Outremer. He carried a poignant letter from the master of the Templars in Jerusalem. "How many and how great are the calamities that our sins require," it lamented. "The anger of God has lately permitted us to be whipped. We are unstable. O sad fate!"

Few could deny that the Christians of Outremer had become at best a soft people— slothful and licentious; languishing in a world of figs, carpets, and dancing girls; intermarrying with Syrian, Armenian, and Byzantine women to produce what some saw as a race of half-castes. "From childhood they are pampered and wholly given to carnal pleasures," mourned the bishop of Acre. He portrayed a depraved society, heedless of the church, with crime rampant, men strangling their wives if they didn't like them, and wives killing their husbands with poisons, sold freely on the streets, to take other lovers. No one trusted anyone else, he charged, and church properties were turned into whorehouses, which proliferated everywhere.[1]

Though his zeal for the crusade never faltered, the frail Pope Gregory died of fever two months after his investiture while striving to unite the warring Pisans and Genoese behind the cause. His successor, Clement III, turned to Europe's monarchs for support, appealing directly to the emperor Frederick Barbarossa and dispatching Josias of Tyre to petition the kings of England and France.

Barbarossa, now in his sixties but as powerful a soldier as ever, readily accepted the call and began to assemble a crack German army numbering one hundred thousand men. Unhappily, he would die on his way to the Holy Land, gravely fragmenting his forces and leaving those of France and England to play the pivotal role (see chapter 4).

When Josias crossed the Alps in January of 1188, Henry II was king of England; duke of Normandy, of Aquitaine, and of Gascony; count of Anjou and of Nantes; lord of Ireland; and the richest monarch in Europe. In atonement for his role in the assassination of Thomas Becket, archbishop of Canterbury (see sidebar, pages 96–97), Henry had been sending sizeable annual stipends to support Outremer. His relations with King Philip II of France were cordial but strained, partly because of a lingering dispute over control of Vexin (the area between their domains in what would eventually become northeastern France) and partly because Philip's half-sister Alice was, in unreliable palace gossip, Henry's mistress, which is why his son Richard wouldn't marry her, a thesis that finds no support in the French chronicles.

After hearing Josias's woeful account, both Henry and Philip vowed to raise armies and depart for Outremer within a year, with Philip's men wearing red crosses, Henry's white, and the Flemish green. But Henry would not live to complete his vow. Upon his death in July 1189, his son would succeed him as King Richard I and effectively become leader of the Third Crusade.

The third of the five sons of Henry and the inexhaustible Eleanor of Aquitaine, Richard had not been expected to become king but had otherwise notably distinguished himself. Tall, lithe, and powerfully athletic, with handsome, ruddy features and reddish blonde hair, he had been dubbed "the Lionheart" for his courage and matchless strategies in wars both for and against his father. He had also been accused by one acknowledged enemy of cruelty and rape, having allegedly commandeered wives, daughters, and sisters of his own freemen and, when he was finished with them, turned them over to his troops as prostitutes. His father disliked and distrusted him (with reason), and the sentiment was mutual (also with reason). Richard was his mother's favorite and supported her in her recurrent rebellions against her husband, whose heir he became only on account of the premature deaths of his two older brothers.

Philip, though eight years younger than Henry, had been king for almost ten years when he took up the cross. He had grown up a close friend of the more charismatic Richard, but the crusade would strain and eventually crack any bond between them. This was not only because they would become rivals for its leadership but also because their attitudes, their mannerisms, their proprieties, their intuitions, their pleasures, their displeasures, and their entire concept of what constitutes acceptable conduct for a king were not only different but actively alien.

Richard, for instance, wore a two-handed battle sword with a golden grip, carried a shield appointed with the single lion of Aquitaine, and rode a massive Spanish stallion using golden stirrups. From his mother he had acquired an appreciation for music and poetry. He also loved fine food and drink, hunting, jousting, and hawking. He told bawdy stories, liked to swear obscene oaths on Jesus' body, and would insult his clerics, knowing they dared not respond. Like his father, he was mercurial, given to snap decisions he would later regret, and although he loved to organize, he hated to administer. War was his métier, and as a strategist, general, and leader of men he had no equal.

Much of Richard's behavior shocked or cowed Philip, who, though the more effete of the two, was slovenly in dress and grooming, blind in one eye, pale, and rather ugly, evidencing few of the

Philip II of France, a childhood friend of Richard's, embarked on the Third Crusade as a co-commander, but his relations with Richard soon soured. In the crusade Philip gave little evidence that he would become one of the great kings of France, honored with the title Philip Augustus. This nineteenth-century portrait of Philip is by Stefano Bianchetti.

2. Some historians present Richard and Philip as homosexual lovers, citing contemporary chroniclers like Roger of Hovedon, who portrays them as sleeping in the same bed, eating from each other's plates, and otherwise doting upon each other like young lovers, much to the horror of Henry. However, Richard's twentieth-century biographer John Gillingham posits that such shows of affection were customary at a time when male friends often held hands and shared the same bed, with no erotic connotation. None of Richard's enemies, Gillingham observes, accused him of sodomy. What Henry more likely feared in his son's relationship with Philip was not sexual perversion but treason.

3. Richard's mother, Eleanor, had encountered Berengaria, eldest daughter of Sancho VI of Navarre and Sancha of Castile, while sojourning in Spain. She hoped the twenty-six-year-old princess could produce an heir to prevent her fifth son, John, whom Eleanor loathed, from succeeding to the throne. Since this broke Richard's vow, the enraged Philip threatened war on Richard, but Richard produced affidavits asserting that Alice had borne Henry's child, disqualifying her as queen of England under church law. He also offered Philip ten thousand marks to release him from his vow. Philip accepted but remained angry.

Richard liked to dress the part of a valiant crusader, wearing a two-handed battle sword with a golden grip and a shield with the single lion of Aquitaine. He rode with golden stirrups a massive Spanish stallion. Here he is portrayed in an 1841 oil painting by Merry-Joseph Blondel.

qualities that in later years would see him acclaimed as Philip Augustus, greatest of the Capetian kings. But in Outremer he possessed neither Richard's charm nor his daring. He hated risk, had no interest in hunting or any other rugged sport, knew no Latin, and was seemingly paranoiac and delusional. By the conventions of the day, he was a notable prude, once ordering a man dunked three times for swearing and thereafter prohibiting swearing everywhere in his kingdom. "The French king goes about so daintily that I am afraid he may spring on me," smirked the poet Bertran of Born. To Philip, Richard came on as an arrogant, foulmouthed boor.[2]

The two set off from Vezelay, in central France, in the summer of 1191 with their armies numbering a combined one hundred thousand. If one were killed, the other was to take over his command. If either broke this pledge, he was to be excommunicated. Richard also promised to marry Philip's half sister Alice within forty days of his return, whatever her relationship with her father.

Richard traveled to his ships in Marseille, Philip to his in Genoa. After much adventure and misadventure (including Richard's subduing of Sicily, his capture of Cyprus from its Byzantine king, and his marriage there to Berengaria of Navarre), the two kings and their fleets finally arrived at Acre, the Muslim-held fortress on the Mediterranean coast—Philip in April and Richard in June of 1191.[3] There they joined in the siege of the city that had begun in the fall of 1189.

Meanwhile, Saladin, with Jerusalem securely in his possession, had released its erstwhile king, the ever-bungling Guy of Lusignan. Perhaps to regain respect, Guy had recruited other knights liberated by Saladin after ransom and had laid siege to Acre. This city, jutting westward into the sea on two sides and facing the Plain of Acre on the east, had been the traditional port of disembarkation for Christian pilgrims, a great marketplace of the eastern Mediterranean, and home to the Hospitallers' biggest hospital and hostel. After taking the city from the Christians, Saladin had fortified its east-facing walls.

There Guy and his army grimly maintained the siege. Near starvation after two winters without success, his rank and file was subsisting on grass and dry bones while his knights bought what provisions they could from unscrupulous entrepreneurs at a hundred times the fair value. Saladin, communicating with Acre's besieged garrison by means of carrier pigeons and swimmers, was encamped on a hill to the southeast, separated from Guy's forces by a trench across which he would make occasional forays. Such was the situation when first Philip and then Richard arrived in their galleys with their troops and siege engines.

Landing on April 20, Philip did a workmanlike job with his army's giant mangonels (a type of catapult) and rams. In fact, he twice breached the walls of the Accursed Tower (so named because it was believed to have been there that Judas's thirty silver pieces were minted). But the city held, and Philip had already failed as a commander before Richard arrived in June.[4]

Besieging castles was one of the two main forms of battle in the Middle Ages (the other being the skirmish). Richard's miners soon weakened the walls by tunneling beneath them. His mangonels, although smaller than Philip's, lobbed harder and denser granite boulders, which Richard had expressly transported from Sicily. His Norman archers atop wooden siege towers fired bolts from their crossbows, a weapon that Richard valued above all others despite papal encyclicals against its use as inhumane.

Then he moved in the "Mategriffon," the wooden castle he had first built for his battle in Sicily. Its walls were covered with vinegar-soaked cord, the only substance that could withstand that petroleum-based ancestor of napalm known as "Greek fire." Aloft on this perilous structure with his crossbow, Richard could serenely pick off Muslims on the city walls. Even when ill with a serious case of scurvy, though feverish and with his hair falling out, he had himself carried to this tower to resume the sport.

Shortly after his arrival, Richard relayed word to Saladin, whom he admired as a chivalrous enemy, that he wanted to parley; perhaps they could reach a settlement. Saladin refused but sent him a gift of fruit and also arranged for his brother

4. Richard was delayed in Cyprus, where several of his ships ran aground. The island's self-appointed king for the previous seven years, Isaac Ducas Comnenus, a rebel against Constantinople, looted the wrecks and refused shelter to Richard's future wife, Berengaria, and his sister Joanna. So Richard perforce landed, subdued the defending forces, and seized the island as a crusader kingdom. Cyprus would become a staging and supply point for the Christians still in Outremer and serve as their refuge when they were driven out of it.

The first order of battle for the crusaders was the recapture of the city of Acre—shown here in a mid-nineteenth-century engraving—which jutted westward into the sea on two sides. The city was among the Christian possessions taken by Saladin following the Battle at the Horns of Hattin in 1187.

In the Battle of Acre in 1189, Guy of Lusignan's besieging forces were attacked outside the city walls by Saladin's much larger army. The Muslims attempted to encircle the Christians, as shown here. Guy's soldiers won this clash, but Saladin regrouped and remained not far away, poised to strike at the besiegers. This reconstruction of the battle is by the mid-nineteenth-century French engraver Gustave Doré.

Malik al-Adil to be available to conduct talks on Saladin's behalf. Thus, although Saladin and Richard would never meet face to face, an unlikely friendship developed between the English king and Saladin's brother.

The long siege had taken a fearful toll on the occupants of the city. By early July of 1191 Acre's emirs, facing starvation and an ever-strengthening force outside their walls, offered to surrender despite Saladin's assurances, conveyed via pigeon post, that provisions would arrive any day from Egypt. This independent action by the emirs, along with the flat refusal of Saladin's army on July 5 to attack the crusader camp, was the first hint that the sultan's grip on his forces was slackening. On July 11 the emirs accepted Richard's terms, which included demands for the payment of two hundred thousand gold pieces, the release of fifteen hundred Christian prisoners, and the return of the true cross, which Saladin had captured after the defeat of the Christians at the Horns of Hattin (see pages 78–79). When a swimmer arrived and told Saladin the terms that he would be called upon to implement, the infuriated sultan began an answer forbidding the emirs to accept. Even as he was composing the letter, however, he saw the Christian banners being unfurled on the towers of Acre. Now he was bound to honor the accord, and Richard held twenty-seven hundred members of the garrison to ensure compliance.

After the crusaders took up residence in Acre, squabbles erupted when Richard refused to split the spoils with anyone but the French. The duke of Austria, who had taken command of Barbarossa's depleted German forces, claimed equal status and raised his banner on one of the towers, only to have it torn down by Richard's troops. The duke marched home in disgust, and this insult would later return to haunt Richard.

Philip, never a particularly enthusiastic crusader and resentful of Richard's preeminence, now fell ill with a malady that would afflict him for the rest of his life, while the same scourge nearly killed Richard then and there. Philip announced that he must return immediately to France. Leaving most of his troops under the command of Duke Hugh of Burgundy, he promised not to molest Richard's kingdom in Europe while the latter remained in the Holy Land, a promise he was reluctantly obliged to keep.[5] Conrad of Montferrat, whose Christian forces from Tyre had joined the siege, wanted no part of an army now controlled by Richard. He also stormed home.

Before advancing the eighty miles south to Jerusalem, the English king had to complete negotiations with Saladin, and conditions were agreed upon. Saladin began defaulting on them, however, upon which Richard refused to release his twenty-seven hundred prisoners. Unless the accepted terms were honored, he threatened, he would execute them all. Saladin, perhaps thinking this a bluff, let the deadline for compliance pass, so Richard had the captives tied together and marched out onto the plain. There, in full view of the Muslim army, they were butchered along with their wives and children. Ambrose, Richard's poet/balladeer (*jongleur* in French), in his *History of the Holy War*, blames this atrocity on Saladin, who by defaulting "had no regard whatsoever for those who had defended Acre for him." Muslims, however, saw this slaughter as an infamous act that they would on no account forget, and Saladin would no longer be merciful toward Christian captives.

Through parched and spider-infested land Richard headed south, leading tens

5. Philip paused in Rome, where he complained to Pope Celestine III about Richard's "rudeness," claiming that Richard had forced him to leave Outremer against his will. He asked to be released from his oath not to attack Richard's lands, but Celestine forbade him on pain of excommunication to do any such thing. Philip had better luck in Germany, however, where kinsmen of the spurned duke of Austria, upon hearing of Richard's refusal to grant equal status to the Germans, resolved to seize him if his homeward journey should lead through their territory.

Out of tragedy arose holiness

Grief, loss, and a cruel confessor, but the light still shone from Thuringia's St. Elizabeth

Even amidst the recurring darkness of the later crusades, some lights shone brightly—one of them in German Thuringia, where in 1211 a four-year-old girl was sent to be raised as the bride of Thuringia's next ruler, then eleven. This little girl, although known to history as St. Elizabeth of Hungary, would spend most of her life in Germany, where many would regard her as the greatest woman of the German Middle Ages.

Life for little Elizabeth was far from easy. News soon arrived of her mother's death amidst political turmoil back in Hungary, and in the high mountain castle of Wartburg, home of the counts of Thuringia, she was mocked and chided for her deep Christian devotion. But she had a champion who silenced her tormenters: the boy who was to marry her, the future Ludwig IV, landgrave of Thuringia. They were wed in 1221, when Elizabeth was fourteen and Ludwig twenty-one, and the next few years were probably the happiest of her life.

They had three children, and Ludwig strongly supported her extensive charitable work among the poor. He used to hold her hand, it was said, as she said her nighttime prayers. When famine and plague struck during Ludwig's absence in the service of the emperor, the landgravine Elizabeth led the relief work, selling castle furnishings to finance a hospital in the town of Eisenach. She also came under the influence of the Franciscans (see chapter 10), eventually joining their third order.

The first great calamity of her life struck in 1227, when Ludwig died of the malady that struck down the Sixth Crusade. Elizabeth was devastated. "The world with all its joys is dead to me now," she said. The second soon followed when a certain Conrad of Marburg became master of the Franciscans in Thuringia and also confessor to the landgravine. Master Conrad, says the *Catholic Encyclopedia*, was "a rough man, of inexorable severity."

This severity he imposed full force upon the young widow, demanding of her spiritual exercises that were harsh even by the standards of the mendicant orders. At one point Conrad took her children from her so that she could become wholly devoted to Christ, and he ordered her subjected to physical punishment. Elizabeth nevertheless persisted in her charities, spending her dower to build a Franciscan hospital. She had become a heroine to the poor by the time, in the fall of 1231, she died of sheer exhaustion at age twenty-four. Repeated reports of miraculous healing soon made her grave a major place of pilgrimage.

A very different end awaited the relentless Conrad. Two years later, as chief inquisitor in Germany he formally accused Count Henry of Sayn of heresy and bizarre diabolical behavior. A court of the count's peers acquitted him, and Master Conrad was murdered as he rode home from the trial with his entourage. When this news reached Rome, Pope Gregory IX received it as information. Notably, he did not call for an inquiry. ∎

After the capture of Acre Richard threatened to execute his twenty-seven hundred Muslim prisoners if Saladin didn't honor his part of the bargain. Saladin, perhaps thinking it a bluff, failed to meet the deadline and suffered the predicable and gruesome consequences, as shown in this Doré engraving. Hereafter, Saladin would show little mercy toward the Christians.

of thousands of soldiers who were signally reluctant to depart from the delights of Acre. An even grumpier duke of Burgundy brought up the rear with the equally unenthusiastic French. All the way they were harassed by Muslims, who hacked captives to pieces at any opportunity. The plan was to capture Jaffa (a borough in modern Tel Aviv) and secure that coastal city as a mustering point for the final twenty-five-mile push east to Jerusalem.

Saladin chose the Plain of Arsuf, just north of Jaffa, for his first great open battle with the crusaders since he had slaughtered them at Hattin, thereby dooming Christian Jerusalem. But Richard had been forewarned of his plan. On the morning of September 7, 1191, he arranged his army in a strategically constructed series of concentric circles. The bowmen were in the outer circle, the knights were behind them, and he and his Norman troops took the center.

The Muslims attacked in midmorning, thirty thousand of them, according to Ambrose. First came wave after wave of lightly armed African and Bedouin foot soldiers. Hurling arrows and darts, they threw Richard's first circle of infantry into temporary disorder but could make no impression on the heavily armed knights behind them. The infantry was followed by Turkish horsemen armed with axes and sabers. But as Saladin's troops withdrew to muster for each new attack, Richard's outer circle re-formed and the whole process started anew.

Richard's strategy was to tire the enemy before ordering his knights to charge, but the knights grew impatient, begging him to let them advance. Though he insisted they hold back, finally two knights defied him and charged anyway. Richard, demonstrating his commander's instincts, instantly rode out ahead and led the charge, thus preventing chaos. The Muslims were overwhelmed. They fled, and by evening the Christian army commanded the field. Continuing its march, it easily took Jaffa and began preparations to move on the Holy City.

What followed became the abiding mystery of the Third Crusade, for Richard the Lionheart would never capture Jerusalem. In the coming year he would twice approach it and twice turn back, once coming within five miles and gazing upon

Saladin, imagined here by Gustave Doré in glorious triumph over a fallen enemy, was in fact starting to lose the support of his emirs following the initial victories of the Third Crusade.

Richard's skill as a commander was clearly demonstrated at the Battle of Arsuf, near present-day Tel Aviv, where Saladin's forces descended on and seemingly boxed in the crusaders. Richard, forewarned of the attack, arranged his troops in a series of concentric circles that held firmly against the repeated Muslim assaults, exhausting the attackers so that a charge by Richard's knights routed them. Gustave Doré portrays the clash. Jerusalem now lay wide open to Richard's assault.

its walls and the Mount of Olives from Nebi Samwil, with tears of frustration in his eyes. For eight centuries historians have searched the record of events to find the reasons. For his first default there is some convincing explanation. In the winter of 1191 to 1192 the rains were torrential. The Templars and the Hospitallers told him that a siege in the hills of Judea would quite literally be a washout. Moreover, they advised, if Richard did capture Jerusalem, who would remain to man it? His weary troops would want to return home. Reluctantly, and to the disbelief of both the Muslims and his own Christian soldiers, Richard retreated.

That winter he busied his disconsolate men with the rebuilding of Ascalon, the port south of Jaffa that Saladin had demolished for fear that the crusaders might use it as a departure point for an attack on Egypt. During that winter and spring Richard won two celebrated battles: one to capture Darum, the southernmost coastal fortress; the other to foil, with just fifty knights, a Muslim reoccupation of Jaffa. But back in Acre the chronically warring Pisans and Genoese, the crusade suppliers, went at each other again, with the Pisans seizing the city and the Genoese and French fighting to repossess it. Richard arrived and effected a shaky truce but came away convinced of a grim reality: peace must somehow be made with Saladin.

Saladin, meanwhile, had his own problems. Having suffered two major defeats, he had become unpopular with his emirs. In bad health and weary of war, he was ready to talk terms. He even considered Richard's bizarre proposal that Saladin's brother al-Adil marry Richard's sister Joanna and they jointly rule Jerusalem and Palestine. But Joanna, widow of King William of Sicily, swore she would prefer martyrdom to marrying a Muslim, while al-Adil, although entranced by the idea of a Christian queen, was not prepared to convert to Christianity. Richard suggested his virgin niece from France as an alternative, but this proposal failed to appeal because al-Adil's heart remained set on Queen Joanna.

Richard's difficulties grew. Back home, his younger brother John, dissatisfied with the territory assigned him by Richard, was gathering a cadre of nobles to usurp the throne. Richard was also tiring of the noisome politics of Outremer. He had appointed the hapless Guy of Lusignan as king for life of Christian Palestine, to be succeeded by Tyre's Conrad of Montferrat, but Outremer's council of nobles objected. They wanted Conrad as king immediately. Richard agreed and mollified Guy by selling him Cyprus, which the Lusignan line would control for the next three hundred years. As fate would have it, Conrad's reign would be cut short when he was stabbed on the streets of Tyre by a pair of assigned killers from the Assassin sect (see sidebar, pages 76–77). So Richard made his nephew king of Jerusalem, marrying him into the bloodline of the former monarchy.

The circumstances of the Lionheart's next approach to Jerusalem, in June of 1192, deepen much further the mystery of his second withdrawal. His troops, positioned in Beit-Nuba, were within twelve miles of the prize. Morale was high even among the duke of Burgundy's hitherto recalcitrant French, and the crusaders

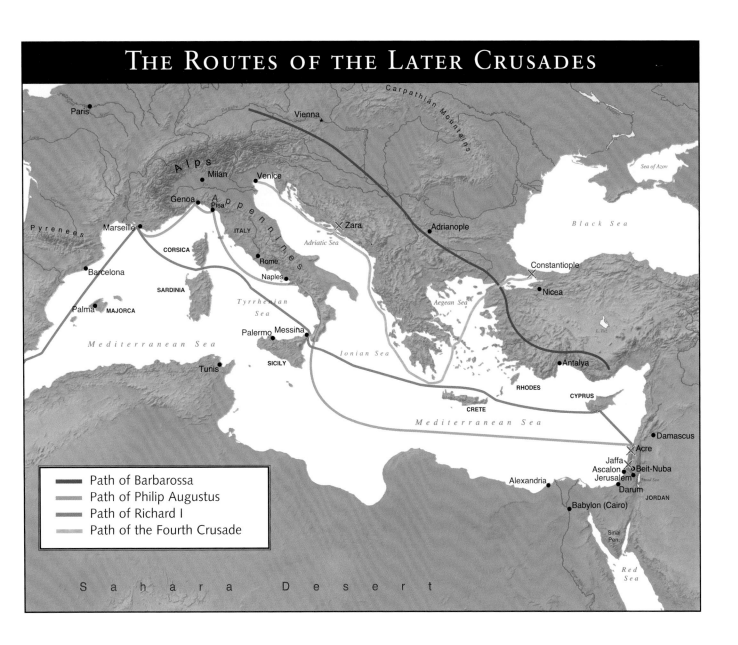

THE ROUTES OF THE LATER CRUSADES

Path of Barbarossa
Path of Philip Augustus
Path of Richard I
Path of the Fourth Crusade

had just captured a caravan from Cairo with a veritable cornucopia of supplies: three thousand horses, three thousand camels, an arsenal of weapons, and food and gold aplenty for a long siege. Moreover, the garrison within the city had been gravely weakened. Saladin had posted his main fighting force outside and planned a flank attack on the besiegers—although he later conceded that he had believed himself incapable of defeating them and had already considered Jerusalem lost.

Then, on June 24, the utterly unforeseen occurred. As his forces eagerly planned which walls they would breach and on which towers place their triumphal banners, Richard called together his commanders and gave them the news. The attack was off. They were going home. Their dismay and astonishment challenge description.

What had caused this change of heart and plan? Was it, as the derisive French would later have it, cowardice? Was it the prophecy of the crusade's impending doom, which Richard had heard from a Cistercian abbot? Was it the perennially vexed question of who could maintain Christian Jerusalem after the crusaders departed? Was it the alarming news from his chancellor that the perfidious Philip was now attacking English lands, threatening Richard's kingdom? Was it just Richard's paradoxical caution when preparing for battle—a trait much at odds with his dauntless ferocity when actually fighting it?

James Reston, Jr., in his eminently readable account of the Third Crusade (*Warriors of God*), discerns an "element of self pity" in Richard's own recorded explanation. The Lionheart told his grim-faced nobles, according to one chronicle, "If I should lead the host to besiege Jerusalem the way you advise and the endeavor should come to defeat, all my life long I should be blamed, even shamed and reviled. I am aware, of course, that there are people here and in France who would love to see me make such a mistake, so that they might broadcast it far and wide and bring infamy to my spotless name. But with such a doubtful result, I deem it wrong to rush rashly forward."

In any event, he signed the five-year peace treaty with Saladin that would allow him to leave. The Christians retained all the coastal cities south to Jaffa, and both they and the Muslims gained free access through each other's lands. Ascalon was to be demolished again. Two Latin priests and two deacons were authorized to serve at the Holy Sepulchre.

In October 1192 Richard sailed from Acre, vowing to return, but he never did. A shipwreck forced him to travel overland through Austria, where the Germans, still smarting over their rejection at Acre, arrested him, charging that he had paid the Assassins to murder Conrad. He was imprisoned for fifteen months until a large ransom was paid, then spent the next five years confounding John's intrigues in England and Philip's hostilities in France. Dying of a crossbow bolt wound on April 7, 1199, he was succeeded by the generally unsatisfactory John, signatory of the Magna Carta (see sidebar, page 139). Richard was "pleasant, upright, magnanimous, and excellent," one admirer asserted, namely Saladin. He would rather have the Holy Land fall into Richard's hands, said the great sultan, as recorded by an Arab chronicler, "than those of any other prince he had ever seen." Saladin himself, exhausted and sick, had died on March 3, 1193.

By then the Third Crusade, too, was all but dead. Edward Noble Stone, translator of balladeer Ambrose's versified account of it, summed it up as "heroic and useless," but perhaps "useless" is too strong. Although wildly disproportionate to the money and manpower expended, and although it failed to recapture the Holy

Richard's tomb at Fontevrault Abbey, in France. After Richard quit the crusade and was ransomed from his German captors on the way home, he spent the rest of his life fighting to hold his territories in the future France and foiling the plots by his brother John in England.

6. For about a thousand years the chief magistrate and ruler of Venice had been styled the "doge," a rare but not unique title derived from Latin *dux*. In Italian it became *il duce*, and in English *duke*. The doges of Venice were elected for life by the city-state's aristocracy. Commonly the person selected was the shrewdest elder in the city.

Having made a strategic decision to recruit dukes and counts rather than kings to fight the Fourth Crusade, Pope Innocent III needed a source of funds. He turned for financing to the Serene Republic of Venice. This decision would lead to a disastrous outcome in which serenity was significantly absent. The great city of canals, shown here at dusk, retains many of the attributes of its fascinating past.

City, it secured a strip ten miles wide stretching ninety miles along the Mediterranean coast from Tyre to Jaffa that would remain Christian for almost all the ensuing century. It also secured Cyprus, and it ended Saladin's career of conquest. Upon the death of the great sultan, the Muslims, respecting none of his seventeen squabbling sons, fell again into disunity.

Pope Celestine III had few illusions about the crusaders. They were driven, he declared, "not by the fear of God or any stirring of penitence. Pride and vainglory directed all their enterprise." His successor, the astute and powerful Innocent III, had a different diagnosis. The Second and Third Crusades failed, he concluded, because kings ran them, not Rome. Had not the First succeeded without the help of kings? Innocent therefore called for a fourth, to be fought by counts and dukes under the strict control of the pope and his legates. But the Fourth Crusade was to prove infinitely the worst disaster of all. Not only would it utterly fail to penetrate Islam, it would also commit an atrocity that would embitter eastern Christians against western for centuries to come, catastrophically widening the gulf between them.

Since no kings meant no big money and the Muslims had by now closed the overland route through Anatolia (modern Turkey), major funding would be needed for sea transport. Equally inescapable would be a key role for Venice, renowned for its shipbuilding and mercantile fleet. Therefore, in 1202, ten years after Richard's dumbfounding withdrawal from Jerusalem, the Venetian city-state was designated as a mustering point for the French and Flemish troops of the Fourth Crusade. The French were led by the massive and fiery Boniface of Montferrat, brother of the assassinated king of Jerusalem. The Flemish leader was the smaller, calmer, weaker, and much more amiable Baldwin of Flanders.

Venice, majestically known as the "Serene Republic," was controlled by the blind and conniving old doge Enrico Dandalo.[6] In his eighties but undiminished in vigor and guile, Dandalo had no demonstrable interest whatever in the crusade's stated objective—returning Egypt to the Christian fold—or in alienating Muslim authorities there.[7] Egypt was crucial to Venice's Mediterranean trade, and the doge had promised Sultan al-Adil, who had succeeded Saladin, that he would never attack Egypt, a commitment he neglected to mention to the crusaders. Dandalo's real objectives were to regain territory lost to the Christian Byzantines at Constantinople, to improve the security of Mediterranean trading routes, and to humiliate and subjugate the Eastern Empire. In the 1170s the government at Constantinople had imprisoned all Venetians in its domain and seized their goods. For this the doge sought retribution.

Enrico Dandalo, doge of Venice and preserved in both mythology and fact as one of the great villains of Christian history, is shown here in this Gustave Doré engraving preaching the Fourth Crusade in full, if hypocritical, fervor. More than eighty years old and blind, he was driven by vengeance and greed, as events would soon demonstrate. It is unlikely that he expected the ships he provided to the crusaders to ever reach the Holy Land. In fact, he already had a secret treaty with the Muslims that they would not.

Gathered in Venice, the crusaders found themselves unable to pay the eighty-five thousand marks needed for passage to the Egyptian coast. Doge Dandalo offered to provide free transport, supplies, and additional troops if they would stop at the Adriatic city of Zara and take it back from the Hungarians, who were Byzantine allies. All booty would be split fifty-fifty, thus paying the passage bill. To the crusade's secular leaders, this offer was irresistible; to the church, it was unthinkable. As titular head of the crusade Innocent had stipulated that it must never attack Christians; the Hungarians not only were Christians, they were *western* Christians. The crusade's military leaders, however, regarding this as an unfortunate but unavoidable circumstance, accepted the doge's offer, attacked Christian Zara, and, after four days of fierce fighting, seized and sacked it.

The crusade's next ostensible objective was the Egyptian port of Damietta, in the Nile Delta, but the doge now had another idea. Why not first seize the seat of Byzantine power, seemingly imperishable Constantinople?[8] Innocent, although he

7. Up to the Muslim invasion in the seventh century, Egypt had played a major role in Christian development, producing key figures like Clement of Alexandria, Origen, and Athanasius. Even in the eleventh century most of Egypt's population was still Christian, although they had long lived under varying degrees of Muslim oppression. Deemed under Qur'anic law to be second-class citizens, they were subject to special taxes, ineligible for high government office, sometimes required to wear special identifying clothing, forbidden to ring church bells or ride horses, and forbidden on pain of death to preach the Gospel to any Muslim.

longed to amalgamate the two churches under Rome's banner, could hardly countenance such an attack on the ancient Christian city. The doge, however, soon came up with a pretext. The current Byzantine emperor had gained the throne by deposing and blinding its legitimate occupant. But the daughter of the deposed emperor was married to the king of Germany, so his son fled westward to seek aid from his sister and his brother-in-law. Here, surely, was a chance to see justice done by putting the young man on his father's throne, a service the crusaders could perform in passing.

The twenty-one-year-old pretender, designated to rule his father's domain as Emperor Alexius IV, added an explicit and potent promise. "If God allows you to restore me to the throne," he told the crusaders, "I will place all my empire under obedience to Rome." Unable to stop the assault, Innocent could do nothing more than stipulate that no Christians be attacked.

Some few crusaders quit at this point, but most sailed on to Constantinople. They disliked the Byzantines anyway. Had they not deliberately betrayed and helped destroy the French contingent in the Second Crusade? (There is historical

8. The realm ruled from Byzantium (original name of the city of Constantinople) was arguably the world's longest-lived empire, lasting 1,123 years (AD 330–1453). The commercial empire of Venice held sway almost as long as Byzantium: eleven hundred years (AD 697–1797). Byzantium, softened by the crusaders' attack in 1204, would finally be overrun by the Ottoman Turks. Napoleon's army would end the trade ascendancy of Venice.

For centuries Christians bewailed a crusade that never happened

It was awful, those children starving and dying as they struggled toward Jerusalem, except they weren't children, and most were soon turned back

For some seven hundred years the story of the "Children's Crusade" provoked tears and horror in readers of history. It told how a shepherd boy known as Stephen of Cloyes had a vision in which Jesus commanded him to lead an army of children to Jerusalem to convert the Muslims. So Stephen, twelve years old at most, began preaching throughout France and Germany, causing what has been regarded as the greatest tragedy of the whole tragic crusading era.

Wherever he went, runs the story, boys and girls ran away from their homes and followed him; as many as thirty thousand are mentioned. Why their parents did not stop them always remained an unanswered mystery in the story. In any event, by the summer of 1212 the child army set out for the Mediterranean. Its waters, Stephen assured them, would part as the Red Sea had for Moses, and they would walk dry-shod to Jerusalem.

Reality quickly set in, however. There was drought that year, and many areas were devastated by famine. Roads were primitive, and bridges had fallen. The people they encountered could be downright nasty. "Is this Jerusalem?" the children would pitifully ask at each new town as they struggled onward. More and more of them fell behind and died of exhaustion or disease or criminal attack. When

they reached the Mediterranean and it disappointingly refused to part, most of the children went home. Five thousand supposedly found passage on merchant ships; however, their fate remained utterly unknown for eight years, until a priest spotted some of them on the Muslim slave markets in Alexandria.

In the late nineteenth century, when scholars began raising questions about the Children's Crusade, the relevant documentary evidence turned out to be flawed, contradictory, or written long after the event. Twentieth-century studies further reduced its credibility, and in 1977 Peter Raedts of Radboud University, the Netherlands, examined sixty-odd supporting sources and published his conclusions in the *Journal of Medieval History*.

For a start, he writes, much of the account must be regarded as pure legend. The participants were likely not children but young servants, newly displaced members of society, and youths who as the youngest in their families would be excluded from inheritance. All sought "an escape from the dreary misery of their daily lives." One cause of the legendary aspect may have been misinterpretation of descriptive terms used by the chroniclers. "Boys," for instance, was used then, as now, to mean "men" (as in "good ol' boys" or "He's gone out with the boys" or the First World War song evidence for this.) Further, as Antony Bridge puts it in his 1980 book, *The Crusades*, the westerners tended to look upon the Byzantines with "the sort of angry scorn felt by country bumpkins for supercilious and unmanly city dwellers."

On July 17, 1203, the Venetian armada of 450 warships, merchantmen, and transports dropped anchor outside the walls of the city considered the world's most beautiful. Here lay much of Christendom's accumulated learning and literature; here were its most magnificent works of art; here were the relics of countless saints, including, most people believed, the head of John the Baptist and the rod of Moses; and here, according to one contemporary chronicler, reposed three quarters of the world's wealth. So the crusaders marveled as they sailed up Constantinople's seven-mile-long Golden Horn, one of the finest natural harbors in the world. "The men in the ships regarded the grandeur of the city," wrote Robert of Clari, a French soldier, "so large it was and so long, and they were dumb with amazement."

Though trouble did not erupt immediately, the citizens failed to welcome the pretender as that young man had confidently asserted they would. The crusader

"Tramp, Tramp, Tramp, the Boys are Marching").

Moreover, Raedts found, two very different movements had been combined into one story. The first grouping assembled in Germany under the leadership of a man named Nicholas, possible model for the shepherd boy, and much of the depiction of this campaign does resemble that of the legendary child crusaders, except that they were not children. The few participants who eventually returned home did so "one at a time, silently, barefoot and hungry, fools in everyone's eyes, and a number of the girls had lost the flower of their virginity." Nicholas was reported either to have died, causing his grieving father to commit suicide, or, alternatively, to have fought valiantly at the fall of Acre.

The second movement arose in France and "caused much less shock and sensation than did its German counterpart." It was, indeed, attributed to a certain Stephen, who in this version claimed that Jesus Christ himself had given him a letter for the king of France. Preaching and performing miracles, Stephen gathered many thousands of people and embarked for Paris. He was halted by the king, however, who, having consulted with his bishops, ordered the whole throng home.

Given that they concerned adults, not children, these campaigns were not as unusual as they might sound to the modern ear. After all, the poor had been involved from the outset, when Peter the Hermit triggered the Peasants' Crusade (see sidebar, pages 16–17). That was a veritable army of beggars, observes Raedts, whose

In this nineteenth-century engraving by Gustave Doré, fresh-faced children gather in Cloyes, near Orleans, at the bidding of a charismatic young shepherd boy called Stephen to embark on an unarmed crusade to Jerusalem. But since Doré's day, historians have become virtually unanimous in concluding that such a crusade did not occur.

"indiscriminate savagery aroused at least as much fear among the Christian knights as among the Muslims." The so-called Children's Crusade was probably much the same. ■

In the Doré engraving above, Murzuphlus, a rebel Byzantine general styling himself Emperor Alexius V, attempts to negotiate from the shore with Dandalo in the stern pulpit of a ship the terms by which the Latins would leave Constantinople. The negotiations proved futile, of course, because conquering and looting the eastern imperial capital was Dandalo's principal reason for undertaking the crusade. Unable to save the city from the ensuing Latin attack, Murzuphlus was captured and executed by being thrown from the sixty-five-foot-high column of Theodosius.

leadership therefore offered the usurper, reigning as Alexius III, a choice: immediate abdication or annihilation. Alexius III complied, but court officials dragged the old blind king from his dungeon and reinstalled him as emperor, hoping the crusaders would be satisfied with this and would leave. But Boniface, the French leader, insisted that the young pretender share the throne with his father, and the Byzantines perforce acquiesced. On August 1, 1203, in the Church of Holy Wisdom (Hagia Sophia) he was crowned Alexius IV Angelus.

But his subjects did not take kindly to Alexius IV, nor did they appreciate the drunken Frenchmen and swaggering Venetians who camped outside their gates and made regular forays into the city to drink, whore, and assault people. The final atrocity came when crusaders burned down a mosque used by visiting Muslims and the fire spread to destroy a quarter of Constantinople. In February 1204 a general named Murzuphlus, proclaiming himself Alexius V, led a revolt. Alexius IV was deposed and strangled, and his aged father soon died of grief in the dungeon to which he was returned.

The crusaders sailed their ships to the head of the Golden Horn and began assaulting the walls, some of them from towers built on their ships. The Greeks held them off for a time, but on April 12 the walls were breached and the French and Venetians poured into the city. Doge Dandalo, who led them all, notwithstanding his blindness, took up residence in the five-hundred-room Great Palace. What followed was something that Steven Runciman, twentieth-century historian of the Crusades, calls "unparalleled in history." Nicatus, a contemporary Byzantine chronicler who watched it all before making his escape, claimed that the Muslims would have been more merciful.

The Venetians looked after looting; the French and the Flemish took charge of destruction. Thousands were killed as drunken crusaders stormed through the narrow streets, brandishing their swords. Nuns were raped in their convents. Children were lifted by their feet and swung against walls, their heads cracking like coconuts. In Hagia Sophia, the preeminent church of eastern Christendom and still one of the seven architectural wonders of the world, soldiers tore down silk curtains, ripped silver from the sanctuary screen, and swilled down the sacramental wine. A prostitute sat on the patriarch's throne and sang bawdy French songs.

Fabulous bronze statuary dating back to ancient Rome and Greece was melted down for its copper. What wasn't looted or put to the furnace was destroyed by raging fires that melted the city's renowned mosaics and enamels. Crusader Geoffrey of Villehardouin wrote in his chronicle, "More houses were burnt in these fires than are to be found in any of the three largest cities in France."

Relics from the Holy Land, gathered during Byzantium's nine centuries of proximity to it and three centuries of jurisdiction over it, were collected. They would be distributed among the churches of Italy, France, and England.[9] A Cistercian abbot called Martin threatened to kill a Greek priest in the Church of the Pantocrator (or Almighty) unless he yielded its relics to him. Abbot Martin reportedly pranced out of the church cradling in the bulging skirt of his cassock bits and pieces of twenty-eight men and eight women saints, including, it was said, a fragment of the true cross, an entire arm of St. James, and much of an arm belonging to St. John.

"Never in Europe was a work of pillage more systematically and shamelessly carried out," wrote the Victorian historian Edwin Pears in *The Fall of Constantinople: A Story of the Fourth Crusade.* "Never by the army of a Christian state was there a more barbarous sack of a city than that perpetrated by these soldiers of Christ, sworn to chastity, pledged before God not to shed Christian blood, and bearing upon them the emblem of the Prince of Peace."

9. The authenticity of some of the relics purloined by the crusaders at Constantinople would be disputed for centuries, disputes that were not soothed by inevitable duplications. There were, for example, two heads of John the Baptist returned from Constantinople.

Constantinople, known as Istanbul since the city's fall to the Muslims in 1453, is dotted with the minarets of mosques in this nineteenth-century painting by Edmund Berninger. Many of these were once Christian churches. The sack of the city by the Fourth Crusade in 1204 and consequent Latin occupation for the next fifty-seven years mortally weakened it, so it fell victim to the oncoming Ottoman Turks.

The affable and malleable Baldwin of Flanders was assigned the dubious job of emperor, and control of Byzantium's valuable territories was divided between Dandalo and Boniface. Rebellions would roil in the captured lands. Baldwin would be killed a year later. The Byzantine Empire, which for nearly six hundred years had stood as Christendom's great bastion against Islam, would continue to stand for another 250 before ultimately falling to the Muslim Turks, but it had been irrevocably weakened by the Fourth Crusade.

In Rome, Innocent III was at first glad to hear that Rome's control now extended over its eastern sister—until he heard, to his horror, how this was accomplished. The atrocities committed by the crusaders were shocking enough. Worse yet, they turned an already hostile Orthodox clergy into implacable enemies of Rome.[10] By the time the Ottomans finally captured a much-diminished Constantinople in 1453, a sardonic saying had gained currency: "Better the sultan's turban that the cardinal's hat."[11]

Thus, by 1204, more than a century after their hopeful inauguration, the Crusades had become a catalog of disaster. The Turks were gaining strength in Anatolia. The Mongols were menacing both Islam and Christianity from the Asian plains. Islam reigned undisturbed and largely unchallenged in the Levant, while the Christians clung to the coast. There would be three more crusades in the thirteenth century, none of which would significantly change the status of 1204.

What did change radically was the Muslim leniency of Saladin's rule. Slave soldiers called the Mamluks, purchased as children from the Turkish peoples north of the Black Sea and raised as vicious fighters, rebelled and took over the sultanate in Egypt. In the mid-1260s a ruthless red-haired Mamluk sultan named Baibars began an intensive campaign to exterminate the surviving Christians of Outremer. This enormous, dark-skinned Turk, notable for one blue eye and one blind white one, razed Caesarea, Beirut, and Antioch, slaughtering much of their populations and taking inordinate pleasure in beheading and mutilating nobles. He captured and enslaved so many Christian boys and girls that it was said the bottom fell out of the slave market. Baibars was a man, notes historian Runciman, "unimpeded by scruple of honor, gratitude or mercy."

In 1277 Baibars accidentally drank some poisoned koumiss (mare's milk liquor) intended for an enemy and died. His thoroughgoing policy of Christian extermination was taken up by his successors, however, who sacked and razed Tripoli in 1289, leaving Acre as the last major Christian fortress in what had been Christian Outremer. On April 5, 1291, the Mamluk sultan al-Ashraf and a great army of Egyptians and Syrians—Arab chroniclers claim a quarter million—surrounded the forty thousand men, women, and children then inhabiting the city Richard had taken a hundred years earlier. This time the Muslims had big siege engines, including a new kind of mangonel that catapulted clay pots of gunpowder, which exploded on impact. The defenders held out for just over a month, during which time Christian subjects of King Henry of Cyprus were able to evacuate some of the women and children to that island in their supply ships.

In mid-May the Accursed Tower was breached and Muslim soldiers poured in, slaughtering everyone they found on the street. Comely women and girls in the hundreds disappeared into the harems of Mamluk emirs. The price of child slaves dropped to its lowest level ever: one dirham each. By May 18, 1291, al-Ashraf

10. Pope Innocent's legate on the crusade, Peter of Capua, seemingly did nothing to thwart the deed. Indeed, Peter reversed a papal excommunication order on the Venetians after the sack of Zara. He was also accused of absolving the crusaders from their vow to fight in the Holy Land. But whatever Peter's errors, it is dubious whether Dandalo or Boniface would have paid him the least attention anyhow. Papal direction of the crusade was, in other words, a farce.

11. At the close of the second Christian millennium, Pope John Paul II would twice express sorrow for the events of the Fourth Crusade. To Archbishop Christodoulos of Athens he would write, "It is tragic that the assailants, who set out to secure free access for Christians to the Holy Land, turned against their brothers in the faith. The fact that they were Latin Christians fills Catholics with deep regret." And during a visit of Ecumenical Patriarch Bartholomew I of Constantinople to the Vatican in 2004, the pope would rhetorically ask, "How can we not share, at a distance of eight centuries, the pain and disgust?" That April, in a speech on the eight hundredth anniversary of the attack on Constantinople, Patriarch Bartholomew would formally accept the apology with the words, "The spirit of reconciliation is stronger than hatred."

The sack of Constantinople in 1204 by the Fourth Crusade is portrayed here by Gustave Doré. Many see this event as the most disastrous in the entire crusading epoch. The crusaders stole thousands of icons, relics, and works of art from Christendom's most beautiful city, looted the great houses, slew clergy and citizens, enthroned a prostitute on the patriarchal chair in the Hagia Sophia cathedral, and installed their own emperor. The Latins would rule the eastern church and empire for fifty-seven years before the Greeks finally expelled them, but East-West Christian relations had been gravely damaged, and the schism would last to this day.

Acre, now occupied by the last vestiges of Christendom in the Holy Land, vainly attempts to ward off the attacking Mamluk Muslims in 1291. When Acre fell, so many Christians were sold into slavery that the slave market collapsed. Never again would there be a beachhead for crusades against Islam.

12. A combination of domestic concerns and increased worldliness among a western European population grown more prosperous and less fervent had quenched any thirst for further expeditions. Then, too, trade was increasing with Islamic countries, so warfare was being supplanted by more peaceful and even friendly modes of contact. Besides, the beachheads were no longer there. Armenia remained Christian, and Christian enclaves held on in the Muslim countries much as they had before the crusaders arrived. In one last gasp, in 1365 one Peter of Cyprus led an expedition to Egypt that brutally sacked Alexandria, after which his army dispersed with its loot.

controlled the city and set about its systematic destruction; never again would Acre be a beachhead for crusades against Islam. The remaining Christian cities of Tyre, Sidon, and Haifa, along with three Templar castles, were quickly accorded the same treatment, and al-Ashraf burned the orchards and poisoned the soil all along the coast to discourage further Christian incursions. Crusades against the Holy Land, for all intents and purposes, were over.[12]

Viewed seven hundred years later, the Crusades are a self-evident failure. Their aim was the Christian recovery of the Holy Land, and it didn't happen. There was another irony as well. In the first call to arms in 1095, Pope Urban II had spoken of "a barbarous people, estranged from God" that threatened the empire of eastern Christendom, desecrated churches, raped women, and mutilated their victims. The crusaders themselves, in many cases, turned out to be just as bad and sometimes worse. The eastern and western churches were split asunder. Between one and two million people (estimates vary wildly) were killed in the fighting or by accompanying disease.

"Seen in the perspective of history," Runciman concludes, "the whole crusading movement was a vast fiasco." As a military venture they unarguably were a catastrophe. When they began, the Muslims were barely beyond Syria. A century after Acre fell, the Muslim Ottoman Turks would be on the Danube. Others, however, hold that the Crusades, by checking the advance of the Seljuk Turks, at least postponed by a century or two Islam's invasion of eastern Europe. One lesson seemed conclusive: Christians must resist Islam by force of arms when necessary, but by force of arms they will never conquer it. That's a job for missionaries, not soldiers, and they will have to be very dedicated missionaries indeed. ■

The man who made the law rule

Archbishop Langton riled first the king, then the pope, but his Magna Carta remained

In popular lore, modern democracy's founding document is the Magna Carta, and it came about when a bad king was defeated by a good archbishop. Popular lore is probably right, though the barons who signed the Great Charter could not have imagined modern democracy and would have been horrified if they had.

However, John I of England, successor to Richard the Lionheart, by all but the most recent accounts, deserved the reputation the old rhyme bestows: "John, John, bad King John, shamed the throne that he sat on." He combined cowardice, arrogance, and tyranny—a fat, black-bearded man who, it was said, made an enemy a day, although late-twentieth-century scholarship treated him more positively.

Stephen Langton, made archbishop of Canterbury by Pope Innocent III, was a quietly charismatic product of Lincolnshire, as respected by England's barons as John was loathed. John had rejected the pope's choice of Langton for archbishop, and in response Innocent had imposed an interdict on England prohibiting all church services and excommunicating John. After Innocent recruited King Philip II of France to amass an invasion force, however, John relented, agreeing to make England a fief of the papacy, and Langton took office.

Langton, meanwhile, had framed the concept that a king should not be above the law but be subject to it, like his barons. With John fighting in France, the archbishop called a secret meeting of the nobility and wealthy Londoners. He laid before them a charter formulated a hundred years earlier under Henry I but never enacted. The document chiefly concerned the matter of wills and inheritances but also required the king to recognize certain restraints in his treatment of his barons. Then it added this revolutionary clause: "And I enjoin on my barons to act in the same way toward the sons and daughters and wives of their dependents."

For the first time, the common man was to have some rights conferred by law. All those present swore their support for this charter.

John returned from his campaign to a determined nobility, which early in 1215 presented him with their demand for the charter. He stalled, considered a civil war, realized he couldn't win one, and agreed to meet with them. Thus, on June 15, 1215, in a field called Running-Mead (later Runnymede), on the Thames bank near Windsor, the united barons and their loathed liege lord thrashed out the seventy clauses of the Great Charter, and John signed it.

Three clauses recognize principles that would descend into the laws of the constitutional monarchies and republics. One forbids detaining a man without trial (*habeas corpus*). Another foresees trial by jury. The third forbids taxes without the approval of the "common council," which would come to mean Parliament.

Still resisting, John took his case to Pope Innocent, who declared the charter void. With England a papal fief, a rebellion against John was a rebellion against the church, so Innocent suspended Langton from office. A civil war thereupon broke out in England; however, Innocent died in July 1216 and John three months later. The succeeding king and pope approved the Magna Carta, and Langton was restored to his office in 1218. ■

A reluctant King John signs the Great Charter (or Magna Carta) at Runnymede in 1215 in this nineteenth-century engraving by an unknown artist.

A crusade lost and a nation won

Rather than abandon his sick and wounded, Louis IX becomes a Muslim prisoner, then back in France he sets a pattern for monarchy that will endure through the ages

1. Blanche was one of two eligible daughters of King Alfonso VIII of Castile. Although the other daughter, Urraca, was a year older and prettier, the practical Eleanor decided that her name would be unpronounceable by the French, so she chose Blanche instead.

Below is a nineteenth-century statue of Blanche of Castile by Antoine Etex. Chosen by her grandmother Eleanor of Aquitaine to wed the French monarch Louis VIII, Blanche would give birth to Louis IX. After the unexpected early death of her husband, she would act as her son's regent until he came of age, skillfully thwarting several attempts at her son's throne.

It was a strange irony that brought together the girl and that elderly lady in the rugged Spanish mountain town of Burgos, capital of Castile, on a February morning in the year 1200. Granddaughter and grandmother, they were headed for the snowbound Pyrenees and France aboard a sturdy royal coach with a heavily armed escort. The older woman, now aged eighty, was Eleanor of Aquitaine, arguably the most controversial woman of the now-departed twelfth century (see sidebar, pages 72–73). The girl, aged twelve, was Blanche of Castile, possibly the most virtuous woman of the oncoming thirteenth.

Three months later in Normandy Blanche would marry the future King Louis VIII, age thirteen, and with him would give birth over the ensuing twenty-six years to twelve children. Four of them would die in childhood, but the fifth, as King Louis IX, would provide a model for monarchy for the rest of the Middle Ages and a model for political rectitude that would last for all time. He would also greatly advance the creation of modern France, would lose two crusades yet be revered both by his own soldiers and his enemies as the perfect warrior, and would finally pass into history as St. Louis, the only French monarch ever canonized. And as Louis himself and every historian would readily acknowledge, the greatest influence upon him all his life was his mother, Blanche of Castile.

Her grandmother Eleanor had been sent to Spain to pick a future queen for France in the fulfillment of a treaty.[1] Though polar opposites in their views of what constitutes acceptable royal conduct, both she and Blanche were driven lifelong by a fierce determination: Eleanor to serve her sons and herself, Blanche to serve first her husband, then her sons, and always her adopted country, France. The latter would not only influence Louis' character; in his childhood and beyond she would also repeatedly and explicitly save his throne.

When her husband, the eighth Louis, died unexpectedly in 1226 after reigning just over four years, his heir was the eleven-year-old Louis IX. A cabal of French nobles, led by the count of Brittany and backed by King Henry III of England, moved swiftly to liberate themselves from any allegiance to the boy king. The inexperienced Blanche, acting as regent, moved more swiftly still. She hastened to have young Louis crowned, forced any wavering barons to swear allegiance to him, and, with the help of the papal legate in Paris and the friendly Count Theobald of Champagne, organized a royal army. Its utterly unexpected appearance chilled the conspirators. They yielded immediately, Henry withdrew his troops to England, and the rebellion was, for the moment, over.

Twice more in the course of the king's youth, Blanche had to muster troops to suppress similar baronial mutinies led by the count of Brittany and England's Henry. In one the barons tried to kidnap young Louis, but he took refuge in a royal castle. The people of Paris arrived in their

> *The people of Paris turned out to protect the young king. He would never forget that.*

thousands to rescue him, their armed men lining the roads as he returned home. It was a demonstration of loyalty Louis would never forget. To fight the last baronial insurrection of his youth, his mother launched a midwinter surprise attack. (Nobody fought wars in the snow.) She herself accompanied the army, sometimes collecting wood to keep her soldiers warm. This time Henry went back to England and stayed there.

Meanwhile, young Louis dutifully survived the arduous Christian and cultural education his mother provided for him—everything from poetry to geometry to the memorizing of all the monastic offices. He also played an increasing role in the government of the country long before his formal assumption of power. His task, he understood, was to unify France from the English Channel to the Mediterranean and from the Pyrenees to the lands of Germany, and to curb the English control of large parts of France.[2]

His grandfather Philip II had been known as "Augustus" because he had greatly enlarged the French kingdom, gaining control of Normandy, Maine, Anjou, and much of Poitou. Young Louis' father, in his brief reign, had furthered the work. Following the brutal suppression by Simon de Montfort of the Cathar heresy in the south (see sidebar, pages 230–233), Blanche's son brought peace, French culture, and Christianity to embattled Languedoc, securing the submission of the rebellious count of Toulouse, who eventually stood barefoot and penitent in Notre Dame Cathedral. He also accepted the submission of rebellious Brittany to the crown, and he cemented by marriage a claim to the rich region of Provence and its great port city of Marseille.

With Louis' marriage to the beautiful Marguerite of Provence, however, came a predictable problem. There were now two women in his life: Blanche, so accustomed to the exercise of power, and Marguerite, who earnestly sought it. Blanche brooked no competition from her daughter-in-law, whose duties she saw as confined strictly

to the bedchamber. There Marguerite duly conceived for Louis eleven children, Blanche meanwhile strenuously striving to prevent husband and wife from meeting for any other purpose. But Louis loved his wife. Palace lore describes how they would meet secretly to talk, with guards posted to warn of his mother's approach.

Suddenly, at age thirty, Louis' life appeared to have come to an end. So stricken was he, probably with erysipelas (a bacterial skin infection), that he was given up for dead. Indeed, the sheet was being pulled over his face when suddenly he awoke, rapidly recovered, and declared himself obligated by God to launch a cru-

2. The English claim to this region of the future France originated when William of Normandy conquered England in 1066, thereby making the duke of Normandy also king of England. William's granddaughter married the count of Anjou, Touraine, and Maine, tying three more French titles to the English crown, and his great-grandson married the countess of Aquitaine, adding yet another. It took France until the sixteenth century to push the English out of the country.

Louis IX holds high the cross before Paris in this equestrian statue by Hippolyte-Jules Lefebvre at the Basilica of the Sacred Heart in Paris.

Louis as a crusader, seen surrounded by his men in this nineteenth-century Doré lithograph. He was fiercely loyal to them. After the successful capture of the port city of Damietta, the French set off to take Cairo. To secure that victory, however, they needed first to take the lesser city of Mansourah. It was during this siege that Louis was captured because of his steadfast refusal to leave his sick and wounded soldiers.

to see him fulfill his perceived debt to God, once again became regent. Queen Marguerite and the children accompanied the crusaders to Damietta, the ancient port in the estuary of the Nile.

Damietta was gradually being supplanted by Alexandria but was still so vital to the economy of the Islamic heartland that at one point the Muslims had offered to surrender Jerusalem in exchange for it. On June 4, 1249, one quarter of Louis' force drew up among the perilous sandbars at the Nile's mouth, the other three quarters having been driven off course by storms. Though cautioned against it, Louis personally led his army onto the beaches, where in a fierce battle a foothold was won. The city, scarcely defended, fell the next day. Its great mosque became a Christian cathedral, and Damietta became the effective capital of Outremer.

Now a decision must be made. Should the invaders strike for Babylon, later named Cairo? Or should they seize the great port of Alexandria and seal off Egypt from the Mediterranean coast? They decided upon Cairo, which meant first taking another key city, Mansourah. Here an ill-timed attack by part of the French army resulted in a major defeat, although its worst consequences were overcome by Louis himself, who prevented the Muslims from further exploiting their victory. But for the next six weeks, while the crusader army laid siege to Mansourah, it was critically enfeebled by the diseases of a torrid summer.

Meanwhile, the Muslims were able to besiege the besiegers by setting up a blockade, cutting off their food supplies. King Louis' best strategy now would have been to retreat to Damietta, but this would mean abandoning his sick men—which he would not do. Thus, defeat was inevitable, and the king himself made prisoner. His captors alternately waved knives in his face and offered him life and luxury if he would abjure the Christian faith. Steadfastly he refused, causing the Muslims to admire him so much that some

sade. Much of France took up the cause with him, while England not only agreed to refrain from attacking her habitual enemy but also contributed troops. The story of this, the Seventh Crusade, is told more intimately than almost any other through the diary kept by John of Joinville, who became Louis' closest friend and sometimes severest critic.

With characteristic prudence Louis took more than three years to make preparations for the conquest first of Egypt, breadbasket of much of the Mediterranean world, then of Jerusalem. Special taxes were levied. Genoa and Marseille were contracted to supply transport. Queen Mother Blanche, torn between anxiety for her son and a desire said they wished he were their sultan. The ransom set for the invalid soldiers was one year's revenues of the French crown; King Louis' ransom was the surrender of Damietta. Both were paid and the king was freed, but the Muslims nevertheless slaughtered some thousands of sick French and English soldiers.

Moving his headquarters to Acre, Louis stayed in Outremer two more years, diligently strengthening the defenses of the few Christian cities remaining along the coast. But then the death of his mother made necessary his return. He realized that the crusade had been a complete failure, but more chilling still was a thought that occurred to many a Christian mind: if God denied victory to a man as plainly virtuous as Louis IX, might this imply that the whole concept of the crusades was ill conceived from the start?

Whatever the skepticism of others, however, failure had the reverse effect on Louis. Men should thank God for tribulations, he said, because these can lead to repentance. His personal devotion remained unwavering. He loved sermons, fasted twice weekly, and liked listening to minstrels but preferred hymns. He enjoyed good conversation, read avidly, and, following the example of a sultan he admired, organized a public library in Paris. Joinville once asked him if he would rather be a leper than commit a mortal sin. Hideous though it is, the king replied, leprosy is preferable because it leaves us when we die. Sin is leprosy of the soul, and it may not.

Back in France he was notably frugal in clothing, food, and drink, and wore a hair shirt under his outer garments as a constant reminder that men were still suffering in Outremer. On three projects, however, he spent lavishly. One was a ring of thorns—the same, the authorities assured him, that Jesus wore on Calvary. (First mentioned in the fifth century, the "crown of thorns" was preserved at Jerusalem until Saladin's time, then moved to Constantinople and pawned by the impoverished Latin emperor. It is now

kept at Notre Dame in Paris.)

The other two were building projects. The new royal chapel, Sainte-Chapelle (Holy Chapel), is described by his biographer Margaret Wade Labarge (*Saint Louis: The Life of Louis IX of France*) as "the greatest architectural achievement of his reign." The second was the Cistercian Abbey of Royaumont, some of which still stands at Val-d'Oise, twenty miles north of Paris.

Nevertheless, writes historian Labarge, faithful Christian though Louis undoubtedly was, "he was very far from being a clerical puppet." He repeatedly collided with the papacy when he saw bishops seeking to exercise purely temporal power or ignoring their obligation to obey the temporal courts in temporal matters. He described the members of the Roman curia as "treacherous people," and his assertion of royal authority left old Pope Gregory IX describing himself as "astounded."

It was in his very concept of monarchy, however, that his Christian convictions proved most telling. Joinville depicts him sitting beneath a great oak tree at Vincennes, now an eastern suburb of Paris,

Right: *The reliquary of the crown of thorns, bought from the Latin emperor in Constantinople at great expense by Louis IX. It was considered one of Christianity's greatest relics and is kept at Notre Dame Cathedral in Paris.*
Left: *Garments worn by Louis IX. This unadorned white tunic would have been worn over his hair shirt. Hair shirts were a common form of penance during the Middle Ages, especially in western Europe. They were distinctly and intentionally uncomfortable, causing constant itching, and would usually become a breeding ground for lice.*

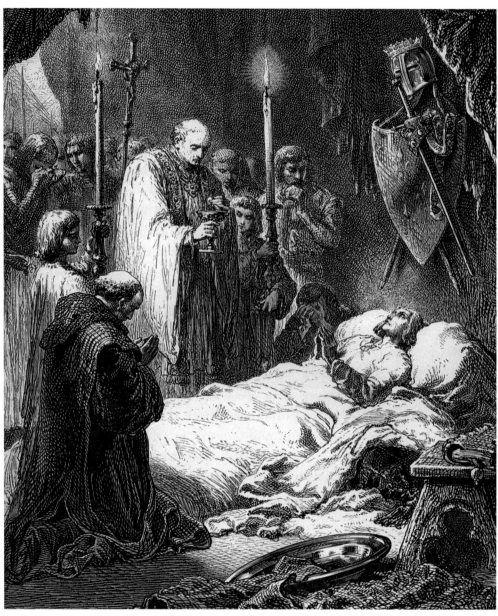

discussing justice with his court and permitting his humblest subject access to the king himself for redress of a personal wrong. Legend though this may be, its import is altogether factual. No king before or after Louis was more acutely aware that, whatever else it does, government must act fairly. Royal officers were strictly forbidden to receive "gifts" (meaning bribes) or levy fines except in open court or sell government offices or levy unauthorized taxes— all radical reforms at the time.

When a priest was charged with killing three government officers who had been robbing the people, the king pardoned the priest and took him into the royal service. When a feudal baron was found robbing travelers and pilgrims, he had the man's

castle destroyed. He strove hard for peace between individuals or feuding barons, and became an international arbiter between nations because he was so universally trusted. A determined opponent of usury (charging interest on loans), he cracked down on the Jews for practicing it, then set up programs to aid their wives and children left bereft as a result.

His compassion seemed boundless. He set up almshouses for the poor and a home for the blind in Paris. He visited leper colonies, frequently washing the feet of the lepers as he frequently washed the feet of the poor. When Joinville protested that a king should not do such things, he replied that a king already had (meaning, of course, Jesus at the Last Supper). As he returned from the Crusades, a monk is said to have told him that no kingdom ever fell except through the failure of its monarch. Louis believed him and acted accordingly.

But his last years are a sorrowful tale of rejection, tribulation, failure, and tragedy, which began in 1260 when the Muslim victory over the Mongols at Ain Jalut ultimately doomed Acre, the last Christian foothold in the Holy Land. As Acre's frantic appeals for help echoed through Europe, Louis, at age forty-seven, resolved on a second crusade. Although he was so weak physically that he sometimes had to be carried from place to place, no one could dissuade him—not his closest advisers, his wife, his unenthusiastic barons, or even the devoted Joinville.

At a glacial pace the crusade inched its way across France, slowed by the feeble king and disrupted by brawls between French troops from north and south in which some hundred men were killed. The goal this time was the capture of Tunis as a preliminary to an attack on Egypt, a strategy that most historians agree was engineered by Louis' brother Charles of Anjou. Accumulated delays kept the army from Tunis until July, the beginning of the torrid season, and dysentery soon spread among them. Its victims included several of France's nobles, among them King Louis' son John Tristan. Born in the failing days of his father's first crusade, the young prince died twenty years later in the failing days of his last. (His name, probably drawn from the hero of a popular song, means "John the Sorrowful." It proved tragically prophetic.)

At length the king himself neared death. As was customary at the time, he had had himself laid upon a bed of ashes with his arms outstretched as on a cross. His final prayer was an appeal for his fellow crusaders: "Gracious, good God, have mercy on this people who stay here, and lead them to their country, that they do not fall into the hands of their enemies and are not constrained to deny thy holy name." His last words were, "Jerusalem, Jerusalem."

Thus died King Louis IX of France on August 26, 1270, at the age of fifty-six. He could never have guessed that centuries later, at the confluence of two mighty rivers an ocean and half a continent away, his name—St. Louis—would be commemorated by a city twenty times bigger than the Paris he knew (and also, in fact, by twenty-one other cities, nearly all in the Americas).

Even Steven Runciman, definitive modern historian of the Crusades and certainly no admirer of them, sheds his skepticism when he comes to Louis IX. "In an age when virtue was so much admired and so seldom achieved," he writes, "few human beings have ever been so consciously and sincerely virtuous. As king, he felt that he was responsible before God for the welfare of his people; and no prelate, not even the pope himself, was allowed to come between him and his duty."

What might have pleased St. Louis more, however, was a tribute from a most improbable source, who would describe him as "a prince destined to reform Europe, had it been capable of being reformed, to render France triumphant and civilized, and to be in every respect a model for mankind . . . in council prudent and firm, in battle intrepid but not rash, and compassionate as if he had always himself been unhappy. In a word, it is not in the power of man to carry virtue to a greater height."

This was the assessment of Voltaire, critic supreme of the French monarchy, the Middle Ages, and the entire Christian religion. Not even his supreme cynicism could withstand the light that shone from this one remarkable Christian soul. ■

Sculpted by James Pradier in the nineteenth century, this statue of St. Louis stands in Aigues-Mortes, near the Mediterranean coast in southeast France. It was here that Louis set up the first French port on the Mediterranean and set forth on the Seventh and Eighth Crusades.

In this undated illustration from the Bettman Archive, Emperor Frederick II parades on horseback through Vienna in January of 1237. He now stood at the pinnacle of his power, having seen his son Conrad made "king of the Romans" (which meant king of Germany). He would now set about the suppression of the Lombard League.

CHAPTER 6

How the wonder boy of the world became a fiery foe of the faith

Frederick II dazzled Europe in acquiring Jerusalem by negotiation, but his harem, his zoo, his arrogance, and a near 100-year-old pope triggered his downfall

O n September 27 of the year 1197 the emperor Henry VI, eldest surviving son of the great emperor Frederick Barbarossa and the most powerful ruler in Europe, did the one thing no one expected of him. He caught malaria and died. He was only thirty-two, and his early death set off a chain of events that would disrupt the whole continent for the next century and would place on center stage a figure often portrayed as the most extraordinary in medieval history. Whether this man was even minimally Christian historians have been debating ever since. That he was no friend of the thirteenth-century Christian church is beyond all argument.

The dead emperor was the third of eight children born of the long marital love affair between Frederick Barbarossa and Beatrix of Burgundy (their story is told in chapter 3). Their first two children, Henry's older sister and brother, died young, so Henry became the heir. In probably the greatest coup of Barbarossa's career, he saw this son of his, already emperor-designate over Germany and northern Italy, married to Constance of Sicily. Thus, when Constance inherited the Sicilian throne, Henry was able to unite nearly all Italy and much of western Europe under the imperial crown.

While Henry's early death cut short his own role in that vast empire, it did not end the probability that his family, the mighty Hohenstaufens of Germany, would continue to rule his far-flung domain. Three years earlier Constance had given birth to a son whom she and Henry had named Frederick in honor of his grandfather.[1]

1. Since Constance of Sicily was about forty when Frederick was born, she feared that when her child grew up he could be called an imposter because his mother had been too old to have given birth, an altogether sensible concern in those times. Accordingly, she arranged to have witnesses at the birth—a group of local ladies by one account, a whole assembly of barons and other dignitaries by a less reliable one. In yet another, she is recorded as having shown her milk-laden breasts to local officialdom, so that there could be no argument; she was, indeed, a mother.

Constance of Sicily gives birth to the future Frederick II in this medieval painting. Constance feared that since she was forty, her child's foes could one day claim her too old to have given birth and her son therefore an imposter. So she arranged the birth as a public event. When Frederick's father died, Constance named the pope as her son's guardian. That pope was Innocent III, whose painting (below) is preserved in the cloister at Sacro Speco (Holy Grotto), the cave in which St. Benedict lived as a hermit. The painting dates from the early thirteenth century.

But now the child heir was fatherless and defenseless, vulnerable to the sort of cruel fate—blinding or poisoning, among the possibilities—so likely to befall a young ruler in such circumstances. Who could foresee that this boy would one day become the emperor Frederick II, known as *Stupor Mundi*—the "Wonder of the World"?

Aware of the peril to her son, Constance wasted no time in seeking a protector who would not deprive little Frederick of his heritage. This guardian must not be German, she decided; for too long she had watched her husband's German comrades despoil her beloved land. So she turned for help instead to the papacy, first to Pope Celestine IV and then, when he died soon afterward, to Pope Innocent III, designating Frederick in her will as a ward of the pope.

Empress Constance's immediate goals were to consolidate her son's position as heir to the Sicilian throne and to neutralize the growing ambitions of Markwald of Anweiler, a former aide to her husband whose army was moving from a base in northeast Italy into the central Italian possessions of the Sicilian crown. She professed indifference to her son's right to rule the German states and northern Italy, meaning the whole northern segment of her husband's empire. It was Sicily that mattered to her.

Her distaste for Frederick's German heritage was of profound significance to Innocent. What the papacy of the twelfth and thirteenth centuries feared most was encirclement by an imperial ruler who controlled both Sicily to the south (whose kingdom included much of southern Italy) and also imperial Germany to the north (whose empire included much of northern Italy). Wedged between them were the papal states, ostensibly but rarely more than loosely controlled by the pope. For more than a century reformist popes had struggled to shore up the sphere of papal independence. How could a pope fulfill his divinely ordained role as guardian of the moral law, effectively guiding kings and emperors, from a position of temporal helplessness? It was deemed crucial that, at the very least, the papal states preserve their autonomy. "The papacy could not function successfully as a homeless, wandering power at the mercy of some secular ruler," writes Innocent's biographer Jane Sayers. "It needed freedom from secular control and power enough to enforce its message."

Given, therefore, the prospect that Markwald might well deprive Frederick of much, if not eventually all, of his inheritance, Innocent hastened to rally allies who might stop the ambitious German. Yet no sooner had the pope's relationship with Constance begun to bear fruit than fate once again stacked the odds against

Constance knew that now her child was fatherless and defenseless, vulnerable to the sort of cruel fate—blinding or poisoning— so likely to befall a young ruler in such circumstances.

little Frederick. Constance fell ill and died, depriving the boy of his most devoted guardian. It was November 1198, and he was not quite four.

By now ensconced at Palermo, Frederick was completely at the mercy of a council of men with no loyalty to him beyond a pledge to the pope, and he well may have discerned, child though he was, that events were moving with chaotic speed. Sicily would be fought over during the next several years by a welter of armed adventurers, with the Germans under Markwald eventually seizing the upper hand. The young monarch's capture was only a matter of time and would become a signature event in his life, revealing both the brazen audacity and the haughty awareness of his own majesty that he would display so often as an adult. Describing his capture at age seven, an admirer wrote to the pope that Frederick "threw himself upon those who were about to seize him, trying with all his force to ward off the arm of him who dared to lay his hand upon the sacred body of the Lord's anointed."

The Lord's anointed seemed, by all odds, doomed, however: Markwald could never permit the kingdom's rightful heir to survive. But Markwald had problems of his own. Wracked with pain from a kidney stone, he consented to surgery, and it killed him. Frederick was transferred for a time to the custody of another German functionary, one less ruthless than Markwald, and eventually to a representative of the pope.

Though the years until he reached his majority at fourteen are among the least documented of his life, there is little doubt he was trained by the finest tutors, including a cleric who would become Innocent's successor. But Frederick was far from a sedentary bookworm. He had the run of Palermo's exotic streets, and he made the most of it, soaking up the cultures of Norman Sicilians, Germans,

Greeks, Jews, and Arab Muslims. Here is where his apprenticeship in languages took place. He would master six, some sources say. Here, too, may have begun his drift toward religious skepticism or, in any event, his lifelong respect for the Islamic faith. He also spent time at summer palaces opening on vast royal parks that teemed with wildlife, where he roamed at will, nurturing a love for nature and for the hunt that would remain lifelong passions. Thus he grew up, heir apparent to his father's immense empire but with a firm hold on none of it.

The pope was his sole ally, and even the pope's support was of necessity conditional. He could scarcely watch papal authority wither under the bullying of an omnipotent temporal tyrant. As Frederick soon perceived, the pope must strongly support his claim to his mother's heritage in the south while somehow thwarting him from asserting his claim to his father's heritage in the north. This would require of Innocent a deft exercise of papal power. Still, power and academic competence came naturally to Innocent; he had grown up surrounded by them. Born Lothar dei Conti of Segni in a family of well-connected Italian aristocrats, Innocent had studied with some of the most cultivated minds of his day in the schools of Paris. At one point he even crossed the channel to visit the shrine of St. Thomas Becket, the martyr who had defied the English crown in defense of church prerogatives (see sidebar, pages 96–97). Becket was an international symbol of clerical courage, and Innocent had clearly admired him.

Even as a cardinal Innocent had begun to spell out his conception of the unique status of the pope as St. Peter's successor. When he was elected to the highest ecclesiastical office in 1198, at about age thirty-seven, he left no doubt about his views. "Who am I myself or what was the house of my father that I am permitted to sit above kings, to possess the throne of glory?" he exclaimed in his consecration sermon. "For it is to me that the words of the prophet apply: 'I have placed you above people and kingdoms that you may uproot and destroy as well as build and plant.' . . . See therefore what kind of servant he is who commands the whole family. . . . He is the mediator between God and man, less than God but greater than man."

Palermo as seen from Monte Pellegrino. In Frederick's time it was what a later generation would call a multicultural city, with a vibrant mix of Italian, Greek, Arab, and other Mediterranean peoples. To Frederick, it was his beloved hometown where he spent his formative years learning to speak several languages and gaining a familiarity with the Muslim faith, a knowledge he would later put to effective use.

Less than God but greater than man. For centuries historians have chewed over this and similarly sweeping pontifical declarations by Innocent, with some scholars describing his ambition for papal power as infinite. Yet this is most certainly false. Innocent did not doubt that temporal power was inferior to religious power, as the moon relied on the sun for light, or that he had the right to rebuke and punish kings for moral transgressions or for interference in the church's sphere of influence. But he was also a shrewd and practical person with little desire, for the most part, to meddle in strictly temporal affairs. Moreover, he still believed in the old doctrine of the "two swords," meaning that although the spiritual power was superior to the temporal, the spiritual authority must not seek temporal control over temporal kingdoms. Such was the man to whom Frederick would be required, again and again, to turn for assistance.

Needless to say, the German aristocracy had not been waiting quietly for Frederick to come of age. No sooner had Henry VI died than a destructive civil war erupted in Germany, with Henry's brother Philip of Hohenstaufen at first fighting on behalf of his young nephew's claim to the German imperial throne against the forces of Otto of Brunswick, nominee of the rival Welf family for emperor. But Philip's supporters were not about to risk their lives for a boy in Sicily they had never seen, and they elected Philip emperor instead. This presented Innocent III with three options. He could uphold the claim of Frederick, a boy with apparently no prospect of asserting authority in the empire's northern lands (fortunately, of course, from the papal point of view). Alternatively, he could throw in his lot with Philip, who seemed to command the support of a majority of German princes, though his relations with the papacy were abysmal. Or, third, he could attempt to boost Otto of Brunswick, who was on much better terms with the church. In 1201 Innocent made his decision. He proclaimed Otto emperor-elect.

Otto certainly seemed like a reasonable choice. Even with the pope on his side, however, he took years to consolidate his support in Germany and would have failed altogether had not his rival Philip been murdered in 1209 by a Bavarian count. And how could a self-respecting Welf emperor like Otto rest comfortably in Germany with a Hohenstaufen upstart like young Frederick on the loose in Palermo? Otto therefore turned his back on Germany and struck south at Frederick, violating an oath Innocent had required him to make. The pope's prompt response was to excommunicate his man and later to depose him.

This sixteenth-century bust of a youthful Frederick II shows him resolute but also pensive. At that age he would have had a great deal to be pensive about. The pope, his protector, fearful of Hohenstaufen control of both the empire to the north of Rome and Norman Sicily to the south, had supported the bid of a member of the rival Welf family to become emperor in his stead. To acquire the imperial office, Frederick would later have to reconquer much of the empire left to him by his father.

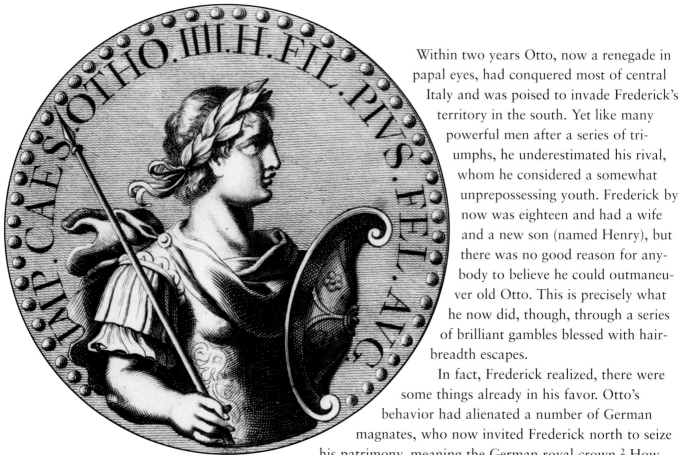

Otto of Brunswick, seen above in a seventeenth-century French engraving, was able to secure the initial support of the pope in his ambition to become emperor. But when he broke an oath and invaded Frederick's lands in Norman Sicily, he, too, threatened to "surround" Rome, north and south, with imperial control, so the pope excommunicated him. Otto would die deposed and dethroned and smitten with guilt.

Within two years Otto, now a renegade in papal eyes, had conquered most of central Italy and was poised to invade Frederick's territory in the south. Yet like many powerful men after a series of triumphs, he underestimated his rival, whom he considered a somewhat unprepossessing youth. Frederick by now was eighteen and had a wife and a new son (named Henry), but there was no good reason for anybody to believe he could outmaneuver old Otto. This is precisely what he now did, though, through a series of brilliant gambles blessed with hairbreadth escapes.

In fact, Frederick realized, there were some things already in his favor. Otto's behavior had alienated a number of German magnates, who now invited Frederick north to seize his patrimony, meaning the German royal crown.[2] How could he manage to do this with such limited forces as he commanded bottled up in Sicily? Against the emphatic pleadings of his wife and nobles, he slipped out of Palermo bound for Rome, his first goal being to secure the blessings and bullion of the pope.

Innocent's options, as Frederick well knew, were narrowed down to two. Would he support Otto, the man who had already betrayed him once? Or would he support Frederick, the man he had sustained through a perilous childhood and had consistently supported as king of Sicily—even if this did mean uniting north and south under a single ruler? The choice was obvious. Arriving in Rome, Frederick happily declared the papacy his "protector and benefactor," gave every evidence of a lifetime allegiance to it, easily won the pope's blessing and bullion, and headed for Germany. Meanwhile, Otto left his army in Italy and also hastened northward to head him off.

It was now that Frederick would first establish his reputation for theatrics and spectacle. Lombard cities such as Milan, allied to Otto and lying like wolves along his path, would be richly rewarded if they caught him. Even if Frederick somehow got past them, Otto could remain confident that the narrow Alpine passes beyond could easily be rendered impenetrable. But some towns were friendly, and Frederick, driven by that wellspring of energy that would fuel his whole life, slipped from one to another like a fox. On the banks of the Lambro River after a lengthy night's trek, however, all seemed lost. He and his small escort rode straight into a Milanese trap. His guards were slaughtered. Frederick, it seemed, was finally caught. But suddenly he leaped, like a lithe gazelle, onto a riderless horse, rode bareback into the Lambro, and escaped on the other side.

He then zigzagged through the Alps, taking trails barely marked, bypassing Otto's vigilant posts on the main road, and ultimately showing up with a recruited

2. By custom, the emperor of Germany first won election as "king" by the German nobility. His official title was King of the Romans, and his coronation took place on Charlemagne's throne at ancient Aachen. At a later point he would be crowned emperor by the pope, usually at Rome.

escort of three hundred before the gates of neutral Constance, where the Rhine broadens into a lake of the same name. Inside the city walls the chefs of Otto's advance party had prepared a big dinner for the emperor, expected shortly. Here Innocent's help again proved decisive. When the local bishop refused to open the gates, a papal nuncio accompanying Frederick read out the pope's sentence of excommunication against Otto. The wavering bishop was won over, the gates were flung open, and Frederick's party moved in and (presumably) ate the dinner. Otto's fury when he arrived an hour or so later can be imagined.

From that moment Frederick's fortunes soared. With a major assist from Philip Augustus of France, whose military victory over Otto at Bouvines in 1214 cost the excommunicate emperor any remaining credibility, Frederick marched through Germany from one triumph to another on his way to the historic seat of German kings, the city of Aachen. There, on July 15, 1215, he took his place on the throne of Charlemagne and was crowned "king of the Romans" by the archbishop of Mainz. In the same year, Otto was deposed as emperor.[3]

At his coronation Frederick did something that has baffled historians to this day. Taking the cross, he vowed to lead a crusade. Was this the spontaneous gesture of a still-impulsive youth, as some have maintained? Not likely. The coordinated preaching throughout the following day suggests a planned event. Or was Frederick bent on ingratiating himself with Innocent III? There was no need for that. He had already conceded just about everything the pope wanted.

So what did propel this indifferent son of the church, a man fluent in Arabic and no ideological enemy of Islam, known for lavishing money on just about anything but churches, to take up the crusader cross? Surely it was his sense of high destiny. What better way to signal his elevation as the unrivaled leader of Christendom, heir to Charlemagne and Frederick Barbarossa, than an expedition to the Holy Land? But the oath he took soon became a thorny burden. As pope after pope demanded he fulfill it, he balked.

A year and a day after the crowning of Frederick at Aachen, on July 16, 1216, Pope Innocent III died of a fever at Perugia, Italy. He departed this life with what he doubtless saw as his greatest endeavor magnificently completed. The Fourth Lateran Council of 1215 had attracted the largest gathering of bishops of any assemblage in the Middle Ages and had addressed a host of issues dear to Innocent's heart, among them the vanishing Christian presence in the Holy Land, the rapid growth of heretical teaching, and the corruption and indolence of many clergy.

An engraving of Frederick II from a medallion preserved in the church of Porto Santo in Andria, Italy. After defeating the ill-starred Otto (opposite page), Frederick rode triumphant into Aachen for his coronation as "king of the Romans," a title given to those who are expected to be crowned emperor by the pope. Remarkably, and seemingly without reason, Frederick also declared that he would embark upon a crusade, an undertaking he would later resist.

3. Excommunicated as a Christian, deposed as an emperor, and rejected by most of the German nobility, Otto died in Harzburg Castle, in Brunswick, on May 19, 1218. According to Frederick's biographer Ernst Kantorowicz, Otto was received back into the church the day before by a Cistercian monk and then submitted himself to the monks, asking to be thrown to the floor and beaten as an act of penitence. Otto died of the beating, reciting "Lord have mercy," adds Frederick's biographer Georgina Masson, who calls Otto's death an instance of "medieval barbarity." Thus perished the only Welf to become emperor.

Above: *two surviving accoutrements of Frederick's reign. Above, the crown worn by Roger II, king of Sicily, Frederick's grandfather. Frederick is believed to have worn the crown at his own coronation as king of Sicily. It has twelve precious stones and four icons. It is preserved at the Church of St. Nicola in Bari, Italy. Below: The throne of Charlemagne at Aachen cathedral in Germany, where Frederick was crowned. The same throne was used at the coronation of twenty designated emperors between 936 and 1531.*

Historians would later castigate Innocent III for his role in two major Christian calamities, the Fourth Crusade (see chapter 5) and the brutal suppression of the Cathar heresy (see sidebar, pages 230–233). His later defenders, while conceding his imprudence in trusting untrustworthy people, vehemently deny that he had any role in the Fourth Crusade's attack on Christian Constantinople and insist that the penalties imposed by the Inquisition on the Cathars and the inquisitional system that tried them were fair and reasonable. It is also noteworthy, they say, that Innocent approved the founding of the Dominican and the Franciscan orders, both widely deplored at the time but resolutely supported by Innocent.[4]

Perhaps, as things would turn out, Innocent's worst miscall was his failure to perceive the true nature of the man he had raised to European ascendancy, the redoubtable Frederick. Innocent's successor, Censio Savelli, who became Pope Honorius III, was the first to discover what Frederick's success portended. He may have suspected it already, having been Frederick's papally appointed tutor. Right from the start the new pope began calling the emperor's attention to his promised crusade, typically causing Frederick to renew the promise and then continue to ignore it. Other things interested him more.

Germany was not one of them, however, although he felt obliged to remain there for a few years. He discovered that generations of civil war had allowed the aristocracy to wrest too much power from the crown for his taste. He would put in place his own ideas of governance in his beloved kingdom of Sicily, to which he decamped in 1220, leaving behind his son Henry to run Germany.

He established his seat of government at Capua, twenty-five miles north of Naples. Like most medieval monarchs, however, he spent much of his time on the road, moving from fortress to fortress with his court and the elaborate menagerie of birds and animals that became his trademark eccentricity. Foremost in his mind were two goals: the suppression of all resistance to his authority and the creation of a central-ized imperial state such as Europe had not seen in centuries.

To Frederick it was intolerable that tens of thousands of Muslims on the island of Sicily enjoyed de facto inde-pendence. His answer: a pitiless policy of ethnic cleansing as he battered down their strongholds. His sympathy with Islam, that is, did not extend to allow-ing Muslims or anyone else "indepen-dence." But soon another thought occurred to him. Why not put their tal-ents to use on his own behalf? In 1223

he began a mass deportation of Muslims, some fifteen thousand or more, to the town of Lucera on the Apulian plain in southern Italy. Isolated there and com-pletely dependent on the emperor's favor, these Islamic serfs were to provide some of his most trusted light troops and bodyguards during the rest of his reign.[5]

The emperor was just as harsh in his other administrative measures. For exam-ple, he seized almost every castle of strategic importance. He established extensive imperial trading monopolies. He even founded a university at Naples to provide him with a lay-educated bureaucracy untainted with Christian assumptions and used them to replace local officials.

But what about his pledge to lead a crusade? The pope, naturally, wanted to know. Not yet, Frederick replied again and again. And finally, give him two more years, he said at last; all would be ready in 1225. This time Honorius was sure Frederick possessed the needed spur. The emperor's first wife had died in 1222, and he had subsequently betrothed himself to the young Yolande of Brienne, hereditary queen of Jerusalem. What better incentive for a crusade than to claim another kingdom as his own?

As the promised year approached, however, it became apparent that Frederick was no closer to departure, and another two-year deadline was fixed. This time, though, the agreement between pope and emperor included a cudgel: if Frederick dallied, he was to be excommunicated. But when 1227 arrived, it was not pro-crastination that thwarted the promised Crusade; it was disease. As throngs of knights and retainers gathered midsummer in the scorched camps outside the port of Brindisi, a deadly epidemic broke out. Hundreds died, one of them the hus-band of the saintly Elizabeth, landgravine of Thuringia (see sidebar, page 123); many others, including the emperor, hastily boarded ships and left. But by this time he, too, was sick. He returned to his kingdom—just in time to receive word that Honorius was dead.

4. The bishop-historian-crusader Jacques of Vitry saw Innocent's body the day after his death. Noting that it had been left alone, lying in the cathedral of Perugia awaiting burial the following day, Jacques writes, "That was the day when I really understood the nothingness of earthly grandeur. Incredibly, the pre-ceding night, thieves had entered and stripped the pope of everything he had on. With my eyes I saw his half-naked body lying in the middle of the church, already smelling." The members of the curia, he observes, "were so taken up by tem-poral affairs and lawsuits and so preoccupied with everything that had to do with kings and states that one can scarcely touch upon ques-tions pertaining to religion. All this caused me much grief." The Franciscan Thomas of Eccleston adds, "No one dies as solitary and forsaken as a pope."

5. In the following century the Muslim Ottoman Turks would insti-tute the Janissaries, an elite guard that for centuries would spearhead Ottoman victories over the Christian West. This guard was composed entirely of Christian boys taken from their parents as children and raised to be devout Muslims, ideologically dedicated to the tri-umph of Islam. Frederick did not bother with conversion. His special soldiers, drawn from a Muslim community, remained devoutly Muslim while brutally imposing Frederick's rule on recalcitrant cities in Christian Italy.

Pope Honorius III, whose tireless nagging and threatening would finally persuade Frederick to embark on the crusade he had sworn to make. Smitten with disease, however, the expedition was aborted, and Frederick returned home so ill he verged on death, only to discover that Pope Honorius himself was already dead. The illustration is from Science and Literature in the Middle Ages and the Renaissance. *Both the book, published in 1878, and the illustration are ascribed to the author, Paul Lacroix.*

Frederick had regarded the old pope as a man in his dotage and may now have expected his successor to be considerably younger. But Ugolino of Conti was not younger. He was five years older than Honorius when, at the age of eighty-four, he became Pope Gregory IX. He was (and is) regarded by fervent admirers of Frederick as a "hateful" old man who began his pontificate by excommunicating the emperor as an oath breaker and malingerer, and continued to harangue, deplore, and thwart him for the ensuing fourteen years.

Gregory IX simply would not believe that Frederick's illness was real, and, unlike Honorius, he was not a man to bite his tongue. He also possessed the iron will of Innocent III; indeed, he was Innocent's nephew and was fiercely loyal to his uncle's basic policies. So Gregory soon established himself as an octogenarian activist. He canonized Francis of Assisi in 1228, having first saved the Franciscan order from almost certain disintegration after Francis's death (see chapter 10). He ramped up the papal campaign against heresy. He ordered a compilation of canon law that would remain in use for centuries. To quail before anyone playing games with a crusader oath was not in his character.

What galled him most, however, were Frederick's larger pretensions. As Frederick strengthened his hold over the southern half of his empire, gathering every rein in his imperial fist, Gregory saw that Rome, too, would soon wind up in the imperial harness. He resolved that when the inevitable contract was drawn between Frederick and the papacy, his own indelible stamp must appear on the terms.

Frederick seems to have been baffled at first by the pope's decision to excommunicate him. He was in uncharted waters here, but that is where he excelled. It occurred to him that no excommunicate had ever led a crusade. In theory, at least, no excommunicate could, for if he tried, no knight or soldier could obey his commands. Be that as it might, Frederick resolved, he would call Gregory's bluff and see what the pope wanted more: a liberated Jerusalem or a humiliated Holy Roman Emperor.

The army that shipped to the Holy Land in 1228 and is recorded historically as the Sixth Crusade consisted of Muslim bowmen, fifteen hundred knights, and about ten thousand infantry—a relatively paltry force for such an undertaking. They joined a nearly equal number of crusaders waiting at Acre, but even the two forces together were no juggernaut. Frederick had an ace up his sleeve, however. For a leader of Christendom, he boasted a remarkably close relationship with a powerful Muslim ruler, al-Kamil, the sultan of Egypt, the same sultan who had befriended Francis of Assisi ten years before (see chapter 10). They had exchanged embassies, lavished gifts upon each other, and discussed the possibility of a deal before Frederick had even left Italy. What al-Kamil had to offer was Jerusalem itself. What Frederick could supply in return was aid in al-Kamil's struggle with the sultan of Damascus.

By the time Frederick disembarked in the Holy Land, however, the political landscape had shifted. The sultan of Damascus had died, and al-Kamil no longer wished to treat with Frederick. No matter. Frederick would not be put off. His representatives cajoled, flattered, reasoned, and threatened. At one point he menacingly marched his army south with orders issued not in his own name but in the name of God and Christendom so that the Templars and Hospitallers would obey them without qualm. And to the enduring shock of Europe, al-Kamil came around. He agreed to turn over the three original Christian holy cities—Nazareth, Bethlehem, and Jerusalem (minus the Temple Mount)—to the crusaders' control, along with a corridor to the coast.

This scene of the aging Pope Gregory IX excommunicating for the second time Emperor Frederick II hangs in the Vatican Palace. It is polemical, not historical, representing Frederick shirtless and prostrate before the old pope and pointing out something in the Scriptures. The pope's feet are planted on the emperor's torso while other admiring clerics look on. The painting is by the sixteenth-century artist Giorgio Vasari. No such scene ever occurred, of course, though in one sense it reflects reality. Old Gregory, just under one hundred years of age, by an extraordinary appeal to the Roman people, thwarted Frederick's occupation of Rome and began the chain of events that led to the emperor's downfall.

Gifts were often exchanged between medieval monarchs to bolster relationships and hold together alliances. In the run-up to Frederick II's negotiation for the throne of Jerusalem, he exchanged gifts with Sultan al-Kamil. The two men are seen in this medieval painting, with Frederick at left and al-Kamil on the right. These gift exchanges could have included such items as this decorative horn, created in the eleventh century in Sicily, now preserved in Berlin.

Critics of Frederick would never let him forget that the Treaty of Jaffa, which he signed with al-Kamil, left Jerusalem defenseless, that it included no enforceable guarantees, that it was based on the word of a Muslim ruler who might repudiate it on a whim. Even so, it was a colossal achievement, fully justifying Frederick's state entry into Jerusalem in March 1229 with his knights and several Catholic bishops. There, in the Church of the Holy Sepulchre, he was crowned king of Jerusalem—or rather, more precisely, crowned himself.

Even at this moment of triumph, however, Frederick's position remained precarious, writes his biographer David Abulafia (*Frederick II: A Medieval Emperor*). The eastern Christians would have nothing to do with him, and the loyalty of some in his own camp was in doubt. Furthermore, he was inadvertently alienating the Muslims by his indifference to his own faith. They were shocked, for instance, at his mockery of Christians. "What is the point of the grill over the doors of the mosque?" the emperor asked his hosts at one point. "To keep out the sparrows," they replied, upon which Frederick reportedly quipped, "Yet Allah has brought swine among you after all." On another occasion he assured the Muslims that they need not silence the muezzins on his account since "my chief aim in passing the night in Jerusalem was to hear the call to prayer given by the muezzins, and their cries of praise to God during the night." His last moments in the Holy Land became a jarring reminder of the ugly crosscurrents he had weathered: as his company made their way to the harbor in Acre, they were pelted with pig guts and offal by a riotous group of butchers.

Frederick's success put the pope in an awkward position. Gregory had spent the year of the emperor's absence fomenting rebellion, recruiting and subsidizing armies to invade Frederick's realm, sabotaging the crusade, and spreading rumors of its failure and even of Frederick's death. With Frederick's triumphant return and the rapid collapse of opposition, Gregory had little choice but to reach an understanding with him. It is a measure of the papacy's moral authority and the stigma of excommunication that even at this stage Gregory could wrest concessions from

Frederick on behalf of the Sicilian clergy. Relenting at last, he lifted the ban of excommunication in August 1230, after which he and Frederick dined together at Anagni, about thirty miles southeast of Rome, an amicable interlude amid years of bitterness.

Restored as a Christian communicant, with Jerusalem now in his territory and with Pope Gregory at least briefly acquiescent, Frederick could return to his court at Capua and enjoy the fruits of his labors. Not that he actually slowed down. Only one year later, after prodigious research into all the laws of the land as well as other legal systems, Frederick promulgated the Constitutions of Melfi, which stand as the preeminent legal code of the Middle Ages. Whether the Constitutions deserve comparison with the Code of Justinian is a matter of debate; probably not. But they unquestionably confirm much about Frederick the man and his conception of royal power.

Thus, they vigorously embraced the principle of imperial authority as sacred: "To discuss the Emperor's judgments, decrees, and statutes is sacrilege." So was any questioning of the worthiness of his officials. After all, the emperor was "the

Stories spread of Frederick's indulgence in grotesque experiments. To discover whether a soul could be seen fleeing a body, he had a man die sealed in a wine vat. The result was unsurprising.

terrestrial incarnation of divine justice, the supreme representative of God's will" in the sphere of political order. Nor would any questioning be permitted in the religious sphere. Heresy, too, amounted to treason, and if inquisitions were required to root it out, so be it. Frederick's attitude toward heresy would become a matter of profound embarrassment to later admirers trying to present him as the embodiment of enlightened secular indifference toward theological squabbles. Some try to explain his crackdowns as sops to the pope, but, in fact, his stern suppression of heresy is simply consistent with his attitude toward dissent of any type.

Also much admired has been his habit of objective inquiry. He communicated with the best minds in the world, whatever their background, including Jews in Spain, Muslims in Egypt, and his own celebrity-laden court. What proof is there, he wanted to know, of the eternity of matter? What is the true nature of volcanoes and geysers—and of paradise too? His biographer Patience Andrewes (*Frederick II of Hohenstaufen*) depicts him as embracing the Cistercians for their advanced methods of farming, borrowing their expertise and experimenting with various crops, including indigo and henna. He picked the brain of Leonardo of Pisa, known as Fibonacci, perhaps the age's leading mathematician. He abolished trial by ordeal for the sound reason that "these judgments of God by ordeal which men call 'truth revealing' might better be styled 'truth concealing'."

His intellectual curiosity knew no bounds, it was said, and, unhappily, this seems to have been literally true; it became apparent that Frederick's vaunted intellectual virtues were offset by dark and sometimes monstrous flaws. Stories were widely told of his indulgence in grotesque experiments. He was said to have had children raised by nurses who never spoke to them, for instance, to see how they

This Renaissance image of Frederick II's imperial court at Capua, Italy, is from the Hulton Archive. Frederick, sitting enthroned, is surrounded by turbaned advisers and clutched by a member of his harem as he pronounces judgment upon a hooded miscreant, presumably accused of attacking the girl. The severity reflected in the emperor's face suggests his final years, when, he said, he would play the role of "the hammer" rather than "the anvil" and began a reign of terror in his own court that saw some of his longest-serving and most loyal servants sent to their deaths.

would communicate on their own. (They died.) He had a man sealed in a wine vat to test whether a soul could be spotted escaping upon his death. (It wasn't.) To determine whether food digested better in a man at rest or a man at work, he had two such men cut open. (Conclusion unrecorded.) And although he incorporated relatively advanced provisions regarding women into his legal code, he treated his wives in the manner of a pasha, isolating them from the life of his court by means of menacing eunuch guards.

The emperor's interest in other religions is justifiably extolled, as well as the lengths to which he went to disprove a blood libel against German Jews. But although he granted Jews economic privileges, he also attempted to expand his official authority over them, stipulating that they were "serfs of our chamber," and he had no qualms about enforcing a rule that they wear special clothing. His attitude toward Muslims was similarly complex: from their persecutor in Sicily he evolved into their protector in Lucera, so long as their fate was utterly dependent upon his whim. He stocked his court with Muslim dancing girls—his "harem," whispered the justly suspicious critics—and even slaves, who included black African page boys.

Without doubt, however, Frederick's singular personal achievement in intellectual terms, completed in the late 1240s, was the treatise *De Arte Venandi cum Avibus* (*The Art of Hunting with Birds*), a book that is far from the genial description of royal leisure its title might suggest. Indeed, this ornithological study, the first of its kind, is the distillation of thirty years of careful observation of birds, especially falcons and their prey, from nesting habits to diseases.

Yet no matter how much time Frederick managed to spend roaming the forests of Europe with his falcons, more pressing matters always intervened. He had last seen Germany in 1220, after ensuring the election of his son Henry as king of the Romans (which meant king of Germany). By 1231, however, he was hearing rumblings from German princes regarding the behavior of his heir. Henry, now a young man who hardly knew his father, had developed decided views on how Germany should be governed. For the first time not everything was going Frederick's way.

Unamused by his son's gestures of independence, he summoned a diet at Ravenna, in northern Italy, for November 1231, which he expected Henry to attend. What he did not anticipate, although perhaps he should have, was that several Lombard cities, led by Milan, would choose this moment to challenge his authority in a manner he could not dismiss.

In the relationship between some Lombard cities and Frederick, it was hard to say which side more heartily detested the other. At the cost of decades of strife, some of these cities had developed as largely self-governing republics. Barbarossa, Frederick's grandfather, had exhausted himself trying to force them to adhere to

The emperor's son would spend the rest of his short life in one dungeon or another until he could endure it no longer. Finally at the age of thirty, he killed himself by riding off a cliff

imperial rule; now they mounted resistance to his grandson.[6] They could imagine no fate worse than to be brought to heel like the towns of southern Italy, with imperial bureaucrats replacing their local administration.

For his part, Frederick considered municipal self-governance an abomination. If that weren't enough, he had never forgiven Milan for its lack of enthusiasm at his accession and for its refusal to honor him with the iron crown symbolic of kingship over Italy. Further stoking his resentment was a bitter historical memory: the defeat of Barbarossa at Legnano.

Milan and its allies seem to have considered the gathering at Ravenna a threat, another imperial move against their liberties. Whatever the reason, they blocked the major passes through the Alps and thus the path to Ravenna. Frederick rescheduled his meeting with Henry for Easter in ancient Aquileia, a Roman city in northeast Italy near the Adriatic, northwest of Trieste and not far from fateful Legnano. This, he knew, his son would have no excuse for missing. Henry dutifully, if reluctantly, attended upon his father's court there in the spring of 1232 and was quickly put in his place. If he wished to retain his crown, he would have to agree to strict rules of behavior, pledge to govern entirely in accord with Frederick's wishes, and even agree to write a letter to the pope welcoming his own excommunication in the event that he disobeyed the emperor.

Such humiliating terms, far from settling the emperor's German affairs, stoked resentment in young Henry's proud heart. Within two years his agents were in secret negotiations with the Milanese. Shortly thereafter he took his defiance public, siding with the Rhineland cities against their overlords and thus

6. In the century-long struggle between the Hohenstaufens and the Welfs, the Lombard cities allied themselves with one house or the other. Milan, the largest and richest, was traditionally and often violently Welf and in its vicious conflicts with Barbarossa had at one point been all but destroyed. It was against these same Welf cities that Frederick II was now contending.

Frederick's intense interest in birds far exceeded that of a hunter or falconer. His treatise The Art of Hunting with Birds *is recognized as one of the foundational texts of ornithology. This illustration, taken from his book, shows him with a falcon perched beside his throne. Below is one of the hunting forts that he built throughout Italy as residences for his hunting parties and habitations for his bird collections. This one is Castel del Monte in the province of Bari, in southeastern Italy.*

instigating a civil war. But he had disastrously misjudged the spell that Frederick might still cast in the coming showdown.

Cool as always, the emperor swung into action. After securing Henry's excommunication from the pope, he proceeded north in 1235 with a modest military escort and his ever-present menagerie, banking on his personal prestige and old loyalties to recruit an army on the spot. Henry's support swiftly melted away, however, and the son found himself prostrate before his father, hoping for a clemency that could never be granted. He would spend the rest of his short life in one dungeon or another, until he could endure it no longer. At the age of thirty, during a transfer to yet another prison, he killed himself by riding off a cliff.

Three matters now remained that required Frederick's attention. Heading the list was his third marriage, to twenty-one-year-old Isabella of England in a ceremony at Worms attended by a stunning list of nobles and churchmen.[7] Second, in early 1237 he arranged for his son Conrad to be elected king of the Romans, supplanting the ousted Henry and again securing the succession. And last but certainly not least, he was resolved to teach the Lombards a lesson.

The German princes did not have to be prodded into assisting Frederick, especially given the way he deployed the gold of his English wife's dowry as payment. Nor was the pope in any position to openly help the Milanese, given their allegiance with the now-excommunicated Henry. In September 1237 Frederick left Germany for the final time, joining an army of perhaps fifteen thousand that he had amassed in northern Italy. By November they were engaged in a complicated duel with a Milanese army of ten thousand, which kept the emperor at bay by using the region's marshes and rivers as shields.

Frederick knew he must break the deadlock or squander the year, so his army noisily feinted in the direction of winter quarters, thus persuading the Milanese to drop their guard. Moving leisurely back toward their city, they were ambushed at Cortenuova by Frederick's troops, who rushed into the fray shouting, "Soldiers of the emperor" and "soldiers of Rome." The imperial forces not only cut down the Milanese in droves; they captured Milan's symbolic *carroccio*, a sacred wagon emblematic of the city. This he deftly exploited to drive a wedge between the pope and the people of Rome by dispatching the *carroccio* as a gift to Rome, where it was received with an ecstasy befitting an oncoming conqueror.

Frederick was now at the height of his power. The conquest of all Lombardy seemed within his grasp, but at this point his thirst for vengeance unhinged his judgment. When Milan sued for peace on favorable terms for the emperor, he rejected the offer out of hand—probably the greatest mistake of his career. Only unconditional surrender would satisfy him, but to the Milanese such a demand was too ominous to contemplate. The Milanese stood fast, and when Frederick attacked Brescia, a Milanese ally, he was blocked there too, and he lost the advantage of momentum.

At this point Pope Gregory saw his chance and pounced, though it seems incredible that he would dare to openly challenge the emperor's still formidable position. But beneath the superficial amity between the papacy and the imperial court lay deepening mistrust. The pope had watched with growing alarm as Frederick brought much of northern Italy to heel and began to install across all Italy his centralized lay bureaucracy. Surely, he would soon cast covetous eyes on Rome, the logical capital for the new caesar.

Gregory might be in his nineties, he might be hated by much of Rome's citizenry, and his policies might be resisted by a growing cabal of cardinals, but the doughty old man never flinched. He began patiently building a case (pretext, his critics would call it) for Frederick's second excommunication. Meanwhile, he quietly worked to bring Genoa and Venice into alliance with Milan and the Holy See, and he succeeded. Thus, in 1239 he dramatically renewed his excommunication of Frederick, releasing all Christians from their oaths of loyalty to him and committing his body "to Satan." He categorically condemned the emperor for his treatment of the crusading orders, for his iniquitous personal behavior, and for his reportedly heretical views, and most especially rebuked him for his abuse of the Sicilian church. Lombardy was not mentioned.

Frederick, too, took his case to the world. Not only did he respond in a rare public speech in Padua, full of wounded indignation; he even sent a letter to all the kings of Europe, warning that "the abomination of Babylon goeth forth from the elders of the people . . . into wormwood they turned the fruits of justice" (Amos 5:7). Yet in this war of rhetoric the pope still ruled supreme, dishing out a papal bull of stunning vehemence, drawing heavily from the language of the Apocalypse. "Out of the sea rises up the Beast," it began, "full of the names of blasphemy who, raging with the claws of the bear and the mouth of the lion and the limbs and likeness of the leopard, opens its mouth to blaspheme the Holy Name and ceases not to hurl its spears against the tabernacle of God and against the saints who dwell in heaven."

Unable to ignore this galling challenge, Frederick upped the ante by declaring

7. Frederick's first wife, Constance of Aragon, was married to him for nearly thirteen years. Mother of his son Henry, she died in 1222 at the age of forty-three. His second wife, Yolande of Jerusalem, who brought him the crown of the Holy City, died giving birth to the future Conrad IV in 1228 after three years of marriage. His third, Isabella of England, died in 1241 at age thirty-seven after six years of marriage, during which she bore him four children. Two died in infancy and one at age sixteen; the fourth, a daughter, became the margravine (or marquise) of Meissen.

the pope the Antichrist and moving his army, often headed by his Muslim troops, against the papal states, with Rome itself as the ultimate objective. This was the final act so long feared by Gregory and his two predecessors. If Frederick took Rome, the papacy would very soon become a mere department in his government. What to do? Though the city had formidable defenses, most of its citizens seemed to be on the emperor's side. Who would rally them?

Pope Gregory IX would. As the imperial forces reached Rome's outskirts on February 22, 1240, this pope—nearly one hundred years old—issued one of the most remarkable calls to action in the history of the Holy See. Following a dramatic procession through the city, he took his tiara and placed it with the reliquary skulls of Peter and Paul, brought out on display for the occasion. This was a holy war against a renegade emperor, he thundered, a crusade against an excommunicate—and the saints themselves would defend Rome if no man among them had courage for the deed! An unfathomable and utterly unforeseen delirium swept the crowd. They took up crosses as signs of the holy cause, and at that

Old Gregory, in his tiara and displaying the reliquary skulls of Peter and Paul, declared holy war on a renegade emperor. An unfathomable, utterly unforeseen delirium swept the crowd.

moment Frederick's advantage completely vanished. He had no appetite for conquering Rome if it would require a devastating siege, for that would confirm every charge the papacy had ever leveled at him.

He would have just one more chance to best this pope, whom he now hated with every fiber of his being. A year later he assembled his forces for a second attempt to march triumphantly and unopposed into the city. But fate or fortune or the will of God once again intervened: Pope Gregory IX, inconveniently, died. Frederick could hardly seize the city prior to the election of another pope: such blatant opportunism would permanently blacken his reputation.

Nor was this process speedy. The city's most powerful layman, the senator Matteo Orsini, was pushing for a quick election of someone who would mirror Gregory's anti-imperial stance. To that end, he had locked the ten available cardinals in the decrepit Septizonium Palace, where their deadlocked debates degenerated into a two-month living nightmare. Oppressed by the heat and the stench of overflowing lavatories, harassed by Orsini's threats and by guards who made their contribution to the discomfort by urinating onto the leaky roof above the episcopal heads, the cardinals became weak and ill. One of them, the Englishman Robert of Somercote, actually died. When they at last elected one of their number as Pope Celestine IV and were set free, the new pope, too, was so drained that he expired seventeen days later. By then the cardinals had fled to Anagni, whence they refused to return for another hellish conclave.

In the long months that followed, public sentiment throughout Europe gradually turned against Frederick. He was blamed at first for blockading Rome to hasten the election of a new pope and thus to make possible his own triumphal entry, then accused of tampering with the election by holding one of the cardinals prisoner. Not until June 25, 1243, nearly two years later, did the cardinals finally elect Sinibaldo of Fieschi as Pope Innocent IV. Frederick had great hopes for this highly intelligent, resourceful canon lawyer from Genoa, but of this optimism he was rapidly disabused. Innocent IV turned out to be Gregory IX all over again, except much younger and with sharper teeth.

Nevertheless, during the early months of Innocent's pontificate he and Frederick appeared poised to settle a number of longstanding differences, agreeing at last to a face-to-face meeting at Narni, about sixty miles north of Rome. Whether the pope ever intended to appear on the appointed date is unknown; perhaps rumors that the emperor had resolved to take him prisoner changed his mind. Given the planning necessary for the plot that unfolded, however, it is likely that Innocent had been chafing under the terms of the proposed settlement and realized how difficult it would be to rebuff the emperor in person.

His failure to appear made him a fugitive from the imperial wrath. With his nephew and two cardinals in tow, he made a dash for the coast, where waiting galleys sped him to Genoa. From there he journeyed even farther, arriving in Lyon near Christmas of 1244. Though nominally part of the empire, it was beyond Frederick's effective control. According to one contemporary chronicle, Frederick "ground his teeth like a satyr in his rage" when he heard of Innocent's flight, but this was nothing compared to his anger at what transpired next, when Innocent called a general council of prelates for June 1245 to deal with the crises facing the church.

Although the emperor sent eloquent spokesmen on his behalf, the outcome was foreordained. On July 17 Innocent IV read out the judgment of the council, with particular emphasis on Frederick's scandalous personal conduct.[8] And this was a mere prelude. The pope stunned the world by announcing that the emperor was henceforth deposed, that his titles had been stripped from him, and that his subjects had no need to obey his commands. Frederick understood it as a declaration of war. "I have not yet lost my crowns, and I shall not lose them without shedding blood . . ." he raged. "For too long I have been the anvil; now I wish to be the hammer."

Being the hammer involved, first of all, a propaganda onslaught in which he railed against the worldliness and wealth of the church. "Our priests," he declared in one of his manifestos, "are slaves to the world, drunken with self-indulgence, who put God in the second place; the stream of their wealth has stifled their piety." But the hammer was physical, too. Frederick's cruel streak had always lurked just below the surface, and now it burst forth with indiscriminate abandon as he began to sense traitors in his midst. He accelerated a purge of the clergy, confiscating the property of anyone under suspicion; allied himself with regional strongmen whose brutality was notorious; stuffed his dungeons with hostages; bragged about the mass execution of prisoners; cut off the hands and feet of anyone with papers from the pope; and treated every anti-imperialist as a revolutionary who must be hanged—or perhaps blinded with a hot poker, stuffed into a sack with snakes, and thrown into the sea.

When he uncovered a plot (hatched by Innocent, he believed) to kill him and his illegitimate son Enzio, his fury was monumental. Anyone suspected of

When Innocent IV (above) succeeded to the papal throne, Frederick assumed that this learned and scholarly cleric would finally bring relief from the tough old hard-liner Gregory IX, who, though approaching a hundred years of age, had successfully checked Frederick's plan to take over the city of Rome. To Frederick's chagrin, however, Innocent proved a far more formidable foe than Gregory. He slipped out of Rome before Frederick could capture him and assembled at Lyon the council that would help work Frederick's final downfall.

8. In the formal charges the pope did not go into the specifics of Frederick's "personal misconduct," dwelling instead on his persecution of the clergy that he could not control in Sicily and his treatment of the bishops and cardinals he had captured at sea to foil a church council called by old Pope Gregory shortly before his death. However, it happened that a terrible letter from Cardinal Rainer of Viterbo, a fierce critic of Frederick, had arrived just as the excommunication documents were being made public. The letter charged Frederick with every sordid vice, even with the murder of his own son Henry and of all three of his wives. Most of its contents were read aloud by the pope.

involvement was blinded, mutilated, and either burned to death or dragged throughout the countryside as a horrifying example of the fate to befall all would-be regicides. Eventually the emperor decided to strike directly at the source of his woes by rousting the pope from his sanctuary in Lyon. Yet even as his army wheeled in that direction, he received word from Enzio that Parma, a strategically vital city, had been seized in a coup led by a nephew of Innocent. He had no choice but to change plans; soon the walls of Parma were surrounded by his troops, preparing for a long siege.

Frederick made no secret of Parma's likely fate. It would be razed, and in its place would rise a new city, Vittoria, whose construction he ordered begun even during the months in which his forces were reducing Parma's citizens to a diet of scraps while terrorizing them with the daily spectacle of public executions outside the walls. But unfortunately for the emperor, his brutality made him irrational; his recklessness was matched by his folly. His entourage included not only the ubiquitous harem and menagerie and the imperial library but also a vast store of gold, jewels, and other treasures, a priceless crown among them. Furthermore, the fortifications of opulent Vittoria were unwontedly slipshod. On February 18, 1248, the emperor confidently rode off with his falcons and several

boon companions for a fine winter hunt. Parma's defenders thereupon feigned a sortie that duped the garrison and led it away from the town. With the imperial force out of sight, Parma's desperate population raced out of the city, slaughtered Vittoria's remaining forces, and carted off every last item of value.

Frederick reacted with his usual élan, riding through the night for nearly forty miles to Cremona to gather reinforcements, a feat of magnificent endurance for a man of fifty-three. He returned with troops to renew the assault on Parma, but there was

9. Two of Frederick's most favored sons were illegitimate in the eyes of the church, though not in Frederick's. Both met sad ends. Enzio of Sardinia was the product of a relationship Frederick had established with Adelaide of Urslingen. He was captured in the wars with the Welfs and died in prison twenty-three years later. Manfred, the son of Bianca Lancia, was killed in 1266 in the Battle of Benevento (see chapter 8).

no hiding the fact that he had suffered a staggering defeat, the worst of his career. The looted treasury, needed to pay his troops, could be refilled only through another levy on the already-resentful subjects of his southern realm. Even before Vittoria fell, his grip on Germany had weakened to the point that some northern princes had actually elected Count William of Holland as the new king of the Romans.

With pressure squeezing him from all sides, Frederick even began to imagine enemies where none existed. He had lost one of his two closest confidants at Parma when Thaddeus of Sessa was captured defending the treasury and then horribly executed. Now he himself turned on Pietro of La Vigna, who for twenty years had served him in a host of capacities, most memorably as ghostwriter of his polished proclamations. Three explanations have been offered. One, that Pietro conspired with the imperial physician to poison him, is almost certainly false—or if at all true, he may have been put up to it by the emperor's enemies in Parma, where the doctor had been prisoner. More likely, Pietro was a victim of ugly rumors and of Frederick's increasing paranoia. Another possibility, even more despicable, is that he was sacrificed so that the financially desperate monarch could get his hands on the wealth that Pietro had accumulated during his long service.

Blinded on Frederick's orders and publicly abused, Pietro had no illusions about the further agony awaiting him before his inevitable execution. In April 1249, while being led to what he no doubt feared was some new horror, he reportedly asked his jailors if there was a clear path to the stone wall. Told that there was, he took it at full speed, smashing his skull with such violence that he died.

Now, too, Frederick's body began to betray the toll of stress and physical hardship, succumbing with alarming frequency to a skin disease and other illnesses. But the worst blow of 1249 was the capture and imprisonment in Bologna of Frederick's beloved son Enzio, an inspiring leader possessed of the same fearless energy as his father.[9] Remarkably, however, the year 1250 began with the imperial forces holding their own against papal-backed troops and an outbreak of municipal insurrections. By September the situation had further improved, and Frederick, too, had revived during a summer in southern Italy. Confronting the pope in Lyon appeared a possibility again.

But by late fall, however, the emperor was beset by dysentery, eventually fell seriously ill with a fever, and in December summoned his chief officials to his side. To his dismay, he learned that in his stricken state he had been transported to Castle Fiorentino, a place he had never visited for the same reason that he had always avoided Florence. However irrationally, he feared an oracular prophecy foretelling the manner of his death: "You will die near the iron door in a place whose name will be formed by the word 'flower'."

Frederick never left Fiorentino alive. He designated his son Conrad as his heir, had himself clothed in the white habit of a Cistercian monk, and, just before dying, received last rites from Archbishop Berard of Palermo, whose loyalty spanned the emperor's entire career. Buried in Palermo with appropriate magnificence in a tomb of red porphyry, he seemed to have ensured the survival of the Hohenstaufen dynasty. But it was not to be. The turmoil unleashed by his conflict with Innocent IV would spread with his death, and his entire male line—legitimate and bastard sons alike as well as two grandsons—would die off or be slain within a generation. Conrad died at twenty-six, only four years after his father. Conrad's son, Conradin, was captured while still in his teens by the new Angevin masters of Sicily and publicly executed in Naples in an event that scandalized Europe.

In the short term, the papacy had won its deadly joust with the Hohenstaufen family. But Gregory IX and Innocent IV had walked some very dubious lines by deploying every weapon in the church's arsenal—from excommunication to the preaching of crusades to the offer of indulgences to anyone who would take up arms—in what some Christians considered a purely political struggle. Others would argue that what the popes were striving for was a church beyond the control of national monarchies and governments that could prevent wars by acting as a neutral arbiter between nations. However, imperial propaganda further eroded papal prestige, as did populist preachers who followed it. But the papacy, although weakened, nevertheless survived, whereas the House of Hohenstaufen would shortly vanish from history. The Wonder of the World was its spectacular final bow. ■

Frederick's final resting place is this tomb of red porphyry in the cathedral at Palermo. This man, who was able to take Jerusalem without raising a sword and brought to heel much of Italy and central Europe, would be the last successful emperor of the Hohenstaufen line. His male heirs were soon vanquished. It would remain for an heiress, a granddaughter, to provide the family's last hurrah (see chapter 8).

A key Christian victory assures the doom of Muslim Spain

Two violent but short-lived Islamic revivals fail to save Andalusia as the Christians advance inexorably south to the Battle of Las Navas

It had been three hundred years since the Muslims ousted Spain's Christian Visigoths and occupied nearly four fifths of the Iberian Peninsula. Called Andalusia, Muslim Spain reached its cultural, military, and economic summit under the brutal regime of the rulers al-Mansur and his son Abd al-Malik at the end of the first Christian millennium. After Abd al-Malik's death in 1009, it split into an array of city-states called taifas, run by an assortment of amiably decadent Arab, Berber, and other sultans.

With the Muslims thus weakened, the Christians in the north slowly but resolutely moved into attack mode. By then they consisted of the sparsely populated but militarily competent principalities of Galicia, Leon, Castile, Navarre, Aragon, and Catalonia. These ran across the craggy top of Spain from the Atlantic along the south slope of the Pyrenees to the Mediterranean. The Muslim taifas were wealthier, more peopled, and potentially able to assemble bigger armies, but the Christians were more unified and better organized.

Thus, under Sancho III the Great, king of Navarre from 1000 to 1035, they were able to exact tribute from the adjacent Muslim taifas of Badajoz, Toledo, and Saragossa—protection money guaranteeing them against Christian attack. This brought Muslim gold flowing northward, making Christian Spain an economic rival to flourishing Flanders and Lombardy.

Sancho III reestablished regular contact with the Roman curia, and French Benedictine monks gradually supplanted the traditions of Spain's old Visigothic church. With the new monasteries came new towns, peopled by immigrants from France and Italy, who also took up the cheap farmland of the rugged north and of the Trans-Duero region, the big wedge of cattle country that included the La Mancha plateau. The latter was the key to further expansion into the city and taifa of Toledo that dominated the economic life of central Iberia.[1]

Reconnection to Rome and Europe brought another, and especially dubious, benefit. In a forerunner of the Crusades, the king of Christian Aragon, with the blessing of Pope Alexander II, imported fifty thousand Normans, French, and Italians to take the Muslim city of Barbastro in 1063. What the pope did not bless, however, was the outcome. In the Muslim account, these foreign troops broke the terms of the city's surrender and

The cityscape of Toledo still shows the fingerprint of Alfonso VI. After retaking the city from the Muslims, Alfonso converted mosques into churches and furthered the re-Christianization of Spain, known to Spanish history as the Reconquista. *The spires of these churches can still be seen on the Toledo skyline.*

THE *RECONQUISTA*

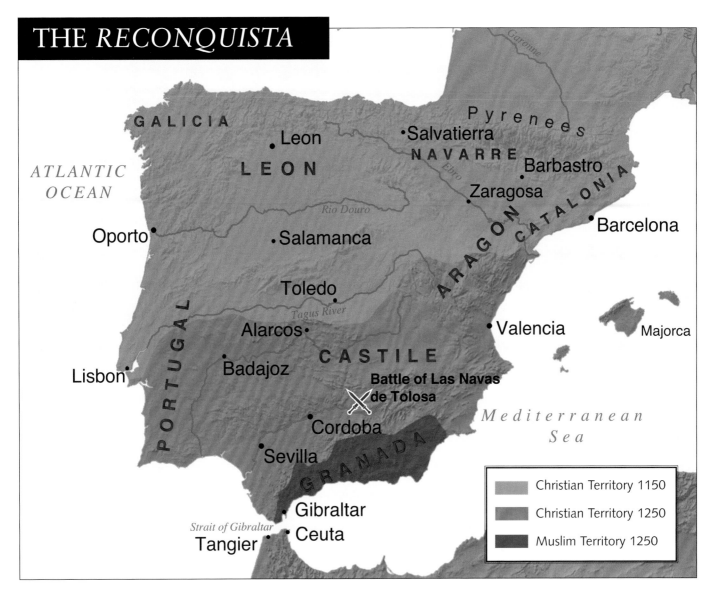

GALICIA

ATLANTIC
OCEAN

•Leon

LEON

Pyrenees

•Salvatierra

NAVARRE

•Barbastro

Zaragosa

ARAGON

CATALONIA

•Barcelona

Oporto•

Rio Douro

•Salamanca

Toledo

Tagus River

Alarcos•

•Valencia

Majorca

PORTUGAL

Badajoz

CASTILE

Battle of Las Navas
de Tolosa

*Mediterranean
Sea*

Lisbon•

•Cordoba

GRANADA

•Sevilla

Gibraltar

Strait of Gibraltar

•Ceuta

Tangier

	Christian Territory 1150
	Christian Territory 1250
	Muslim Territory 1250

slaughtered all the defenders plus an additional six thousand male inhabitants, all of them first made to watch the rape and enslavement of their wives and daughters and the murder of their children.

This was considerably at odds with Spanish precedent. The northern kings tended to preserve conquered populations, allowing residents to continue practicing their trade and religion. They realized that the Andalusian cities had no strong loyalties to either side and would fight for whoever paid them. Spanish Christians, too, had been known to switch sides—even the great Cid (volume 6 pages 252–253).[2] Barbastro, incidentally, was recovered by the Muslims a year later.

In the 1080s Alfonso VI of Castile set his sights on Toledo, the ancient Visigoth capital. Still half Christian, it was now the

capital of a vast Muslim taifa, also called Toledo, that sprawled over the center of the Iberian Peninsula. Contending that Toledo had been paying tribute with debased coinage, Alfonso laid siege in 1085 and with the help of Toledo's Christians brought about its surrender. He offered generous conditions: self-government for the taifa plus freedom of religion for Muslims and Visigoth Christians alike. There was a price, however: steeper tribute payments from neighboring sultans, or the Christians would seize the taifas of Saragossa, Seville, and Granada as well.

This put the sultans into a painful quandary. They knew they could not defeat Alfonso's formidable armies, which, after Toledo, had gone on to take the taifa of Valencia. Moreover, another immediate danger was threatening them from the

1. La Mancha, home of Cervantes' fictional seventeenth-century knight errant Don Quixote, is an arid but fertile area that in the time of Alfonso VI was the home of bandits and cattle herders. Its name means "the stain" in Spanish, but the etymology is Arabic, from the word *al-mansha*, "dry land."

2. By the second half of the eleventh century, the standard surrender procedure for Spanish Christian kings was as follows. Residents of a town under siege who surrendered promptly were allowed to remain, with full freedoms, under the new regime. Those who delayed surrender for very long would be allowed to leave, taking only such goods as they could carry. If they waited for the town to fall by force, they faced death or enslavement.

Left: *Rodrigo Diaz de Vivar, known to history as El Cid Campeador (see volume 6, pages 252–253), is one of the great heroes of Christian Spain, revered to this day. This equestrian statue of him is located in the Spanish town of Burgos, six miles from his birthplace. Right: A statue of Alfonso VI of Castile stands in the Sabatini Gardens in Madrid. The gardens are considered part of the Royal Palace in Madrid and were opened to the public in 1978.*

south. Across the Strait of Gibraltar in North Africa, poised to strike, were the Almoravid Muslims, an Afro-Berber dynasty that had sprung up in the Sahara in the 1040s and had taken over northwest Africa. Under their devout, warlike, and pitiless leader, Yusuf ibn Tashfin, the Almoravids practiced a Qur'anic literalism that glorified *jihad* and strict asceticism. This appealed not at all to the pleasure-loving taifa sultans, who typically neglected even military spending while lavishing money on the glorification of their courts. Their wealth was far better spent, in their view, on the poets, artists, and musicians who so magnificently adorned their palaces.

These splendors, however, were not always appreciated by the masses, whose taxes paid for them. Further, devout Andalusian imams tended to share the Almoravid moral outlook. To them, the sultans' courts were cesspools of sin and squalor, unhealthily influenced by Christianity, where homosexuality, harlotry, and adultery were accepted or winked at and alcohol freely consumed. These things, expressly forbidden by the Qur'an, were openly indulged in by Andalusia's nobles and celebrated by its poets in ever more lubricious verse. "One cannot help sensing among the literate ruling class a widespread boredom and cynicism, an appetite for novel sexual sensations, and a striving after

verbal cleverness for its own sake," writes historian Gabriel Jackson in his *The Making of Medieval Spain.*

Caught between Islamic fundamentalism, which they loathed, and Christian conquest, which they dreaded, the sultans of Seville, Granada, and Badajoz reluctantly chose the former. They called in the Almoravids, hoping that they would prove reasonable as well as helpful. So the aging Yusuf arrived with his crack Berber troops and began taking over one taifa after another, willing or otherwise. Within fifteen years the Almoravids had added Andalusia to their empire. They also in short order took back Valencia from the Christians.[3]

Strict Qur'anic rule did not last, however. When Yusuf died in 1106, reputedly at the age of one hundred, his empire had peaked. Under his son Ali bin Yusuf, described by one historian as "a pious nonentity who fasted and prayed while his empire fell to pieces," decadence began a recovery. Meanwhile, the northerners, reinforced by Christian refugees from Andalusia fleeing the strictures of Islamic law, were gaining strength. Furthermore, to replace their lost taifa tribute revenue, the northern kingdoms sought and found money and manpower in Europe beyond the Pyrenees. So Christian forces repeatedly defeated Almoravid leader Ali bin Yusuf, and after

Ali's death in 1142 his son fared no better, perishing four years later in battle.

Meanwhile, another kingdom, to be known to history as Portugal, had struggled into being on the Christian side. Originally called Portucale, it began life after its recapture from the Muslims in 868 as a county in southwestern Galicia. In the late eleventh century, during a war between the Spanish Christian kingdoms, Portucale ruler Count Henry declared independence. This became a recognized fact after his son won the curious Battle of Sao Mamede in 1128—curious because he waged it against his own mother and her lover.[4] When Portugal captured the port of Lisbon, at the mouth of the Tagus River, with the help of a few boatloads of soldiers on their way to the Second Crusade, Lisbon became its capital. In 1250 it expanded southward by again defeating the Muslims.

By the mid-twelfth century Christian Spain had resolved into three relatively stable kingdoms that would last to the end of the Middle Ages: Portugal, Leon-Castile, and Aragon-Catalonia. The Almoravid Empire was in rapid decline, and the end of Muslim Andalusia seemed at hand, but such was not yet to be. Out of the rugged Atlas Mountains, in what would become Morocco and Algeria, there emerged another Islamic movement: the Almohads, founded by a pious Berber named Ibn Tumart, who, invoking Qur'anic law, began by trashing wineshops and attacking unveiled women. Recruiting an army of like-minded apostles, he made ready to take on more formidable foes than women and bootleggers.

After Ibn Tumart's death in battle, the title of caliph was assumed by one of his generals, Abd al-Mumin, who rapidly overwhelmed the now dissolute Almoravid Empire. By 1149 he had extended his rule across North Africa to Egypt. His successor, Yusuf II, crossed the straits, established a base in Seville, and

began terrorizing the Almoravid, Christian, and Jewish populations of Andalusia, many of whom fled north. The Almohads quickly pushed the Christians back farther north, recovering the territory lost by the Almoravids.

Before long their initial zealotry evolved into a pragmatic rule characterized by an efficient bureaucracy and impressive feats of engineering, which included the Giraldi mosque tower in Seville and the new port of Gibraltar. Berber armies were regularly shipped in from Africa to contain the Christians, who, in any case, were now occupied with a dispute over the succession in Castile and Leon.

Significantly, however, the Almohads were not able to defeat the northern kingdoms in a major battle until the year 1193, when the caliph Ya'qub trounced Alfonso VIII of Castile at the Battle of Alarcos. Most of Alfonso's army of eight thousand was killed; he himself barely escaped with

> The pious Berber Ibn Tumart began by trashing wineshops and attacking unveiled women

his life. But Ya'qub either could not or did not exploit the victory, and six years later the turn of the tide began that would ultimately see the Muslims expelled from Spain.

Ya'qub died in 1199 and was succeeded by his less gifted son, Muhammad al-Nasir, who unwisely signed a truce with the defeated Alfonso VIII. Then, assuming the Christians thoroughly vanquished, al-Nasir left Andalusia to deal with a revolt in Tunisia. It was a catastrophic mistake: Alfonso took advantage of his absence to rebuild his army, strengthen border defenses, and repair relations with the other Christian kings (who had bitterly blamed him for the defeat at Alarcos).

By 1210 al-Nasir realized what was going on and hastened back across the strait with an army estimated in the notoriously exaggerated contemporary accounts at six hundred thousand men. Marching north, he captured the castle at Salvatierra, where the first truly Spanish

3. The Almoravid army adopted a modified phalanx formation whereby a front rank knelt behind long spears and tall shields, bulwarking a cavalry armed with bows and shields and mounted on horses or camels. The front rank, meant to weaken the oncoming enemy, would periodically part to allow the cavalry to rush out. Many of the cavalrymen were black, recruited from Senegal, on the southern frontier of the Almoravid Empire. These troops, together with their ominously booming war drums, tended to unnerve opponents.

4. In the Battle of Sao Mamede (June 24, 1128), Portuguese forces led by Afonso I of Portugal defeated an army led by his mother, Teresa of Leon, and her lover, Fernao Peres de Trava, who sought to retain Portugal as a county of the kingdom of Leon. This victory is considered Portugal's foundational event. Afonso styled himself "prince of Portugal" thereafter and by 1143 was recognized by his neighbors as king of Portugal.

The gorge of Despeñaperros, which translates literally to "where dogs are thrown over," is the pass through which the Christian coalition stole to surprise the Muslim army camp at Las Navas. The gorge was renamed after the battle to commemorate the Muslims' being overthrown.

5. The military order of the Calatrava was founded early in the twelfth century by Don Diego Velazquez, a Cistercian monk from the monastery of Fitero, in Navarre. He and several colleagues received their abbot's permission to arm themselves in defense of Calatrava, which the Templars had abandoned as indefensible. The Order of Calatrava expanded swiftly and was later made independent of the Cistercians.

military monastic order, the Calatrava, was based.[5] Alfonso, thoroughly alarmed, sent an anxious request for support to Pope Innocent III, who responded with an appeal to the French nobility, offering indulgences to those who joined the "Spanish Crusade."

The major contingents of the international Christian army that gathered in Toledo were nobles, town militias, military orders, and mercenaries from Castile, but Peter II of Aragon brought three thousand knights and almost as many crossbowmen. There was a large group of Portuguese and a smaller one of Leonese—albeit without their kings, who still distrusted Alfonso on account of Alarcos. King Sancho VII of Navarre brought two hundred retainers. Finally, over the Pyrenees there marched or rode sixty thousand assorted crusaders. Arriving in Toledo, they had to be restrained by the Castilians from trying to kill all the city's Jews.

This army, the greatest of the *Reconquista*, moved south toward the enemy on June 20, 1212. Although short of rations, they crossed the baked

Gadiana plains and fought a hard battle to win the town of Old Calatrava. Finding little there by way of plunder to reward their efforts, the French troops embarked upon slaughter but were ordered by Alfonso to leave the townspeople alone. For the foreign crusaders this was a final frustration. On July 3 they abandoned the Spanish army to its fate and headed back home across the Pyrenees.

The Spaniards, being inured to tough fighting on the parched plains of Spain's interior, marched on and retook Alarcos. On July 12 they reached the pass at Muradel but found it already blocked by the massive Almohad army. Its warriors held the high ground on either side and far into the distance, with the Ittabalan musicians beating their huge kettledrums from the rock ledges. But a local peasant, it is said, showed the Christians an alternate route around the blocked pass to the plains (*las navas*) on the Andalusian side of the Sierra Morena. Here the greatest battle of the Reconquista was about to take place.

Al-Nasir's army was arranged in three lines. Cavalry and heavily armed foot soldiers were in the center, screened by archers and a row of Berber lancers. At the rear sat al-Nasir beside his red tent, dressed in a black cloak and surrounded by bodyguards. In one hand he held a sword, in the other the Qur'an. An unknown scribe writes in the *Latin Chronicles of the Kings of Castile,*

> Then the Christians arose after midnight, the hour at which Christ, whom they worshipped, rose up victorious after death. After hearing the solemnities of masses, and being renewed by the life-giving sacrament of the Body and Blood of Jesus Christ our God, they fortified themselves with the sign of the cross. They quickly took up their weapons of war, and with joy rushed to the battle as if they were invited to a feast. Neither the broken and stony places, nor the hollows of the valleys, nor the steep mountains held them back. They advanced on the enemy prepared to die or conquer.

The Christians moved forward in a three-line flanking attack, militia to the front, cavalry behind, and the three kings—Alfonso of Castile, Peter of Aragon, and Sancho of Navarre—in the rearguard. They crashed through the front line of Muslim defense and into the heavy core of troops behind, where hand-to-hand fighting with axes and swords continued inconclusively for hours. Then the caliph called in his reserve troops and the Christians fell back, but Alfonso hastened to return to the fray, and the rest followed. Under this last thrust the Andalusians first gave way, followed by the Berbers and, finally, the Arabs. One of the earliest to depart, on a fast mare, was Muhammad al-Nasir. "Who can count how many thousands of Moors fell that day and descended into the depths of hell?" the chronicler wonders.

The hard part was over. Caliph al-Nasir took ship back to Maghreb. Behind him he left most of his army on the plains of Tolosa, destined to be slaughtered in the Battle of Las Navas de Tolosa. The Christians did not immediately occupy towns near the battlefield, in part because of drought but chiefly because of stench and disease from the unburied corpses.

The Almohads had been dealt a blow from which they would not recover, and the path to the Reconquista was now clear. In the next thirty-six years Spanish Christians led by Ferdinand III of Leon would take back all Andalusia save the kingdom of Granada, a foothold in Iberia that Islam would retain for the next two and a half centuries. At length it, too, would be lost, but that is a story for a future volume. ■

Below is a nineteenth-century painting of the Battle of Las Navas de Tolosa by Francisco de Paula van Halen. In this battle a coalition of Christians from Leon, Castile, Navarre, and Aragon dealt the Muslim Almohads a blow from which they would not recover.

"There!" boomed the fat man. *"There is the final conclusive argument against the Manichaean heresy!"* Such an outburst at the banquet table of the king of France was outrageous. But ignoring the disruption, Louis IX had a different interest: what was this conclusive argument against the Manichaean heresy? After all, the heresy had been around since the days of the apostles.

CHAPTER 7

The fat man of Aquino who helped Christians unite reason with faith

The jovial friar they once called "Dumb Ox Thomas" set forth a case for Christian truth that was extolled and denounced in his lifetime and for centuries after

A thirteenth-century banquet, judging from the description in the *Encyclopedia of the Middle Ages*, must have been a joyous yet semi-sacramental affair, and a banquet hosted by the king of France an occasion demanding especially strict regard for one's conduct. How very regrettable, then, was the sudden outburst by the gigantic guest seated on a bench not far from King Louis IX himself.

This obtrusive gent wore the black-and-white garb of a Dominican friar, and a great deal of garb there was, for he was a very corpulent man. Powerful, too: his fist slamming down upon the delicacy-laden table made the dishes jump and clatter. "There!" he boomed out. "*There* is the final and conclusive argument against the Manichaean heresy!"

A Dominican colleague tugged the man's sleeve, whispering, "Master Thomas, Master Thomas, do be careful. You are sitting at the table of the king of France!" We do not know the big man's response, but from his conduct on similar occasions, we can guess it. "Good heavens!" he would have said. "What have I done? What a dreadful way to behave! But I was thinking, you see. I was thinking."

The king, who was thinking too, immediately ordered a secretary to go speak to this man. "To reprimand him, your Majesty?" "Oh no," replied the king, "to take a note. Find out what *is* the conclusive argument against the Manichaean heresy."

This, King Louis knew, mattered far more than a disturbance at a royal banquet. Ancient Manichaeanism, the belief that eight centuries earlier had initially prevented the mighty Augustine from embracing Christianity and four hundred years before that had troubled Christians in apostolic times, lay at the root of the current Cathar heresy. Spreading like an epidemic, this curious religion, much at odds with Christianity, now threatened the unity of his kingdom and all Europe.

The king also knew that if anyone could rebut it, that man was his noisy guest, Thomas of Aquino. Thomas was admittedly radical and eccentric in some of his teachings, and known for disrupting more things than a royal banquet. Nevertheless, in an age of crusaders, few doubted that Thomas was a soldier of Christ who fought with mind, not muscle.

What neither the king nor his guest could have known, incidentally, was that they would one day share a notable distinction. Both would be canonized by the church. King Louis would be credited with setting a model for Christian monarchy and justice rarely equaled in the centuries to follow (see sidebar, pages 140–145). The philosophy and theology of Thomas Aquinas would become so deeply entrenched that six hundred years later the Church of Rome would embrace it as the summation of Christian belief against which all truth claims can be measured. Whether Thomas himself would have approved quite such unequivocal recognition some of his many admirers of later years have doubted. But he strongly believed in truth, particularly scientific truth as revealed by reason, even if it appeared to conflict with some interpretations of the Bible, and he insisted that there could never be two conflicting truths.

Thomas of Aquino was no stranger to distinguished company. The eighth and youngest son of Count Landulf of Aquino, he was a grandnephew of the emperor Frederick I Barbarossa (see chapter 4) and a cousin of Barbarossa's grandson the emperor Frederick II, known as *Fridericus Stupor Mundi*, "Frederick Wonder of the World" (see chapter 6). The Aquinas family estate was centered on the castle of

In another view of the Manichaean incident, Aquinas (second from right) discusses his insight with a Dominican colleague while a secretary takes notes. The scene is a fifteenth-century tempera on a panel by Niklaus Manuel.

Roccasecca (Dry Rock), high above the main road between Naples and Rome, and it followed that the family was deeply involved in politics and war. They had joined Frederick II's army in attacking the nearby Benedictine abbey of Montecassino, which was allied to Frederick's bitter enemy the pope. When one Aquinas brother deserted and joined the papal army, he was put to death on Frederick's orders.

Count Landulf decided early that his youngest son, born about 1225, was unsuited to political or military life. At age five he was large, uncommunicative, placidly acquiescent, and seemingly dull witted. He was naturally pious, however, spontaneously distributing the castle food to local transients and poring for hours over the Bible. Clearly, he was meant to be a monk, so the count enrolled him in Montecassino, the same abbey he had helped the emperor assault. Family influence might someday make him abbot, although it seemed unlikely. His fellow students called him "Dumb Ox Thomas" because he kept asking such stupefyingly dumb questions as "What is God?" And he really wanted to know.

His father abruptly removed him from Montcassino at about age fourteen, fearing that the monastery might become further involved in the wars between pope and emperor, and sent him to study in Naples. Later on, the Aquino family would switch to the papal cause, forcing them to abandon Roccasecca and take refuge in the papal states. But meanwhile came truly devastating news from Naples: Thomas, now nearly twenty, had joined one of the new mendicant orders. That is, he had become a preaching beggar in what many regarded as a religious cult, called the "Dominicans" after their fanatic founder, Dominic (see sidebar, pages 192–193). Eventually, his family was sure, the church would condemn the whole mendicant movement, but at present this exhibition by their youngest son was an unthinkable humiliation. Something, plainly, must be done, said his mother, the countess Theodora.

The quiet joy and fascination Aquinas derived from books is reflected in his eyes and mouth in this portrayal by the fifteenth-century painter Fra Bartolomeo, who himself, like Thomas, became a Dominican.

Much as Aquinas must himself have done, a group of clergy walk beneath the arcade at the Monastery of Monte Cassino. Aquinas was sent there by his father until he was fourteen years old. Fearing the monastery's involvement in the wars between the pope and the emperor, his father removed him from the monastery and sent him to finish his studies at Naples.

According to one account, she herself hurried to Naples. However, the Dominicans, already accustomed to raids by the outraged noble families of young applicants, had dispatched Thomas to Rome. Knowing that two of his soldier-brothers were stationed near his route, the countess urged them to intercept him and bring him home until he recovered his senses. They encountered him on the road and struggled to rip the Dominican habit right off his back, but they couldn't do it; he was so very strong. Peasants used to stop and stare, it was said, when this enormous man passed by. In the words of one of the old records, "They came near to look at him, filled with admiration for a man of such compliance and beauty."

Thomas finally agreed to go home. Wrapped tightly in his shredded habit and riding a donkey, he was escorted to a nearby family castle and locked up. Soon the brothers reappeared with what the old account describes as "a young and pretty damsel, attired in all the blandishments of love." Thomas, furious, seized a brand from the fire, chased the terrified young woman from the room, slammed the door behind her, and used the brand to inscribe a charred cross on it. Then he knelt before it to pray.

This persuaded his brothers that Thomas's chosen vocation, though crazy, must be deeply sincere. They moved him to Roccasecca, where he remained for a year, with his four adoring sisters waiting on him. Countess Theodora, although beginning to yield, still opposed his vocational begging, however. She appealed to both the emperor and the pope to intervene but was thwarted by her daughters (one of whom would later become a nun). In one account, they lowered their gigantic brother by rope from the castle walls so that he could join what their mother saw

Upon discovering that her son had joined the Dominicans, who begged for their subsistence, Aquinas's mother, the Countess Theodora, sent his brothers to intercept him on the road to Rome and bring him back to the family estate, where he could be "brought to his senses." His overzealous brothers attempted to rip his habit off of his back, something that Aquinas, who was very strong, did not allow them to do. He did, however, agree to return home.

as his fellow cultists in Rome. But Thomas also remained a devoted family member, cherished by his sisters and loyal to his brothers, and later served efficiently as executor of a family estate. But by then the family had come to see what others saw so readily. Dumb Ox Thomas was an intellectual giant as well as a physical one.

He appears at one of the great turning points in the Christian faith. During most of the early thirteenth century the mention of a single Greek term could arouse either profound respect or deep suspicion in the rapidly proliferating universities of western Europe. That term was "Aristotelian physics." The work of Aristotle, the greatest philosopher and scientist of the ancient world, who lived in the fourth century before Christ, had been familiar to Greek-speaking eastern Christians from the earliest times, but a Latin version had been available in the West only for the past two centuries. By Thomas's time most educated people had no trouble at all with Aristotle's works in logic or ethics. The sticking point was Aristotelian physics because it conflicted with the biblical account of the Creation.

The Christian whose thought piloted western Christianity during all the dark years of semi-barbarism in devastated Europe and then through the long revival of western civilization was Augustine of Hippo (see volume 4, chapter 5). The Greek influence on Augustine came from Plato, Aristotle's teacher. But Aristotle dwarfed Plato in range and depth, and the Nestorian Christians of Persia had passed on his work to their new Muslim rulers. They, in turn, conveyed it to Muslim scholars in Spain, so when the great libraries of Toledo fell to the Christians in 1085, Aristotle's philosophy, in Arabic, began spreading to western Europe's rising universities. The response to it was overwhelming, if divisive. To some it represented a foreign religious intrusion that in some respects threatened to return Christianity to paganism by supplanting divinely revealed truth, particularly regarding Creation, with supposed "truth" revealed through human reason.

To others, however, both Plato and Aristotle offered a new and powerful approach to Christian truth. This approach did not arise suddenly. A slow, steady growth in more methodical thinking about the faith had begun back in the 1050s with the brilliant Archbishop Lanfranc of Canterbury, senior ecclesiastic in England, whose celebrated treatise on the Holy Communion drew on both the Bible and logic. His pupil and successor, Anselm, wrote a defense of Christianity founded entirely on reason. By Thomas's time a whole new academic approach to faith, known as scholasticism, had been established.

In Thomas scholasticism would reach its pinnacle. Though he cited Augustine more than he cited Aristotle and cited the scriptures more than he cited either of them, he was determined to "baptize" those parts of Aristotle that had been considered incompatible with Christianity by rereading Aristotle in the most accurate translations and by rejecting those parts that could not be reconciled with biblical Christianity. This work would define his life—a life embroiled in bitter controversy. He would be denounced as a purveyor of paganism, threatening the integrity and authority of the Bible, a dabbler in scientific magic. Most irksome to his critics, however, he rarely lost his temper. All accounts describe him as courteous in debate—charming, clear, and unruffled—but so logically devastating that he frequently reduced opponents to helpless rage. Even so, writes his biographer Jean-Pierre Torrell (*Saint Thomas Aquinas: The Person and His Work*, translated by Robert Royal), it is a mistake to conclude that Thomas was an icy, self-secretive intellectual without zeal or fervor. However dispassionate he was in debate, his writings exhibit vehemence and downright belligerence. They show him as a feisty intellectual scrapper, taking undisguised pleasure in reducing the rival case to absurdity.

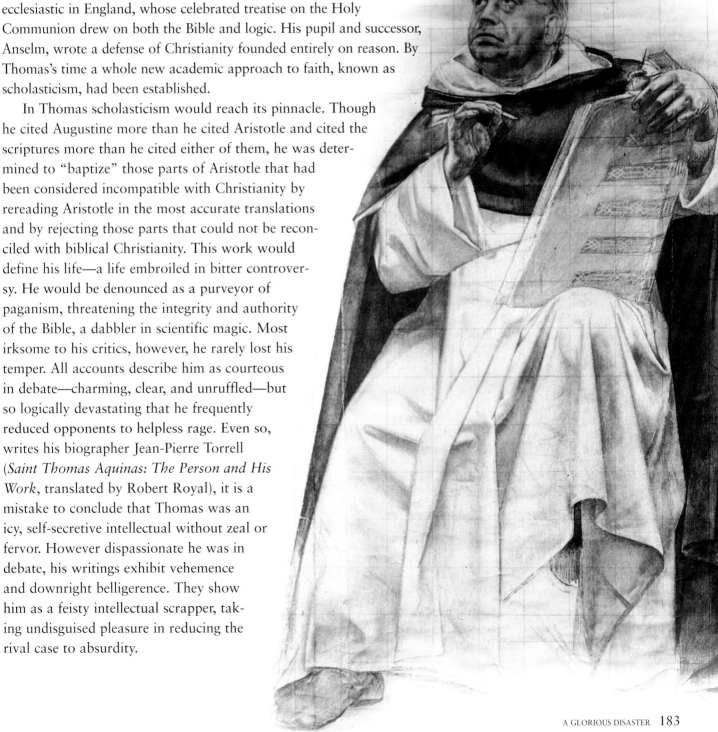

Having been freed from the family's Roccasecca castle by his adoring sisters, Thomas joined his fellow Dominicans in Rome, where he began the massive volume of work that he would leave to posterity. He is shown below in a twentieth-century charcoal sketch by Pietro Annigoni.

ONE OF THOMAS'S PRAYERS—VIRTUE WITHOUT THE ATTENDANT FLAWS

O Lord my God, make me submissive without protest, poor without discouragement, chaste without regret, patient without complaint, humble without posturing, cheerful without frivolity, mature without gloom, and quick witted without flippancy.

Thomas's sharpest and angriest critics were known loosely as "Augustinians." (The term described a school of thought. The Augustinian order of monks, which was then being formed, was not involved in the controversy.) These critics saw Thomas's focus on Aristotle as a movement intended to supplant the teaching of the great Augustine. Although Thomas vigorously denied this, the Augustinian attack on him would go on for nearly fifty years after his death.

As Aristotle's work became better known in the West, its staggering dimensions enthralled a whole generation of Christian students in the mid-thirteenth century, for it embraced philosophy, biology, animal genealogy, astronomy, meteorology, physics, morality, and what today would be called psychology. "We are dwarfs sitting on the shoulders of the ancients as on those of giants," the twelfth-century teacher Bernard of Chartres had declared. "If we see more things than they did, it is not by perspicacity of our view, nor by our size, but because we were elevated by them and brought to a gigantic height."

By Aquinas's time, noted the twentieth-century Christian historian and theologian Jacques Maritain, Aristotelian thought had been making "fearful inroads" into Christianity for half a century. "It was not merely that he brought in his train a crowd of Jews and Arabs whose commentaries [on Aristotle] were fraught with danger: the noble treasure of natural wisdom which he imported was full of

Though dispassionate in debate, Thomas's writings exhibit vehemence. They show him a feisty, intellectual scrapper, taking overt pleasure in reducing a rival case to ashes.

pagan poisons, and the mere dazzling glitter of the promises of pure reason was sufficient to bewilder an ingenuous and inquisitive world."

The "pagan poisons" were things like the denial of human free will, the denial of the Creation, and the eternity of matter. As Aristotle's opponents well knew, such Aristotelian assertions were plainly heretical. He taught, for instance, that the world had always existed, the human soul did not survive death, and God has left the world to run itself. To Christians, the universe had a beginning, the individual soul survives death, and God definitely intervenes in the affairs of men. How, they asked, could Christian teaching be grounded in Aristotle?

Thomas countered these objections. Christian teaching must be grounded in revelation, in Jesus Christ as recorded in the New Testament and in the Hebrew law and prophets, he said. But Aristotle provided a foundation for how to think about these things. Moreover, some things, like the concept of a purely autonomous universe and the denial of the individual soul's survival, he argued, did not come from Aristotle; they had been interpolated into his writings by the Muslim scholar Ibn Rushd, known to the Christians as Averroes, called "the Commentator." As for the contention that there was no "beginning," Aristotle was simply wrong. If the world was to have an end, as Aristotle himself believed, then it must also have had a beginning. But was this sole error adequate grounds for disqualifying the whole rational approach? Was this a reason to deny Christian teachers the boundless potential of reasoned argument in defense of the faith?

Convinced that the Aristotelian approach offered a persuasive new way to convert literate people to Christianity, Thomas (shown at left in a fifteenth-century painting by Sandro Botticelli) had first to refute the Aristotelian interpretation of the Muslim scholar Averroes (pictured above in a statue located in Cordoba, Spain).

The whole Aristotelian approach, Thomas insisted, offered a new and convincing way to present Christianity to literate and thinking people. To Thomas, notes his biographer Ralph McInerny (*Aquinas*), it presented a kind of "clinical specimen" of what the world would look like to a thoughtful man uninfluenced by the Christian religion. This opened a door, as it were, to the non-Christian mind, providing an access for the Gospel.

For Thomas there could be no true conflict between conclusions reached by human reason validly employed and those conveyed by the scriptures and creeds. Reason, like the five human senses, was given to us by God. So were the scriptures. So were the creeds. Just as there could be only one God, not several, there could be only one truth, not several. Therefore, what our senses tell us—what we see, hear, smell, touch, taste, and otherwise observe—unless perverted by sin,

A fifteenth-century portrait by Joos van Gent and P. Berruguete of Albert the Swabian, who would later be known as Albert the Great. Albert taught Thomas in Cologne for several years and was one of the first people to correctly predict that Aquinas's teachings would one day "fill the world."

must be taken as true and real. The world we behold is not merely a transient sensation of the mind, as Plato contended. It is really there.

The twentieth-century Christian essayist and poet G. K. Chesterton saw this assertion of the ultimate credibility of our senses and, therefore, of the reality of nature as Thomas's greatest contribution to the Christian faith. This is how Chesterton paraphrased what Thomas was saying to Aristotle's critics:

> I am not ashamed to say that I find my reason fed by my senses; that I owe a great deal of what I think to what I see and smell and taste and handle; and that so far as my reason is concerned, I feel obliged to treat all this reality as real. To be brief, in all humility, I do not believe that God meant man to exercise only that peculiar, uplifted and abstracted sort of intellect which you are so fortunate as to possess: but I believe that there is a middle field of facts, which are given by the senses to be the subject matter of the reason; and that in that field the reason has a right to rule, as the representative of God and man. It is true that all this is lower than the angels; but it is higher than the animals and all the material objects man finds around him. True, man can also be an object; and even a deplorable object. But what man has done man may do; and if an antiquated old heathen called Aristotle can help me to do it, I will thank him in all humility. (*St. Thomas Aquinas*, published posthumously in 1943)

Thomas, concluded Chesterton, was "more of a theologian, more of an orthodox theologian, more of a dogmatist, in having recovered through Aristotle the most defiant of all dogmas, the wedding of God with man and therefore with matter." He had provided, that is, a philosophical rationale for the incarnation of the Word of God in the person of Jesus Christ.

Thomas had done something else as well, although probably unintentionally. He had contributed significantly to the philosophical foundation of modern science. If conclusions reached through empirical observation (i.e., through our senses) could be taken as credible, it followed that thought, discussion, and eventually experimentation with physical nature could be considered a valid exercise for Christian universities. He was encouraged in this line of thought by his first teacher among the Dominicans, who focused particular attention on Aristotle's "natural philosophy," the study of nature, soon to be known as "science."

This man, some twenty years older than Thomas, was Albert the German, who came from Swabia and who taught Thomas for at least three years (and perhaps as many as five) at Cologne. Even within his lifetime Albert would become known as Albertus Magnus (Albert the Great), and the heavy emphasis he laid on "the evidence of the senses," along with his early experiments with siphons and vacuums, cause some to regard him as a father of modern science. Albert himself saw Thomas as a far greater figure. "You call him a dumb ox," said Albert. "I tell you this dumb ox shall bellow so loud that his bellowings will fill the world."

Albert and Thomas were in total agreement, however, about avoiding the "theologization" of natural philosophy because, as Albert wrote,

> Anything that is taken on the evidence of the senses is superior to that which is opposed to sense observations; a conclusion which is inconsistent with the evidence of the senses is not to be believed; and a principle that does not accord with the experimental knowledge of the senses is not a principle but rather its opposite. (William A. Wallace, *Causality and Scientific Explanation*)

As Aristotle's (and Thomas's) critics pointed out, a dangerous principle was being asserted here. What would happen if human reasoning, now so sanctified, were to be applied to the scriptures and the Christian creeds? If the latter were found to be irrational, which view would prevail?

At the University of Paris,[1] where Thomas taught after he left Cologne, work on "natural philosophy" was at first forbidden. Later it was authorized but only if those studying it stayed away from theology. This was a fortuitous decision, observes Edward Grant in his comprehensive study *God and Reason in the Middle Ages*, since its effect was to liberate the study of natural philosophy (i.e., science) from the vigilance of ecclesiastical critics. The Aristotelian avalanche soon created such a rapidly rising interest in the physical sciences that it would be more true to say that the scientific revolution began in the thirteenth century, not the sixteenth or seventeenth, the centuries usually assigned to it.

By Thomas's time Europe's universities were at work on geology, oceanography, meteorology, physics, and mathematics. And yet, notes Grant, medieval scholars were not scientists in the modern sense. They speculated, but they did not experiment. They were absorbed, for instance, by the question of whether anything is ever at rest. Throw a ball up in the air, and it will go up and come down. Is there an instant between its ascent and descent when it is not moving either way? Or watch a sphere rotate. A location on its widest circumference (its "equator") will travel a considerable distance with each rotation. One close to its "pole" will hardly move at all. The closer you come to the axis, the slower a particular spot on the surface will move. Is there a point, its real axis, which is motionless? All fascinating, but the idea of setting up an experiment and observing actual results hardly ever occurred to them.

This reliance upon reason was by no means confined to the students of natural philosophy. Theology also quickly became rationally focused. "Reason in the university context of the [Middle Ages] was not intended for the acquisition of power over others, or to improve the well-being of the general populace," writes Grant. "Its primary purpose was to elucidate the natural and supernatural worlds . . . [They became] a society obsessed with reason . . . Nothing like it had ever been seen."

1. The name "Sorbonne," commonly used to refer to the University of Paris, is derived from the college founded in 1257 by Robert of Sorbon, a significant addition to the University of Paris, which predated the college by roughly a century. Sorbonne College was shut down during the French Revolution, reopened by Napoleon in 1808, and closed for good seventy-four years later. Meanwhile "Sorbonne" became a colloquial term for the entire university.

The costly pride of Peter Abelard

The brilliant prof who dazzled the young meets catastrophe in a tragic love affair; then, amid failures, he resigns the struggle to find peace and, in posterity, fame

Whether Peter Abelard was the most brilliant man of his times or a failed saint or an exhibitionist nuisance, all three views were held by his critics and admirers in the twelfth century, as they would be held by his critics and admirers in all the centuries that followed.

That his life was a tragedy, however—embracing, as it does, a tragic love affair, his repeated failure in monastic life, and the condemnation of his teaching by a church council—has been universally acknowledged. But he died at peace with God and his enemies, it is said, so perhaps his real story, if it ever be known, will not turn out to be a tragedy after all.

It begins at the little village of Palet, near Nantes in Brittany. The eldest son of a minor noble, Abelard early evidenced an extraordinary ability in dialectic (rational argument). He elected an academic career at age fifteen and entered the famed cathedral school of Notre Dame in Paris, where he became so adept at the argumentative put-down that he humiliated the school's leading philosophical authority and was asked to leave. Undiscouraged, he established his own competing school near Paris (first at Melun, then at Corbeil), where he attracted the adulation of the youngest and brightest scholars.

Within a few years he moved his school to the top of Mount Saint Genevieve, today considered more of a hill than a mountain but nevertheless symbolically looking down on the old Notre Dame. (Construction of the present cathedral did not begin for another fifty years.) By now he had switched to theology and was soon besting his own teachers in this field as well. Inevitably, he came down from the mountain in 1115 to head up the theology faculty at the cathedral school.

He was now enormously popular, his lectures attracting huge crowds, and by his own later admission he became vainer, more arrogant, and cordially detested by fellow academics. One fervent admirer, however, was a certain Heloise, niece of Canon Fulburt of the cathedral faculty. She was beautiful and rendered more attractive still, Abelard writes, by her wide knowledge of Greek, Latin, Hebrew, and classical letters. Abelard became her tutor, then her lover.

When she became pregnant, he sent her to Brittany, where their son was born. Then, over Heloise's objections (she did not want to destroy his clerical career) they were secretly married, and to escape the rage of her uncle, she took refuge in a convent.[1] Canon Fulburt, believing Abelard intent on abandoning her, broke into his bedchamber one night with several companions and castrated him, thus barring him from the priesthood and episcopal office. Heloise, at Peter's bidding, then became a nun. Their secret love letters, discovered in the fif-

teenth century, have since become classics.

From there, though he was still idolized by thousands, the path of the brilliant dialectician led irreversibly downward. With his position at the cathedral school already lost, he decided to become a monk at the royal Abbey of St-Denis, where he loftily informed his new colleagues that the St. Denis they revered was actually three different men conflated into one (see page 42). The monks in their fury seized on one of his scholarly papers and charged him with heresy; a provincial synod forced him to burn that paper and transferred him to an abbey at Soissons. But there, too, he took particular delight in teasing the other monks with erudite exposures of their primitive beliefs until, as he perhaps had hoped, they demanded he be sent somewhere else.

Adopting the life of a hermit, Abelard then built himself a cabin of reeds near Nogent-sur-Seine, naming the place the Oratory of the Paraclete (Holy Spirit), and students began flocking from Paris and beyond to hear him teach. However, his enemies, who were many, also discovered his whereabouts, and fearing for his safety, he asked to be sent to another monastery. He accepted the post of abbot in a wild and lawless coastal region of Brittany, where even the monks were undisciplined and uncontrollable.

In one of the rewarding triumphs of his life, however, he was then able to establish a Convent of the Paraclete on the site of his oratory and have Heloise installed as abbess. During those trying years, he also wrote his autobiography, *The Story of My Calamities*, attributing his downfall entirely to his pride. He describes his love life with Heloise in graphic language, but by now their relationship had become like that of a brother and sister.

But Abelard had not yet confronted his greatest challenge. This would be posed by Bernard of Clairvaux, who, though an admirer of Abelard, was persuaded to bring his writings before a church council at Sens and with telling eloquence accused him of teaching "error." Surprisingly, Abelard did not contest the charge but instead appealed to Rome. The council, meanwhile, condemned his writings. En route to Rome to defend his case, Abelard collapsed at the abbey of Cluny, where his friend (and Bernard's) the abbot Peter the Venerable persuaded him to quit fighting and make his peace with God and with Bernard.

This Abelard did. With death close approaching, he was moved for his comfort to the Priory of Chalon-sur-Saone and died there in 1142, at the age of sixty-three. Soon afterward his remains were removed to the Oratory of the Paraclete, where Heloise was buried beside him when she died twenty-one years later.

Abelard and Heloise, two iconic lovers seen together in this nineteenth-century painting by Edmund Blair Leighton. After spending an early life at odds with authority, Abelard surrenders and repents, meanwhile establishing Heloise as abbess of a convent. Their letters, now as between brother and sister, survive. In the century after his death his writings strongly influenced a new generation of Christian scholars.

His influence, notes the *Catholic Encyclopedia*, was far greater in the thirteenth century than it was in his own, the twelfth, when the church's rejection of some of his works and the fierce animosities inspired by the haughty sarcasm of his days of triumph still inhibited support for him. But as the years passed and the young people who thronged to read and hear him became the dominant generation, many came to emulate his approach to theology and philosophy, overlooking the fact that his vast array of scholarly work sometimes "savored" of Arianism, Pelagianism, and Nestorianism. Later admirers would hail him as the "first modern man" and as "founder" of the University of Paris—opinions that should be discounted, says the *Encyclopedia*.

"His intellectual independence and dialectical methods," says the *Oxford Dictionary of the Christian Church*, "naturally aroused the opposition of authoritarian mystics like St. Bernard. But his influence, through his lectures, was enormous. His success came rather through the brilliance and freshness with which he handled particular problems than in the propagation of an elaborate system." It concludes cryptically: "His distrust of authority, where it was genuinely traditional, must not be exaggerated."

Perhaps Abelard himself best summed up his position. "I would not be a philosopher," he wrote to Heloise, "if it implies disobedience to Paul. I would not be an Aristotle and separated from Christ. For there is none other name under heaven wherein I must be saved." ■

1. Nothing definite is known of Abelard's son, Astrolabe (named for an astronomical instrument), who, says historian Betty Radice, "played so small a part in his parents' lives." It seems he led a monastic life and eventually had a stipend at a cathedral secured for him by Peter the Venerable after Heloise urged the abbot to assist him.

Thomas became fast friends with the Franciscan Bonaventure, shown above in a sixteenth-century Renaissance painting by Alessandro Bonvicino. The fact that they represented two mendicant orders that would long tend toward rivalry does not appear to have eroded their friendship.

2. The term "secular clergy" originated in the twelfth century to distinguish the priests living in the world and serving parishes from those who belonged to religious orders (called "regular clergy" because they lived by a rule, in Latin "regula"). Members of the former were bound only by vows of chastity and could own property but were subject to the authority of their bishops. A "secular" priest took precedence over a "regular" priest of equal rank.

Indeed, reason played a greater role in theology than in the more secular subjects. In the twelfth and thirteenth centuries it was viewed as a tool to reinforce faith. Not until the seventeenth century was it adopted as a weapon to attack faith."

The "schoolmen," as scholasticism's practitioners came to be called, ferociously applied the laws of logic to debate such questions as the proofs for the existence of God, the implications of man's fall from grace, the inevitability of human sin, the atonement, the factor of "personhood" in the Trinity, and the value of faith as against good works. What was the nature of the Eucharist, or Lord's Supper? Could the saints answer prayer? What was the role of the Virgin Mary in salvation? In the eighteenth century, Grant observes, when reason was invoked to discredit faith, such unbelievers became known as "rationalists," but if reliance on reason denotes a rationalist, "then you could equally say that Thomas Aquinas was a rationalist."

Thomas did not much engage in natural philosophy, however. "What is God?" he had asked as a child, and he spent most of his life providing an answer. And however skilled as a controversialist, he was primarily a writer and teacher. Torrell calculates that he produced 4,061 handwritten pages of work at Paris between October 1268 and April 1272, the equivalent of nearly thirteen close-typed pages daily. This included massive work on his primary project, a summation of Christian teaching known as the *Summa Theologica* (still being drawn on by Catholic thinkers in the third Christian millennium as one of the credible sources of church teaching), plus 331 other articles. A twentieth-century study of Thomas's thinking by the German philosopher Martin Grabmann (*Thomas Aquinas: His Personality and Thought*, translated by Virgil Michel) assessing the whole corpus of Thomas's work counts twenty-two "philosophical writings," three major works "chiefly theological," thirteen books on various theological questions, twelve on "points of dogma," three on apologetics, six on "practical theology," eleven on "religious life," and ten scriptural commentaries.

He reputedly began each day before dawn by saying one Mass and hearing another, then worked straight through to the service of compline, around nine in the evening. He is said to have toiled on as many as five projects at a time, dictating to as many secretaries. He began each undertaking with a prayer and when confronted with an intractable problem would drop to his knees and seek divine help. His abstractions were legendary. His meals were brought to him, but he seemed scarcely conscious that he was eating them. His dress was slovenly, and caustic remarks about his appearance amused him. Comments on his great girth he found extremely funny, especially references to the crescent-shaped cut that had to be made in his desk to accommodate his stomach. Though he could deal with the most abstruse questions of Christian theology, he repeatedly warned future teachers to "keep it simple" and strove mightily to do so himself. He endeared himself to many; Albertus Magnus reportedly missed him so much after Thomas moved to Paris that he would weep at the mention of his name.

Thomas's skill as a debater could extend well beyond theology and philosophy into church politics. In 1229, when Thomas was about four, the mendicant orders, the Dominicans and Franciscans, had set up schools at the University of Paris. Their welcome had been anything but hospitable. The students and secular clergy[2] teaching at the university had rioted; several students had been killed in the resulting crackdown, and the students had just gone on strike to protest such heavy-handedness. So the mendicants had unexpectedly found themselves cast in the role of strikebreakers. The resulting conflict would rage for the next thirty years, sometimes violently, with the friars occasionally beaten up on the streets or teaching under armed guard. Thomas arrived from Cologne in 1252. He was chosen at the unusually young age of thirty to deliver the inaugural lecture two years later, at a time when another student-faculty strike had been called to protest the mendicants' getting too many appointments. Thomas delivered the lecture while the king's archers protected the building and a student mob blocked many from hearing him.

So persistent was the mendicant-secular conflict that Rome repeatedly intervened to make peace, one pope deciding for the seculars, his successor for the mendicants. Finally, a formal hearing was called. The mendicants had two advocates: Thomas represented the Dominicans while John of Fidanza became the Franciscan representative. John was another distinguished academic, one day to be canonized as St. Bonaventure. (Though divided on a number of theological issues, the two would become fast friends.) The seculars were represented by the fevered William of Saint-Amour, described by one of the twentieth century's senior historians of this affair as "irascible, violent and obstinate" (Marie-Michel Dufeil, *William of Saint-Amour and the University of Paris Polemic, 1250–1259*).

Many major background issues were involved. First, it was widely believed that monks should remain in monasteries, not wander about preaching and begging. Second, it was argued that Christians living in community should hold all property in common as in the apostolic age (Acts 4:32). The mendicants, having no property, could not do so. Third, the rule of Benedict, which had established the basic requirements for monastic life seven hundred years earlier, required that monks *work*, and begging didn't qualify. Therefore, it was argued, these mendicants should be dispatched into monasteries, put to work, and ordered to stay there.

Thomas was not the dispassionate and humorless scholar that his writings portray. He seemed to find his great girth comical, for instance. This was especially true of his custom-made desk with a crescent-shaped cut in it to accommodate his paunch so that he could bring his arms close enough to write. When anyone would mention this, he would laugh uproariously.

Born of the battle they lost

Dominic's Order of Preachers failed to convert by preaching the Cathar heretics,
but the letters OP would follow the names of distinguished Christians to this day

With a sparkling academic record, disciplined habits, a stubborn but generous nature, a strong faith, and a proven ability to resolve intractable problems, Dominic de Guzman Garces had every reason to be confident about his mission in the south of France in 1206. Yet nothing, it seems, could have adequately prepared this accomplished and dedicated man for what he would find there. For the first time in his life, he would suffer a major defeat.

He was sent to Toulouse to thwart the seemingly irresistible advance of the Cathar heresy. The challenge was not to persecute the *Cathari* but to restore them to the Christian fold. A contingent of Cistercian teachers sent by Pope Innocent III to do so was failing miserably and wanted to leave. The regular clergy of Toulouse, accustomed to soft living and unable to match the zeal and magnetism of their chief heretical adversary, the abstemious and energetic Cathars, could make no gains either. "Our watchdogs," Innocent bitterly commented, "have lost their bark."

Dominic soon concluded that the Cathars could only be reached intellectually. They specialized in what they advanced as reasoned theology. In argument they could triumphantly make fools of any Christian adversaries they encountered. This, along with their austere and outwardly holy lives, was winning them converts everywhere. What was needed, Dominic reasoned, was a team of men grounded theologically, convincing rhetorically, and sharp in argument but living lives every bit as abstemious as those of the Cathars.

So he went among them, not as a well-fed missionary from the affluent church, nor as a polished academic from one of the respected universities, but as a beggar. The scorn they poured on the clergy couldn't be applied to him. He had nothing. But neither, he found, could he convince them. For two years he tried, and but for a few converts he failed. His failure was wholly underlined in 1209 when the pope declared a holy crusade against the Cathars (see sidebar, pages 230–233).

However, in one other respect he succeeded magnificently. Perhaps even to his own astonishment, others began joining him, most of them men of high intellectual capability. They agreed with and shared in his commitment to total poverty. They begged and they studied and they honed their skill with words, and they became known as the "Dominicans," after Dominic de Guzman Garces.

The de Guzmans were an unusually devout family. Dominic's mother, Juana, was said to have dreamed before his birth of a dog carrying a torch that set fire to the world.[1] Juana would be beatified, as would Dominic's elder brother, renowned as a saver of souls; another brother was much admired for his work among the poor. But it was Dominic himself, the youngest, who would leave the strongest imprint on Christian history, and this began when he was sent to Toulouse to contend with the Cathars.

Dominic had certainly heard about these people (variously known in France as the Albigensians, in Italy as the Patarini, and in eastern Europe as the Bogomils) and about their extreme dualistic beliefs and their penchant for suicide and, occasionally, murder or assassination. Still, nothing in his background had particularly fitted him to deal with them. The Cathars reveled in theological argument, for example, whereas Dominic had never considered himself a theologian, having dropped out of the University of Palencia for a time when famine struck that city. He could not stand idly by while famished parents watched their children starve, he protested; he sold all his possessions, even his precious book collection, to help them. "Would you have had me study off these dead skins," he would demand, flipping through the parchment pages of a book, "when men are dying of hunger?"

Neither, for that matter, would his subsequent work at Osma, near Spain's northeast corner, seem of much application. Before he was twenty-five Dominic had been summoned there by its bishop to reform the priests of the cathedral chapter, who had become corrupt, unproductive, and lazy, and he succeeded well enough to become superior of the chapter. But how would these experiences help him deal with the quick-tongued, sharp-witted Cathari? They were not starving, and, heaven knows, not lazy. In fact, they were bursting with energy. That, indeed, was part of the problem.

An insurmountable problem, as he and his Dominicans found, and they discovered something else. They found that they could not define the purpose of their growing community as one of refutation. They could not become specialists in disproof, denial, contravention, and contradiction. They could not build on negatives. They must focus on what's true rather than what's false. They had their own message to deliver. In short, they must advance the Gospel of Christ; they must preach the Word. They must become an order of preachers. And when in 1216 they took their case to be recognized as an order to Pope Honorius III, that is what he called them. They became *Ordo Praedicatorum*, the Order of Preachers.[2] And who taught them to preach? Jesus Christ, they would say, Jesus Christ and the Cathars.

Over the ensuing centuries, tens of thousands of men all over the world would carry the letters OP after their names, signifying that they were Dominicans, successors in the work of Dominic de Guzman Garces. Pope Honorius offered them Rome's Church of St. Sixtus as a home base, and before long preachers in the Dominican order, living as beggars and known as friars—as distinct from monks—had spread through western Europe, expounding the Gospel and establishing schools. The black robe they wore over their white habit made them known as the "Blackfriars," the name of their college at Oxford.

They also began serving in senior ecclesiastical positions; within a century 450 Dominicans had been appointed to the high offices of the Church, a total that included two popes and some dozen cardinals. Furthermore, the two most brilliant medieval scholars—Thomas Aquinas and Albert Magnus (see foregoing chapter)—both carried the letters OP after their names, as did Meister Eckhart of Hochheim, known widely as the father of German mysticism.

Dominican literary output included theological treatises, biblical translation, poetry, and the largest medieval encyclopedia, while artistic Dominicans exerted a profound influence on late medieval painting and on the development of Gothic architecture. Finally, they also served the monarchies of Europe as confessors, advisers, and ambassadors, often negotiating treaties between hostile Christian nations.

Especially in view of their origins as combatants against heresy, they inevitably played a role in the medieval Inquisition. Indeed, Dominic's later critics would accuse him of launching it, but Henry Charles Lea in his *History of the Inquisition of the Middle Ages* asserts that this is not true. Though Dominic might "stand by the pyre" to see a stubborn heretic burned, it was not until more than ten years after his death in 1221 that such an institution as the papal Inquisition can be said to have existed. Even so, counters the *Catholic Encyclopedia*, there can be little doubt that inquisitors were disproportionately drawn from the Dominican order.

By the fifteenth century there was a world of Dominicans to draw from—Persian Dominicans, Dominicans in Africa, Dominicans on the Indian subcontinent. The friars would be somewhat eclipsed in the dazzling light of the Renaissance but would recover with the discovery of the New World; in the seventeenth century their numbers would peak and their missions reach from Japan to Cuba. The order would decline once again during the anti-Christian violence of the French Revolution, then revive to produce a nineteenth-century Dominican renaissance that would do much to restore Christianity in continental Europe.

In short, like all genuinely Christian initiatives, and indeed like Christianity itself, Dominican vigor rises and wanes. So, too, does their love-hate relationship with their nearest Christian cousins, the Franciscans, the other order of friars founded in the same era and likewise mendicant servants of Christ (see chapter 10). Though Francis and Dominic saw eye to eye, often their disciples have not, and their chronic feuds have been far from edifying. "Too many obvious grounds for jealousy" observes historian R. F. Bennett (*The Early Dominicans*). "Nothing could prevent petty irritation and minor feuds in the lower ranks."

Still, the Dominicans continue their original mission as effective preachers who, in obedience to their rule, must "go forth and behave everywhere as men seeking their own salvation and that of their neighbors, in all perfection and with a truly religious spirit, as evangelical men, that is, men following in the footsteps of their Savior." ∎

1. The word "Dominicans" later became a Latin pun—*Domini canes*, "dogs of the Lord"—which also took into account the dream of Dominic's mother. This metaphorical dog arguably did set his world on fire in a real sense.

2. More than a decade before Pope Honorius officially recognized the Order of Preachers, Dominic had already begun establishing the Dominican Sisters. The Monastery of Prouille, in the Diocese of Toulouse, was founded for the women whom he and the other missionaries converted from heresy. According to the *Catholic Encyclopedia*, Dominic used this establishment as "the center of union of his missions and of his apostolic works." The ascetic life of the sisters is the same as that of the friars. They celebrated their eight hundredth anniversary in 2006.

Pope Honorius III approving the rule of the Dominican order in 1216, as envisioned by Leandro Bassano in the sixteenth century. These men, whose name later became a pun—Domini canes, or "God's dogs"—would be used widely by the popes to fight heresy. Though skilled in logic and debate, their forte lay in their eloquence, and therefore they still carry the designation OP, for Ordo Praedicatorum (Order of Preachers), behind their names.

THOMAS ON MAN'S THREE NECESSITIES FOR SALVATION:

Three things are necessary for the salvation of man: to know what he ought to believe, to know what he ought to desire, and to know what he ought to do.

3. In his biography *Saint Thomas Aquinas* historian Jean-Pierre Torrell vigorously defends Siger of Brabant. Thomas's ideas of what the Averroists were saying came, he said, not from Siger, nor from Averroes's own writings, but from the attacks on them being made by anti-Aristotelians at the University of Paris. Averroism, in other words, was a theology invented by its detractors. Siger was not an Averroist at all, says Torrell. Indeed, he had read Thomas's works assiduously and as he grew older became a dedicated Thomist.

4. Despite Thomas's best efforts, missionaries to Muslims, both Protestant and Catholic, report that reasoned argument and rational presentations rarely persuade Muslims of Christian truth. They are far more likely to be impressed by the spirit of Christ they see reflected in the lives of the missionaries and other Christians.

Deftly, gently, and devastatingly, Thomas tore William's case to shreds so thoroughly that the pope vindicated the mendicants and asked King Louis IX to banish William and his three chief supporters from France. Louis declined, perhaps considering such a penalty too severe. Later, however, William published a paper portraying the mendicants as the false preachers who would appear before the coming of the Antichrist (1 John 2:18). When the church condemned this document, Louis relented, and William departed from France.

Thomas's next confrontation was even more formidable, as was the challenger. The Englishman John Peckham, regent of the Franciscans in Paris and a future archbishop of Canterbury, destined to work sweeping reforms within the church in England, was probably the most vigorous foe Thomas ever faced. The issue was now Aristotle. Should study of his work be banned in Christian universities? Many thought so; indeed, it seemed at one point that nearly everybody thought so. Thomas found himself heatedly opposed by the Augustinians, many Dominicans, most Franciscans, the bishop of Paris, and nearly all the masters at the University of Paris. Peckham, arguing that Thomas's work should be condemned as heretical and burned, castigated him personally in a long and violent harangue. Thomas responded courteously and logically, thus further enraging Peckham. The issue finally came before a church court presided over by the firmly anti-Aristotelian bishop of Paris, where all hope for Thomas must have seemed lost. Chesterton describes what happened:

> The prospects of any Aristotelian culture in Christendom looked very dark indeed. Anathema after anathema was thundered from high places; and under the shadow of the persecution, as so often happens, it seemed for a moment that barely one or two figures stood alone in the storm-swept area. They were both in the black and white of the Dominicans; for Albertus and Aquinas stood firm.
>
> In that sort of combat there is always confusion; and majorities change into minorities and back again, as if by magic. It is always difficult to date the turn of a tide, which seems to be a welter of eddies; the very dates seeming to overlap and confuse the crisis. But the change, from the moment when the two Dominicans stood alone to the moment when the whole Church at last wheeled into line with them, may perhaps be found when they were practically brought before a hostile but a not unjust judge.
>
> Stephen Tempier, the Bishop of Paris, was apparently a rather fine specimen of the old fanatical churchman, who thought that admiring Aristotle was a weakness likely to be followed by adoring Apollo. He was also, by a piece of bad luck, one of the old conservatives who intensely resented the popular revolution of the Preaching Friars. But he was an honest man; and Thomas Aquinas never asked for anything but permission to address honest men.
>
> It would seem that the triumph of Thomas was really a personal triumph. He withdrew not a single one of his propositions; though the reactionary bishop did condemn some of them after his death. On the whole, we may say that [with the Tempier decision] the great Greek philosopher entered finally into the system of Christendom. The process has half humorously been described as the Baptism of Aristotle.

But Thomas's wars were not yet over. He had one more to fight, one he did not expect. As noted above, the versions of Aristotle reaching western Christendom in the thirteenth century came largely from Muslim Spain in the form of commentaries by Averroes. Indeed, many Aristotelians at Paris called themselves "Averroists." Their chief spokesman, Siger of Brabant, now hailed Thomas's victory as a victory for Averroism and triumphantly produced a paper to this effect. Thomas was appalled. Fundamental to his defense of Aristotle was his insistence that Averroism was a perversion of what Aristotle actually taught. His enemies had warned that if Aristotle were approved, the Averroists would claim their beliefs ratified. Now it was happening.

Armed with new translations of Aristotle by one of his fellow Dominicans, Thomas produced a refutation of what he established as the two chief errors of Averroism. The first error was that reason is a collective entity shared by the soul of mankind as a species. No, Thomas contended, there is no collective human soul; each of us has his own and through it is endowed individually with the power to think, to know right from wrong, and—up to a point, anyhow—to exercise a free will. The second Averroist error concerned him even more, namely the claim that there could be two kinds of truth, that a man could believe one thing theologically yet base his daily life on something quite incompatible with it. Philosopher McInerny sums up Thomas's objection to this idea in twenty words: "It would be impious to suggest that God presents for our acceptance as true something we know to be false." The bishop of Paris again came down on Thomas's side. The Averroist propositions were condemned.[3]

There yet remained another adversary, one that Christians had been opposing for six centuries: Islam. For more than 175 years men had been dying in the Crusades to reverse its spread. But even if such offensives succeeded, which by the year 1259 was looking less and less likely, what would really be accomplished? Although stopping the Muslims might be necessary, the clear Christian duty was not to kill them but to bring them to Christ. So Thomas produced his second-greatest work, *Summa Contra Gentiles*, a manual for missionaries to Islamic peoples.[4]

His masterpiece remained uncompleted, however. He knew that Aristotle and Aristotelian methods could be an effective new means of preaching and teaching the Gospel of Jesus Christ but would first require a whole new presentation of what Christians believe. This was the role of the *Summa Theologica* (properly the *Summa Theologiae*, though the other title is popularly used). By the 1270s two of its three parts were finished. The first is a reasoned explication of the essential

The Triumph of St. Thomas Aquinas, *by fifteenth-century artist Benozzo Gozzoli. The uppermost inscription ascribes a quotation to Christ that translates, "You have written well about me, Thomas." Aquinas himself is shown seated, holding his works, between the philosophers Aristotle and Plato, while the Muslim scholar Averroes lies beaten at his feet. The image along the bottom appears to be a discussion of scripture at a church council.*

A page from an original copy of Thomas's Summa Theologica, his life's work. These tomes were so all encompassing that centuries later they would still be used as one of the fundamental bases for Catholic theological teaching throughout the world.

concepts of Christian belief based on scripture: the unity of God, the Holy Trinity, the creation of the universe, the distinction between good and evil, angels, the dual nature of man (physical and spiritual), and the laws that make it possible for men to live with one another. The second deals with Christian morality: God's plan for man, how what we believe and do determines our destiny, our passions and habits, the law, and the grace of God. It then focuses on the seven Christian virtues: fortitude, justice, temperance, prudence, faith, hope, and love (see subchapter, page 202). The third part, opening with the Incarnation, Thomas had to leave unfinished.[5]

He had labored on the *Summa* at all the schools to which the Dominicans assigned him—at Paris, Rome, Orvieto in Italy, back to Rome, and then back to Paris. He traveled frequently (some nine thousand miles, Torrell estimates), nearly all of it on foot. In 1272 he returned for a further term at Naples, and there, in December 1273, he underwent a profound transformation that shocked everyone who knew him and has puzzled historians ever since. It seems to have occurred when he was celebrating Mass in the Chapel of St. Nicholas. The closest friend of his later years, the Dominican Reginald of Piperno, noticed the change immediately and asked him what happened. "I cannot do any more," was Thomas's inexplicable reply. He began disposing of his writing materials, and again Reginald, now "stupefied," asked him why. "I cannot do any more," Thomas repeated. "Everything I have written seems to me as straw in comparison to what I have seen."

His strength, hitherto so robust, now rapidly failed. He was taken to the home of his sister the countess Theodora, near Naples, but when summoned to a church council at Lyon, where Pope Gregory X was seeking reunion with the Orthodox Church, Thomas responded. Now frail and faltering, he tripped and fell on the road but assured his companions that he was fine.

As they passed Montecassino, the monastery of his childhood, the abbot asked him to visit and help resolve a problem the monks there were pondering. Thomas agreed even to this, though it meant a steep six-mile detour. He heard their question and noted down the answer—the last thing he would ever write.[6] Laboring onward, he stopped at the Benedictine Abbey of Fossanova, where he lay for several weeks, becoming gradually weaker. On March 4 or 5, 1274, Reginald heard his final confession. It was, he wrote, "like the confession of a five-year-old child." Three days later Thomas of Aquino died.

Death did not resolve the controversies that swirled around him. By then Frederick II also had died (some twenty years before), and the church, turning to the French as a relief from the Germans, had placed its confidence in Charles of Anjou. For the Aquino family, already refugees in the papal states, this was not good news. When Charles chased them out of there, they claimed that their celebrated son, Thomas, had actually been murdered by imperial agents. This allegation long persisted, affirmed by Dante Alighieri, preeminent poet of the late Middle Ages who was eight years old when Thomas died. Twentieth-century historians, says Torrell, give it no credence whatsoever.

Much more interesting is the question surrounding Thomas's strange transformation of December 1273. Did a mystical experience occur at that Mass? Did his long habit of abstraction turn into anorexia, so that in effect he was starving himself to death? Was it a cerebral stroke? Was it a physical and mental breakdown from overwork? "We must have the honesty to recognize that none of these explanations seems convincing," Torrell concludes, adding that if he had to choose, nervous exhaustion coupled with a mystical experience seems most plausible.

Where Thomas Aquinas should be buried remained controversial for centuries. The monks of Fossanova first buried him near their main altar. Then, lest Dominicans demand the body or relic-seeking grave robbers steal it, they secreted it within their cloister. When a monk particularly friendly to Thomas said he had

5. Thomas did not live long enough to complete the *Summa*. The third part was finished for him by his Dominican successors. It deals with the Incarnation, the sacraments, and the Resurrection.

6. The monks' problem was one that has dogged Christians down through the ages: How can a man sin unless his will is free? But if God already knows the future, how can man's will be free? Thomas's answer, recorded in the margin of a text by Reginald, in effect points out that all time is spread out before God. He is outside time, so all is (so to speak) the present with him. In one glance he sees what you are doing now, what you did twenty years ago, and what you will be doing twenty years from now. Yet at every point on that time line, your will is free, just as it is right now.

An aerial view of the monastery at Monte Cassino. It was here that Thomas's life in Christ began, and it was near here that it ended. While on his way to a council to end the schism between eastern and western Christians, Thomas was asked to stop and answer a question for the monks at Monte Cassino. He assented and detoured to see them, solving their problem. Only a few days later and several miles down the road, he made his last confession at the Benedictine Abbey of Fossanova.

The room at Fossanova where Aquinas died has been turned into a chapel and has become such a popular place of pilgrimage that the adjoining room has been enlarged to accommodate the steady influx of pilgrims. This bas-relief, situated above the altar, envisions Thomas's deathbed. His last confession, said the priest-friend who heard it, was like that of a little child.

appeared to him in a dream, they moved him back to the main altar. Ninety-five years later, despite urgent pleas from the University of Paris, the Dominicans prevailed after all, and Thomas's remains were moved to their church at Toulouse. In 1791, during the turmoil of the French Revolution, they were transferred to the Basilica of St. Sernin, where they remained until 1974, when they were returned to the Church of the Jacobins in Toulouse.

The fiercest fight of all, however, broke out within weeks of his death between the old Augustinian conservatives in the theology faculty and the new Aristotelians in the arts faculty. In this collision of extremists, both sides were notably anti-Thomas. The theology faculty objected to him as too Aristotelian, the arts faculty because he wasn't Aristotelian (meaning Averroist) enough. Finally, the new pope, John XXI, asked the elderly archbishop of Paris, the same man who had favored Thomas back in 1270, to adjudicate. This time Stephen Tempier went the other way. It took him less than a month to conclude that 219 propositions favored by Aquinas should be condemned.

The pope acquiesced and urged the archbishop to "cleanse" the arts faculty.[7] While the Augustinians joyously noted that a great many of these men had been taught by Thomas, his old enemies eagerly moved in for the kill, the Franciscan John Peckham pressing to have the condemnation of Aquinas made specific. This controversy is usually portrayed as a battle between the two mendicant orders, but some notable Dominicans were actively anti-Thomas, prominent among them Robert Kilwardby, the archbishop of Canterbury, and others in the order's Oxford chapter. Most Dominicans soon rose to Thomas's defense, however. The Oxford chapter came under severe criticism from the rest of the order, and with the new century, the fourteenth, the attacks on him waned. On July 18, 1323, he was canonized as St. Thomas Aquinas, and in 1568 Pope St. Pius V named him a doctor of the church, Catholicism's highest theological distinction.

Even so, he remained a storm center. After his death scholasticism swiftly began to atrophy and broke into competitive factions. The Franciscans came to be represented by Duns Scotus and, from the mid-fourteenth century, by the nom-

7. This hasty decision by Pope John XXI has been subject to question and criticism ever since. Torrell lists eight twentieth-century historians who have "returned to it to evaluate its bearing and consequences."

inalist William of Ockham. The Dominicans were divided into Albertists and Thomists, though Albert and Thomas had never been divided. Thomism itself, now squarely backed by the church, became a closed system, shutting out new ideas and always answering challenging questions with pat quotations from the *Summa*. "Those who followed his methods degenerated with a great rapidity," writes Chesterton (though not all Catholic historians would agree with him). "Of some scholastics we can only say that they took everything that was worst in

The foundations for science are laid

By insisting that all truth must be one, Thomas paved the way for scientific advance

Professor X teaches biology at a top-ranked American university and worships devoutly at a local church. How does he reconcile his scientific beliefs with his religious ones? "Very simply," he would explain. "Scientific truths are one thing, Christian truths quite different things." Yet Thomas Aquinas would say that Professor X is wrong. There cannot be two truths, he insisted, but only one—though finite human minds can never knit that infinite truth into a single formula.

Professor X is fictitious, but his position—that there is more than one kind of truth—is not fictitious at all. It has been held by many Christians, not all of them scientists. However, in the thirteenth century Christians found themselves particularly divided, with some advocating a distinction between scientific truth and religious truth, others holding that only divine revelation can disclose what's true. Thomas offered a way of resolving the controversy. He united what we can learn from thought (i.e., reason) with what God has revealed to us directly (i.e., revelation). But they must both be considered truth, he said, because there can be only one truth.

It wasn't a popular answer. Both sides accused him of compromise, but it gradually became the accepted view, and thus the Christians set the stage for a truly progressive, modern science. But neither was it an altogether new answer. As far back as the sixth century the Christian philosopher Anicius Manlius Severinus Boethius had insisted, "*Fidem rationemque coniunge*"— "Join faith and reason."

Yet even in Boethius's day, it had been a departure from the human norm. Nearly all civilizations have implicitly divided themselves into "two truths"—with the learned holding an elite philosophy and everyone else a folk myth. But Christians have tended to resist this division. If God created the material world and nature "proclaims his glory," they say, then Christianity should nurture science. While physical science must progress by its own rules, they regard dogmatically atheistic science as unscientific. It has moved out of the scientific field into the theological to voice a plainly unscientific antagonism toward faith.

What raised the issue in the thirteenth century was the rediscovery in the West of Aristotle's "natural philosophy." In the fourth century BC, the great philosopher had developed a philosophy of nature, based on the reproduction of species: trees reproducing trees, dogs reproducing dogs, and rational human beings reproducing rational humans. All these, he said, expressed the "*logos*," or "reason," of nature. This eternal logos of the material world, he concluded, requires that there exist an eternal Mind, or Divine Reason. Though not the loving Creator of later Christian revelation, here lay that which was ultimately responsible for the order, beauty, and permanence of nature.

However, Aristotle's teaching reached the West via Muslim philosopher Ibn Rushd—latinized into "Averroes"— who had died about a quarter century before Thomas was born. To Averroes, divine revelation was merely a poetic popularization of natural reason. True human bliss lay in philosophic contemplation, but this was reserved for the wise. The populace needs myths like personal immortality, heaven, and hell to make them live moral lives in decent societies. So religion is simply the poetic expression of abstract philosophic truths. Theologians must learn from philosophers the truths of nature and translate them into divine myths—but otherwise leave philosophers alone in their contemplation.

When western followers of Averroes made the same claims for natural science within Christendom, the knee-jerk reaction of many Christians was to ban Aristotle altogether. After all, had not the great Augustine himself stressed the total dependence of creation on its Creator? But Thomas realized that God has granted creation a qualified independence, governed by natural laws and discoverable by natural reason. He saw that when focused within the limits of nature, Aristotle's natural philosophy could become a most useful tool.

Even so, many theologians resisted Thomas's effort to "baptize" Aristotle, lest science come to erode the authority of revelation. To them, it didn't matter what a man thinks about creation, so long as he has the correct opinion about God. But Thomas objected. An error about creation ends as false thinking about God, he maintained, because there can only be one truth. Eventually, his teaching prevailed and Thomas thus endowed western civilization with a solid faith in the intelligibility and benignity of the natural order, the cultural precondition out of which natural science arose in the western world. ■

Even death could not keep the tireless Thomas Aquinas from traveling. Originally interred in an unornamented tomb at Fossanova's abbey church, his relics were shipped to Toulouse on the orders of Pope Urban V in 1368. There they were placed in the Dominican Church of the Jacobins, which crosses the background, its three spires at the right of the picture. The violence of the French Revolution necessitated another move, this one to Toulouse's Basilica of St. Sernin, whose spire can be seen in the foreground. In 1974, the seventh centenary of his death, Thomas was returned to the Jacobin church, where he remains.

8. Twentieth-century historian Michael Root notes that Luther later came to give "grudging" recognition to Thomas, and some later Lutherans, in fact, became Thomists. The turning point came in the early seventeenth century, says Root, when Johann Gerhard, "the greatest of the Lutheran scholastics," often quoted Thomas to clarify or illustrate a point (*Aquinas in Dialogue: Thomas for the Twenty-First Century*).

scholasticism and made it even worse. They continued to count the steps of logic, but every step took them farther from common sense. They forgot how Thomas had started almost as an agnostic, and they seemed resolved to have nothing in heaven or earth about which anybody could be agnostic. They were sort of rabid rationalists who would have left no mysteries in the faith at all."

By the Renaissance, scholasticism was widely viewed as an entrenched establishment that in the name of reason forbade most reasoned argument. The sixteenth-century humanist Desiderius Erasmus, an unabashed foe of scholasticism, vented fury upon it: "They set up as the world's censors," he stormed. "They demand recantation of anything that doesn't exactly square with their conclusions . . . As a result, neither Paul, Peter, St. Jerome, Augustine, or even Thomas, the greatest of the Aristotelians, can make a man Christian unless these learned bachelors have given their approval." Meanwhile, one Augustinian monk focused his attention not on the scholasticism but on Thomas himself, castigating him as "the fountain and foundation of all heresy, error and obliteration of the Gospel." That monk was Martin Luther, though in later life he softened his opinion.[8]

For much-debated reasons, Thomism (see sidebar, page 199) enjoyed a startling revival in the nineteenth century, first in the Catholic Church and then beyond it. Some see this as a response to the general slide of modern philosophy into nihilism (the belief that an objective truth or existence is impossible). Having long ago parted company, that is, with the Thomistic insistence that the evidence of sense perceptions must be taken as real, philosophy was left with the pertinent question: then what *can* be believed? The response—nothing—did not seem entirely satisfactory, causing some to begin reexamining both Aristotle and Aquinas.

Thus, Chesterton, in the twentieth century, saw the renaissance of Thomism as a return to reality. The great philosophers almost all agree that we cannot accept as real that which we can see, feel, hear, taste, and smell, Chesterton noted. But in order to see a car bearing down on them or kiss their beloved or follow a delicious smell to the roast beef, they still must act as if such things are real after all. Thomas merely faced that fact.

In an encyclical issued in 1879, Pope Leo XIII formally adopted Thomism as a means of clarifying Catholic teaching. The entire Catholic world did not immediately follow the pope's wishes, but gradually Catholic schools began basing their curriculum on Thomism. One product of this was the Institute of Medieval Studies at the University of Toronto, Canada. Modern Thomists, McInerny writes, come in three types: transcendental Thomists, existential Thomists, and Aristotelian Thomists. They vary from the erudite Jesuit Karl Rahner to the earthy novelist Flannery O'Connor, who called herself a "hillbilly" Thomist.

As in his lifetime, however, Thomas's teachings continued to arouse significant wrath. For example, the introduction to a collection of essays by Mortimer Adler, a twentieth-century Jewish scholar sympathetic to Thomism, recounts in *What Man Has Made of Man* the typically dismissive definition offered him by one colleague: "Scholasticism, a sterile form of deductive thinking, developed as a harmless outlet for the reasoning powers of man in a period of intellectual servitude when man could not observe the world around himself, lest any observation come in contradiction with prevailing dogma."

Thomism's detractors, observes Adler, are rarely responding to what Thomas actually wrote. "They have not read him, nor tried to understand him; they are prevented from doing so by an evil rumor of what Thomism is, spread by the malicious, or caused by our own poor rhetoric."

Thomas himself might have had another response. He knew well how speaking the truth can attract condemnation, ridicule, scorn, and hatred. The best response is prayer. In fact, he himself had written such a prayer that closes the greatest of his hymns:

> *The heavenly Word proceeding forth,*
> *Yet leaving not the Father's side,*
> *Accomplishing His work on earth*
> *Had reached at length life's eventide.*
> *By false disciple to be given*
> *To foemen for His life athirst*
> *Himself, the very Bread of Heav'n,*
> *He gave to His disciples first.*
> *He gave Himself in either kind,*
> *His precious flesh, His precious blood,*
> *In love's own fullness thus designed*
> *Of the whole man to be the Food.*
> *O saving victim, opening wide*
> *The gate of Heav'n to men below,*
> *Our foes press on from every side,*
> *Thy grace supply, Thy strength bestow.*

The seven virtues and the seven sins

As the Christians came to see that what Christ wanted was not obedience to a set of rules but people of godly qualities, they set forth the desirable and undesirable in Christian life

1. Psalm 15 reads in part:

Who shall sojourn in Thy tabernacle? Who shall dwell upon Thy
holy mountain? / He that walketh
uprightly, and worketh righteousness, and speaketh truth in his
heart / That hath no slander upon
his tongue, nor doeth evil to his fellow, nor taketh up a reproach
against his neighbor.

A further verse adds,

He that sweareth [i.e., makes a
promise] unto his neighbor / and
disappointeth him not, though it
were to his own hindrance.

*The seven virtues as portrayed
on these pages were conceived
by fourteenth-century artist
Bondone di Giotto and are
taken from the Cappella
Scrovegni (Arena Chapel) in
Padua. The seven deadly sins are
portrayed by the sixteenth-century painter Jacob de Backer.*

Justice

Christians through twenty centuries
and more have sought to explain just
how Jesus Christ wants them to
behave. Jesus had as his background Moses'
Ten Commandments, the writings of the
Hebrew prophets, and "the Law," or the
Torah, the myriad regulations of the Jewish
tradition, from many of which Gentile
Christians were exempted. Instead, the
Christians had the Jewish scriptures, the
Christian scriptures as they came into being,
and preeminently Jesus' own example: what
he himself called "the Way."

But the Way was difficult to teach,
they soon realized, because what Jesus
plainly wanted was not simply adherence
to a set of rules so much as people of distinct qualities and character that would
dispose them to adhere to such rules. As
the Christians began to describe these
qualities in letters ("epistles") addressed to
the churches and later collected in the

New Testament, they increasingly found that many of the
behavioral traits they strove
to produce were already
revered by the best of the
pagan society around them.
The pagans called them
"virtues" (in Latin *virtus*, in
Greek *arete*) and considered
four to be "cardinal," or pivotal: justice, courage, temperance, and prudence.

Justice encompassed the
concept of "fair play" and
honest dealing. The just man
would tell the truth even to
his own disadvantage, for
instance, and keep his
promises. Justice required
people to follow the rules of

Fortitude

the game, the whole game of life. And
Christians rapidly realized that the Jews'
fifteenth Psalm was also written to extol
what pagans recognized as the virtue of
justice.[1]

Courage, or fortitude, meant two
things. It meant facing danger—standing by
your post when you're terrified or standing
by your convictions with a whole crowd
laughing at you—but it also means sticking
to the task, not giving up when everything
in you seems to be urging you to quit.
Obviously, a serious attempt to practice
any virtue would also involve this one.

Temperance meant going the right
length and no farther. For example,
overindulgence in liquor or food constitutes "intemperance," but you can also be
intemperate in work or in play. Golf or
bridge may be as spiritually dangerous to
one person as whiskey or cigarettes to
another. The effects might not show on

the outside; golf won't slur the speech or cards damage the lungs, but for anyone captive to them, they can just as surely corrupt the soul.

Temperance was not the same as abstinence, however. A good man may abstain from something because he can't do it at all without overdoing it or because he wants to save money for some other purpose or because he believes it is jeopardizing his whole society, without believing the thing itself—in moderation—to be wrong.

Prudence essentially meant using the brains God gave you. A virtuous man does not hide from the facts but contends with them. He does not pretend that something (or some person or some cause) is good when it is quite obviously bad. He considers thinking things through, especially in religion, to be a definite responsibility since religious belief should not entail shutting one's eyes to obvious fact. Nor would he "take a positive attitude" toward something that plainly called for a negative one.[2]

The greatest factor in the conversion of the pagan world to Christianity was the way in which Christians themselves, both under fearful persecution and in their own community life, exemplified these much admired pagan virtues. Conversely, as

Temperance

Christians such as Justin and Clement (volume 2), Ambrose and Augustine, Chrysostom and the Cappadocians (volume 4) came to see these parallels in the pagan culture, they gradually absorbed the four pagan virtues into Christian teaching, a process that was completed by Aquinas in the thirteenth century.

But they discerned something else as well. The four cardinal virtues, admirable though they are, do not embrace some of the key traits needed in a Christian life. They saw that there must be three more that the pagans did not recognize but which were identified by St. Paul in the most quoted of all his letters: "And now abideth faith, hope and charity, these three. But the greatest of these is charity" (1 Corinthians 13:13). So to the four "cardinal" virtues the Christians added three "theological" virtues, for a total of seven. They also noticed that these three all led to and reinforced the first four. For Christians, that is, the theological virtues lay behind the cardinal virtues. "The theological virtues are the foundation of Christian moral activity," says a Christian catechism. "They animate it and give it its special character. They inform and give life to all moral virtues."

Charity commonly came to be translated as "love" because the meaning of the term "charity" gradually narrowed down to what the Bible calls "alms," that is, giving to the poor, and nothing else. However, the English word "love" poses still another problem since it is used to designate four quite different forms of behavior.[3]

The essence of charity for a Christian is what theologians like Aquinas and many of his forerunners defined as the love of God; to love God is a state of mind, just as loving ourselves is a state of mind. It is wishing our own good. If we learn how to

Prudence

2. As C. S. Lewis put it, "[God] has room for people with very little sense, but He wants everyone to use what sense they have. The proper motto is not 'Be good, sweet maid and let who can be clever,' but 'Be good, sweet maid, and don't forget that this involves being as clever as you can'."

3. In *The Four Loves* C. S. Lewis defines four different categories of love: affection (*storge*), fondness such as family members feel toward one another; friendship (*philia*), the bond shared by people with similar interests; romantic love (*eros*), which he distinguishes from purely sexual desire (*venus*); and charity in the Christian and biblical sense (*caritas* or *agape*), unconditional love of one human being for another or of a human being for God.

Faith

Hope

Charity

love our neighbors as ourselves, in the sense of wishing good for them too, then we are learning how to love God and are thus practicing the greatest virtue.

They emphasized, however, that "loving" someone in the Christian sense does not necessarily mean "liking" him. It does not mean trying to believe his conduct "good" when it is plainly "bad," or trying to persuade yourself he is "likeable" when his conduct is obviously detestable. Rather, it means hoping the best for him, wishing his good. Some Christian teachers even have a kind of test for this. If you discover that a person you dislike has done something that demonstrates him not quite as bad as you had thought, do you sense a certain disappointment? This would indicate you are not loving him. But if you are gratified to discover this, that probably means you are.

It is also true, they found, that sometimes by actively pretending to like someone we dislike, we can begin to genuinely like them after all and, more astonishing still, *they* may come to like *us*. The pretense, in other words, has become a reality. Conversely, when we hurt someone we dislike, we usually discover ourselves disliking him more. The same goes for our love for God. We may not feel it is possible to love God, but if we behave as if we love him, we may be surprised to discover that genuine love for him follows.

The theological virtue of hope is learning to live with the idea of eternal life, usually thought of as heaven, or paradise. Aquinas called it the contemplation of the perfect Good. It represents a deep human need, and just as food satisfies our hunger and copulation satisfies our sexual desire, the future life satisfies our yearning for permanence that earthly life cannot provide. Thus hope, for Christians, means striving for confidence in God's ultimate and everlasting mercy. Not that they despise the earthly pleasures he provides, but they realize that these are the foreshadowing of better things to come, to be enjoyed as such—like an appetizer preceding the heavenly feast. If one accepts the pleasures of this world as a gift of God, one must also recognize the longings they trigger as coming from the same source.

As a virtue faith seems a bit of a stretch. Taken at face value, it may appear to be something that one either has or doesn't have, based on the weighing of the evidence. Where is the virtue in that? But if you have weighed the evidence and conclusively decided that Christianity is true, there will still be moments when you doubt your conviction. You may also be drawn away from it by circumstances if, for instance, you have an opportunity to make some money by slightly shady means or feel that it is in your best interests to tell a lie. When it becomes temptingly convenient

Gluttony

Lust

the natural human capacity for enjoying life's pleasures, but it is not the act of eating or owning a house or wearing good clothes that constitutes gluttony; it is doing these things to excess. We seldom really need to eat until we can hold no more, after all, or to acquire a ten-thousand-square-foot house. Gluttony is the perversion of that free, careless, and generous mood that wants enjoyment from life for us and for others. And the perversion kills the good, for it is a vain effort to satisfy the above-mentioned longing, which should be directed toward the hereafter and not the here and now.

Similarly, lust (*luxuria*) is the exaggeration of the natural desire to procreate and the natural pleasure that comes from sex. Aquinas taught that God gave us the ability to procreate and to enjoy the process. But it is by its nature designed to regenerate the species and must therefore be practiced only within the bonds of marriage. "Chastity is the most unpopular of the Christian virtues," observed the twentieth-century Christian writer C. S. Lewis in his *Mere Christianity*. "There's no getting away from it; the Christian rule is, 'Either marriage, with complete faithfulness to your partner, or else total abstinence.' Now this is so difficult and so contrary to our instincts that obviously either Christianity is wrong or our sexual instinct, as it now is, has gone wrong. One or the other. Of course, being a Christian, I think it is the instinct."

Wrath (*ira*) is anger and hate taken to damaging levels. It is right and just to hate

to forget that Christianity is true, then faith, derived through prayer and other spiritual means, must come into play.

A second and even more important aspect of faith involves entrusting one's entire life to Christ. This happens when we realize that we can never on our own reach the moral perfection that Jesus epitomized, or even sometimes meet the bare standard of conduct we expect of other people. We discover, that is, our own moral bankruptcy. Only then does the endlessly repeated Christian prayer "Lord, have mercy" begin to have meaning for us. We have discovered that if we are ever to get to heaven, the grace of God will have to figure centrally in our getting there.

Pagan culture, of course, dealt with bad behavior as well as good, recognizing seven major flaws in human conduct that the Christians, in turn, would recognize as the "Seven Deadly Sins." The seven—gluttony, lust, wrath, greed, envy, sloth, and pride—were adopted by Christian teachers in the West at the time of Pope Gregory the Great in the sixth century. They have been part of a Christian's moral education ever since and are usually subdivided into three so-called warm-blooded sins and four cold-blooded.

Gluttony (Latin "*gula*"), the first of the warm-blooded sins, is an exaggeration of

Wrath

Greed

Envy

evil, to become angry at those who practice evil, and even to punish evil through violent means, including war. The problem begins when we enjoy the hating and take pleasure in the punishment and pain it inflicts out of a sense of vengeance. Vengeance is not justice; it is the sin of wrath.

Nevertheless, the four cold-blooded sins are considered far more serious because of their origin. Where the warm-blooded sins are perversions of some good, the cold-blooded are considered "sins of the spirit." They do not originate in the natural world, the Christians say—they are purely diabolical.

Greed (*avaritia*) is the first one. Also known as covetousness or avarice, it is an unhealthy preoccupation with possessions, often money or the things money can buy.[4] In mild form it might be referred to as thrift or niggardliness, but while the village miser is guilty of this sin, far more is the rather more attractive, swashbuckling billionaire who ultimately measures everything and everybody only in dollars and cents. For avarice is driven by competition and pride: the greedy man wants more, not because it increases his pleasure but because he needs to prove himself smarter, richer, and generally superior to anyone else, and to preserve that status.

Envy (*invidia*) is the sin that wants us all miserable together and resents anyone being happier. "If avarice is the sin of the haves against the have-nots, envy is the sin of the have-nots against the haves," writes mid-twentieth-century Christian essayist Dorothy L. Sayers in an essay entitled "The Other Six Deadly Sins." In its lesser form, envy can inspire social climbing or snobbism, but the envious can also be destroyers. The trade unionist who would rather that the company go broke than that he forego a salary increase or ease a clause in

the collective agreement might well be acting out of envy. The wife who cannot abide her husband's success and nags a marriage to its death commits the same sin.

Sloth (*acedia*), which in most ages was simply condemned as laziness, would gain sympathy and even respectability in the late twentieth century, when apathy and indifference to life's problems would come to be rather admired or else diagnosed as depression in need of drug therapy. The pagans called it "sadness" and the romanticists "melancholy," but they nonetheless thought it sinful. For sloth is the sin that rejects God's creation, the sin, says essayist Sayers, that "believes in nothing, cares for nothing, seeks to know nothing, interferes with nothing, enjoys nothing, loves nothing, hates nothing, finds purpose in nothing, lives for nothing, and only remains alive because there is nothing it would die for."

But perhaps the greatest surprise in secularist eyes is the first-place ranking that both pagan society and the Christians assigned to pride (*superbia*), which C. S. Lewis describes as "the one vice of which no man is free; which everyone in the world loathes when he sees it in someone else; and which hardly any people except Christians ever imagine they are guilty of themselves . . . There is no fault which makes a man more unpopular and no

4. Avarice has often been cited as the root sin, as in the famous passage from the apostle Paul's letter to Timothy: "The love of money is the root of all evil." But note that it is not the money that is at issue but the love of it.

Sloth

Pride

fault which we are more unconscious of in ourselves. And the more we have it ourselves, the more we dislike it in others."

But surely, a man might object, there's nothing sinful about being proud of my country, or my family, or my golf club. This depends, however, upon what he means by "being proud of." If he means he admires his country, loves his family, and revels in the camaraderie and skill of the golf course, this is not "pride" as Christians use the word. But if he tends to look down on other, "inferior" countries or to put on airs because of his family lineage or because he belongs to the "right" golf club, this would be a very different matter. It would be pride.

Pride, like sloth, would gain some respectability in the late twentieth century, when "looking out for number one" began to be seen as virtuous, along with the quest for "self-fulfillment" and the seeking for "empowerment." But the old realities would remain, of course, as people would discover whenever they actually needed help from someone who was looking out for number one and saw them as number two or three or possibly fifty. Marry someone forever searching for self-fulfillment or hire someone intent on "seeking empowerment," and the diabolical origins become evident as ever.

The outstanding twentieth-century entertainer Frank Sinatra won accolades for a captivating song, written by Paul Anka, in which he looked back on his life and declared, "I did it my way." Few of his admirers stopped to think that every marital breakup, every family feud, and much other human misery come about because somebody is determined to "do it my way."

The sin of pride comes when you don't care what others think because you consider yourself above them. It is the most competitive of sins, getting no pleasure out of having something, only of having more of it than the next man. The proud person, more than any other, hates to be snubbed or ignored or outshone. Thus, Christians believe pride to have been the main source of woe in every nation and every family since time began.

Pride is pure antagonism, both between human creatures and between humans and God. For when a man looks down on everyone, he cannot see something that is above him. Pride, through which the devil became the devil, comes straight from hell. Therefore, observes Lewis, the proud, self-righteous prig who sits in the front pew of the church every Sunday may be closer to hell than a prostitute. However, he concludes, "it is better to be neither." ∎

Charles of Anjou glares coldly out across the Palazzo Reale in Naples, Italy. This man, whom the papacy originally viewed as the savior of the church, was discovered by later popes to be a relentless foe. Under his watch the papacy began its switch from the Germans to the French, a transition that would spell catastrophe.

CHAPTER 8

The Sicilian Vespers: an event that doomed the medieval papacy

The popes, fearing encirclement by the Germans, call in Charles of Anjou, who proves even worse; then a duel between king and pope changes history

When news of the death of Emperor Frederick II reached the Roman curia, it occasioned not mourning but unrestrained jubilation. "Wonder of the World," some called him, but to most in the papal circle Frederick was the "Horror of the World." He was evil incarnate, the supposed champion of Christianity who routinely sneered at its gospel, sacraments, and priests; who traveled Christendom with his oriental court, his troops of hired Muslim killers, and his harem of concubines; and who used living human beings in his sordid "scientific experiments."

So, at any rate, his enemies accused him, and with good evidence, though they generally ignored the fact that this man also had succeeded in regaining Jerusalem from Islam without losing a single life. Whatever Frederick "*Stupor Mundi*" might have been, however, now he was no more. "The tyrant's fall," cried Pope Innocent IV to the church, "has changed the thunderbolts and tempests that God held over your heads into gentle breezes and fertile dews."

But Frederick's many kinsmen were not gone—that virulent Hohenstaufen brood (as Innocent saw them) with all their unholy horde of relatives, retainers, and sycophants. Known in Italy as the Ghibellines (after one of their castles), they had dominated the imperial government for more than a century, and there were powerful nests of them everywhere. True, they were generally opposed by the Guelph clan (or Guelf, from their German name, Welf) who customarily backed the pope, but the Guelphs were seldom successful. In any case, this bloody factional conflict was

tearing Italy apart. "How can Christendom defeat Islam if it is chronically beset by internecine warfare?" was the anguished demand of pope after pope. And therefore how long could it be until Islam again invaded Christendom?

But who in Christendom was powerful enough to supplant the Hohenstaufen and their cabal of German aristocrats? Eleven years after Frederick's death, the frantic curia, swayed by the French cardinal Simon of Brie, would come up with one possible answer by allying itself with France in 1261. This calamitous leap from frying pan to fire would eventually see the pope a hostage in France, indentured for seventy years to the French king. It would also spell the end of the medieval papacy, the birth of European nationalism, and the beginning of the end of Christian unity in the West. During these eleven years, moreover, the Hohenstaufen era, seemingly imperishable when Frederick died, would fade into near extinction.

The emperor Frederick's three wives had borne him three sons. Henry, the eldest, had rebelled against his father, had been deposed, and had died, probably by suicide. Conrad, the second, was already "king of the Romans," meaning king of Germany; his father had also named him king of Sicily, a domain that included both the island and the southern half of the Italian peninsula. To his third son, another Henry, Frederick had bequeathed two effectually empty titles. But Pope Innocent was now inspired to nominate this Henry king of Sicily, thereby putting himself on a collision course with Conrad.

Desperate to rid himself of the Hohenstaufen yoke, Pope Clement IV crowned Charles of Anjou king of Sicily, as seen in this medieval illumination. Charles was able to wipe out all male Hohenstaufens within a mere three years of arriving in Rome as the pope's protector. Unfortunately for the papacy, Charles would prove just as hostile to papal control.

The collision was not long delayed. Naming his own infant son, Conradin, titular king of Germany, Conrad headed south to claim the title bequeathed him by his father. Once again, the curia realized, the Hohenstaufen would bracket the papacy, north and south. At this point the politics turned outright criminal when young Henry was fatally poisoned. Innocent accused Conrad of the murder. Conrad publicly condemned Innocent as a usurper and heretic. Innocent responded by excommunicating Conrad. War was inevitable.

Then came another shock. Conrad himself suddenly died of malaria at age twenty-six. Only one possible Hohenstaufen claimant seemed to remain: Frederick's illegitimate son Manfred, whom he had designated prince of Taranto, the port city in the "sole" of the Italian "boot," with responsibility to act as Conrad's representative in the south. Taking this assignment seriously, Manfred had been putting down rebellions there, which he claimed were fomented by Innocent. Twice defeating papal armies sent to suppress him, he was reasserting Hohenstaufen control across Italy. Innocent excommunicated him, just as he had excommunicated Conrad, but that was one of his final acts. Pope Innocent IV died in 1254, four years after his bitter enemy Frederick.

By then Manfred had declared himself representative in Italy of the child Conradin. Hearing a report in 1258 that six-year-old Conradin was dead, however, he crowned himself king of Sicily and, upon discovering the report false, refused to abdicate. The new pope, Alexander IV, declared this coronation void. More distressing to Alexander's successors was Manfred's feeble attempt to save the Latin empire in the East. Having contracted a marriage with a Greek princess, he sent some troops to defend the impoverished Latin emperor at Constantinople,

The frantic curia's decision to ally itself with France was a calamitous leap from frying pan to fire that would eventually see the pope a hostage in France, spelling the end of the medieval papacy.

but they were far from adequate. The Greeks swiftly regained control of their empire, and the eastern patriarchate regained its capital city—a humiliating reversal for the Western Church and the West generally.[1]

But the last straw came when Manfred was proclaimed "senator of the Romans" by that city's antipapal faction, which looked like a certain preliminary to a takeover of Rome (as had twice been threatened by Manfred's father). Pope Alexander's successor, Urban IV, grew desperate enough to listen to Cardinal Simon of Brie. Perhaps, Urban reasoned, the French were indeed the only answer.

Certainly nothing else had worked. Successive popes had tried and failed to find a king for Sicily who would dependably rule it as a papal fief. But this proposition, in the words of one unenthused candidate, was also like being offered the moon provided you could hook it. Nevertheless, when Charles of Anjou was asked to come to Italy as the church's champion against Manfred, he accepted. Oust Manfred, he was told, and he would be free to inaugurate a French regime in southern Italy.

Twelfth and last child of the devout and iron-willed Blanche of Castile, Charles was the youngest brother of the remarkable King Louis IX of France (see subchapter, pages 140–145), who now encouraged him to accept. The olive-skinned and muscular Charles was a cultured, competent, and energetic prince. Like King Louis, he was always ready to sacrifice his amusements for higher purposes. Unlike Louis, however, he seemed to see himself as God's sole instrument to fulfill those purposes. He also tended to be cold and self-contained, and often harsh in his dealings for fear of looking weak.

Urban died before Charles could get started, and Manfred, utterly confident, neglected (or perhaps failed) to block the election of Clement IV, who, like his predecessor, was French. Fearing assassination by Manfred's agents, Pope

1. The Latin patriarchate of Constantinople was sustained as a titular ornament of the papal court well into the twentieth century. Pope Paul VI in January 1964 suppressed it as well as similar titular patriarchates of Alexandria and Antioch.

Clement pleaded with Charles to hasten to Rome to protect him, so early in 1265 Charles sailed from France with an advance party of one hundred knights. He slipped past Manfred's naval blockade and paraded triumphantly as the pope's rescuer into the papal city, where Clement crowned him king of Sicily. That was the easy part.

"Aha," trumpeted Manfred, "the bird is in the cage." But the bird was more powerful than he knew. By July much of central Italy was backing Charles, and Manfred's own lieutenants began deserting him. Still unheeding, however, Manfred relaxed and went hunting while Charles and Clement, both cash strapped, pawned church plate to augment and pay Charles's twenty-five-thousand-man force. By October this army was moving relentlessly out of France and into Lombardy, where city after city either greeted it joyously or fell before it. By May of 1265 his army was in Rome.

Still underfunded, he could not delay until spring and so immediately started south. Manfred, awaiting reinforcements near Naples, expected his fortresses to slow the French advance, but Charles rolled relentlessly over these dispirited garrisons. Then he abruptly swerved east into the Apennines, forcing Manfred to move inland as well. When Charles came down from the mountains, Manfred was waiting for him at Benevento, forty miles northeast of Naples, his men posted strongly behind a swollen Calore River.

Above: Manfred (right) is shown with the tip of a French knight's lance impaling his head. He was killed at the Battle of Benevento when, refusing to flee, he charged with his bodyguard into the heart of the melee in a vain effort to wrest victory from defeat. Below: Manfred's headless body is dragged behind a French soldier's horse. Both frescos are located in Pernes-les-Fontaines, France, about seventy miles northwest of Marseille. They date from the thirteenth century.

Given enough time, hunger might have destroyed the French army, but Manfred's own allies were wavering, and he dared not wait. To Charles's delight, he began threading his army across a narrow bridge over the Calore. Next morning, February 26, 1266, Manfred launched first his Muslim troops (inherited from his father) at the well-entrenched enemy, then his Germans, and finally his Italians. But adequate reinforcements, slowed by that bridge, could not reach them in time. Charles's troops soon cut them down so badly that when Manfred ordered a charge, even his Italian cousins gave up and simply rode away. Manfred himself, refusing to flee, plunged with his bodyguard into the melee. Fewer than six hundred of his thirty-six hundred Germans survived this battle, and days later a military straggler led a sack-laden donkey into Charles's camp. "Who wants to buy Manfred?" he shouted.

Excommunicated by two popes (Alexander IV and Urban IV), Manfred of Sicily could not be buried in consecrated ground. Charles had him buried at the foot of the bridge at Benevento, and each soldier who crossed over threw a stone on his grave. Out of these stones a cairn was erected. Thus Sicily acquired a new king. "Holding the putrid corpse of that pestilent man, our dear son Charles holds peacefully his kingdom," the pope exulted. With positively indecent haste, city after city and family after family sent their submission to the new monarch, a process eased by his remarkable clemency. Few estates were confiscated, no cities sacked, and Charles's French administrators quickly spread over the realm to implement an honest tax system.[2]

Yet within a year Italy began to sour on "our dear son." The somber Charles was personally less attractive than the affable Hohenstaufens, his taxes grew more onerous, and his French officials soon turned hard and arrogant. Although the Guelphs were ascendant in Tuscany and Lombardy, he would not let these northerners settle their own affairs. Instead, he campaigned ceaselessly there, seizing stubborn towns, provoking a Ghibelline coup in Rome, and alarming even his Guelph allies.

Perhaps, many people began saying, the Hohenstaufens were not so "putrid" after all—and one of them still lived. Conrad's son, Conradin, now fifteen, was handsome, bright, and proud of his illustrious blood. By July of 1266, fed up with Charles's supposed clemency, Manfred supporters were slipping over the Alps to Bavaria and fanning Hohenstaufen ambition. At the year's end, the citizenry of Rome was ready to declare for Conradin, and much of Sicily was in spontaneous revolt against what was now seen as French intrusion. In September 1267 a melodramatic manifesto was published over Conradin's name, condemning papal tyranny and demanding his rightful inheritance.

The boy king, ignoring his mother's fearful pleas, led four thousand knights over the Alps and proceeded across Lombardy, gathering gold and supporters. The following summer he marched on Rome, past the papal castle at Viterbo, where mutterings of "lamb to the slaughter" were heard from Clement's balcony. Rome welcomed Charles's youthful challenger with hymns, bouquets, and torchlight processions, and then the lamb marched out to conquer Italy.

Conradin's army collided with that of Charles at Tagliacozzo, fifty miles east of Rome, on August 23, 1268. Though they were separated by a river, Conradin's Italians found a hidden ford and outflanked Charles's main body, shattering it at

2. The initial clemency demonstrated by the triumphant Charles of Anjou did not extend to heirs of his vanquished enemy. The three bastard sons of King Manfred of Sicily were imprisoned at Nocera, twenty-five miles southeast of Naples, whence they never emerged, although one was still alive in 1309, forty-four years later. Manfred's daughter by his second wife, Helena, however, was freed in 1284 to marry an Italian marquis. Constance, his daughter from his first marriage, was already the wife of Peter of Aragon, a circumstance that would ultimately lead to Charles's ruin.

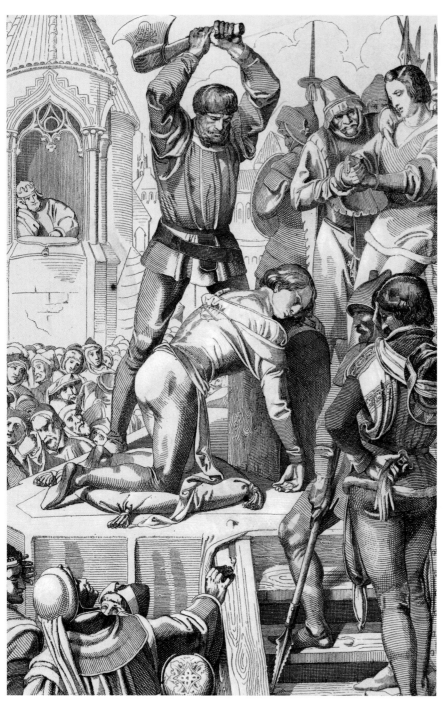

In the upper left corner of this nineteenth-century sketch, Charles of Anjou languidly watches Conradin of Swabia being beheaded in 1268. Conradin was the last male Hohenstaufen and seemingly the final threat to Charles's power in western Europe.

first shock. But Charles had hidden a reserve of some thousand knights in a distant hollow. When Conradin's army scattered to seek plunder, the boy was left almost alone—and Charles's reserves charged from ambush to slaughter his bodyguard. As his army melted away, the royal youth escaped down the road and three days later appeared before Rome. But that fickle city refused to open its gates, and on he fled until he was seized by a local baron.

Charles's supposed mercy did not include such a rival as this. He had Conradin convicted of treason and publicly beheaded in a piazza at Naples. Many people thought the execution appalling, one of them Pope Clement. Now dying, he was said to be "deeply troubled"—not just about the fate of Conradin but also about the emerging ambitions of "our dear son." Charles, on the other hand, saw no need for penitence. God had given him this throne to eradicate the vile Hohenstaufens, which he had done. What was there to repent of?

The papacy now went into one of its periodic spasms of paralysis, with the cardinals deadlocked for three years as they could not agree on a successor for Clement. This void at Rome gave Charles a free hand. He crushed the resistance in Sicily, sparing none of the disaffected, and settled seven hundred French squires on confiscated estates alongside his French governors. Demonstrating undisguised disdain for the place, he rarely bothered even to visit the island himself.

This negligence he would one day have cause to regret, but by now his eyes were focused on an altogether new horizon. Baldwin, the deposed "Latin emperor of the East," was canvassing the courts of Europe for a new crusade to win him back his empire. Charles had quietly subscribed to the Baldwin cause even before his involvement in Italy—on the condition, of course, that he, Charles, be Baldwin's successor. To this end, he had carefully woven a network of marriages and treaties through Greece and the Balkans. The imperial throne in the West had been vacant since the death of Frederick Stupor Mundi. If he could gain the eastern imperial throne, Charles reasoned, how could any pope refuse him the western one? A second and greater Charlemagne would have fully restored the ancient empire of Rome.

Moreover, Constantinople seemed an easy target. Michael Palaeologus, the man whom Manfred had failed to defeat, had gone on to oust poor Baldwin, with all the dire consequences foreseen by Rome. Michael had reasserted the independence of the Eastern Empire from the Latin West, reinstated a Greek patriarch and eastern worship, repaired the walls of Constantinople, and rebuilt its fleet and had begun to repopulate the city. Finally, though neither he nor anyone else could know it at the time, he had founded a dynasty that would rule the Eastern Empire for another two centuries, until its final fall to Islam. Nevertheless, as Michael must have realized, his restored empire hung by a hair. If the Latins attacked again, Byzantium might hold on but would be so weakened that it must surely fall to Islam's next westward surge.

What Michael needed most was a "patriarch of the West" (the term eastern Christians applied to the pope) who was more interested in reconciling with the Orthodox Church than in conquering the Eastern Empire. In 1271 there appeared just such a pope. After their three-year deadlock the cardinals finally agreed on Tebaldo Visconti, who took the name Gregory X.[3] He was a man who fully understood the peril in which Outremer now stood—in fact, he was on a pilgrimage in the Holy Land when told of his election. His sermon on departing for Rome took its text from Psalm 137: "If I forget thee, O Jerusalem, may my right hand forget her cunning." As Gregory X he immediately issued a blanket order: there must be no further crusades against Constantinople. Charles, needless to say, was not pleased.

Further, Gregory summoned an ecumenical council in Lyon to heal Christianity's "Great Schism" and to call for another crusade against Islam. Five hundred bishops attended, although among Christendom's monarchs only the decrepit James of Aragon showed up.[4] Michael eagerly selected an eastern delegation. Half his delegates perished en route in a storm at sea, but those who made it to Lyon declared their loyalty to Pope Gregory, and a number of Orthodox bishops participated in a western Mass, using the western version of the Nicene Creed.[5] This done, the council confidently declared the Great Schism between East and West officially over.

But it was not over. In the aftermath of the council Emperor Michael faced bitter opposition, even among his royal nieces and nephews, to union with Rome. When he forced into exile the stubborn Patriarch Joseph, who adamantly opposed such a union, Joseph became emblematic of the anti-Latin movement.

3. At Viterbo the cardinals were evenly divided between those who wanted another French pope and those who wanted an Italian. The deadlock was finally broken when the citizenry of Viterbo, acting on the advice of Bonaventure, minister general of the Franciscans, ripped the roof off the building where they met and also locked them in. Three days later Pope Gregory X was elected. One of his first acts was to establish the "conclave," a procedure under which the cardinals are locked up during the election of a pope that has been in effect ever since.

4. Thomas Aquinas, teaching in Naples at the time, was not on good terms with Charles of Anjou but was summoned to the ecumenical council of Pope Gregory X to persuade the Orthodox East of the merits of the theology of the Catholic West. When he died on his way there on March 1, 1274, some suspected Charles of poisoning him, but history records no evidence to substantiate the charge.

5. The Nicene Creed, adopted during the fourth century as a definitive statement of the Christian faith, deals with the mystery of the Holy Trinity by declaring that the Holy Spirit "proceeds" from God the Father. Some two and a half centuries later, the Latin churches in Spain began amending this to read "proceeds from the Father *and the Son*" (in Latin *filioque*), and eventually the Catholic Church fully accepted the change. The Orthodox Church to this day rejects it.

The large public piazza at Naples was, and is, the perfect place to hold large public gatherings to hear or witness large public declarations. That's why Charles of Anjou chose this place more than seven hundred years ago to behead Conradin.

Historically, when a Roman emperor was crowned, he was first raised up on the shield of the troops. This symbolized the support of the army, always integral to the success of the imperial ruler. Michael Palaeologus is shown above being raised by his soldiers following this ancient tradition. He would then take back Constantinople from the West, rebuild its walls, and reinstitute the Orthodox patriarchate.

And when Michael sent an army to suppress a pro-Orthodox rebellion in Macedonia, the army itself rebelled against him, the soldiers avowing sympathy with the rebels. Some Greek bishops even excommunicated him.

Though the Council of Lyon declared no crusade against Islam, the ban on attacks against Constantinople continued until Gregory's death in 1276. After that things slowly turned in Charles's favor. Four popes held office over the next five years, the third dying when his bedroom ceiling collapsed during renovations of the Viterbo palace. With each new election, tensions between Italian and French cardinals grew, and the popes became more hostile to the Eastern church. Finally Charles won a key round. With the cardinals again deadlocked, his troops moved in and forced a decision. Intimidated, the cardinals elected none other than Simon of Brie, veteran leader of the French faction, who became Pope Martin IV.

Blindly a French patriot, Martin had no concept of the papacy as a mediator between princes. He disliked Germans, distrusted Italians, and saw the East only as a field for French conquest. When Emperor Michael's envoys arrived in Rome with congratulations and submission, they were met by Pope Martin and King Charles, both French and unmistakably evidencing the new church-state partnership. The pope denounced Michael Palaeologus as a heretic and demanded he surrender his empire. Charles, with Martin's blessing, began assembling a fleet of forty men-of-war, two hundred galleys, and transports for ten thousand knights and even more infantry. The crusade against Constantinople was set to sail in April 1282.

King of Sicily and lord of much of France, Italy, and Greece, Charles was now the most powerful man in Christendom. He had beheaded the last male Hohenstaufen contender fourteen years earlier. Who could stop him now? The answer was a female Hohenstaufen. Manfred, long before his fall, had arranged for his daughter Constance to marry Peter of Aragon. Peter's kingdom, lying along some three hundred miles of the Mediterranean coast from the Pyrenees to Cape San Antonio, reached far enough inland to include about one fifth of modern Spain. This granddaughter of Stupor Mundi could make a claim to the Sicilian throne, a fact that most of Europe, Charles included, either had forgotten or never credited.[6]

Not quite all Europe, however. John of Procida had been Frederick's gifted physician and Manfred's chancellor. After Conradin's defeat at Tagliacozzo, John first tried without success to enlist the Germans against Charles. Then he began advancing Constance's claim. When King Peter assumed his throne in 1276, he, too, made John his chancellor, specifically charged with the destruction of Charles of Anjou. With any luck, John no doubt reasoned, Charles would make the mistake of all ruthless politicians by acquiring more enemies than he had friends.[7]

Pope Gregory X, who presided over the Council of Lyon, worked out with the eastern emperor Palaeologus the terms by which the great schism between East and West could be ended. However, neither subsequent popes in the West nor the populace in the East accepted this agreement, and the eastern and western churches have remained divided to this day.

6. Manfred of Sicily was Frederick's illegitimate son by Bianca Lancia, an Italian noblewoman, but by marrying her on her deathbed, Frederick contended, he had legitimized Manfred. This could equally be argued to legitimize the claim of Manfred's daughter Constance to the throne of Sicily. To the popes, however, all this was irrelevant. Since they considered Sicily a papal fief, its ruler must be a papal designate—in this instance, their nominee Charles of Anjou.

7. Legend has it that after the Battle of Tagliacozzo, when one of Charles's knights seized the lands of Manfred's chancellor, John of Procida, he also abused John's wife, killed his son, and raped his daughter.

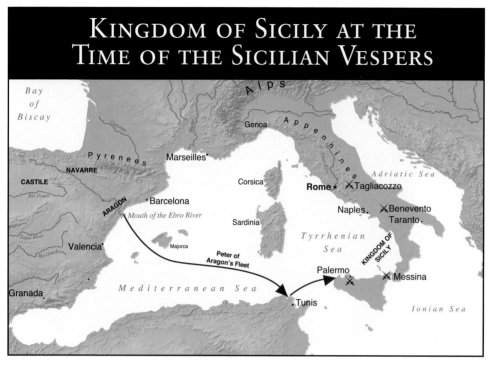

KINGDOM OF SICILY AT THE TIME OF THE SICILIAN VESPERS

Bay of Biscay

Alps

Genoa

Appennines

Pyrenees

Marseilles

NAVARRE

CASTILE

Corsica

Adriatic Sea

Rome ★ ✕Tagliacozzo

Rio Douro

ARAGON

• Barcelona

Mouth of the Ebro River

Naples • ✕Benevento
Taranto •

Sardinia

Tyrrhenian Sea

KINGDOM OF SICILY

Valencia

Majorca

Peter of Aragon's Fleet

Palermo
✕

✕ Messina

Rio Guadiana

Tagus River

Granada

Mediterranean Sea

• Tunis

Ionian Sea

John accordingly dispatched agents, chief among them one of his own sons disguised as a friar, to flit like shadows between Constantinople, Aragon, and Sicily, using gold provided by Michael Palaeologus to foment rebellion against their common enemy, Charles. The latter was entirely absorbed with the grand fleet he was assembling at Messina, Sicily, and stocking with supplies confiscated from sullen Sicilian farmers. He scarcely heeded intelligence reports that another armada was gathering in the mouth of the Ebro, ninety miles down the coast from Barcelona.

His agents will have inquired, of course, just where this fleet might be bound. For Tunis in North Africa, was King Peter's answer, which indicated the Crusades and must have seemed safe enough. But there were two forgotten factors. First, from Tunis, with a fair wind the Sicilian coast was just a two- to three-day sail. Second, Charles's French officials had become so despised in Sicily that the whole island was ready to explode.

On Easter Monday, March 30, 1282, it did. Thousands were celebrating the festival with song and dancing, and there had been a wedding at Palermo's Church of the Holy Spirit. French soldiers joined in the jollity, drinking deeply and ignoring the scowls of Sicilians as they jostled the local girls. Eventually a certain Sergeant Drouet dragged the bride from the wedding party and began to make free with her. This proved to be a mistake that would change the whole history of Europe, in the incident known as the Sicilian Vespers.

Within seconds Sergeant Drouet fell with the groom's dagger in his heart. Someone yelled, other Sicilians drew their blades, and within moments many French soldiers were bleeding on the ground. As the church bells rang for vespers, mayhem erupted throughout the city, with youths running through the streets shouting "*Moranu li Franchiski!*" ("Death to the French!") Once begun, the killing continued in ungovernable rage. Sword-wielding Sicilians poured into the streets, slaughtering anyone French, ransacking their homes and favorite inns, impaling their wives and children. Mobs burst into monasteries, ordering the monks to pronounce the peculiar Sicilian word "*ciciri*" (chickpeas). This was a test: anyone who couldn't say it properly must be French and was butchered on the spot. By dawn two thousand French bodies lay cooling on the cobblestones and the rebels held Palermo.

Messengers ran from village to village, militias assembled and marched, and within a fortnight Sicily's French overlords had either fled or were dead. Only strongly garrisoned Messina, sheltering Charles's fleet, hesitated to join the rebellion.

But when its governor nervously tried to replace his Sicilian troops with French ones, rioting broke out, and Messina, too, fell to the rebels. The ships, trapped at anchor, were burned to the waterline. In Naples, Charles learned that his dreams and his supposedly indestructible empire now lay in ruins. "Lord God," he cried, "since it pleases you to ruin me, let me down only in small steps."

The Sicilians immediately sent ambassadors to Pope Martin to beg his protection. They approached his throne smiting their breasts and chanting, "Lamb of God . . . have mercy on us." But the pope answered bitterly with the words from the Passion, "And they smote him." He angrily excommunicated the rebels and their allies. Then he proclaimed yet another crusade, this one against Sicily, an action some see as the final discrediting of the whole crusading ideal.[8]

The Sicilians quickly found another protector, however: none other than King Peter of Aragon, whose fleet lay mere days from Palermo. In late June, when Charles ferried his troops across the strait and laid siege to Messina, the Sicilian "rabble" managed to repel five successive assaults. Then Charles got the news that King Peter's army had landed at Palermo. As it crossed the island to relieve Messina, the besiegers fled, and Sicily acquired a new king and queen.

Thus ended the Latin threat to Constantinople. Now old and ill, Michael Palaeologus died two months later. He had restored a fallen empire, a rare achievement. He had also done as much or more than any man to heal the East-West schism among the Christians, acting with a pope, Gregory X, who shared his vision of a workable union. But now Michael's heir repudiated his plans to end the Great Schism, and his bishops refused to bury in consecrated ground a man they considered a heretic. (By contrast, Pope Gregory was beatified and is

8. "Not even Pope Martin IV," writes Catholic historian Warren H. Carroll (*The Glory of Christendom*) "could contend that Sicilians were heretics, schismatics or pagans . . . There could be no excuse for calling such a war a crusade. Everyone knew it. It is hard to imagine how Pope Martin could justify it to himself." In four years, Carroll concludes, Martin did "as much harm to Christendom as any pope in two millennia."

Eruli Erulo's magnificent painting of the Sicilian Vespers is seen below. An unplanned yet spectacularly coordinated assault on their French overlords was carried out by the Sicilians on Easter Monday, March 30, 1282, after a French sergeant went too far with a bride on her wedding day and was promptly killed by the groom.

Charles of Anjou

Pope Martin

revered as a saint in Rome and several European dioceses.)

Meanwhile, the War of the Sicilian Vespers descended first into farce and then into stalemate. Pope Martin demanded the unconditional surrender of Sicily, which was, of course, refused. Peter crossed into southern Italy and skirmished there with Charles, but neither could prevail. With Peter poor and Charles debt ridden, military activity declined.

To economize (and perhaps also glamorize), Charles proposed a "trial by combat" with a hundred picked knights on each side so that "God could decide." Martin said that as pope he acted for God in these matters, and he had already decided. With most of Europe either appalled or amused, on June 1, 1283, both royal entourages showed up at Bordeaux, the appointed place of combat, as arranged. Peter and his band arrived at dawn, roared their challenge to an empty field, declared the French cowards, and rode away. Charles and his troop showed up at noon, shouted their challenge to a field still empty, declared the Aragonese cowards, and rode away. Pope Martin called for a crusade against Aragon.

If this war had a hero, it was Roger of Lauria, Peter's commander at sea and the greatest admiral of the age, whose repeated naval victories prevented Charles from invading the island. Finally, Charles's son and heir, disobeying paternal orders, took his father's fleet out of Naples harbor to confront Roger. The fleet was captured, the son was captured, and the disgusted father was left muttering that he thought the boy might at least have had sufficient courtesy to get killed rather than get caught.

The great Louis IX of France was by now dead from the dysentery that destroyed the Eighth Crusade, leaving the throne of France to his ineffectual son, Philip III. He was known as "Philip the Bold" for his personal courage and fighting dexterity—but not for his performance as king. Having followed the wishes of his father all his life, he now followed the wishes of his father's brother Charles

Philip III

Peter of Aragon

of Anjou, who suggested that he please the pope by invading King Peter's Aragon. This Philip did with great cost and calamitous result, a purposeless and useless war, in the view of observers then and later. It ended with his army sick and fleeing Aragon, Philip himself dying in their midst. Meanwhile, there came news that Charles of Anjou was also dead. Long sinking, toward the end he prayed, "Lord God, you know I took the kingdom of Sicily for your holy church, not for my own gain. So you will pardon my sins." It sounds less a plea than an instruction.

That year, 1285, unfolded like the last scene of Hamlet. All the major players died: Charles in January, Pope Martin in March, Philip III in October, and Peter of Aragon in November from wounds suffered in hand-to-hand combat in the defeat of Philip's French invaders. The Sicilian war smoldered on for another eighteen years in raids, riots, and sieges, eventually petering out because the participants lost interest. Disenchanted with the defense of Christendom from enemies within and without, monarchs increasingly pursued the wealth and glory of their own realms. After the funerary year 1285, the whole conflict between state and church came to center on two determined, intelligent, and (in many respects) ruthless men. One was a king and the other a pope.

On the French throne was the seventeen-year-old son of Philip III, whose handsome face would earn him the sobriquet "Philip the Fair." In all other respects, Philip IV was distinctly unfair, however, and hidden behind his great beauty lurked a cold, disdainful reserve. He resembled an owl, critics jibed, "the handsomest of birds . . . who does nothing but stare." A childhood marred by tragedy perhaps explains his icy view of life: three years old when his mother died; eight at the death of an older brother, possibly murdered by their stepmother; father tainted by the charge of "unnatural intercourse" (i.e., sodomy). In any case, though punctilious in religious observance, Philip IV recruited ministers of sacrilegious brutality. And while he reputedly admired his revered grandfather, he

In 1285 all of the major players in the war begun by the Sicilian Vespers died in quick succession. From left to right, Charles of Anjou died in January, Pope Martin in March, Philip III in October, and Peter of Aragon in November. However, the Sicilians, having liberated themselves from the French yoke, would continue the war for eighteen more years.

King of France Philip IV, known as "the Fair," in a nineteenth-century painting by Jean-Louis Bezard. Philip became the Fair from his youthful beauty, decidedly not because of his respect for justice.

9. By one account, the unfortunate Pope Celestine was imprisoned in a cell so small that he could not lie down in it and died within a year. Although an impossible pope, Celestine became a model for friars trying to follow the tough rules of the mendicant orders. Even before his death, thirty-six monasteries were named for him, and eighteen years later he was canonized by Pope Clement V.

used France's central bureaucracy, created by Louis IX to ensure more effective judicial equality, chiefly to ensure more effective tax collection.

After the death of Pope Martin, the Italians regained control of the papacy under two popes: Honorius IV, who served two years, and Nicholas IV, who served four. But the Italians themselves were divided, not only by the old Ghibelline-Guelph conflict but also by two powerful families in Rome, both of which tended to treat the papacy as a private family affair. Perhaps it was the embattled deadlock following the death of Nicholas IV that led the cardinals to seek this time a man of indisputable holiness—thus bringing briefly to the papacy one of the most extraordinary figures ever to hold the office.

Pietro da Morrone (Peter of the Mountain) was a Benedictine priest-monk living as a hermit, an occasional option for Benedictines. He came from the hill country of the Abruzzo region fifty miles east of Rome. He fasted every day but Sunday, observed four major fasts a year (three of them on bread and water alone), and draped his scrawny frame with an iron chain. When three cardinals from Rome approached him in his mountain fastness and asked him to become pope, he prayed fervently and then accepted, styling himself Celestine V. Immediately falling under the influence of the French, in four tumultuous months he named twelve new cardinals, seven of them French. He was taking steps to move the papacy to French-controlled Naples when the horrified College of Cardinals persuaded him to resign, the only pope since Rome had become Christian ever to abdicate. Having done so, the erstwhile Celestine V fled Rome by sea but was caught and cruelly imprisoned by the man who persuaded him to quit.[9] This was Cardinal Benedict Gaetani, an individual as distinctly unencumbered by religious asceticism as poor Celestine was given to it. Gaetani then became Pope Boniface VIII, and in him Philip the Fair would find a formidable adversary.

The Gaetani family came from Anagni, forty miles east of Rome and not far from Peter's mountain. They were old nobility, though second ranked behind Rome's warring Orsini and Colonna families. They counted three popes among their ancestors but were politically Ghibelline, young Benedict once getting his head broken in a partisan brawl. Tall, bullet headed, and big jawed, he came to the papacy rude, combative, and with clearly defined goals. He aimed to renew the crusade against Islam, resolve the Sicilian war, pacify feuding Florence, make peace between Venice and Genoa, and save Scotland from the avarice of England's King Edward I. He would fail in all five.

Even in Rome Boniface proved unable to make peace, blatantly promoting his Gaetani clan and thus stoking aristocratic resentment. In May 1297 the Colonnas seized a convoy of Gaetani gold, defying Boniface's order to return it on the grounds that he was a heretic who had effectually usurped the papacy from Celestine. Civil war broke out, which Boniface classified as a "crusade" and which raged for a year. When the Colonnas lost, Boniface was able to destroy their castles and seize their goods, dividing them between the Orsinis and the Gaetanis, and making the Colonnas his bitter lifelong enemies.[10]

His one notable success was neither political nor ecclesiastical but theatrical. In 1300 he proclaimed Christianity's first "jubilee" year. In a surge of pious enthusiasm, pilgrims came from all over Europe and even from distant Asia. A Florentine eyewitness recorded that two hundred thousand people packed Rome for the festivities and that part of the city wall was leveled to accommodate them. Ominously, however, no kings showed up for this celebration.

By then Boniface had already fought and lost his first battle with Philip. Both France and England were paying for their wars of expansion, and with one another, by pirating church revenues. Philip was levying the same tax to pay his troops, whom the pope needed for his crusades. Since a power to tax was also a power to destroy, Boniface issued a bull, known as "*Clericis laicos*," forbidding taxation of church property without prior papal permission, on pain of excommunication.

In England both the clergy and the nobility endorsed the papal ultimatum, which forced the king to accept. Not so in France, however, where the language of the bull rather than its principle evoked outrage. "Toward the clergy, the laity have always been hostile," it declared, a proposition clearly false but potentially self-fulfilling. Philip's ministers raged, the French clergy waffled, one abbot loudly branded Boniface a "heretic and usurper," and the nobles hungered to harvest church revenues themselves. So Philip took a dire step: he embargoed any export of gold or valuables from France and expelled the papal collectors, starving Boniface financially.

Philip had by now flanked himself with two antipapal zealots: the one-eyed lawyer Peter Flote and the law professor William of Nogaret. The former was dispatched to Boniface, by then so hard up that he had to yield by issuing a new bull recognizing the king's right to take church revenues in a "national emergency." The pope also announced the canonization of Philip's grandfather but sent the triumphant Flote home with the parting observation that he "would rather be a dog than a Frenchman."

Although Philip lifted the embargo, the conflict quickly escalated. Under royal pressure the clergy doubled the church tithe to the French crown. The Colonnas, expelled from Rome, found welcome at the French court, where they pressured Philip to depose Boniface. A manifesto was published urging the king to make the church a department of his government. French bishops expressed loyalty to the pope but obeyed the king. "Your power is made of words," Flote taunted Boniface. "Ours is real."

In response, Boniface appointed as his legate in France a man as confrontational and loose tongued as himself, Bernard of Saisset. Bernard, who hailed from rebellious Languedoc, proceeded to speculate publicly on the possible secession of that region from France. Further, he fumed with imprecations against the French

After the resignation and imprisonment of a saintly predecessor, Cardinal Benedict Gaetani was named Pope Boniface VIII by the College of Cardinals in 1294. He began by boldly proclaiming five objectives for his papacy, then failed in all five. But his most disastrous failure came in his bitter conflict with the ruthless Philip the Fair, which changed the course of Christian history.

10. During the "crusade" against the Colonnas, Boniface excommunicated the entire family "to the fourth generation," an unprecedented condemnation of unborn children and a melodramatic excess that became typical of the man.

The fair Philip's final outrage

The Knights Templar, once heroes of Europe, become instead Europe's rich bankers; France's king liquidates them; their last master meets a fiery death, fuming defiance

That the Knights Templar had in their day been Christian Outremer's most courageous and dependable defenders few by the dawn of the fourteenth century would have denied. Yet times had changed, and so had they. Outremer was gone, they were based now on the island of Cyprus, and they had acquired a strange quality that excited intense envy and suspicion. That quality was wealth. They had become, in fact, the world's first international bank.

The order, officially known as the Poor Knights of Christ and of the Temple of Solomon, had changed considerably since its inception after the First Crusade (see sidebar, pages 35–37). What once was a small troop of devout pilgrim protectors had become a secretive multinational company, numbering ten thousand people or more. By bankrolling crusaders, taking their property as collateral, they had become rich through inheritance. Their extensive land holdings and more than one hundred branch offices (or temples) stretched from Scotland to the Middle East. There was no richer organization in Europe.

This guaranteed them covetous enemies. One in particular was King Philip IV of France, who ruled what was now Europe's largest kingdom and whose expenses far outstripped his revenues. His people were being taxed to the limit; he had already expelled the country's Jews and seized their property. Philip (called "the Fair" for his looks, not his ethics) saw the Templars' wealth as the solution to all his problems.

Therefore, on the pretext of launching a crusade and setting up his own order of knights, Philip recruited the help of the papacy, which he now regarded as a French possession since his victory over Pope Boniface VIII (see accompanying chapter). The new pope, Clement V, a Frenchman much in Philip's thrall, approved the plan to destroy the Templars and seize their treasure. As justification the king cited ostensible depravity and heresy, which, he charged, had come to characterize the order in its latter years.

Thus on Friday, October 13, 1307, King Philip unleashed an impressively choreographed police action. Every Templar in France was rounded up, and the torturers went to work. Limbs were slowly racked from their sockets, feet smeared with fat and set on fire, fingernails pulled out one by one. Soon Templars were confessing to all manner of depravity, which included spitting on the cross, black magic, sodomy, and initiation rites involving the "kiss of shame" (wherein initiates supposedly had to kiss the genitals, buttocks, and lips of the order's prior).

This undated illustration shows Jacques de Molay, last grand master of the Templars, being burned at the stake. While the flames licked at his feet, he famously uttered three curses—against Pope Clement, King Philip, and France.

Though Pope Clement registered discomfort with this process, at Philip's behest he nevertheless ordered the rulers of all countries where Templars were resident to arrest and try them. Most complied. At Templar headquarters King Henry II of Cyprus insisted on a fair trial, which acquitted the order. Pope Clement immediately ordered a second trial, however, and sent along a legate to make sure that "justice" was done. Its proceedings remained unrecorded, but the Cypriot Templars were jailed for life.

On March 12, 1312, Clement formally decreed the suppression of the Templar order and the distribution of their goods to their rivals, the Hospitallers. Sensing that they would be the next target for plunder, the Hospitallers set up a monastic state on the island of Rhodes, guarded by the strongest fortress in the Middle East.

Jacques de Molay, grand master of the Templars, by then was in his late sixties. Arrested by Philip four years earlier, he had confessed under torture to heretical acts, but he now recanted these confessions. The enraged king ordered him burned at the stake. The execution took place on March 13, 1314, on an island in the Seine in Paris. As the flames rose around him, de Molay is said to have called down a curse upon Pope Clement, Philip, and France.

Pope Clement died suddenly a month later. Seven months after that Philip died at age forty-six, mauled by a wild boar while hunting. The following year brought the Great Famine, followed by the death of Philip's heir, Louis X, and then a peasants' revolt. Louis's brother and successor, Philip V, died prematurely in 1323, followed five years later by his youngest brother, Charles IV, who died without heir.

Thus ended the direct Capetian line of French kings, though not necessarily the Capetian dynasty. (Since their successors, the Valois, were themselves Capetian descendants, some regard the Capetians as having reigned right through into the nineteenth century.) In any event, what lay ahead for the French kingdom was the Hundred Years' War and a century of agony for all France. ■

This work, entitled Reading of the Sentence Condemning Members of the Templars, *is by nineteenth-century painter Alexandre Fragonard. It is a highly romanticized view of the event. The Templars were questioned behind closed doors while under torture.*

This depiction of the meeting of France's Estates-General in Paris was painted in the eighteenth century by Jean Alaux. It shows the alarmed members meeting in Notre Dame Cathedral after King Philip had declared on the basis of a fake document that Pope Boniface was about to seize all their property on behalf of the church. The session set in motion a chain of events that would culminate in a French-led attempt to kidnap the pope from his home at Anagni, Italy.

monarch, portraying him as "surrounded by corrupt, lying courtiers" and "as bad as any of his men." Worst of all, he questioned Philip's legitimacy. Predictably, Bernard was arrested in his bedchamber one night, tried for treason with Flote as prosecutor, and found guilty in the church courts by a royalist abbot. Both Flote and Nogaret then set out for Italy to demand that Boniface "degrade" his legate and turn him over to the secular courts for sentence.

At that, Boniface boiled over. Previous popes, he reminded Philip, had deposed three emperors and, if necessary, he himself would dump the king of France "like a stable boy." He barraged France with bulls demanding Saisset's freedom, withdrawing all concessions to the crown, and forbidding churches to surrender any tithes. He also summoned the French bishops to Rome for a council the following year to discuss the state of their church and to reform their monarchy. A letter to Philip, *"Ausculta fili"*—literally, "Listen, son"!—chastised him for oppressing the church, debasing the coinage, and hiding behind his ministers. The church is one, Boniface proclaimed, and while the king is responsible for France's temporal affairs, the pope is responsible for the discernment of his sins. For Philip to think that he had no earthly superior was madness. Indeed, it was heresy.

Philip burned the letter and substituted a forgery over Boniface's name. It showed the pope claiming full temporal jurisdiction over France, the French treasury, and virtually all private wealth in the land. Then Flote organized town meetings throughout the country to warn the major families that the church was about to seize everything they had and to present their king as the true defender of the faith in France.

To preempt Boniface's council, set for November 1302, Philip convened in April the country's first "Estates-General" of the nobles, clergy, and townsmen (akin to the English Parliament). He flaunted the forged ultimatum and begged national support for his "defense of the faith" against papal aggression. The nobles enthusiastically denounced Boniface as the Antichrist. The clergy dithered but then, under threat from Flote, sent a plea begging Boniface to make peace.

Boniface castigated the French clergy as cowards, denounced the forgery, denied that he was invading royal jurisdiction, and added a personal message for Flote—namely, that he was headed for hell. Wherever Flote was headed, it didn't take him long to get there. About two weeks later, in a bloody clash with rebellious Flemish militia, the French army was defeated and Flote was killed. Some hoped that this would bring peace with the church. It did not. With Flanders in rebellion, Philip needed more money than ever, and it was William of Nogaret's job to get it.

Only thirty-six of France's seventy-eight bishops attended Boniface's council at Rome in November, thirty-one of them without royal permission, causing their fiefs to be confiscated by the king. The council achieved little, although it did try to resolve a long-disputed ambiguity in the ancient doctrine of the "two swords." There are two swords all right, Boniface declared, one spiritual and one temporal, but the spiritual must instruct and judge the temporal. Moreover, salvation requires that "all be subject to the Roman pontiff."[11]

Boniface then fired his last shot. He sent another legate, Cardinal Jean Lemoine, to Philip with a twelve-point ultimatum, warning that if it went unanswered, the king would be excommunicated and deposed. Receiving no reply, he dispatched a messenger to Lemoine with two more letters, the first excommunicating Philip and the second summoning France's bishops to Rome. The messenger was arrested and the letters burned. Lemoine protested, then fled France.

Meanwhile, at a French council of state Nogaret avowed that Celestine V was still alive, condemned Boniface as a "master of lies," and urged Philip to convene an assembly to condemn the pope. Philip complied. Before an assembly of bishops and nobles at the Louvre, Nogaret read a list of twenty-nine charges against Boniface, including heresy, simony, gross and unnatural immorality, idolatry, magic, loss of the Holy Land, and, finally, the murder of Celestine V. Little of this has been substantiated by evidence, then or since, but Philip declared himself conscience bound to depose the pope. A third of France's bishops concurred. One dissenting abbot was imprisoned.

Fighting back, Boniface, under solemn oath, denied all charges, suspended a rebellious Cypriot bishop for supporting Philip, canceled the right of the French church to appoint its officials, and declared that only popes can call ecumenical councils. He also announced that, failing Philip's repentance, a bull would be promulgated on September 8, 1303, excommunicating the king of France and absolving his subjects from their oath of fealty.

11. Historian Warren H. Carroll describes this missive as "the last, worst example" of Boniface's "tendency to overstatement." In fact, he writes, the Catholic view is that claims of papal authority in "faith and morals" must be supplemented by a qualified independence of judgment in both the pastoral and political spheres.

How far had respect for the papacy fallen when Pope Boniface VIII was struck with a mailed fist at his home in Anagni, Italy, and told to "consider the goodness of [his] lord, the king of France"? (Some records say that the pope was not actually struck, though he was certainly attacked in his bedchamber.) The attackers were driven from Agnani the following day. The scene is portrayed in a nineteenth-century lithograph by Gustave Doré.

But Philip and Nogaret moved first. Furnished with a French warrant to bring Boniface to the "king's justice," bands of armed Italians, under a deposed Colonna cardinal and led by William of Nogaret, crept up to the walls of Anagni on the night of September 3, 1303. The town gates were traitorously opened. Sudden shouts and rattling weapons awakened the populace. "Men and women leapt from their beds, opened the doors, and asked the cause of such hubbub," wrote Boniface's English secretary, William Hundleby of Lincoln. "They discovered that [the Colonnas] had entered the town with a great force from the king of France, that they might seize the pope and give him to death."

Bells clanged and people rushed into the marketplace, but the town captain, brother of one of the intruders, offered no resistance. The crowd, realizing the circumstances, became an opportunistic mob that plundered the villas of the cardinals, then laid siege to the papal palace. Under truce Boniface appeared before them. What, he demanded, did they want? Reinstatement of the Colonnas, they replied, plus the whole church treasury, plus the pope himself as their prisoner. Boniface refused. The truce expired. The mob attacked the adjoining cathedral, barricaded by Boniface supporters, set fire to the doors, broke in, murdered a visiting archbishop, plundered the place, then burst into Boniface's palace. "Long live the king of France!" they shouted. "Long live the Colonna! Death to the pope!"

In the papal chamber they found Boniface seemingly very ill, lying on a couch, crucifix at his breast. "Come forward!" he challenged. "Strike my head. I want martyrdom. I want to die for Christ. Here is my neck. Here is my head." A Colonna lunged forward to oblige, but others restrained him and repeated their three demands. Angrily, Boniface refused. The old pope was then struck, according to one chronicle, with a mailed fist.[12]

Moments later, Nogaret arrived. "What are you doing here, you son of Patarine?" Boniface challenged him, referring to a Cathar heretic. "I arrest you," Nogaret retorted, "by the public law, in defense of the faith. You are a

12. Some accounts deny that Pope Boniface suffered physical abuse. Boniface biographer T. S. R. Boase (*Boniface VIII*) affirms that he did, however, citing the account of Cardinal Nicholas Boccasini, the future pope who supported Boniface.

sad pope! Consider the goodness of your lord, the king of France!" Then Boniface's ornaments were ripped away and his palace plundered, while throughout the town the mob broke into wine cellars and most of Anagni got drunk. "*Papa habuit malem noctem*," the Englishman Hundleby wrote home. ("The pope had a bad night.")

The following morning, while his assailants debated whether to kill Boniface or imprison him, Anagni's citizenry woke up, sobered up, and began repenting. Soon fighting broke out with the intruders. Nogaret was injured. The crowd began shouting for the pope. The intruders scattered. The pope was found and brought down to the market, where citizens dragged the French banner through the mud and implored his forgiveness. Much of the plundered treasure was returned.

A week later a well-guarded Boniface left for Rome, but he was, writes Hundleby, "a broken man." Some accounts describe him as behaving like a madman, gnawing his hands and bashing his head against a wall. On October 12, forty days after Anagni, came the death of Pope Boniface VIII—of "exhaustion," it was said. Ten days later the cardinals gathered in conclave and elected a Dominican, Cardinal Nicholas Boccasini, as Pope Benedict XI. William of Nogaret, with staggering audacity, attended as the representative of France.

Significantly, the near murder of a pope occasioned no general protest, clear evidence of the papacy's declining prestige since Martin IV. In the next six months Pope Benedict, although he lifted the censures against Philip, also demanded that Nogaret appear before him as a public penitent by July 7, 1304, on pain of excommunication. That very day the relatively young and healthy Benedict XI was found dead in his bed. Was he poisoned? No evidence was offered and no such charge ever laid. Nogaret called the death "a miracle."

What very nearly was murdered was the papacy itself. Benedict's successor moved it into France, where for the next seventy years the entire church would become little more than a department of the French government. Nogaret lived nine more years—and died, according to one account, with his tongue sticking out. Philip the Fair would last another ten, during which he would commit one crime more, a crime that some declare worse than the Anagni episode (see sidebar, pages 224–225). ■

The Death of Pope Boniface *is the title of this much-acclaimed nineteenth-century painting by Nicolo Barabino. Boniface was said to have died of exhaustion forty days after the attack on him at Anagni. It left him, in the words of one witness, "a broken man."*

In fury and fire a heresy perishes

The teaching that long thwarted Augustine's conversion breaks out anew; cities are burned, and tens of thousands die in the harsh campaign to destroy it

The town of Beziers, nestled beside the marshlands of the Mediterranean shore west of Marseille, had never before figured prominently in European affairs. In the early thirteenth century, however, something very strange was going on in Beziers—something that appalled the nobility of northern France, seriously alarmed the Roman curia, and was about to issue in a historic tragedy deplored for the next eight hundred years.

For Beziers had become a hotbed of a strange religion called Catharism, whose fanatic adherents actually ran the town and which was spreading throughout the whole region of Languedoc, with powerful people either supporting it or joining it. Something had to be done, and therefore on the evening of July 21, 1209, an army of ten thousand crusaders assembled at the city gates. Their purpose was to take the town and exterminate its Cathars.

But they encountered an immediate difficulty. All the Christians living in Beziers had been asked to evacuate the town and leave the Cathars to their fate, but this warning had been rejected. So how were the invaders to distinguish them from Cathars? They were not there to exterminate Christians.

Next morning, while crusade leaders continued to debate this problem, the town gates suddenly burst open and Beziers' militia charged out and attacked the crusader camp. The crusaders' so-called camp followers—cooks, valets, blacksmiths, workmen, stable hands, armorers, and prostitutes—fought off the militiamen. Then they chased them back into the city and ran wild through the streets, bludgeoning everyone in sight, breaking into houses, stealing, raping, and burning.

The crusader knights, meanwhile, hastily armed themselves and joined the fray,

snatching plunder from the grip of their camp followers—who then resolved to destroy what they couldn't steal and set the whole town on fire. By now women and children were being butchered. Nuns, aged priests, and other Christians cowered in churches, clutching crucifixes. As the flames spread, many were buried under the burning timbers. The slaughter ended only when the heat of the blazing city drove the marauders out. Some would claim that twenty thousand died that day at Beziers.

As for that original problem about identity, one account of the slaughter records a particularly distressing claim. How, someone is said to have shouted amidst the melee, could they know who were Cathars and who were Christians? A voice rang out in reply: "Kill them all! The Lord will know who are his!" This allegedly was the voice of Abbot Arnold Amaury, the legate (i.e., representative) of Pope Innocent III, who had ordered the crackdown on Catharism. Could this be true? Quite possibly, although the claim is a frail one. History, however, repeatedly records how men in the throes of such mayhem—even, perhaps, papal legates—can be led by mob hysteria to do terrible things.

Thus began what is known to history as the Albigensian Crusade, the name taken from the city of Albi, another major Cathar center. The war on the Cathars would claim as many as a million lives in Languedoc, their major region; many of the dead would be orthodox Christians. The crusade would last twenty years, and an inquisition established to complete it would go on for another thirty. One outcome would be the absorption of Languedoc into France.

While many have condemned this crusade, few would defend Catharism. It is usually referred to as a Christian heresy, but it is more, in fact, an echo of ancient Manichaeanism, the religion that diverted young Augustine of Hippo from Christianity in the fourth century. It held that spirit alone is good, while the body and the entire material world are evil. Muslim conquerors had almost wiped out Manichaeanism in the seventh century, but a remnant, the Paulicians, lingered in Armenia. The belief later spread to the Danube basin, where a priest named Bogomil preached it to the Bulgarians. By the tenth century it had appeared in southern Italy, where its followers called themselves the *Katharoi* in Greek, or "Pure" (hence Cathar). By the eleventh Catharism had moved with alarming vigor into Languedoc.

Alarming because of what the Cathars believed. In 1167 they held a public synod at Saint-Felix, where they declared that the humanity of Jesus and his crucifixion were illusions. Jesus was pure "spirit," they said, and came to free souls from the abomination of natural life. Marriage was evil. Homosexuality was preferable because it produced no children. Ordinary Cathars faced few moral restrictions, but the elite of the sect, known as the *perfecti*, lived in such dire austerity that most believers delayed becoming "perfected" until they lay on their deathbeds. Suicide, especially by starvation, was the noblest death.

How is it that such a life-denying faith could flourish in, of all places, carefree, life-celebrating Languedoc? The early thirteenth century was a restless age, a period of wild nonconformity in which the church, sunk in luxury, was widely scorned. Innocent III presided over a Christendom in which monastic abbots lived like dukes, their affluent abbeys often sitting like foreign colonies in impover-ished lands, where the people of the cities flourished in ever-greater isolation from their cathedrals, where children went untaught in the Christian faith, and where superstition ran rampant. "Discipline breeds wealth, and then wealth destroys discipline," mourned the chronicler-monk Caesarius of Heisterbach. He saw this as the "tragic law" of civilization.

Biblically based disgust with clerical luxury provoked anticlerical paroxysms everywhere. In Italy Arnold of Brescia demanded that the clergy return to the poverty of the apostles (see sidebar, page 101). In the Low Countries women known as Beguines lived upright Christian lives in poverty and were slandered and pilloried as lesbians. By contrast, Tanchelin of Antwerp, calling himself the Son of God, roamed Flanders plundering churches and soliciting concubines yet went unmolested because he was protected by a three-thousand-man bodyguard. Flagellants paraded through the streets, thrashing their backs into bloody ribbons, while Peter Waldo's "Poor Men of Lyon" also strove for biblical poverty and were suppressed because they rejected the sacramental priesthood.[1]

The need, Pope Innocent realized, was for evangelism. But the austerity and apparent holiness of the perfecti contrasted so sharply with the life of luxury-loving prelates that even gifted mendicant preachers like Dominic de Guzman, founder of the Dominican order, could not quickly succeed in reaching them (see sidebar, pages 192–193). The preachers needed time, and time was running out.

Already some Languedoc nobles had become Cathars; others, like Toulouse's Count Raymond VI, were sympathizers.[2] His wife, Beatrice of Beziers, was herself a

1. The Waldenses, whose movement began in the 1170s, at first were received sympathetically by Pope Alexander III, but they were prohibited from preaching except with the authority of a bishop in 1179 by the Third Lateran Council. Defying this rule, they were hounded into the Alps and almost eradicated. Their descendants two centuries later would join the emerging Calvinists.

2. Languedoc was a province in medieval France, but the term "province" denoted only a region. It was not a politically defined area. At the beginning of the thirteenth century, Toulouse was a large county, independent of the French crown, that included Languedoc and parts of several other provinces. After Toulouse came under the French crown, largely as a result of the Cathar war, its area was significantly diminished.

Beziers, seen below in this twentieth-century photograph, presides in pastoral serenity over the coastal lands of southern France, giving no clue of the horror that beset it seven hundred years earlier, when it was a center of the Cathar heresy. In one terrible night the Cathars were slaughtered and the town destroyed as the Albigensian Crusade began.

3. Count Raymond VI of Toulouse was the vacillating, luxurious son of a strong father. A patron of troubadours, he is said to have seduced his father's mistress, committed incest with his sister, and repudiated two of his five successive wives. Beatrice, his second, left him to join a Cathar convent. Count Raymond tolerated the Cathars in his lands but considered himself an orthodox if sinful Christian.

Simon de Montfort, Earl of Leicester, in an eighteenth-century sketch. His brutal persecution of the Cathar heretics would long live in infamy. He would blind them, stone them, and burn them at the stake while taking their lands and possessions as his own.

perfecta and very enthusiastic about the prospect of a Catharist Languedoc, free from association with the brutish northern Franks and from Rome's legalism. For eight years papal legate Peter of Castelnau had been pleading for the cooperation of Languedoc's barons in suppressing the Cathars, only to be refused or ignored, threatened with assassination, and, eventually, forced to flee. Finally, on January 14, 1208, came the explosion. After an argument with Raymond, the legate was assassinated by one of the count's knights.

That did it. Pope Innocent declared the crusade and arranged a meeting with the French nobility, at which Raymond, a practiced penitent, sought and gained forgiveness.[3] The attack on Beziers followed, and its horrific destruction brought the quick surrender of such other Cathar centers as Albi and Narbonne. Finally, their strongest city, Carcassonne, capitulated. Here the lives of the citizenry were spared, but their property seized. They marched out, one chronicle laconically remarks, "in their shifts and their britches."

Significantly, the French nobility refused all title to the conquered properties, plainly realizing that if Catharism remained active despite the military defeat, they would be left with a costly and probably unsolvable problem. So papal legate Amaury persuaded the harsh but devout Englishman Simon de Montfort to take over the Cathars' lands and the leadership of the crusade.[4]

De Montfort proceeded to carry out this responsibility with a ferocity that would darken Christian history even in this bleak era. As each city surrendered, the tally of executions mounted. At Minerve 140 unrepentant Cathars were burned at the stake. At Montlaur many were hanged. At Bram de Montfort's men blinded the entire garrison, sparing only one man so that he could lead the others to the next Cathar stronghold. At Lavaur Cathars were stoned and burned by the hundreds while

Dominic, the preacher who had tried to convert them but had failed, looked on in horror. Meanwhile, Count Raymond, recanting his recantation, finally threw himself entirely behind the Cathar cause and regained thirty towns before de Montfort could contain him.

As atrocities and betrayals multiplied on both sides, peace became impossible to achieve. In 1213 the ambitious Pedro II of Aragon led an army across the Pyrenees to support his brother-in-law Raymond, trapping de Montfort at Muret. But de Montfort, although vastly outnumbered, attacked at dawn and scattered them "like dust before a gale." Within minutes Pedro was dead, and Raymond was left to negotiate his exile to England.

Four years later Raymond slipped back into Languedoc and raised the Cathar standard over Toulouse. De Montfort attacked and was killed in the ensuing siege; Raymond died four years later. Both men were succeeded by their sons, neither of whom compared in competence to his father. But now the French monarchy, which had hitherto refused any role in the crusade, appeared as the ultimate victor. Louis VIII rapidly subdued one town after another, and by 1229 his indefatigable widow, Blanche of Castile, had put all Languedoc under French suzerainty. Further, its nobility had agreed to help suppress what was left of Catharism.

But this task, in fact, fell to the church. In 1229 a council at Toulouse began the systematic eradication of Catharism by obliging every adult to swear an explicit oath as a faithful Christian to denounce its teaching. Each parish would provide two laymen and a priest, all called "inquirers" (hence "inquisition"), to search out secret Cathars. When a former adherent named William of Solier argued that public accusation would endanger the lives of accusers, secret indictments were approved.

Implementation was sporadic at first. Toulouse's bishop caught nineteen Cathars worshipping in a forest by night and had them burned, but prosecution was generally erratic. Besides, the system was abused

by private feuds, and unescorted inquirers were beaten or murdered. Therefore, in 1233 Pope Gregory IX declared the first "General Inquisition." To conduct it, he assigned the Order of Preachers—the organization specifically founded to use reasoned argument, not compulsion, on the misguided. In their new role, however, the Dominicans would prove only too efficient.

On their first visit to Moissac, fifty miles north of Toulouse, the new inquisitors condemned 210 to burning. At Toulouse itself, several prominent citizens went to the stake. When the new inquisitors began to exhume and burn long-dead Cathars, however, they became increasingly unpopular. Caught without bodyguards, they were sometimes beaten or lynched, and when twelve members of the Toulouse nobility were indicted, their retainers sacked the Dominican convent.

Pope Gregory ordered the General Inquisition moderated in 1236 and suspended in 1237, but within three years the Cathars at Beziers were once more in open rebellion. It was crushed again by a fresh royal army, and the Inquisition was reestablished. Now only those refusing to recant were burned, but penitent elders and nobles were imprisoned—often for life—with the proceeds of their lands going to the crown. More cooperative penitents were sometimes required to undertake pilgrimages. The humble were fined or made to wear yellow crosses. Within four years such efforts had reduced Catharism to an impotent secret society.

Their last major stronghold, the aerie of Montsegur, was largely ignored until a sortie from this fortress hacked to death four inquisitors billeted in a nearby town. A year later, intent on wiping out this last embarrassment, a royal army besieged the rocky

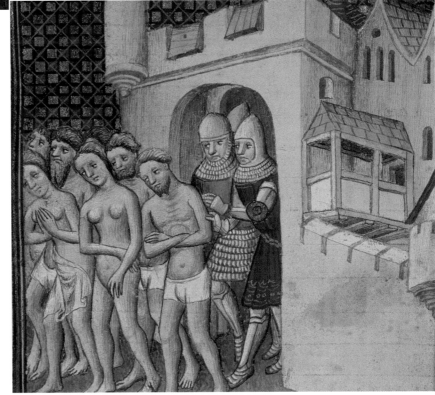

citadel, and within nine months, in March 1244, it capitulated. Much of the garrison consisted of hired Christians, who were left unmolested. Unrepentant Cathars were allowed fifteen days' grace. Those not yet perfecti were admitted to that exalted rank, and these, about two hundred in all, were led out and begged to abjure their errors. When they refused, they were chained to a massive pyre, and within minutes it was over.

The Languedoc inquisition suspended systematic activities in 1279. Over fifty years it had executed some five thousand Cathars, meticulously recording their trials (in notable contrast to the vaster and largely undocumented mass exterminations of the twentieth century). A certain William Belibaste, a perfectus, was lured from exile in Catalonia by an enemy in 1321 and became the last Cathar to be burned. With that, the movement vanished from history. ■

Carcassonne, top, as it stands today, still retaining the walls that made it the strongest Cathar stronghold and the last to fall against Simon de Montfort's crusading forces. Below it is a medieval illumination of the Cathars being expelled from Carcassonne "in their shifts and their britches." Their homes and all their other belongings had been seized.

4. Simon de Montfort, Earl of Leicester, had been the foremost knight to refuse to attack the Christian cities of Zara and Constantinople during the Fourth Crusade of 1204. He may have been cruel, but he drew the line at attacking other Christians.

Genghis Khan, depicted here in a Mongolian bronze, was born to a
warlord among the tribes on China's northern frontier, grew up fighting
for his clan, and by age twenty-eight had control of all the Mongol tribes
and was ready to strike first south, then west. While rejoicing in
slaughter and conquest, this tall, burly man with cat's eyes was a
brilliant administrator and politician who died leaving his sons set to
take over most of the world.

CHAPTER 9

Genghis Khan's attack, the horror of history, bursts out of the east

Mounted archers of lethal skill, speed, and efficiency wipe out whole city populations and seem invincible until their dynastic feuding saves Christians and Muslims

Why on earth, complained the knowledgeable Europeans of the thirteenth century, must ignorant people believe such manifest nonsense? If they weren't spreading rumors about fire-breathing dragons, they were fantasizing about werewolves, or gigantic fish swallowing whole ships. But this latest was the craziest yet. Ferocious creatures with dogs' heads were sweeping into major cities, it was said, killing every living thing in them: animal, plant, or person.

This couldn't be true, of course—and yet, very odd things certainly had been occurring in the 1230s. In England, for instance, the herring business had all but collapsed when most buyers from the Baltic just never showed up. Why? It seemed that there suddenly were fewer people left in the Slavic lands to buy the catch—wiped out, some reported, by hideous horsemen appearing like a whirlwind from lands to the east. People with dogs' heads? Well, maybe not that, but they certainly behaved like wild dogs. They usually left nothing alive, and in any case the stench of corpses made whole cities uninhabitable.

Resistance seemed useless. The princes of the Slavic people, then known as the Rus, reportedly had assembled the greatest army in their history, but in a single battle these hard-riding devils had wiped it out. Beyond them and beyond the lands east of Persia, they were said to have left the storied cities of Samarkand and Bukhara in charred ruin. No one knew where they might strike next, and they claimed that their destiny was to rule the whole world.

1. The personal beliefs of Genghis Khan were shamanistic, and his tolerance of any monotheistic religion arose largely from indifference. Although he admired the learning of religious scholars, he was typically Mongol in valuing religious belief chiefly for any practical assistance it might provide in expanding his power or wealth.

Throughout Europe lofty skepticism turned to dread, and people turned to God. How could this be happening to them, and why? The answer seemed clear: God himself must be punishing them for their sins.

But who were these invaders? Some called them Mongols, and others knew them as Tatars, both words that now struck terror everywhere. Whatever their name, they seemed to come from an exotic land of myth, mystery, and little known fact that lay beyond the northern frontiers of China. And one thing was indisputable: they had already conquered much of Asia, leaving untold millions dead—a catastrophe of a magnitude never before experienced.

Moreover, all these disasters were being attributed to the evil genius of a single man, a tyrant called Genghis Khan, who rejoiced in slaughter and commanded the killing of innocent men, women, and children as his mounted minions raped, pillaged, and plundered wherever they went. (For centuries Genghis Khan would stand infamous as history's most ruthless practitioner of genocide, until technology would vastly expand humanity's ability to wipe out humanity.) Europeans did not then know, however, that Genghis was a brilliant administrator who had imposed superb, if suffocating, order across Asia. Tall and burly, with cat's eyes and cheeks creased by scars, he had implemented his people's first alphabet, for instance, introduced a postal system, and tolerated all monotheistic religions.[1] Although he was a polygamist whose concubines ran into the hundreds, he would safeguard the stability of his vast realms by carefully limiting the succession to sons of his first wife.

Genghis was a product of his people, of course, the nomads of the seemingly boundless grasslands of central Asia, who, in pushing westward for thousands of years, wave after wave, had supplied most of Europe's population in the form of displaced peoples. Yet these Mongols differed from their forerunners. For one thing, they were Asiatic, not Caucasian. They were also, as those in their path were about to discover to their grief, the world's finest cavalry soldiers and by far

The Mongolian army was the most advanced fighting machine of its time, its tactics based on unity of command and communication systems that included twenty-five-mile way stations, banner signals by day, and flares by night. By the beginning of the fourteenth century they were using gunpowder cannons and bamboo rockets powered by naphtha and quicklime. The depiction of Mongol horsemen below is from the Heinz Leger's 2004 film Genghis Khan.

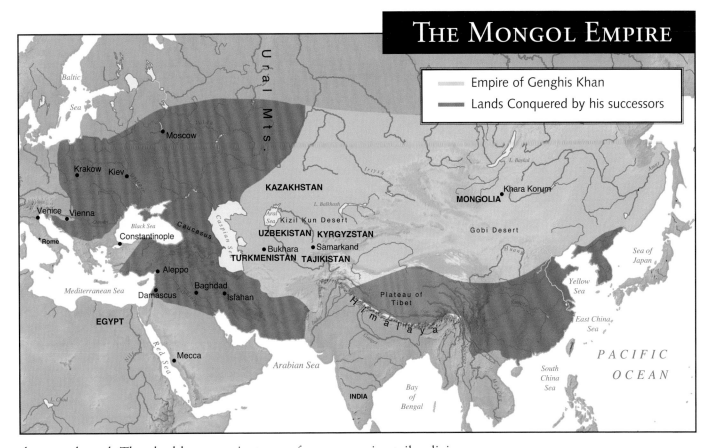

THE MONGOL EMPIRE

Empire of Genghis Khan
Lands Conquered by his successors

the most brutal. They had begun as just one of many warring tribes living on China's northern frontiers, a thousand miles west of Korea. But then came Genghis. Born to a warlord father, he grew up fighting for his life and his clan; by age twenty-eight, through an alliance with the neighboring Kerait Turks, he had subjugated all the Mongol tribes. Then he turned on his erstwhile Turkish allies, killed their leader, and subjugated them, too. Systematically defeating other neighbors, including the Tatars to the east, he built loyalty through rewards of slaves and booty, plus endless promise of new horizons. In 1206 he declared himself supreme khan (king) and all his confederate tribes agreed to call themselves Mongols.

Genghis ruled by superimposing his own family upon one tribe after another as its ultimate authority. From all of them he required heavy tax revenues, troops on demand, and utter obedience to his civil, commercial, and criminal laws. But when he declared that "the greatest pleasure is to vanquish your enemies and chase them before you, to rob them of their wealth and to see those dear to them bathed in tears, to ride their horses, and clasp to your bosom their wives and daughters," he was talking a language that a nomadic horseman could understand.[2]

Driven by the appetite for expansion, he soon led his army against the bordering Chinese states, defeating the weakest, the Tanguts, in 1212, and absorbing the Chin by 1223. After seizing China's westernmost state, Buddhist Kara Kitai, between Lake Balkhash and present-day Kyrgyzstan, he looked westward toward the riches of the Islamic lands of Khiva

2. Despite the Mongols' utter indifference to human life, never-ending butchery, and notorious examples of cruel death, Genghis tended to draw the line at torture. He encouraged this only where he believed he had been personally insulted.

*The inevitably victorious Genghis Khan rides through a conquered
city in an illustration that conveys a sense of the devastation
incurred when a population refused to surrender.*

(Khwarazm), Transoxiana, and Khorasan. These had recently been conquered by the mighty Muhammad Ali Shah, then the most powerful figure in the Muslim world, a man who styled himself "the Second Muhammad" and whose arrogance, as things turned out, was rivaled only by his stupidity.

Genghis first proposed a trade agreement with his new neighbor, but the notoriously vain Ali Shah, who knew little of this nomad khan, was offended by such presumption of equality. His wealthy Khivan domain covered Asia from the Caspian Sea and Persian Gulf to the river Indus and the Hindu Kush Mountains. His subsidiary officials shared his arrogance. When an envoy from Genghis arrived in 1218 accompanied by a huge Mongol caravan intent on establishing trade, the local governor had the merchants all murdered and stole their goods. Then he sent the envoy's head back to Genghis, who, in understandable rage, immediately mobilized an army. Undaunted, Ali Shah confidently posted five hundred thousand soldiers along a five-hundred-mile line in Transoxiana, near his eastern border.

In the first battle, cavalry under Muhammad's skilled son Jalal forced thirty thousand approaching Mongols to retreat. But that sortie was mere theater. Behind it two hundred thousand horsemen were dividing into four armies. Without warning, the first of these descended on the city where the caravan had been massacred and hacked to pieces every man, woman, and child there. All except the governor, that is. He died in slow, screaming agony as molten silver was dripped into his eyes and ears.

All four Mongol armies then converged on the great trading city of Samarkand to capture Muhammad Ali Shah himself.[3] After Genghis's horsemen annihilated fifty thousand foot soldiers, thirty thousand defending cavalrymen tried to switch sides, which left the city completely undefended.[4] The citizens surrendered, and the Mongols took one hundred thousand of them as slaves. They allowed the shah's opponents to keep their lands but executed the thirty thousand would-be turncoats. Muhammad fled but was followed for fourteen hundred miles by Mongol horsemen until, wounded by an arrow, he died of pleurisy on an island in the Caspian Sea, still a fugitive and so poor that he was buried in a donated shirt.

Meanwhile, there was further horrifying news. Bukhara, a hundred miles northwest of Samarkand, had fallen to another Mongol army commanded by Genghis himself. He had surprised the city, hacked its fleeing garrison to pieces, and burned almost the entire place to the ground. The victory at Bukhara is considered one of the most dramatic surprise attacks in all military history. To accomplish it, Genghis apparently conscripted a local guide to cross the Kizil Kum Desert, which the Khivans had believed impenetrable.

Fearing a Khivan resurgence under Jalal, Genghis and his army now headed west from Samarkand, burning crops, razing entire cities, and slaughtering, say the records, virtually every human being they encountered. Although he annihilated Jalal's army at the Indus, Jalal himself managed a daring escape by swimming the river—still holding his standard aloft. So impressed was Genghis by the young

All Mongol boys were trained from an early age in horsemanship and in mastery of a bow with 150-pound tension that could be fired with accuracy on horseback and pierce a moving target three hundred feet away. Mongol warriors, resembling the one pictured in this modern reenactment, could ride for days without food or water and, if necessary, drank blood drawn from their horses' leg veins.

3. Samarkand, about 420 miles southeast of central Asia's inland Aral Sea and 150 miles north of the Afghan border, is the second-oldest city in Uzbekistan. Founded about 700 BC, it was a key point on the Silk Road between China and Europe, and with the Arab invasion of the eighth century AD, it became Muslim. By the thirteenth century Samarkand had reached the zenith of its growth.

4. The figures used in this account—for city populations, size of armies, numbers of dead, mobility of Mongol armies, the totality of Mongol destruction, and so on—are based on contemporary chronicles. Although they are often ludicrously exaggerated, the Mongol invasions were the most ghastly events in history until the technology of the twentieth century made it possible to exceed them.

man's skill and bravery that the khan, watching him flee, was said to have remarked, "Fortunate should have been the father of such a son." Jalal would spend the rest of his life as a roving brigand.

Genghis then dispatched twenty thousand men on a two-year mission to scout the rich lands to the west beyond the Caspian. In 1221 they hit Christian Georgia, now relaxing from the high moral order demanded by its great queen Tamara (see sidebar below). At the time, says James Chambers (*The Devil's Horsemen: The Mongol Invasion of Europe*), Tamara's playboy son, King George IV, was assembling knights for the Crusades. What a fine chance to practice on

The lioness of Christian Georgia

'The lion's whelp is a lion,' wrote the poet, 'be it male or female,' as Queen Tamara vanquished both the Turks and an ex-husband

To George the Rus, officially Prince Yuri of Novgorod, a man not notably inhibited by the knightly virtues—in fact, widely known as an overbearing, brutal, and malicious drunk—here, surely, was an opportunity to seize and rule a great nation. A callow girl, in fact the ex-wife who had divorced him, had continued to reign as queen of ancient Georgia, one of the oldest kingdoms in Christendom. But that any female could rule the rough, tough Georgians? What nonsense! Step one was obviously to get rid of her; it was time to gather an army.

So he did, and in 1190 he marched against the forces loyal to Queen Tamara, heiress of the dynasty that had ruled Georgia for nearly five hundred years. Stirred by their resolute young queen, the royal army quickly quashed the insurrection. The surly George was paraded before the throne he had so recently shared with her and waited the inevitable execution order. But having shown her undoubted courage, the queen now showed her mercy. She banished George otherwise unpunished to Byzantium, a leniency he rewarded by rebelling once more seven years later. Defeated again, he vanishes from history altogether.

By then, however, the queen's capability surprised no one. Running in her blood was the courage of the remarkable Bagrationi dynasty, which would rule Georgia for another seven hundred years, until the Russian conquest in the nineteenth century. She resembled her great-grandfather, King David II, said

A Georgian icon of Queen Tamara. During her twenty-nine-year reign Georgia experienced what would be called its Golden Age, with advances made in science and agriculture, and military victories over the predatory Muslim Seljuks.

to have cleansed his lands of Seljuk Turks and reclaimed cities fallen to the Muslims, who was canonized for restoring Georgia as a unified Christian nation.[1]

The resemblance proved true, for it was during Tamara's twenty-nine-year reign that Georgia enjoyed what historians call its "Golden Age," wherein, it was said, "the peasants were like nobles, the nobles like princes, and the princes like kings." In her reign the Seljuks were pushed out of Armenia farther west into Anatolia and Muslim armies suffered major defeats, in 1195 and 1203.

Tamara's era, says Antony Eastmond (*Royal Imagery in Medieval Georgia*), saw Georgia reach its "cultural apogee," with advances in science and agriculture. But it did not begin easily. The queen, crowned while still in her teens—a mere child, they said, and a girl at that—barely survived her first years in power. It had been two hundred years since the widow of King Gurgen II had tried ruling Georgia, and she had been forced to abdicate by her own Bagrationi relatives. "You, as a woman, cannot control a city," they asserted. But Tamara's father, Giorgi III, thought otherwise, had carefully trained her, and saw that she was crowned as his successor before he died.

Ironically, it may have been the marriage to George the Rus that won her the respect of her people. Whatever his reputation for malevolent debauchery, George was an Orthodox Christian and could these barbarous nomads, he thought, and sent seventy thousand men to confront them. The Mongols soon fled, with the Georgians pursuing them until their horses were exhausted—at which point the Mongols returned, mounted on the fresh steeds they had waiting for them, and wiped out the Georgian army. George escaped but lost again when he challenged the Mongols a second time and died soon afterward.

Riding out of the Caucasus between the Caspian and Black seas, the Mongols emerged on the western steppes, swept up a waiting army of Turkish nomads, and tore a path westward. By the summer of 1222, while their mandarin scholars

Probably the most extolled of Georgia's rulers, Tamara was canonized by the Orthodox Church. She still gazes skeptically from modern-day Georgian currency.

provide the country with an heir. He had orchestrated several Russian victories over Muslim armies, and military achievement mattered greatly in Georgia. But Tamara well knew the marriage had been forced upon her, the contrivance of ambitious nobles preparing to seize the throne. So she swiftly consolidated her power, divorced George, then awaited the predictable coup and destroyed it.

Choosing her own second husband, she bore a son and a daughter, both of whom would later reign. She preserved peace at home by rigorously enforcing the law—"nobody dared to rob a caravan," it was said, while Tamara was queen—and, if need be, she wreaked bloody vengeance on foreign belligerents. The sultan of Ardebil (in modern Azerbaijan) had taken a Georgian city in 1209, slaughtering any civilians his troops could find, thousands of whom were at church for the Lenten services. In response, Tamara waited for the sacred Muslim season of Ramadan. Then her army invaded Ardebil, slaying one Muslim for every Christian who had died. The sultan himself was killed, his wife and children sold into slavery with the rest of the survivors, and Ardebil razed.

Soon, writes Eastmond, "layers of myth, folklore, and romance" gathered about Tamara. To some, she was the "model warrior-queen," to others a "siren-like temptress" who fatally lured men with her beauty. But the most flattering tribute of all was penned by the Georgian poet Shota Rustaveli, called by some "the greatest poetic genius of the Middle Ages," who not only dedicated his masterwork, *The Knight in the Tiger's Skin*, to Tamara but claimed her as its inspiration.[2] "The lion's whelp is a lion," he wrote, "be it male or female."

Tamara, ultimately canonized by the Orthodox Church, was fortunate to have died in 1212, eleven years before the terrifying arrival of the Mongols and the abrupt end to Georgian hegemony. ■

1. King David II's efforts culminated in 1121, when Georgia routed the Muslims near Didgori, conclusively quelling Islamic influence in the region. Known as "the Wonderful Victory," its anniversary is still celebrated as a Georgian holiday.

2. Little is known about Shota Rustaveli, although he may have been a minister at Tamara's court before retiring to a monastery. Georgia has named its highest award for art and literature after him as well as the main street in Georgia's capital, Tbilisi. *The Knight in the Tiger's Skin* is considered its national poem, a work that, as historian Pavle Ingorokva puts it, "trained the Georgian people in the spirit of heroism."

6. The Bulgars appear in history as a Turkish people living northeast of the Caucasus. Overrun by the Khazars, most moved north into the Volga valley, where they formed a Bulgar kingdom that embraced Islam at some unknown time before the tenth century. Others moved west to the Danube valley, becoming Christian and eventually giving their name to modern Bulgaria.

Under the law that Genghis had laid down, all of the leaders of the khanates must return to the administrative capital of Karakorum to elect the next great khan. This halted the Mongol advance during these periods of instability and gave respite to those whom they were attacking. This fourteenth-century Muslim painting depicts the coronation of Ogedei, Genghis Khan's son and successor, in 1229.

mapped and collected data for a projected massive invasion, their scouting army reached the Hungarian border. Before the Slavic princes could organize against them, however, the Mongols began heading home, dispatching a peace envoy to Kiev. Too late, said the prince of Kiev, and he killed the envoy. He wanted a fight.

He would certainly get one. In spring 1223 this Mongol reconnaissance army lured an eighty-thousand-strong Slavic force into a nine-day, 250-mile chase. Then, at the river Kalka, just north of the Sea of Azov, the invaders suddenly turned, confronted the leading Slavic troops, and annihilated them. Slavic contingents coming up from behind were wiped out one after the other by Mongol archers hidden in clouds of dark smoke, making the battleground a black nightmare of slaughter.[5]

By the time the defiant prince of Kiev arrived with his army of ten thousand, half the original force of eighty thousand lay dead, including six princes and seventy nobles. The horrified Kievans turned to flee but were butchered in their entirety, and their prince was suffocated to death beneath the table on which the triumphant Mongols ate their victory banquet. As a further gesture, the conquerors took time to punish the Muslim Bulgars and nomads north of the Caspian, who had sent aid to the "Second Muhammad."[6] This mammoth "reconnaissance," carried out over two full years by men in the saddle riding fifty-five hundred miles and fighting and winning more than twelve major engagements, has been termed the most outstanding cavalry achievement in the history of war. Out of it came the legend of Mongol invincibility.

The aging Genghis now paused to carefully arrange the imperial succession, bequeathing his empire to three sons, Ogedei, Chagatai, and Tolui; and two grandsons, Batu and Orda. (Their father, his eldest son, Jochi, had died young.) He designated Ogedei as supreme khan because he was shrewd and determined but also possessed sufficient friendliness and generosity to maintain army morale and expedite diplomacy.[7] Ogedei's objective was elementary: the Atlantic coast.

To Europeans it did indeed now seem that these heathen warriors would enslave every nation, subjugate every government. Who could stop them? At the heart of their capability were the remarkable tribesmen themselves, toughened and disciplined from birth by their unforgiving nomadic lives. They could ride for days without food or water; if necessary, they drank blood drawn from their horses' leg veins. Sinewy, resilient, and restless, they survived winter blizzard and summer drought. On horseback they could pull a bowstring under 150 pounds' tension to pierce a moving target at three hundred yards. Some fought tigers barehanded to show courage. They were fiercely loyal to their clan, doggedly obedient, and entirely hardened to suffering, their own or anyone else's.

In just twenty years Genghis had harshly subdued clan rivalries, won

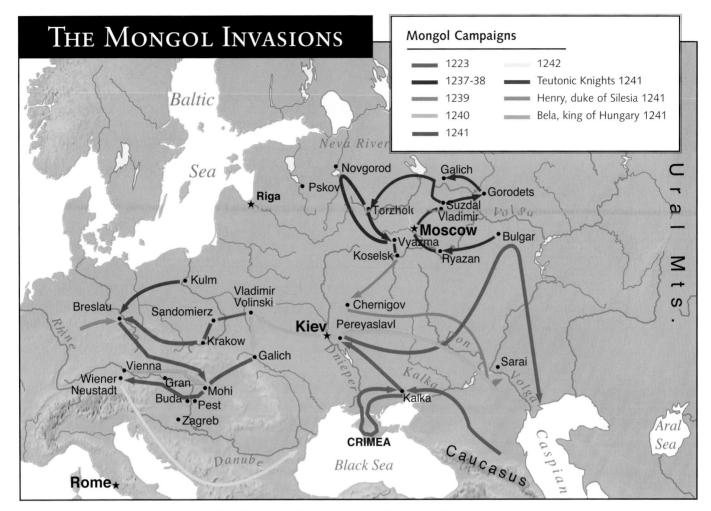

Mongol Campaigns

▬▬ 1223	▬▬ 1242
▬▬ 1237-38	▬▬ Teutonic Knights 1241
▬▬ 1239	▬▬ Henry, duke of Silesia 1241
▬▬ 1240	▬▬ Bela, king of Hungary 1241
▬▬ 1241	

loyalty by sharing spoils, and welded his people into a superbly coordinated fighting force. They could cover 120 miles a day in units of anywhere from ten men to ten thousand. Officers rose via competition, not heredity. Discipline was rigid.[8] Every boy was required to learn archery and horsemanship. Battlefield maneuvers were standardized, and every man from age fourteen to sixty was drilled in them for months.

Administratively and technologically, they now had the most advanced army in the world. Their tactics being based on unity of command, communication systems included horseback messengers and twenty-five-mile way stations, banner signals by day, and flares at night. Camps, always laid out the same way, were run by a quartermaster, who looked after food (likely dried meat and cheese) and communications. Spies performed extensive reconnoitering and mapping. The Mongols could outrace any foe, and their favorite tactic was to feign withdrawal, drawing the enemy past hidden flanks, then crush him from front and back. They created smoke and floods and by 1300 were using gunpowder cannons, incendiary grenades, and arrows and bamboo rockets dipped in naphtha and quicklime.

All this was now directed toward the slaughter, enslavement, and subjugation of Europe. In 1236 Genghis's grandson Batu, with an army one hundred and twenty thousand strong, set about finishing off the northernmost Islamic state, the Bulgar kingdom, on the east bank of the Volga. That done, all territory from the Urals to the Dnieper would be his to seize. To keep open his communications with the Mongol East, he began by destroying or enslaving the nomadic Cuman Turkish tribesmen who roamed the steppes. In the summer of 1237 he overwhelmed the wealthy Bulgarian capital, called Bulgar, exterminating its entire

8. Individual Mongol soldiers were expected to defend one another to the death. If any member of a ten-man unit was captured, for example, all other members of that unit would be killed upon returning to camp. Every soldier was responsible for being fully equipped at all times and was required to keep at least a dozen horses for remounting. Many traveled with up to thirty.

7. The son chosen by Genghis Khan to succeed him as supreme Mongol ruler, Ogedei had one very notable fault: his fondness for wine. This was a trait also exhibited by his father and notoriously shared by most Mongol soldiers. But Ogedei's thirst was sufficiently troublesome to bring complaints from his loyal counselors, especially his chief secretary, who eventually had to take over many administrative decisions as a result of the khan's inebriation. And his death was attributed to a bout of drinking inspired by a plotting wife.

9. At a formal dinner celebrating their success, Batu created discord by violating Mongol custom and drinking ahead of the most senior prince. This so upset his cousins Kuyuk (son of Ogedei) and Buri (grandson of Chagatai) that they stormed out hurling insults. Batu wrote to Ogedei to complain that the two princes had insulted him. They were summoned to the Mongol capital of Karakorum and reprimanded for jeopardizing the campaign but were allowed to resume their commands.

A Mongol march is reenacted in 2006, the eight hundredth anniversary of Genghis Khan's unification of the bickering tribes that thereafter were called the Mongols. During a two-year "reconnaissance" mission westward beyond the Caspian, the khan's forces rode fifty-five hundred miles and won more than twelve major engagements. It has been termed the most outstanding cavalry achievement in the history of war.

population of fifty thousand and razing the place so completely that it was never rebuilt. The vast lands of the Slavic people—fractious, imprudent, and unprepared—now lay open to Batu like fruit ripe for the picking.

As the Battle of the River Kalka receded into the immediate past, the Slavic princelings returned to their ceaseless internecine feuds. The once-powerful state of Kiev, where more than two hundred years ago Prince Vladimir and his wife, Anna, had introduced Christianity (see volume 6, chapter 8), had disintegrated into quarreling provinces. The northern trading center of Novgorod, near the Baltic, had declared independence and was growing rich. Princes fought perpetually with each other over succession and against the free citizens in the emerging cities.

Ryazan, fifty miles east of the Don, was typical. Governed by four feuding cousins, it became the Mongols' first target. Driving an outpost garrison back into the city, the invaders spent a week erecting a wooden palisade all around it to protect their archers and catapults. A three-day barrage of arrows and rocks followed, after which the attackers burst in with battering rams and began their slaughter. Civilians were hacked to pieces with swords, pierced with arrows, flayed alive, impaled, drowned, or burned alive. The Mongols raped girls before murdering them and defiled nuns in churches while priests were forced to watch, and then all were thrown into the fires. They torched the entire city but did allow a few people to run away and tell the rest of the Slavs what awaited them.

As the Mongols burned a bloody path northward in February 1238, the grand duke of Suzdal, the most powerful Slavic prince, traveled the country gathering

vassal armies to defend his capital of Vladimir. The Mongols destroyed his city before he got home, then confronted his army by the river Sit, surrounded it, and annihilated it. Surely, treasure-filled Novgorod, two hundred miles northwest, would be next. But as Batu advanced upon it, heavy spring flooding turned the surrounding fields into marshes. Deprived of his customary mobility, Batu turned southward, and Novgorod escaped.

Now short of supplies, the invaders summered on the grassy plains west of the Don, where they received fresh herds of horses from Mongolia. Through the following winter, they systematically annihilated or enslaved half a dozen nomadic peoples as far south as the Crimea. In autumn 1239 they went north and destroyed the city of Chernigov. Then, following a rare instance of internal discord,[9] they spent the winter on the Kipchak steppes but used the time to reconnoiter Kiev, still the largest and most magnificent city in all the Slavic territories.

In December 1240 they struck. Their army easily battered down the walls, then sliced its way through defenders atop the rubble. The carnage was merciless, and in a horrific conclusion, the weight of people crowding inside the cathedral collapsed its walls. All that remained of the once-splendid metropolis was a hideous pile of writhing and crushed humanity; six years later travelers found Kiev's streets still filled with skulls and other bones. The Rus were close to being vanquished in a stroke. Furthermore, Batu was not the only threat confronting them.[10]

Aggressive neighbors to the north and west saw in the Mongol turmoil a perfect opportunity for themselves. In 1239 a Swedish army swept through Finland

10. The destruction of Kiev ended the city's hegemony over all the Rus peoples. In the coming centuries, these peoples would coalesce into a number of independent principalities, chief among them Muscovy, which would come to dominate all the "Russias." However, the individual peoples maintained their identities right into the late twentieth century, when the country called "Borderlands" (in the Slavic languages "Ukraine"), which had appeared on maps as early as the eleventh century, returned to the maps of Russia with its capital at Kiev.

Above: *The Russian hero and Orthodox saint Alexander Nevsky, as depicted in a promotional poster for Sergei Eisenstein's 1938 film* Alexander Nevsky, *which recounts his landmark victory over the Swedes in 1242. Below: The Imperial Order of St. Alexander Nevsky was introduced by Catherine the Great as Imperial Russia's third-highest military honor. The Soviets abolished it in 1917, then revived it as the Order of Alexander Nevsky during World War II, when it was awarded to forty-two thousand soldiers.*

and began to ravage their northwestern border regions, encouraged by the pope, who viewed the Catholic Swedes as his agents. They aimed at cutting Novgorod off from the Baltic. As has so often happened in the tumultuous history of the eastern Slavic peoples, however, there now appeared the man who could meet the challenge. The Swedes had not reckoned on the leadership or tactical skills of that city's Prince Alexander.

In 1240 Alexander seized the initiative and, though his force was smaller, courageously attacked the advancing army on the banks of the Neva River. Riding at the head of his charging vanguard, he himself cut and seriously wounded the flabbergasted Swedish commander, who barely escaped with his army. In honor of his victory that day, the prince was given the name by which history has remembered him, Alexander Nevsky (meaning "of the Neva"). The Orthodox Church, interpreting the battle as a landmark victory over Catholicism, canonized him.

Yet the heroics at the Neva were only a beginning. A western coalition army spearheaded by a fighting religious order known as the Teutonic Knights was now discerned approaching Novgorod through Estonia, the leading edge of a long-term German drive eastward across Slavic lands. Having begun as crusaders in the Holy Land, the Teutonic Knights were now based on the southern coast of the Baltic and were growing rich and powerful as they fought to impose the "true faith" on schismatics and heathens alike.

Intent upon conversion of the local people to Roman Catholicism, forcible or otherwise, the knights had Germanized or exterminated many Baltic-Slavic and western Lithuanian and Estonian tribes. Lusting after Novgorod's mercantile wealth, they believed its isolation would make for an easy conquest. They were joined by another militant order called the Sword Bearers, formed by the bishop at Riga and allied with the Finns. In 1241 this resplendent but lumbering force captured the city of Pskov, less than forty miles west of their target, Novgorod.

Month after month the knights advanced, but Prince Alexander was delayed by internecine political struggles. Once these were resolved, however, he arrived at speed to drive the invaders out of Pskov. After chasing their larger army back into Estonia, in April 1242 he lured it onto the ice of Lake Peipus, a brilliant choice of battleground. Although his troops barely managed to withstand a furious initial charge by their more powerfully armored adversaries, Nevsky executed a flanking maneuver and then, with the spring ice beginning to crack, a counter-attack. This soon became a rout as the heavy western knights and their big horses broke through the ice and were trapped. The Battle of Peipus would be forever celebrated in Russian history as "the massacre on the ice." It was a defining moment that established the indispensable roles of both Alexander Nevsky and the Orthodox Church in preserving the soul of what would become the Russian nation against its enemies.[11]

Meanwhile, with much of the country in smoking ruins, the Mongols had also invaded the surrounding nations. Their terrible army, like a hurricane gathering

11. Director Sergei Eisenstein's brilliant film *Alexander Nevsky* celebrated the battle and the prince, but the Soviet-produced work entirely ignores Nevsky's deeply held faith in Christ, which was indisputably the mainspring of everything he accomplished.

This 1942 painting by Vladimir Aleksandrovic Serov depicts the celebrated Battle of Peipus Lake, in which Alexander Nevsky's forces lured a far more numerous western army led by the Teutonic Knights onto the spring ice of the lake. The more heavily equipped westerners broke through the ice, and Nevsky's forces went to work.

momentum, had actually grown bigger because of thousands of conscripts, so Batu assigned thirty thousand troops to hold the Rus while he led another hundred thousand across an astounding six-hundred-mile front. His primary target was Hungary, ruled by King Bela IV from Buda, on the Danube. As the main Mongol force under Batu rode directly toward Buda, two others crossed into Poland and Transylvania to wreak havoc among King Bela's potential allies.

The anxious king had tried to strengthen his forces by admitting to his country more than sixty thousand Cuman nomads, but this deluge of pastoral immigrants and their crop-trampling herds caused resentment in Hungary. Some of his barons were determined to drive them out.[12] Did no one, Bela must have wondered, understand the Mongol threat? Apparently not. His war council degenerated into a squabble over compensation. Neighboring rulers ignored his plight. The pope was busy recruiting knights to fight the emperor Frederick II. Only in mid-March, after Batu annihilated defenders in the Carpathian passes two hundred miles east, did Hungary manage to assemble an army at Pest, across the Danube from Buda. Bearing down on them through the mountain snows at an amazing sixty miles per day, the Mongols arrived at Vac, twenty miles from Buda, slaughtered everyone there, and set up camp.

The Hungarian barons responded by blaming Bela and his unreliable Cumans

12. The Cumans had been driven from the steppes of Kipchak Russia by the Mongols. As part of their bargain for Hungarian citizenship, they agreed to become Christians. So eager was King Bela of Hungary to gain their fighting skills that at the baptism of their ruler, Kotian, he volunteered to be godfather.

Fierce fighters against conversion

The western mission to the eastern Baltic peoples began with a martyrdom, was pursued with the sword, and was stopped dead on the ice of Lake Peipus

In 1198 Archbishop Hartwig II of Bremen sent Abbot Berthold of Loccum to Riga, on the Baltic Sea. Along the way, separated from his Saxon escort, Berthold was surrounded by Livonian warriors and ripped to pieces. However inauspiciously, the missionary conquest of the eastern Baltic tribes had begun.

Undeterred, Hartwig sent as replacement his nephew Bishop Albert of Buxtehude, who arrived at the mouth of the Dvina River in 1200 with twenty-three ships and five hundred crusaders to begin his mission to the Livonians. After probing upstream to assess the situation, he finally settled in Riga, a strongpoint easily supplied by sea.

Bishop Albert was no fool. So ferociously did the Livonians resist any effort to convert them to Christianity that he quickly decided a permanent military presence was the only way that his mission would survive. In 1202 he established a small private army of knight-monks called the Brothers of the Knighthood of Christ, or the Sword Bearers, to garrison Riga and the Dvina valley.

The Sword Bearers, however, soon were being accused of every conceivable crime. So plagued were they by scandal, in fact, that contemporaries were not surprised when in 1209 one of the brothers, Wigbert of Soest, went so far as to murder their first grand master, Winno, with an ax. But the end for these infamous knight-monks came in the summer of 1236, when Lithuanians slaughtered most of their army near Siauliai.

Meanwhile, another private army was formed in 1207 by Bishop Christian, a Cistercian missionary to the Prussians who also decided that he needed troops to protect his precarious establishment in Prussian territory. His knight-monks were known as the Knights of the Bishop of Prussia, or the Knights of Dobrzyn, but by 1235, after a lackluster military record, they, too, vanished from history.

But remnants of both groups found their way into the ranks of the older and more stable Teutonic Order of St. Mary's Hospital in Jerusalem. Formed in 1190 to care for German casualties in the Third Crusade, the Teutonic Knights had set up a field hospital during the crusader attack on Acre. By 1198 they had formed into a military monastic community that fought beside the Templars and Hospitallers. Later the Teutonic Knights transferred to the Baltic region to become a key player in the conversion and/or subjugation of the Baltic peoples.

The history of these knights in Europe became somewhat checkered. In 1211 they helped defend Hungary from an attack by the wild Cuman tribes but alarmed Hungary's King Andrew I by petitioning Pope Honorius III to bring them under the direct authority of the Holy See. Viewing this as an attempt for the massacre at Vac and drove the Cumans out of the country after murdering their leader. Nevertheless, the king's remaining army of one hundred thousand was still the largest in Europe, and when Batu failed to attack immediately, Bela began to grow confident. Then Mongol reinforcements arrived from the south, and he watched in amazement as the invading army began a slow departure. They were giving up, thought the king; they must be afraid or in trouble. And so, disastrously, he chased them.

At Mohi, about eighty miles east of Pest, the Mongols sprang their trap. Surrounding the Hungarians, they unleashed a barrage of firebombs and arrows. When a gap finally appeared in the encircling horde and the Hungarians raced through it to escape, they discovered themselves trapped in a gorge where archers could easily annihilate them. An estimated sixty thousand died, though Bela slipped away to exile on the Adriatic. Batu returned to Pest, burned it to the ground, and set up camp.

By then all Europe had been further frightened by news of more mayhem to the north, where the northern wing of the Mongol army had destroyed the Polish cities of Lublin and Zawichost, sacked Sandomierz, and plundered a Cistercian monastery. In Krakow and Wroclaw terrified residents actually burned their own cities and fled. Finally, at Legnica the rampaging horsemen had met an army of

to escape his control, King Andrew expelled them from Hungary in 1225.

The following year the Polish duke Conrad I of Mazovia appealed to the Teutonic Knights to subdue his Prussian enemies, an assignment that they reportedly executed with notable brutality. As the thirteenth century unfolded, they also rolled eastward through the Baltics, crushing in turn the Livonians, the Prussians, the Estonians, and the Finns.

Not that their long campaign to conquer and convert the Baltic pagans was entirely completed, since pockets of resistance and regular revolts by the conquered tribes continued beyond the end of the century. Nor were they able to force Latin Christianity upon Orthodox Russia; their defeat at the Battle of Lake Peipus marked the complete failure of that enterprise (see accompanying chapter).

The eagerness of western Europeans to influence and subdue the Baltic was clearly a product of mixed motives. The papacy sanctioned these military campaigns as crusades, but commercial and political ambitions figured prominently. And as is clearly shown in a document known as the *Erikskrönikan*, describing the expedition of the Swedes against the Finns in 1249, loot and adventure were also important motivators.

Whatever the motives, by the end of the thirteenth century the Baltic Sea had become a "Latin sea" and the political-religious map of the eastern Baltic had been radically reorganized. The cross had been widely planted and eight new bishoprics established. Livonia, Prussia, Estonia, and Finland were emerging from their tribal beginnings. And the frontier of Latin Christianity had been pushed nearly three hundred miles eastward. ∎

A medieval festival in Germany provides a modern depiction of a Teutonic Knight in full battle armor on his warhorse. This order of knight-monks, while founded and active in the Holy Land during the Crusades, was most effective in the Baltics, helping to push the frontier of Latin Christianity three hundred miles eastward.

twenty-five thousand under Henry of Silesia that included Templars, Teutonic Knights, the entire Polish aristocracy, and the full flower of northern chivalry. But even this assemblage was obliterated in short order.[13]

Waves of panic now rippled all the way to the Atlantic. In cathedrals people prayed, "From the fury of the Tatars, O Lord, deliver us." The pope and Emperor Frederick II put their quarrel temporarily aside. The pope called for a crusade against the Mongols in Germany, and Frederick placed his thirteen-year-old son, Conrad, king of Germany, nominally in charge of this operation. Bela, in exile, sent money to build forts on the west side of the Danube. Meanwhile, Bela's chronic enemy the duke of Austria quietly prepared to invade Hungarian territory.

Months went by with no move from Batu—the crusade never materialized either—but then, on Christmas Day 1241, the Mongols exploded with fury against Buda and against Gran (now Esztergom), thirty miles to the northwest. There they reportedly roasted citizens alive to make them reveal the locations of hidden treasure, before riding toward Vienna, about seventy miles farther on. The invasion of Austria had begun. But was Austria the only target? Mongol troops were spotted as far away as Zagreb, east of the Adriatic. These may have been part of an advance contingent of twenty thousand sent ahead in search of King Bela, still in exile off the Adriatic's Dalmatian coast. Panic spread in Italy when some were spotted near Venice.

All Europe, it seemed, lay helpless before them. It would require the combined might of every army in Christendom to stop these horsemen, but such a mammoth, unified force simply did not exist. Then, amazingly, the Mongols vanished. What the Europeans did not know was that Great Khan Ogedei had died of a sudden convulsion. His death had saved Europe, because Batu had to go to Karakorum, where the succession would be contested. However, the dread fear remained, of course; these ghastly marauders would surely return, spelling the doom of Christendom.

But need this, in fact, be so? There were some, indeed, who took a very different view of the Mongols, regarding them not as vanquishers of Christendom but as an instrument by which Christianity

The Mongols under Batu rampaged their inexorable way through the cities of Poland, finally meeting Henry of Silesia's army of twenty-five thousand in Liegnitz. Here the entire Polish aristocracy along with the Templars and Teutonic Knights (shown in the illustration below) were obliterated in short order. Batu's commander ordered the ears of the fallen to be lopped off and bagged to record the number of the dead.

could actually overcome Islam. Might this not be the legendary priest-king Prester John (see volume 6, pages 186–187) become an actuality, killing Muslims because they were infidels and the eastern Slavs because they were schismatics?

For there was another rumor, scarcely credited, that among these horrible, murdering barbarians were many Christians. Europeans were about to discover that this tale was indeed true. Some highly placed officials in the great khan's court were Nestorian Christians. Entirely unbeknownst to most of the Mediterranean world, Nestorian missionaries had since the fifth century established hundreds of churches from Arabia to China and on the steppes had converted nomadic tribes who now formed part of the Mongol confederacy. There were Christian princesses among the wives chosen by the polyga-

Among these brutal barbarians were many Christians descended from tribes long ago converted by Nestorian missionaries. So could the Mongol horror be turned against the Muslims?

mous Genghis Khan both for himself and his sons. One of his Nestorian daughters-in-law, widowed young, was about to engineer control of the entire empire by two of her sons, who would become khans sympathetic to Christianity. Other highly placed Nestorian officials at Karakorum included three chief secretaries and a secretary of state (see volume 6, chapter 7).

When Innocent IV became pope in 1243, his chief question about the Mongols was: would they be back? But two more quickly followed: could their terror be turned against the Muslims, and could they be converted? Seeking answers, in 1245 he dispatched to them a diplomatic embassy led by a portly, sixtyish Franciscan monk called John of Plano Carpini. Friar John made a painful journey to Mongol headquarters in the Slavic lands, only to be directed two thousand miles farther to Karakorum. After a historic three-year adventure, his small party returned as heroes, the first Europeans to have visited the Far East. Unfortunately, the message he brought from the great khan was a humiliating rebuff. Christendom had just two choices, Genghis declared: submit peacefully or perish.

Nor had the friar found any sign of Prester John, although Christians (of the Nestorian variety, unfortunately) were certainly prominent at the khan's court. On the hopeful side, however, an invasion of Europe was unlikely to occur soon because of rivalry between prominent Mongol families. Pope Innocent had sent a second mission, headed by a Dominican, to explore an alliance with Baichu, the Mongol general in Syria. Baichu welcomed the idea and dispatched two Nestorian envoys to Rome, but when no further progress was made by 1248, he recalled them.

There were, in fact, decades of flirtation between Mongol and Christian leaders, led most notably by King Louis IX (the future St. Louis; see pages 140–145) after a Mongol commander in western Asia wrote to him in 1247 offering prayers "for success against enemies of the cross." The commander volunteered to protect the Christians in Persia and proposed that he and the king conduct

13. In both Krakow and Wroclaw annual prayers still commemorate the horror of the Mongol invasion. To record the number of dead at Legnica, Batu's commander ordered ears to be lopped off and bagged. Nine enormous sacks of ears were dispatched to Vac along with the news that Bela now had no nearby allies. Avoiding a large army organized by Wenceslas III of Bohemia because it was too far from Bela to help him, the Mongol forces then broke into smaller raiding groups and rode through Moravia, burning towns as they went.

parallel crusades against the Muslims. Louis immediately sent a friar to affirm such an alliance, but meanwhile the khan had died and his proposal with him.

Reports that Batu's son had been baptized also spurred Louis to send a Franciscan, William of Rubruck, to preach Christ to the Mongols rather than negotiate treaties. But William turned out to be a poor preacher, an ineffectual evangelist, and a severe critic of Nestorian Christianity and of the Nestorians themselves, whom he accused of sorcery, polygamy, immorality, and greed. William's outlook may also have been soured by the fact that his Mongol interpreter, as he complained, was a drunk. His one piece of encouraging news was that the Mongols were preparing to hit Islamic Persia next, not Christian Europe.[14]

Did the popes make a grievous error in not pressing harder for a Mongol alliance? Historians disagree. James Chambers observes that "through lack of trust, Christianity had relinquished western Asia to Islam, and through the paucity

William, a Franciscan, was dispatched to evangelize the Mongols, but he was a poor preacher and a severe critic of the Nestorians. Worst of all, he grumbled, his Mongol interpreter was a drunk.

of its missionaries, the East was to be lost to Buddhism." J. J. Saunders (*The History of the Mongol Conquests*) reaches the opposite conclusion, calling Christian notions of a fruitful alliance with the Mongols "a mirage." If the Mongols had had the chance, he says, they would have destroyed Rome and Florence as they devastated Kiev and Baghdad, and there could never have been a Renaissance based on Christian culture. Steven Runciman, one of the definitive historians of the Crusades, further points out that the Mongols would never have agreed to be subject to anybody. If the Christians had been willing to be vassals of the great khan, they might have got Jerusalem back, but the Mongols would have insisted on ruling it.

As it happened, the man in charge of the great Mongol offensive against Muslim Egypt and the Islamic heartland, the Persian khan Hulagu, actually had significant Christian ties. His principal wife was a devout Nestorian who attended Mass daily and was vociferously anti-Muslim. His chief general, Ked-Buka, was a Christian, and so was his wife. The Christian king of Armenia, not waiting for others to decide, pledged his vassalage and army to Hulagu. Christians from Georgia also joined, and eventually even Bohemond, the crusader prince of Antioch and Tripoli, threw in his lot—for which Pope Alexander IV later excommunicated him.

By January 1256 Hulagu had assembled a force of one hundred thousand. His first objective was to destroy the independent Shi'ite sect called the Assassins in their mountain fortresses near the Caspian Sea (see sidebar, pages 76–77). More than one hundred Assassin castles crumbled over the next year, pounded by a thousand crews of Chinese catapult bombers; every inhabitant, including women and children, was slaughtered. The strongest Assassin bastion, Alamut, about sixty miles north of Tehran, would hold out for

14. Another notable effort at a Mongol-Christian alliance would be made by Kublai Khan, who was fascinated by the story of Jesus Christ and his heroic sacrificial death. He was also impressed by the institution of the papacy, its wealth, and its enormous power. After Venetian merchants Nicolo and Maffeo Polo arrived at his court in 1269, Kublai requested that they return with a hundred learned Christians to instruct his people in Christianity. The pope sent two Dominicans, not a hundred, and both abandoned the mission; Nicolo Polo's son Marco reached Kublai's court without them in 1275.

three years. Thus in some thirty-six months the Mongols eradicated the entire sect, something the Muslims hadn't managed in two hundred years.

Hulagu's juggernaut now rolled toward Baghdad, on the Tigris River, home of Sunni Islam's highest caliph, and drowned defending soldiers by the thousands by breaking a dike and flooding their camp. Then, bursting through Baghdad's weakly defended walls in February 1258, the attackers unleashed one of the biggest and bloodiest single-city massacres in human history. It began after remaining troops voluntarily disarmed, expecting to be conscripted, but instead were systematically marched out of the city and butchered. Then the Mongols killed more than a half million surrendering civilians, although they spared the Christians huddled in the Nestorian church.

After a week of bloodshed, pillage, and plunder, Hulagu burned before the eyes of the caliph what was left of Baghdad, then had him sewn up in a carpet and trampled to death by horses. Muslim historians put the total killed as high as two million; other estimates favor about eight hundred thousand. The cities of Syria fell like dominoes after that, and at one, where a Muslim prince had murdered a Christian priest, Georgian and Armenian troops fed him pieces of his own flesh until he choked to death.

Then further stunning news arrived. The conquest of Egypt was on hold. Hulagu was taking his army away because back in Karakorum the supreme khan Mongke had died of dysentery and because of politics surrounding the succession, Hulagu needed to protect his capital in Azerbaijan. Once again, the death of a khan had saved an empire, this time the Muslim one.

The Mongol target, now abandoned, had been the Mamluk regime in Egypt, the same that had produced the remarkable Saladin, who had taken Jerusalem in 1187 (chapter 3) and had thwarted the attempt of the Third

Hulagu Khan is pictured above in a fourteenth-century painting by Richard al-Din. His principal wife was a devout Nestorian Christian who attended Mass daily and was vociferously anti-Muslim. His chief general, Ked-Buka, was also a Christian, as was the general's wife.

This fourteenth-century depiction of the sacking of Baghdad by Hulagu in 1258 scarcely conveys the horror of what is reputedly the largest and bloodiest single-city massacre in history. Virtually every living thing was killed in an orgy of carnage that lasted a week and claimed, according to one of the accounts, more than eight hundred thousand human lives. The cities of Syria now fell like dominoes.

Crusade to win it back. Nearly a century later the Mamluks would drive the last crusaders from the Holy Land, as described in chapter 5. During that same century, they would perform one further service for Islam. In the events about to unfold, they would drive the Mongols from the Holy Land as well.

After Hulagu called off the offensive against Egypt, he reduced the Mongol force at Damascus to a mere twenty-five thousand men under the command of his chief lieutenant, the Mongol Christian Ked-Buka. The Mamluk general in Egypt, the same Baibars who later, as recounted in chapter 5, would begin the process of driving the Christians out of Outremer, now approached them in their base at Acre. Would they join him, he asked, in an attack on Mongol-held Damascus? Failing that, would they let his army bypass Acre en route to its attack on Damascus? To the latter the crusaders agreed, and they even amiably feasted Baibars as his forces passed by. Meanwhile, Ked-Buka, discovering the peril, conscripted more than one hundred thousand men from the remnants of armies Hulagu had defeated. Marching south, he crossed the Jordan and rode ten miles beyond into the same valley where, it was said, David slew Goliath.

Spotting Ked-Buka's advancing Mongol army near a village called Ain Jalut, the Mamluks under Baibars broke and fled. Ked-Buka pressed close in pursuit but, too late, found he had been trapped; his army was engulfed and slaughtered. The Mongols had been defeated, that is, by their own familiar tactic, the feigned retreat. Moreover, the myth of Mongol invincibility was destroyed forever. Islam now began its resurgence from the near oblivion to which the Mongols had reduced it, and because of continuing power struggles at Karakorum, the Mongols would never again mount a serious attack in Palestine or Syria.

Ain Jalut had worked another fundamental change. In the words of historian Chambers, "The final methodical expulsion of the crusaders from Palestine had begun." The Mongols tended to measure the value of any religion by its results. The Muslims were the first and only people to defeat them on the battlefield, leading them to speculate that God really did favor Islam. When the Muslim conquest of Acre followed thirty-one years later, writes historian Laurence Browne (*The Eclipse of Christianity in Asia*), it doomed Christian prospects all across the East. Even those Mongol rulers who were positively disposed toward Christianity became increasingly hostile to "a religion of proved feebleness." Besides, historian Saunders observes, Christians "did not speak with one voice." Rome,

Constantinople, Nestorians, Maronites, Jacobites, Armenians, Copts, and others all vied against one another.

Always a "religion of foreigners" in China, notes Richard Foltz (*Religions of the Silk Road*), Nestorian Christianity enjoyed a modest surge after Mongols took control of the trans-Asian trade in the 1200s, displacing the Muslim merchants who had dominated these Central Asian cities. After Islamic traders reappeared, Nestorianism began an irreversible decline, not because it was based on heresy, Foltz emphasizes, but for lack of serious missionary effort. This was equally true of western Christians, despite the opportunities revealed by their thirteenth-century embassies to the East.

The Mongols tended to measure a religion's value by its results. The Muslims were the only people to defeat them in battle, leading them to speculate that God really did favor Islam.

However, while Islam had retained most of the steppelands of central Asia, it had missed the biggest prize of all, notably the future Ukraine and Russia. The explanation lies in the practical sagacity of the man who had stopped the Teutonic Knights and the Swedes. Some historians to this day castigate Alexander Nevsky for subjecting his peoples to more than a century and a half of virtual serfdom under the Mongols. Yet his reasoning seems unassailable. He knew that until the Slavic princedoms could be united, they had no hope whatever of defeating the Mongols. Therefore, with great sincerity he made himself a vassal prince of the "Golden Horde," as the Mongols who occupied or controlled the eastern

The Jezreel Valley, shown below, was the site of the first major Mongol defeat near the village of Ain Jalut. In this valley, said to be the locale where David slew Goliath, the Mamluk Muslims under the fearsome Baibars employed the Mongols' own military gambit and reversed forever their advance in the Middle East.

Slavic lands came to be called. For the next century and more, they exacted money and conscripted manpower from the exhausted cities and countryside, thwarting their development and turning them into a feudal backwater isolated from both Europe and Asia.

From a capital set up at Sarai, on the lower Volga just sixty miles from the Caspian Sea, Batu ruled with iron severity and demanded humiliating servitude. (He executed one prince simply because he exported horses without a license.) The Golden Horde shortly emerged as an independent state within the Mongol Empire.[15] Batu's clansmen preferred to roam the steppes, where they enslaved other nomads but had little contact with cities, most of which continued to stagnate in depopulated ruin. But of course he stationed garrisons throughout the north, and his ferocious soldiers thundered in without hesitation if anyone failed to pay tribute or hinted at rebellion. Christians took hope when one of Batu's sons was baptized into the faith. Under the reign of Batu's brother, however, the whole Golden Horde converted to Islam, though their interest was plainly centered in wealth, not God.

On Russia's northwestern frontier, Alexander Nevsky was the first prince to become the Mongols' servant. He had proven his courage at Neva and Lake Peipus, but he knew that the Teutonic Knights and Swedes would keep on attacking and that his people were far too weak and disunited to withstand them or other serious enemies while trying to expel the Mongols. Thus, he gave them the chance to survive by gaining the favor and confidence of their overlords.

Not everyone could see Alexander's point. His own brother Andrew, for example, insisted upon raising a rebel army but wound up fleeing to Sweden after Batu destroyed it. There were others as well whose refusal to compromise turned them into heroes. Prince Michael of Chernigov, for example, arriving before Batu to pledge his service, could not bring himself to kneel before a statue of Genghis Khan when commanded. He was thereupon executed, becoming a saint-martyr in the Orthodox Church.

After the pope failed to deliver on a promised crusade against the Golden Horde in 1253, the wisdom of Alexander Nevsky's course became clearer. While the Mongols dominated and impeded the development of eastern Slavic lands for two centuries, the nation's future history was shaped by the ascent of Moscow in prosperity and power, enabled in part by the relative independence Nevsky had secured for it. By paying tribute money promptly to the Golden Horde, he and his successors kept the Mongols away. Moscow also became the seat of the metropolitan of the Russian Church, which made it a religious as well as a political center. By the mid-fourteenth century Moscow dominated the northern territory and from this base would become the eastern Slavic champion against both the Mongols and covetous western neighbors.

Recognizing that the Orthodox Church was the best instrument for keeping peace among warring Russian princes, the Mongols strengthened it by refusing to levy taxes on it and eventually made it the most powerful force in the land, a role it would play in Russia right into the twentieth century. For all this the church honors St. Alexander Nevsky. In due time

15. Batu was alienated from Odegei's successor, Kuyuk, but supported Great Khan Mongke, who rewarded him with virtually complete independence. Thereafter Russian princes swore allegiance to Batu and his successors. The Golden Horde remained independent for more than two hundred years. In fact, the lower Volga region around Batu's capital was Turkish speaking and partly Islamized before his invasion. Even Batu's fiercely Muslim brother Berke was not interested in further challenging the Christian Byzantine-Slav culture to the north.

A nineteenth-century painting of Alexander Nevsky by Afanasiy Yefremovich Kulikov. Nevsky planted the seeds for a unified Russian state by subjugating himself and his country to the Mongol Golden Horde. The stability created by this decision allowed him the freedom to fight off the Teutonic crusaders and set Moscow on the path to become the most powerful city in his new Russia.

the metropolitan at Moscow, working hand in hand with the grand prince of Moscow, would shake off the "Tatar-Mongol yoke." Fittingly, their expulsion would begin with a signal Muscovite victory on the same river Kalka that had witnessed the first catastrophic Slavic defeat a century earlier. And, like the Muslims at Ain Jalut, this time the Slavs would use the feigned retreat, the very tactic they so painfully had learned themselves from the Mongols. But that story belongs to the oncoming era and to the next volume of this series. ■

St. Francis of Assisi, shown here contemplating death in a painting by Francisco de Zurbaran (c. 1635). He created a quiet revolution in all western Christendom simply by listening to and following the words of Christ.

CHAPTER 10

The man from Assisi who taught the world the realities of Christ

After a young life of wealth, women, and war, Francis suddenly went a little 'crazy,' obeyed Jesus literally, lived as a beggar, healed the sick, and drew thousands to the cause of compassion

He must have cut a curious figure, that slight young man with the beatific smile who spent most of his time dredging stones from crumbled building sites and hauling them out of town in a sack over his back, almost always singing. When kids threw things at him, he would just duck and smile at them. They also called him names, though we don't know what—"Crazy Frank" or something like that.

Everybody knew about him, of course. He was the playboy son of crusty old Peter Bernardone, who had made a lot of money in textiles, and he used to work for his father. But then Crazy Frank got religion and went sort of berserk. He had a terrible row with the old man, started dressing in rags, and began to rebuild the derelict church in the woods just outside town.

Some things about Crazy Frank everybody did not know, however—in fact, nobody knew, including, at this point, Crazy Frank himself. They did not know that the man they were jeering at was about to trigger one of the greatest reforms the Christian church would ever experience, helping to produce what would one day become the most compassionate society in history—namely the western world at the close of the twentieth century. For his name was not Frank, it was Francis, and the name of his town was Assisi.[1]

To be strictly accurate, his name was not exactly Francis either. When he was born, around 1181, his father was in France on a business trip and his mother had him baptized John. But Peter Bernardone so loved the French language and people, it was said, that he nicknamed his son Francesco—"Little Frenchman"—

1. Assisi, whose population was about 25,000 at the end of the twentieth century, is in the Italian region of Umbria, near the city of Perugia, some ninety miles due north of Rome.

2. The wars in which Francis fought were not mere skirmishes. They were bloody, vengeful, and frightful. When Frederick Barbarossa's son succeeded him as the emperor Henry VI (see chapter 4), the German hold on the anti-imperial Italian cities was briefly lost. Assisi rose in rebellion, slaughtered all the German nobility, destroyed the castle that had been occupied by the imperial garrison, and set about enjoying their new-found freedom from the empire. But the holiday did not last. Assisi's long-standing rival twelve miles to the west, pro-imperial Perugia, had lost heavily through the rebellion. So Perugia declared war, the war in which Francis was involved.

3. Leprosy, rampant in Europe in the late Middle Ages, causes sores and oozing boils to break out, result-ing in a putrid odor and sometimes hideous disfiguration. Though lepers occasionally would appear on the roads outside the towns, they were generally confined to lazarettos, or leper colonies, of which, according to one account, there were twenty thousand in Europe at the time.

The magnificent Franciscan center dominates the town of Assisi with its monastery and the Basilica of St. Francis, both created by the Franciscans as a tribute to their beloved founder. Soon after Francis's death, work on these buildings was begun by Brother Elias, later a minister general of the order, who firmly rejected the Franciscans' "begging-bowl" era.

and it stuck. The boy grew up to be a charming youth and a great salesman in the family business because his customers loved him.

But he was also a lavish spender, a leader in the bawdy youthful revelries of Assisi, and a connoisseur of fine wines, troubadour songs, and loose women. "He lives like a prince," his father complained. One of his early biographers went fur-ther, describing Francis as "a slave of sin . . . sated with carnal pleasures," who "did not scruple to go beyond his masters in immorality."

Since he kept company with Assisi's young gentry and cherished ambitions for fame as either poet or soldier, Francis eagerly answered the call to arms when Assisi's ancient enemy, neighboring Perugia, declared war in 1201.[2] He fought bravely in the fierce Battle of Ponte San Giovanni, say the chroniclers, but he and his companions were taken prisoner and spent the next year in a Perugian prison. There, while the others bitterly mourned their fate and continually berated one of their company, whom they held responsible for their capture, Francis kept singing the whole time about how lucky they were to be alive and comforting this man.

Upon release he returned to Assisi and a year later spent inordinate sums to reequip himself fully as a knight. This was something that many even among the nobly born could not afford, but Francis acquired the finest accoutrements avail-able—horse, weapons, and armor, with a finely embroidered robe over all. As he left for battle, however, an odd thing happened. Encountering another knight who was miserably equipped and shivering in the cold, Francis spontaneously removed his splendid cloak and handed it to the man. His comrades were astounded.

As the army moved toward the front, they got another shock. At Spoleto, about twenty miles south of Assisi, Francis suddenly quit and turned for home. Was he afraid? Was this cowardice? Not likely: he had always seemed heedless of death. He mentioned something about a dream, a vision of Jesus Christ that told him to return.

A little later, it came his turn to play the traditional role of host-fool at one of the Assisi party crowd's regular bashes. He obliged but was unusually silent through the evening and lagged behind when everybody spilled out drunkenly into the town. "What's the matter, Francis?" somebody jeered. "Are you in love?" Yes, he replied, he had found a wonderful bride, noble, rich, unmatchable. "Her name," he said, "is Lady Poverty."

That did it. From then on, his conduct became really strange. He began hand-ing out money to beggars. Where he had always shown a particular horror and revulsion for lepers, he now began befriending them, even actually embracing

them.[3] And he kept reciting certain Gospel passages. "Sell all and give to the poor . . . Take no thought for the morrow, what you shall eat and what you shall wear . . . Insofar as you did it to the least of these my brethren . . ." You cannot ever really help the poor, Francis would later write, without becoming one of them.

The humiliation all this caused his father is hard to exaggerate, but the grand climacteric came after Francis visited old St. Damian's Church, overgrown by weeds and falling apart, at Portiuncula, about three miles west of town. As he would later describe his experience there, he was praying before the altar of the tumbledown church when he had a clear vision of Jesus, who said to him, "Francis, as you can see, my church is falling to pieces. Go and rebuild it." Realizing that this would require money, he went to his father's store, seized a great bolt of cloth, sold it, and took the money to the old priest who lived by the crumbling church. The priest, suspecting where it came from, refused to take it, so Francis threw it on the ground.

In the thirteenth-century church fresco above, the young Francis, newly and richly equipped as a knight, astonishes his friends by handing over his tunic to a poor knight. Not long afterward, following a vision, he would quit war altogether and give away all he owned.

His father, enraged beyond measure, soon tracked him down, sprang wolflike upon him, and began beating him mercilessly. Francis fled, hid for a month in a cave, then was arrested. Though his father had reclaimed the money, the young man was arraigned before the civil magistrates. But all he did, he protested to the court, was what Jesus said everybody ought to do. Ah, said the magistrates, so this was not a civil case but an ecclesiastical one, and, doubtless with some relief, they referred the matter to the bishop of Assisi.

Bishop Guido, a saintly man, listened to Francis's Gospel-based argument at what appears to have been a public hearing. Though he clearly admired the impetuous youth, he explained that the Gospel did not empower him to take his father's property. Dramatically, Francis thereupon removed his clothes and handed them to his father. Now, he declared, he had only one Father, "Our Father who art in heaven . . ." and he recited the rest of the Lord's Prayer.

The bishop gave him some clothes as he left, but outside town, going he knew not where, Francis was pounced upon by robbers, who all but stripped him, beat him up, and left him for dead in the snow. Struggling to his feet, he stumbled on to a nearby monastery, where he worked for several days as a scullery hand.

Told by Jesus in a vision to "rebuild my church," Francis immediately set about rebuilding an old debilitated church at Portiuncula, about three miles west of Assisi. Today this old church is preserved within the Basilica of St. Mary of the Angels.

Then, it is said, even the monks rejected him. Only one possibility remained: the leper colony. Welcomed warmly, he remained there, dressing their sores and caring for them.

But this, he soon realized, was not rebuilding the church, so Crazy Frank returned to St. Damian's and, stone by stone, began its reconstruction. Though the records are unspecific, it appears that he completed the job and worked on two other churches in the Assisi vicinity as well.

Then one day he asked Christ in prayer whether this was how he was to spend his life. The answer came in the Gospel for that day: "As ye go, preach, saying, 'The kingdom of heaven is at hand. Heal the sick, cleanse the lepers, raise the dead, cast out devils. Freely ye have received. Freely give. Provide neither gold nor silver nor brass for your purses, nor scrip for your journey. Neither two coats, neither shoes nor yet staves, for the workman is worthy of his meat [i.e., pay]'" (Matthew 10:7–10).

Hearing this, Francis leapt to his feet, shouting, "This is what I have been waiting for! This is what I have been seeking! This is what I long with all my heart to do!" This time he returned to Assisi to seek souls, not stones. He begged for his food and he preached on the street, and the crowds who came to hear him grew larger and larger. Finally, with the bishop's permission, he preached at the church of his childhood

in Assisi, reducing the congregation to joyous tears. From that point on, notes his twentieth-century biographer Omer Englebert (*Francis of Assisi: A Biography*), the scorn and ridicule of Crazy Frank stopped. Whatever his idiosyncrasies, he moved the people of Assisi as nobody ever had before.

Talk about him reached the ears of a wealthy local magistrate, known as a wise and good man, whose house was palatial and whose responsibilities wide. Bernard of Quintavalle, curious whether this preacher was crazy or holy, asked Francis to spend an evening with him. The consequences were astounding. Bernard decided to join him and queried what he must do. He must take everything he possessed, replied Francis, and give it to the poor. So Bernard did just that in the most literal way possible. Standing at the door of his mansion, he handed out money to anyone who wanted it while the poor (along with a great many who decidedly were not) came and stripped the place. Assisi, to put it mildly, was flabbergasted. A third man named Peter, about whom little is known, joined them, and the trio lived together in Francis's reed hovel at Portiuncula.

There, what became the Franciscan order was born. A week later, a farm boy from the area came to Francis, fell to his knees, and begged to follow him. He had not come there on his own, Francis assured him, raising him to his feet; he had been called by a king greater than any emperor, and thus Brother Giles joined the Franciscans. The four lived by begging and working not for money but for food.

Modern-day Franciscan brothers from the friary of Fiesole, about five miles northeast of Florence, Italy, relax with the Florentine hills beyond them. Living much as their master did, they own nothing and practice the vocation of preaching. The Order of the Friars Minor had sixteen thousand members at the end of the twentieth century with fifteen hundred houses in one hundred Franciscan provinces worldwide.

Often when they traveled in pairs to nearby communities to preach, they were mocked, beaten, and stripped of most of their ragged apparel, and women were terrified of them. But they took comfort from this, remembering that Jesus had said, "Blessed are you, when men shall revile you, and persecute you, and shall say all manner of evil against you falsely for my sake" (Matthew 5:11).

Nevertheless, individuals sometimes responded unreservedly to them, and soon their number grew to twelve. Francis named them "the Friars Minor," meaning "the little brothers," the name they would carry through history. They must never hold high office, he stressed (a rule they were not long destined to observe, for many would become bishops and distinguished academics, and four would be elected pope), but their work, he serenely assured them, would soon attract thousands of men.

So confident was he about this that he decided such a massive movement must have the approval of the pope. This was something a new religious order did not officially require; a bishop's approval would have sufficed. The twentieth-century Christian essayist G. K. Chesterton, in his delightful biography of Francis, calls this idea an instance of his "brilliant blindness." In any event, in about 1209 Francis led the twelve to Rome, where Pope Innocent III, taking the ragged figure to be a swineherd, told him go away and tend his pigs. When further informed about Francis's little group and their insistence on literally penniless poverty, he still dismissed them as crazy.

Two things changed the papal mind. One was the case advanced by Cardinal Giovanni of San Paolo, who knew of Francis and admired him. How could the church reject a man, the cardinal argued, for obeying Jesus' specific instructions? Would this not imply that the Son of God was wrong? Moreover, in view of the

This well-known fresco by Giotto di Bondone in the Basilica of St. Francis at Assisi shows Francis famously preaching to the birds. Legend has it that Francis could commune with animals and make himself understood to them. He spent much of his time releasing animals from traps and once reputedly negotiated a truce between a ferocious wolf and a town. Giotto, as the artist is known, is considered the first of the great contributers to the Italian Renaissance.

fact that one of the papacy's greatest current problems was the unbecomingly affluent life now being led by so many of its clergy, this was surely no time to dismiss Christians of the opposite inclination.

Even more decisive, however, was a dream Innocent was said to have had that very night, in which he saw Rome's great Lateran Palace about to collapse and being held up by a solitary man who appeared to be a beggar. So he approved the Friars Minor and their seemingly impossible rule of life. The decision, as things turned out, would felicitously exempt the Franciscans, who were viewed with increasing horror by many senior clergy, from a general ban on new orders passed by the Fourth Lateran Council some six years later. Innocent, once committed, remained resolute in his support.

Pope Innocent III, importuned by Francis to approve his order of friars, initially took the ragged supplicant for a swineherd (as represented in this nineteenth-century English engraving). But how, asked a sympathetic cardinal, can the church reject a group for taking Christ's teaching literally? This, along with a vision he beheld in a dream, convinced Innocent to sanction the Franciscans.

The events of the following eight years, although they strain credulity, yet stand as unarguable fact. As the Friars Minor spread their preaching to other cities in Italy and beyond, their way of life began to capture the imagination of hundreds and then thousands of men, young and old, rich and poor, learned and ignorant. Many came from or even headed noble or wealthy families, many were brilliant teachers, many were members of the "secular" or diocesan clergy.

Some joined and quit. Some broke the rules, refusing to beg, for example, or secretly retaining "possessions," such as a priest's breviary, the volume containing the Psalms and other readings of the Divine Office for each day. For monks and canons the office had always been sung in community, but for the friars, often on the move, it became an individual obligation involving a need to have a book at hand, and therefore they were tempted to own one. Francis worried about the differences this could introduce among the brothers. He pictured one saying to another, "Bring me my breviary." Thus, any ownership involved temptations. Some gave in to them and were expelled. But nearly all remained loyal, meeting or striving hard to meet the stern demands of Lady Poverty.

Whatever the explanation for this explosion (mass hysteria, a subconscious yearning to escape life's more onerous responsibilities, or the grace of God, all of which were suggested at the time), the one integral factor unquestionably was Francis himself. In the earliest days, of course, his friars knew him personally and hung on whatever he said, did, or required them to do. As the movement spread, many would never meet him but would thrive on all the stories about him, many of which no doubt were true and many no doubt legendary.

Clare Offreduccio, the beautiful eldest daughter of a rich Assisi family, was so inspired by Francis's sermons that she abandoned an illustrious future, cut off her hair, and became the founding sister of the "Poor Clares," the order of Franciscan women. She proved an able leader, being practical and level headed in a crisis, and able to win arguments, even with popes.

There was his preaching, for instance. He spoke without notes, without "sermon aids," without dialectical argument, without even notable eloquence, yet he somehow enthralled. Once when preaching before the pope, he broke into a dance, joyous in the presence of God. No one laughed; many began to cry and sing. Bells were often rung as he approached a town. After one of his sermons, thirty men came forward and asked to join his order.

Even more compelling was his unbounded love of the natural world around him and the stories—legendary, factual, or a combination of both—about his relation to furred and feathered creatures. He releases a hare from a trap, for example, and it comes and nestles in his arms. He speaks to birds and they clearly comprehend him. Most celebrated of all is the tale of the ferocious wolf of Gubbio, a beast so large and ravenous that it would come right into town, would attack and devour fully armed men, and was terrorizing the entire countryside. Francis walks unarmed from the city while onlookers watch nervously from their rooftops. The snarling wolf launches his attack. Francis stops him with the sign of the cross, reasons with him, and persuades him that if he will cease to harm the people, they will feed him. He then leads the animal tranquilly through the streets, their treaty is ratified, and the wolf henceforth drops in daily for a prepared dinner. He becomes a civic pet, and when he dies some years later of old age is deeply mourned by all Gubbio.

Truth or pure fiction? Does it matter? asks the American nature writer Edward Allworthy Armstrong (*Saint Francis: Nature Mystic*); the point is that Francis was radically altering the whole medieval concept of nature. Instead of nature being something alien, threatening to man, or even (as the old Manichaeans had said) diabolical, Francis saw it as a further manifestation of God himself. It has fallen along with humanity, but like human beings and like the wolf of Gubbio, it is to be redeemed.

Nor was his appeal confined to animals and male humans. Women, too, soon came under his spell. One swayed by his sermons was the beautiful eldest daughter of the Offreduccios, a wealthy and well-connected Assisi family that had great expectations that she would contract a fruitful marriage within the local nobility. She had been baptized Clare (meaning "bright") because, it was said, her mother had had a vision just before Clare's birth that her child would shine a clear light on many souls.

As she grew up, Clare Offreduccio had evidenced an extraordinary generosity and desire to care for poor and helpless people. She had expressed a strong inclination to become a nun, wearing a rough hair shirt under her fine clothing, but her family, most unsympathetic, insisted that she marry. Thus, Clare, along with a cousin who was similarly inclined, left home by night, sought out Francis at Portiuncula, and asked him what they should do. As they talked, says the Franciscan tradition, such brilliant light shone about them that the people of Assisi rushed to the scene, fearing that the woods were on fire. They found only the two women and Francis talking quietly together.

They should place the leading of God before obedience to their parents, Francis told them, then took them to a nearby Benedictine convent, cut their hair, and clothed them in a coarse robe like his own. Next day family members begged Clare to come home, but when she clung to the altar and showed them her shorn hair, they realized that their objections were futile. However, after she was joined by her younger sister, Agnes, aged fifteen, Francis knew there would be trouble. He moved all three women to the Benedictine Abbey of St. Angelo on a nearby mountainside.

Some twelve armed horsemen followed them there the next day and dragged off the shrieking Agnes until, so the story goes, the prayers of her elder sister miraculously saved her. Agnes's body suddenly became too heavy for them to carry, says the chronicle, and when one of her abductors sought to subdue her with his fist, a sharp pain in his hand briefly rendered it useless. Clare, catching up to them, berated the men so severely that they sheepishly abandoned the whole idea and quietly left. A third Offreduccio sister later joined them as well, and the bishop of Assisi gave them the Church of St. Damian as a refuge.

FRANCIS ON THE VIRTUE OF SERVING GOD BY BEGGING:

As strangers and pilgrims in this world who serve God in poverty and humility the friars should beg alms trustingly. There is no reason why they should be ashamed, because God made himself poor for us in this world.

The order of the Poor Clares has continued into the twenty-first century, consisting of Franciscan women who, like Francis before them, have taken literally the injunctions of Jesus regarding service to others. This nun is a member of the Poor Clares at an educational center for blind children in Warsaw, Poland. At the end of the twentieth century there were over twenty thousand Poor Clare nuns living in seventy-six countries throughout the world.

They all agreed that when they inherited their family's fortune, they would give it all away. However credible all the details of this history, one thing is unarguable. The second order of St. Francis, known as the "Poor Clares," thereupon came into being.

The Poor Clares took up the Franciscan cause as Francis himself had done, begging for their food and caring for the sick, but much of their subsequent story centers on Clare and the strict austerity she imposed upon herself. For example, she communed with God every day from noon to Nones (a monastic service usually said in the late afternoon), often weeping as she meditated on the suffering of Christ. After one such meditation had gone on for more than twenty-four hours, a sister had to startle her into reality and remind her that Francis had forbidden her to remain more than a day without food. On another occasion she spent an entire day sprinkling her sisters with holy water. She slept on a bed of boards and rose first in the morning to help with the menial chores assigned to the younger women who joined the order.

Otherworldly though Clare might be, however, she could rise swiftly to purely mundane necessities. She was eminently practical and level headed in a crisis, she rarely lost an argument, even with popes, and her prayers often brought decisive results. When Muslim troops in the pay of Emperor Frederick II were burning, looting, and raping their way through the anti-imperial cities of Italy, for example, people insisted that it was her petitions to God that caused them to bypass Assisi (see chapter 6).

The monastery at Mount La Verna, in the Apennine mountains near Arezzo, about forty miles northwest of Assisi and forty southeast of Florence. The entire mountain was given to Francis by Count Orlando of Chiusi-in-Consentino as a place of spiritual retreat. It was on this mountain that Francis would later receive the stigmata.

Her personally imposed austerities soon weakened her physically and rendered her frequently ill. She was not proud of this, however. She often required her Poor Clares to ease their fasting rules and forbade them to follow her example. She would die just short of sixty (her birth date is uncertain), reportedly while discussing the beauty of God and his works with Francis, who had died twenty-seven years earlier.

In 1212 after Francis preached in Camara, practically the whole town wanted to join him. This, by one account anyway, gave rise to a third order consisting of laymen and laywomen whose responsibilities prevent them from becoming friars or joining the Poor Clares but who share the commitment of those who do. The early rule of the tertiaries, as they are called, was patterned on that of the Friars Minor, with allowances for the different circumstances in which they lived. Though the locations and identities of their first communities are obscure, historians agree that many people joined. Some tertiary recruits were especially notable, like wealthy Luchesio of Poggibonsi and his wife, who went about with a donkey laden with gifts for the poor, or the Roman widow Giacomina, who was with Francis at his death, or Count Orlando of Chiusi-in-Consentino, who bestowed upon Francis one material gift that he did not refuse.

This was a property atop Mount La Verna, near Arezzo, about forty miles northwest of Assisi and forty southeast of Florence. It was ideal, said Orlando, for the contemplation of God, and it so enchanted Francis that he sought the advice of Clare. Should he now leave his work to others and take up a contemplative life instead? He should not, she swiftly replied. He should go on with the work God gave him. So he did, but thereafter La Verna became a permanent place of retreat and meditation for the Franciscans.

Another diversionary challenge haunted Francis. He lived in the era of the Crusades, when thousands of men were losing their lives in the service of Christ. But it would be better, he reasoned, to create Christians than to kill Muslims. Therefore, when he heard of the Christian victory in Spain at Las Navas, he took this as a sign to act. Three times he tried to reach Muslim leaders, but only on the third try did he actually get to confront one of them. In the first instance he set sail from an Italian port for the Christian posts along the Palestine coast, but his ship was driven up on the Adriatic shore. With no money to get home, he had to stow away on an Italy-bound vessel (thus qualifying as the patron saint of stowaways). Next he sought to reach the Muslims in Spain but was dissuaded and instead recruited a whole host of Spanish newcomers to the Franciscan order.

At last, however, in the summer of 1219 he landed at Damietta, in the Nile Delta, just as a Christian army was about to attack the city in what its commander felt certain would be a successful assault. Francis, warned in a dream, predicted a disaster, which the assault did indeed become. Four thousand Christians were killed, and the town still held. Suddenly Francis found himself revered as a prophet—a number of crusader knights joined the Friars Minor—but Francis persisted in his original purpose. Early that fall, with one Franciscan brother, he approached the Muslim lines.

He was seized immediately and marched before Sultan al-Kamil, who had had tiny crosses strewn across the carpet before him. "If this man walks on the

FRANCIS ON HOW GOD TRANSFORMS THE REPULSIVE:

When I was in sin, the sight of lepers nauseated me beyond measure; but then God himself led me into their company, and I had pity on them. When I had once become acquainted with them, what had previously nauseated me became a source of spiritual and physical consolation for me.

Francis preaches to Sultan al-Kamil of Damietta in this nineteenth-century lithograph by Gustave Doré. Having won the respect of the sultan by responding cleverly to a riddle, Francis was returned to the Christian lines as a distinguished state visitor, albeit unsuccessful in having converted the amused sultan.

crosses," he reasoned, "he will insult his God. If he refuses to walk on them, he will insult me." Francis boldly strode over the crosses, explaining that there was more than one cross on Calvary and one of the others belonged to a thief. The sultan burst out laughing and, in the Franciscan account, began the first of several conversations between them. Francis urged him to take up the real cross and become Christian; al-Kamil protested that his people would destroy him if he did such a thing. At length he sent Francis back to the Christian lines as a distinguished state visitor. "Remember in your prayers your friend the sultan," he besought him, "and ask God to show him how best to please him." Soon afterward the Christians launched another assault on Damietta and conquered the city. Informed of their subsequent massacre of the Muslim defenders, Francis wept bitterly and returned, defeated, to Italy.

Another and very different kind of defeat awaited him there. In his absence the order had been rapidly descending into chaos. It now consisted of several thousand zealously committed members, many of whom had given up everything to join it, and three major issues were dividing the brothers. Did the rule of poverty actually require them to provide no place whatsoever to live? Did it really mean that priests among them must not own a breviary or that none of them should own a Bible? Second, could they actively seek the approval of bishops to preach in any diocese, or would such a request be considered "seeking privilege"? Finally, should they be permitted to study? Francis felt that any learning exposed a man to pride, the greatest of all the sins.

Early on he had taken to calling annual meetings of the entire membership, which were called "chapters," always held at Portiuncula, and at the chapter of 1217 some radical changes had been made. The order had been divided into provinces: six in Italy, two in France, and one each in Spain, Germany, and the Holy Land. Each was to be headed by a "minister," and some were to be subdivided into custodies, headed by a "custodian." Two brothers were designated ministers general, their precise authority undefined. Revision of the rule, which would be needed to resolve any questions, had been set aside until Francis's return from Egypt, an eventuality some doubted because they thought him dead. Meanwhile, for the chapter of 1220 about five thousand brothers somehow crowded into Portiuncula.

A crusader with a very different idea

Converting Islam requires not soldiers, said Raymond Lull, but reason, courage, learning, and faith, and this 'father of computer science' took on the job himself

Aboard the Genoese ship taking him home to Europe from Tunis, Raymond Lull made up his mind. There was no avoiding it—he must go back. He had scandalized the devout Muslims of Tunis with his evangelizing, contravening the Qur'an's decree that to preach Christ to a Muslim is punishable by death. Only with the help of an influential Muslim friend had he escaped with his life.

But what of all those thousands of people whose eternal fate depended on hearing the Christian Gospel? Would they escape? Not likely. So whatever fate might await him there, he must return. Before all else he was a missionary, and his mission field was the Muslim world.

Before all else? There had been a great deal "else." Lull was born in 1232 into a wealthy family on Majorca, largest of the Balearic Islands off Spain's east coast, five years after the Christians recovered the Balearics from Islam.[1] Married with two daughters, he was a noted scholar who had tutored Aragon's future king, served as chief administrator to the lord of Majorca, and written the first novel in Catalan, the Majorcan language. Some authorities consider this the first novel in all western Europe.

Lull's seminal work on the relationship between reason and faith was studied in every major European university. Seven hundred years later his foundational studies on mathematical probabilities would be rediscovered, and he would be credited with contributions to election theory, with election strategists referring to "Lull winners" and "Lull losers." He would also be hailed as a founding father of computer science because his system of logic has been taken as the beginning of information science, which ultimately led to the computer age. But his greatest early delight was in the salacious poems and stories of seduction and lust—based entirely upon his own unbridled and predatory experience of women—with which he titillated the courts of Europe.

But all this had happened before one fateful day when, at about age thirty, he beheld a vision of the crucified Christ in the air beside him. He tried desperately to banish it from his mind, according to his autobiography, but could not. That was half the story; the other half came from a very different experience immediately preceding this vision. While engaged in the seduction of a certain dignified lady, he was thrilled when she

Raymond Lull, depicted here in statue near Palma, Lull's birthplace on the island of Majorca, now part of Spain. Lull left behind a libertine life of carnal questing after, it was said, beholding with horror the corruption of fleshly disease.

opened her bodice before him to disclose her breasts—and he saw that they were both eaten away with cancer.

This, he saw, was the destiny of all flesh, and he wrote no more lustful poetry. He spent five years as a hermit and then became a tertiary (lay member) of the Franciscan order, traveling through Europe to urge a new kind of crusade. The new crusaders, he said, must be skilled not in arms but in reason, able to persuade Muslims of the truth of Christianity. Therefore, they must know the Qur'an as well as any Muslim. They must be fluent in Arabic, Hebrew, and Chaldean, a form of Aramaic, the language spoken by Jesus. And they must be prepared to die, not as soldiers but as martyrs, which they might well become. It was a magnificent message. Few listened.

So Lull, though now over eighty years old, acted on his own, returning twice more to Tunis, and on the second visit he finally made progress when three Muslim imams (preachers) sought baptism. A story of Lull's subsequent martyrdom (that he was stoned to death) was later discovered to be a seventeenth-century falsification. He died in his home at Tunis in 1315.

The church subsequently rejected his teachings on reason as he was found to have a wrong understanding of how faith and reason interrelate. That Lull was a devout Christian no one doubted, however. He was given the titles of "Blessed" and "Illuminated Doctor," and a university in Barcelona was named for him.

Much later, other honors would be bestowed upon him. Martin Gardner, popular twentieth-century mathematics and science author, would write extensively about Lull. Lull would become John Masefield's model for the character Cole Hawlings in his children's novel *The Box of Delights*, adapted by the BBC for television in 1984. He would also, strangely, emerge as a twentieth-century comic book figure, inspiring the character Richard Madoc in DC Comics' *Sandman* series, and in Marvel Comics his 1305 book *Ars Magna* ("the Great Art"), magically enhanced by animation, would become a weapon against the wicked Scarlet Witch.

Raymond Lull would surely have been delighted. He knew a lot about that Scarlet Witch. ∎

1. There are three versions in English of this man's name: Raymond Lull, Ramon Llull, and Raymond Lully. In Spanish he is Raimundo Lulio.

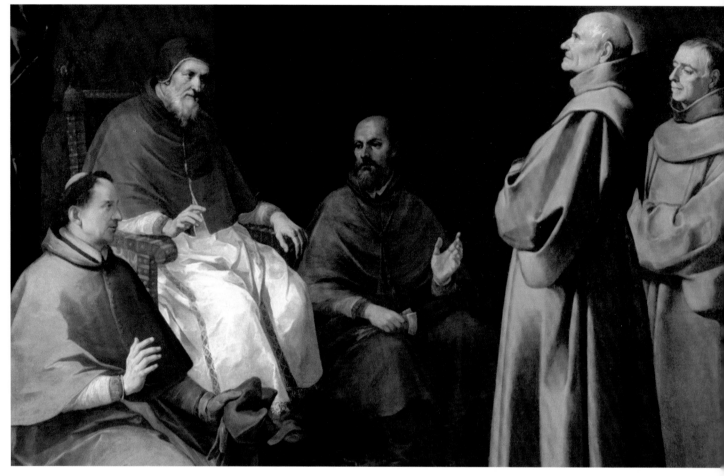

Brother Giles (second from right) appears before Pope Gregory IX in this seventeenth-century painting by Bartolomé Esteban Murillo. One of the first four Franciscans, Giles worked with the pope on the delicate problem of reforming the rule of the order following Francis's death. The task was to make Franciscan life tenable for a large organization without destroying Francis's vision of "holy poverty" in the process. Giles was not always happy with the result.

Francis came home ill from his trials at Damietta, and what he saw drove him into a frenzy. Some of the brothers had begun building a sizeable refuge at Portiuncula. Francis scrambled to the roof and began throwing the tiles down to the ground. Meager buildings today would soon become palaces, he warned. Many brothers were clinging to their breviaries, and many more owned Bibles. Learned brothers—and they were numerous—were hiding their books and continuing to study.

But Francis had also insisted on the "independence" of the friars, telling them that each should primarily seek the guidance of God for his conduct, and this had resulted in abuses. Some had involved themselves with women. Not a few were acquiring housing. One enterprising soul had led a whole leper colony into Rome to visit the pope. Francis now saw his entire work falling to pieces, writes Omer Englebert, and he was about to endure "a unique trial, a torture particularly long and cruel, a distress of conscience, serious and profound." He would have to "walk in darkness, a prey to indecision and doubt."

What saved him from despair and his movement from disintegration was Rome. From Pope Innocent III onward, papal authorities had been carefully observing the Franciscans because they represented both in principle and in practice what was being commonly referred to as "reform." Few disagreed that reform was desperately needed, particularly reform of the clergy, and cries for reformation were heard everywhere. These usually were accompanied by denunciatory rhetoric that sought to destroy the existing fabric of the church while offering nothing very credible to replace it, but the Franciscans were different. They were a positive, not a negative, force, and people loved them for it. The difficulty was that as a formula for such a massive human endeavor as this one, Francis's teachings were, frankly, impossible. Human nature being what it is, they just would not work, Sermon on the Mount or no Sermon on the Mount. Some few men could live by begging; some thousands of men could not.

But who could ever persuade Francis of this? As it so often had done, Rome came up with the right man at the right time. A cousin of Innocent III, Cardinal Ugolino of Conti (called in some English translations Hugolin), who loved and admired the Franciscans, had been designated to act as their link with the rest of the church. At a chapter held while Francis was in Egypt he had instituted a novitiate. A man could no longer simply join; there must be an initiation process. He solved the building problem by getting the chapter to agree that title to every property the Franciscans acquired should pass immediately to Rome. Thus, both

Francis conceded that changes to his rule of life were certainly necessary, but he resigned brokenhearted as head of the order. He had dreamed men could live as Jesus had directed, but it seemed they could not.

collectively and individually they would still own nothing. Finally, Francis's skepticism about a role in learning for his followers was simply rejected. The Franciscan schools at Paris and Oxford would play a definitive role in scholarly development in the High Middle Ages, though this last departure was never universally favored within the order. "Ah, Paris, Paris!" lamented Brother Giles. "It is you who are ruining the Order of St. Francis."[4]

Although Francis conceded that Ugolino's changes were undoubtedly necessary, he resigned brokenhearted as head of the order. He had had a dream that men could live as Jesus had directed, but it seemed they could not, not, anyway, in the numbers who had answered his challenge. For some years he brooded on this, at one instant penitently accepting it, in the next raging against it and condemning those calling for change. "Let them be denounced by you, O Lord, those men whose evil example shames the good friars," he cried. Or, again, "I will go to the chapter and show them who I am!"

Meanwhile, under Ugolino's guidance he worked to revise the rule. He and a brother came up with one revision, which was "lost" by Brother Elias, the minister general, meaning destroyed as hopelessly too strict. A second revision, submitted in 1223, was accepted and is still the rule of the Franciscans.[5] But after Francis's death, Brother Elias with his efficiencies would come as close to wrecking the movement as Francis himself had done with his inefficiencies.

Years of despair, numbering perhaps seven and known as the "Temptations of St. Francis," came to an end much as the years of his great achievements had begun: with a vision of Christ. "Poor Little Man," Jesus said to him, "why are you so sad? Is your order not also my order? Is it not I who am the Chief Shepherd? Then stop being so conflicted, and take care of your own salvation." Francis heard and obeyed, and the agony finally ended.

By now his order, whatever its organizational woes, had spread even more widely. In Portugal the Franciscans were treated as "undesirables" until a royal princess befriended them. In Germany their first missionaries spoke no German

4. Englebert, in his biography, tells how the Franciscan minister at Paris had begun building a magnificent palace called Vauvert. Francis ordered it torn down. It wasn't, but soon afterward, doubtless much to the satisfaction of brothers like Giles, it fell down anyway. Parisians took to calling the place "le démon vert," or "the green devil."

5. While the revised rule of 1223 still required of the brothers their duties to the poor, it reads more like a series of sermon excerpts than a set of regulations. It pleads with the brothers to stand fast in their profession of poverty and humility, writes the Anglican bishop-historian John Moorman (*The Franciscan Order: From Its Origins to the Year 1517*). Gone are the challenging admonitions to take nothing with them on their journeys, as is the requirement to travel on foot. In a final compromise, if the brothers are unable to actually renounce everything they own, "then their good intention shall suffice."

but elicited a remarkably amiable reaction by answering every question with the word "*Jah*," until suddenly amiability turned to fury and they were chased out of town. Later they learned the explanation. Someone had asked them if they were Cathars, that is, heretics. In Hungary the initial reaction was angry rejection, but people later came round. In England, where they centered themselves in London, Cambridge, and Oxford, they went barefoot all winter, sometimes wading knee-deep through icy swamps, and became especially noteworthy for their poverty. So appalling did conditions there become that on one occasion as they contemplated the absurdity of their plight (several having once been rich men), they were reduced to uncontrollable laughter.

With all this, the stories and legends grew, like those about a certain Brother Juniper, who by giving his clothes away, repeatedly came home in his underwear and at least once stark naked. On another occasion he was arrested as a spy and, feeling it wrong to defend himself, was very nearly executed. There is also the story of three robbers who came to a Franciscan house to steal food and were confronted by a gigantic brother, a former knight, who chased them off the property as vicious miscreants who preyed upon defenseless people. But Francis himself, who was there at the time, ordered this brother to follow the robbers with a good dinner. He did so. Next day they returned carrying armloads of firewood for the brothers, and in time all became Franciscans.

Francis's own role in the movement after 1221 rapidly declined. He did not attend the chapter of 1224 but instead retired, very ill, to Mount La Verna with a few of his original followers.[6] There, on a frightening night when the whole forest seemed to come alive with light, as on the night when Clare had fled to him, the wounds of the Lord's stigmata appeared in his hands and his feet.[7]

Soon after this it was time for Francis to return to Assisi, suffering by now from the pain of the wounds in his hands and his feet, from a gastric disease, and from increasing blindness. Plainly, he was dying, and he knew it. His farewell blessing, written to his old friend Brother Leo, was taken from Aaron's blessing to the Israelite people (Numbers 6:24–26) and would be repeated for generations to come by Christians of all denominations: "The Lord bless thee and keep thee: the Lord make his face to shine upon thee and be gracious unto thee; the Lord lift up the light of his countenance upon thee and give thee peace." This he inscribed on a piece of parchment that Leo would carry until his death. It is at St. Francis Church at Assisi, still creased where Leo folded it to put it in his pocket.

At St. Damian's Church, where he had first answered Christ's call, now the center for the Poor Clares, Clare herself had prepared a little reed hutch where Francis could now lie on the ground, as he preferred to do. It was far from comfortable in other respects as well, being infested by mice that shared his meals with him and ran over his body all night.

Such were the circumstances in which Francis wrote the verses known as the *Canticle of the Sun*, and many believe them the greatest tribute to the God of nature ever produced. Based on the 148th Psalm, they portray all the creatures of the Earth united in chorus under the leadership of "Sir Brother Sun"—including "Sister Moon" and "Brother Wind," "Sister Water" and "Brother Fire," and, finally, "Sister Mother Earth" herself—all singing together the praises of the God who brought them into being. Francis sang it first to Clare, say

6. At Christmas that year at Mount La Verna, Francis reconstructed the scene of Jesus' birth at Bethlehem, with the crèche (or crib) surrounded by Mary and Joseph, farm animals, and shepherds, and there they celebrated "Christ's Mass." This was the first recorded crèche scene, which would be duplicated in the churches, in the front yards, and on the mantelpieces of millions upon millions of Christians from that time to this.

7. Francis's experience is the first recorded instance of the phenomenon of the stigmata, wounds that appear in the hands, side, wrists, and/or feet of some Christians. The term comes from the Greek word for a sign, or brand, such as would have been imposed on a slave. Paul used the word in his Epistle to the Galatians when he wrote, "I bear in my body the marks of Jesus." The *Catholic Encyclopedia* cites a nineteenth-century study conducted by Dr. Antoine Imbert-Gourbeyre, who found that twenty such cases appeared in the century after Francis and three hundred by the end of the nineteenth century. All these occurred in Catholics, most of them members of religious orders, in a ratio of seven to one, women to men. By the end of the twentieth century the number had increased to five hundred, the newer cases running five female to four male and including some Protestant Christians. That some of these are fakes seems as certain as that some are also factual. While the existence of the stigmata is no longer challenged, much controversy centers on the cause, with some citing them as miraculous while skeptics and some Christians favor a psychosomatic origin.

*In this modern-day painting, artist Anthony van Dyck portrays Francis
near the end of his life, the stigmata clearly visible on his hand.*

the traditions, and her sisters preserved it for four hundred years before it was published to the world in the seventeenth century. Probably the best-known English translation is a version written by the cleric and hymn writer William Henry Draper for a children's Whitsuntide festival in Leeds, England, in 1919 (see text, page 279).

Not long before his death, Francis was prevailed upon to try treating his blindness, now total, by having the area above his eyes cauterized with a red-hot iron. "Brother Fire," said he as the instrument approached, "God made you beautiful and strong and useful. I pray you be courteous with me." Whether courteous or not, Brother Fire was no help to him. Now in very deep pain, he was

Francis comforts a dying man in this early-twentieth-century painting by Giuseppe Mentessi. "O Divine Master," reads one of Francis's prayers, "grant that I may not so much seek to be consoled as to console."

carried from St. Damian's down to Portiuncula, stopping at the point where the whole town of Assisi came into view. He could not see it but remembered it well and prayed for the city he had loved and made known to the world.

Taken to the bishop's residence in Assisi, he felt the end rapidly approaching, and he joyfully wrote the final verse of the canticle: "Welcome, Sister Death." He died reciting the 41st Psalm: "Blessed is he who considereth the poor and needy; the Lord shall deliver him in the time of trouble . . ." As he drew his last breath, say the chronicles, a flock of larks gathered in a nearby tree and sang their own canticle to the setting sun. The date was October 3, 1226.

Neither the expansion nor the fundamental problems of the Franciscan movement ceased with the founder's death. For the next thirteen years attention centered on the figure of Brother Elias, believed to have been a mattress maker by trade and who had been a teacher in a boys' school before joining Francis in 1210. Recognizing his decisive administrative ability and lacking all such skills himself, Francis bestowed considerable authority on him. Of those in the order who thought the begging-bowl era best buried along with Francis, Elias immediately became the champion.

At the chapter following Francis's death, their numbers were not yet large enough to elect Elias minister general, but his word became law at Assisi. There he began building a magnificent church to contain the tomb of the man some were already hailing as the greatest Christian since the apostles, Francis in the meantime having been buried at Assisi's little Church of San Giorgio. The project was strongly supported by Cardinal Ugolino, who became Pope Gregory IX five months after Francis died. The fact that such an opulent memorial was wholly at odds with some of Francis's most cherished principles was dismissed as no longer relevant. His remains were translated to the new building in 1230.[8] Pope Gregory supervised a revision of the rule to allow the friars to make use of buildings, Bibles, and books, although they must not own them, and to provision themselves with food and other necessities. Though pragmatism argued for the change, it represented a root compromise in what Francis had required, dismaying many Franciscans who had given up so much to abide by it.

They were in part vindicated by Elias's subsequent conduct. Gaining the office of minister general in 1232, he spurred rapid development of Franciscan centers and new missions but at the same time imposed a harsh discipline on those friars who opposed the new liberties, particularly on Bernard of Quintavalle, Francis's first recruit, who was forced into hiding to escape Elias's strictures. Meanwhile Elias, according to his critics anyway, began living luxuriously, visiting society's notables on a fine horse accompanied by servants in full livery and dining sumptuously on food prepared by his private chef.[9] It is significant, however, that throughout this controversy Clare supported Elias, not his critics.

Then came the chapter of 1239, ordered by Gregory and held in Rome, which saw Gregory first pay tribute to Elias for the work he had done in the past, then fire him as minister general. Elias subsequently quit the order altogether, took service with the emperor Frederick II, and as an associate of the excommunicated Frederick was himself excommunicated. He would die reconciled to the church, however, although not to the Franciscan order. In succeeding years the order was

FRANCIS ON WHERE TRUE PEACE MUST BEGIN:

They are truly peacemakers who are able to preserve their peace of mind and heart for love of our Lord Jesus Christ despite all that they suffer in this world.

8. On the great day when the remains of Francis were to be translated (i.e., moved) from little St. Giorgio's in Assisi to the magnificent basilica erected by Brother Elias as Francis's shrine, some two thousand Franciscans and numerous bishops and dignitaries attended, all hoping to see the relics of this great saint. They did not, which caused much indignation. Two explanations are recorded. In one, Brother Elias had them moved earlier by civic authorities, fearing a riot as uncontrollable crowds sought to snatch relics from the body. In the other, the remains were carried in a closed coffin to the doors of the basilica, which were then shut against the crowd. The former is more probable.

9. In one account, possibly legendary, Brother Elias is at table eating a sumptuous meal when there comes a tap at the door. A servant opens it to disclose a beggar with a bowl, asking if he might share some of these delicacies. The beggar turns out to be Bernard of Quintavalle, the very wealthy man who had literally given away everything to become Francis's first follower. What casts doubt on the story is the fact that Bernard, a severe and greatly respected critic of Brother Elias, had to live as a fugitive during the Elias regime because he considered his life in danger.

Joachim of Fiore, who died about a half century before Francis was born, was a mystic and a Cistercian abbot of undeniable piety who set up his own monastery. His teaching, fervently embraced by many among the Franciscan Spirituals, linked human history to the three persons of the Trinity: the era of the Father, which was the period of the Old Testament; the era of the Son, which was to last until about 1260; and the era of the Spirit, which would be ushered in by a host of new Christian movements. Some of his writings were rejected by Pope Innocent III's Lateran Council of 1215 and by the provincial council held at Arles in 1263, but he was nevertheless recognized as a *beatus* ("blessed") by the church.

more fortunate in its ministers general, though one of them—John of Parma, champion of the "Spirituals," those Franciscans who fervently hewed to the Franciscan tradition of poverty—wound up accused of the heresy known as Joachimism and was pressured to resign as minister general.[10]

But it was Bonaventure of Bagnorea, minister general from 1257 to 1274, who undoubtedly did most to hold the order together. His sympathies lay with the Spirituals, but he set forth in his "constitutions" a regimen that sought both to preserve Francis's principles and yet to meet practical exigencies. Franciscan churches must be of simple design, without bell towers; vestments must be plain and not of silk or gold cloth; bowls must not be put out for money, nor friars paid for preaching; they must not beg from strangers; they must not try to persuade rich people to be buried in their churches. At the same time, however, scholarly work must be regarded as labor, not leisure. Bonaventure was later canonized, and Ventura city and county in California commemorate his name, as does a town in Quebec, Canada, which, in turn, provided the name for Canada's last commissioned aircraft carrier.

His constitutions did not satisfy the Spirituals, though, and the Franciscan order would remain divided on the issue well into the fifteenth century. So, too, would perennial inveighing against allegedly luxurious living continue to bring rebuke upon the clergy during the Protestant Reformation of the sixteenth century and the French Revolution of the eighteenth and upon wealthy capitalist Christians in the Marxist revolution of the twentieth and the social revolution of the 1960s. Wealth, in short, would continue to have its critics and Lady Poverty her admirers, though none quite so fervent and so consistent as Francis of Assisi. ■

The Basilica of St. Francis at Assisi little accords with the simplicity that Francis so epitomized in his life. For example, it has a bell tower, an accoutrement Francis had always proscribed. The rift between the Franciscan purists, known as the "Spirituals," and those who favored some concessions to worldly comfort would persist for centuries.

The Canticle of the Sun

Verses from St. Francis of Assisi's *Canticle of the Sun* were translated as a children's hymn by the English hymn writer William H. Draper (1855–1933) and are usually sung to the melody composed by Peter von Brachel of Cologne, Germany, in 1623 with the harmony provided by the English composer Ralph Vaughan Williams in 1906:

All creatures of our God and King
Lift up your voice and with us sing,
Alleluia! Alleluia!
Thou burning sun with golden beam,
Thou silver moon with softer gleam!

Refrain: O praise Him! O praise Him!
Alleluia! Alleluia! Alleluia!

Thou rushing wind that art so strong
Ye clouds that sail in Heaven along,
O praise Him! Alleluia!
Thou rising moon, in praise rejoice,
Ye lights of evening, find a voice!
Refrain

Thou flowing water, pure and clear,
Make music for thy Lord to hear,
O praise Him! Alleluia!
Thou fire so masterful and bright,
That givest man both warmth and light.
Refrain

Dear mother earth, who day by day
Unfoldest blessings on our way,
O praise Him! Alleluia!
The flowers and fruits that in thee grow,
Let them His glory also show.
Refrain

And all ye men of tender heart,
Forgiving others, take your part,
O sing ye! Alleluia!
Ye who long pain and sorrow bear,
Praise God and on Him cast your care!
Refrain

And thou most kind and gentle Death,
Waiting to hush our latest breath,
O praise Him! Alleluia!
Thou leadest home the child of God,
And Christ our Lord the way hath trod.
Refrain

Let all things their Creator bless,
And worship Him in humbleness,
O praise Him! Alleluia!
Praise, praise the Father, praise the Son,
And praise the Spirit, Three in One!
Refrain

PREVIOUS VOLUMES IN THIS SERIES

VOLUME ONE:

The Veil is Torn

A.D. 30 to A.D. 70
Pentecost to the
Destruction of Jerusalem

VOLUME TWO:

A Pinch of Incense

A.D. 70 to 250
From the Fall of Jerusalem
to the Decian Persecution

VOLUME THREE:

By This Sign

A.D. 250 to 350
From the Decian Persecution
to the Constantine Era

VOLUME FOUR:

Darkness Descends

A.D. 350 to 565
The Fall of the
Western Roman Empire

VOLUME FIVE:

The Sword of Islam

A.D. 565 to 740
The Muslim Onslaught all
but Destroys Christendom

VOLUME SIX:

The Quest for the City

A.D. 740 to 1100
Pursuing the Next World,
They Founded this One

BIBLIOGRAPHY

Abelard, Peter, and Heloise. *The Letters of Abelard and Heloise.* Harmondsworth, UK: Penguin, 1974.

Abulafia, David. *Frederick II: A Medieval Emperor.* New York: Oxford University Press, 1988.

Adler, Mortimer J. *St. Thomas and the Gentiles.* Milwaukee, WI: Marquette University Press, 1948.

Allen, W. E. D. *A History of the Georgian People.* London: Kegan Paul, Trench, Trubner, 1932.

Andrewes, Patience. *Frederick II of Hohenstaufen.* Oxford, UK: Oxford University Press, 1970.

Aprem, Mar. *Nestorian Missions.* Trichur, India: Mar Narsai Press, 1976.

Aquinas, Thomas, Albert Magnus, and Philip the Chancellor. *The Cardinal Virtues: Aquinas, Albert, and Philip the Chancellor.* Toronto, Canada: Pontifical Institute of Mediaeval Studies, 2004.

Aquinas, Thomas. *A Shorter Summa: The Most Essential Philosophical of St. Thomas Aquinas' Summa Theologica.* San Francisco: Ignatius Press, 1993.

Armstrong, Edward Allworthy. *Saint Francis: Nature Mystic.* Berkeley: University of California Press, 1976.

Barnes, Harry Elmer. *The History of Western Civilization.* New York: Harcourt, Brace, 1935.

Barton, Simon, and Richard Fletcher. *The World of el Cid: Chronicles of the Spanish Reconquest.* London: Manchester University Press.

Bauerschmidt, Frederick Christian, and Jim Fodor. *Aquinas in Dialogue: Thomas for the Twenty-First Century.* Oxford, UK: Blackwell, 2004.

Bennett, Ralph Francis. *The Early Dominicans: Studies in Thirteenth-Century Dominican History.* Cambridge, UK: The University Press, 1937.

Berman, Constance H. *The Cistercian Evolution: The Invention of a Religious Order in Twelfth-Century Europe.* Philadelphia: University of Pennsylvania Press, 2000.

Bernard, Abbot of Clairvaux. *The Letters of St. Bernard of Clairvaux.* Translated by Bruno Scott James. Kalamazoo, MI: Cistercian Publications, 1998.

Bernard, Abbot of Clairvaux. *Love Without Measure: Extracts from the Writings of St. Bernard of Clairvaux.* Kalamazoo, MI: Cistercian Publications, 1990.

Binns, Leonard Elliot. *Innocent III.* Hamden, CT: Archon, 1968.

Birkhaeuser, Jodocus Adolph. *History of the Church, from its First Establishment to Our Own Times.* Ratisbon, Germany: F. Pustet, 1888.

Bisson, Thomas N. "The Organized Peace in Southern France and Catalonia, ca. 1140–ca. 1233." In *American Historical Review 82* (April 1977), 290-311.

Bloomfield, Morton W. *The Seven Deadly Sins.* East Lansing: Michigan State University Press, 1952.

Boase, T. S. R. *Boniface VIII.* London: Constable and London, 1933.

Bolton, Brenda M. "Philip Augustus and John: Two Sons in Innocent III's Vineyard." In *The Church and Sovereignty, c. 590-1918,* edited by Diana Wood, 113–34. Oxford, UK: Basil Blackwell, 1991.

Bowen, Marjorie. *Sundry Great Gentlemen: Some Essays in Historical Biography.* New York: Dodd, Mead, 1928.

Bradford, Ernle. *The Great Betrayal: Constantinople, 1204.* London: White Lion Publishers Limited, 1975.

Breakspear, Boso. *Boso's Life of Alexander III.* Translated by G. M. Ellis. Oxford, UK: Blackwell, 1973.

Brown, Elizabeth A. R. **"The Prince is Father of the King: The Character and Childhood of Philip the Fair of France." *Mediaeval Studies 49* (1987): 282–334.**

Browne, Laurence Edward. *The Eclipse of Christianity in Asia: From the Time of Muhammad till the Fourteenth Century.* Cambridge, UK: The University Press, 1933.

Bruni, Leonardo. *History of the Florentine People.* Vol. 1. Translated by James Hankins. Cambridge, UK: Harvard University Press, 2001.

Bury, J. B. *The Cambridge Medieval History.* New York: Macmillan, 1911–36.

The Catholic Encyclopedia. www.newadvent.org

Chambers, James. *The Devil's Horseman: The Mongol Invasion of Europe.* London: Weidenfeld and Nicholson, 1979.

Chesteron, G. K. *St. Francis of Assisi.* London: Image, 1987.

Chesterton, G. K. *St. Thomas Aquinas.* London: Houder and Staughton, 1943.

Christiansen, Eric. *The Northern Crusades: The Baltic and Catholic Frontier, 1100–1525.* Minneapolis: University of Minnesota Press, 1980.

Churchill, Winston. *A History of the English-Speaking Peoples.* Vol. 1, *The Birth of Britain.* New York: Dodd, Mead, 1956.

Clari, Robert de, and Ambrose d'Évreux. *Three Old French Chronicles of the Crusades: The History of the Holy War; The History of Them that took Constantinople; The Chronicles of Reims.* Translated by Edward Noble Stone. Seattle: University of Washington, 1939.

Clayton, Joseph. *Pope Innocent III and His Times.* Milwaukee, WI: Bruce Publishing, 1941.

Cleaves, Francis Woodman. *The Secret History of the Mongols.* Cambridge, MA: Harvard University Press, 1982.

Costain, Thomas Bertram. *The Conquering Family.* Garden City, NY: Doubleday, 1962.

Coulton, G. G. *From St. Francis to Dante: Translations from the Chronicle of the Franciscan Salimbene, 1221–1288.* New York: Russell & Russell, 1968.

Coulton, G. G. *Life in the Middle Ages.* Cambridge, UK: Cambridge University Press, 1928–30.

Cowdrey, H. E. J. "The Peace and the Truce of God in the Eleventh Century." *Past and Present 46* (1970), 42–67.

Daniel-Rops, Henri. *Bernard of Clairvaux.* New York: Hawthorn Books, 1964.

Duby, Georges. *Love and Marriage in the Middle Ages.* Cambridge, UK: Polity Press, 1994.

Dunbabin, Jean. *Charles I of Anjou: Power, Kingship and State-Making in Thirteenth Century Europe.* New York: Longman, 1998.

Eastmond, Anthony. *Royal Imagery in Medieval Georgia.* University Park: Pennsylvania State University Press, 1998.

Edgington, Susan B., and Sarah Lambert. *Gendering the Crusades.* New York: Columbia University Press, 2001.

Eliot, T. S. *Murder in the Cathedral.* London: Faber and Faber, 1968.

Englebert, Omer. *Francis of Assisi: A Biography.* Translated by Eve Marie Cooper. Ann Arbor, MI: Servant Books, 1979.

Evans, G. R. *The Mind of St. Bernard of Clairvaux.* Oxford, UK: Clarendon Press, 1983.

Fedotov, G. P. *Peter Abelard: Personality, Self-consciousness and Thought of a Martyr of "Enlightenment."* Belmont, MA: Notable & Academic Books, 1988.

Fenell, John. *The Crisis of Medieval Russia: 1200–1304.* New York: Longman, 1983.

Fisher, George P. *History of the Christian Church.* New York: Scribner, 1895.

Follett, Ken. *The Pillars of the Earth.* New York: W. Morrow, 1994.

Foltz, Richard C. *Religions of the Silk Road: Overland Trade and Cultural Exchange from Antiquity to the Fifteenth Century.* New York: St. Martin's Press, 1999.

Franzius, Enno. *History of the Order of Assassins.* New York: Funk & Wagnalls, 1969.

Frederick II, Holy Roman Emperor. *The Art of Falconry.* Translated by Casey A. Wood. Boston: C. T. Branford, 1943.

Fuller, J. F. C. *The Decisive Battles of the Western World.* London: Eyre & Spottiswoode, 1954–56.

Gautier, Leon. *Chivalry.* Translated by D. C. Dunning. London: Phoenix House, 1965.

Geanakoplos, Deno John. *Emperor Michael Palaeologus and the West.*

Cambridge, MA: Harvard University Press. 1959.

Grabmann, Martin. *Thomas Aquinas: His Personality and Thought.* Translated by Virgil Michel. New York: Russell & Russell, 1963.

Greenaway, George William. *Arnold of Brescia.* Cambridge, UK: The University Press, 1933.

Gregorovius, Ferdinand. *History of the City of Rome in the Middle Ages.* Translated by Gustavus W. Hamilton. New York: Italica Press, 2000.

Gibb, H. A. R. The *Life of Saladin.* London: Saqi Essentials, 2006.

Gimpel, Jean. *The Cathedral Builders.* Translated by Carl F. Barnes, Jr. New York: Evergreen Books, 1961.

Glick, Thomas F. *Islamic and Christian Spain in the Early Middle Ages.* Boston: Brill, 2005.

Goyette, John, Mark S. Latkovic, and Richard S. Myers. *St. Thomas Aquinas and the Natural Law Tradition: Contemporary Perspectives.* Washington, DC: Catholic University Press, 2004.

Grant, Edward. *God and Reason in the Middle Ages.* Cambridge University Press, 2001.

Gray, George Zabriskie. *The Children's Crusade: A History.* New York: William Morrow, 1972.

Habig, Marion Alphonse. *St. Francis of Assisi: Writings and Early Biographies.* Chicago: Franciscan Herald Press, 1973.

Hammer-Purgstall, Freiherr von Joseph. *The History of the Assassins, Derived from Oriental Sources.* Translated by Oswald Charles Wood. New York: B. Franklin, 1968.

Head, Thomas, and Richard Landes. *The Peace of God.* Ithaca, NY: Cornell University Press, 1992.

Herde, Peter. *Colestin V.* Stuttgart: Hiersemann, 1981.

Hiscock, Nigel. *The Symbol at Your Door: Number and Geometry in the Religious Architecture of the Greek and Latin Middle Ages.* Aldershot, UK: Ashgate Publishing, 2008.

Holloway, Julia Bolton, Constance S. Wright, and Joan Bechtold. *Equally in God's Image: Women in the Middle Ages.* New York: P. Lang, 1990.

Innocent III, Pope. The *letters of Pope Innocent III (1198–1216) Concerning England and Wales.* Oxford, UK: Clarendon, 1967.

Isoaho, Mari. *The Image of Aleksandr Nevskiy in Medieval Russia: Warrior and Saint.* Boston: Brill, 2006.

Jackson, Gabriel. *The Making of Medieval Spain.* New York: Harcourt Brace Jovanovich, 1972.

Jarrett, Bede. *Life of St. Dominic (1170-1221).* Garden City, NY: Image Books, 1964.

John, of Salisbury, Bishop of Chartres. *The Letters of John of Salisbury.* Oxford, UK: Clarendon Press, 1979.

Jordan, William Chester. *Louis IX and the Challenge of the Crusade: A Study in Rulership.* Princeton, NJ: Princeton University Press, 1979.

Kantorowicz, Ernst. *Frederick the Second, 1194–1250.* Translated by E. O. Lorimer. New York: Frederick Ungar Publishing, 1967.

Labarge, Margaret Wade. *Saint Louis: The Life of Louis IX of France.* Toronto: Macmillan of Canada, 1968.

Latourette, Kenneth Scott. *A History of Christianity.* London: Eyre & Spottiswoode, 1952.

Latourette, Kenneth Scott. *A History of the Expansion of Christianity.* New York: Harper & Brothers, 1937.

Lea, Henry Charles. *The Inquisition of the Middle Ages: Its Organization and Operation.* New York: Citadel Press, 1963.

Lewis, C. S. *Mere Christianity.* San Francisco: Harper San Francisco, 2001.

MacKay, Angus. *Spain in the Middle Ages: From Frontier to Empire, 1000–1500.* London: Macmillan, 1977.

Maddicott, John Robert. *Simon de Montfort.* New York: Cambridge University Press, 1994.

Mann, Horace K. *Nicholas Breakspear: The Only English Pope.* London: K. Paul, Trench, Trubner, 1914.

Maritain, Jacques. *St. Thomas Aquinas: Angel of the Schools.* Translated by J. F. Scanlan. London: Sheed & Ward, 1948.

Mark, Robert. *Experiments in Gothic Structure.* Cambridge, MA: MIT Press, 1982.

Masson, Georgina. *Frederick II of Hohenstaufen: A Life.* London: Secker & Warburg, 1957.

Maurois, Andre. *A History of France.* London: Methuen, 1964.

McInerny, Ralph. *Aquinas.* Cambridge, UK: Polity Press, 2004.

McNamara, Jo Ann. **Gilles Aycelin: The Servant of Two Masters. New York: Syracuse University Press, 1973.**

Medieval Russia's Epics, Chronicles and Tales. Translated by Serge A. Zenovsky. New York: Dutton, 1974.

Moorman, John. *A History of the Franciscan Order: From Its Origins to the Year 1517.* Oxford, UK: Clarendon Press, 1968.

Munz, Peter. *Frederick Barbarossa: A Study in Mediaeval Politics.* London: Eyre & Spottiswoode, 1969.

Nicholson, Helen. *The Knights Hospitaller.* Woodbridge, VA: Boydell Press, 2001.

Nicholson, Helen. *Templars, Hospitallers, and Teutonic Knights: Images of Military Orders, 1128–1291.* New York: St. Martin's Press, 1995.

The Nikonian Chronicle. Vol. 2, *1132–1240.* Translated by Serge A. Zenkovsky and Betty Jeab Zenkovsky. Princeton, NJ: Kingston Press, 1984.

Otto, Bishop of Freising and Rahewin. *The Deeds of Frederick Barbarossa.* Translated by C. C. Mierow. New York: Columbia University Press, 1953.

Pacault, Marcel. *Frederick Barbarossa.* New York: Charles Scribner's Sons, 1967.

Packard, Sidney Raymond. *Europe and the Church under Innocent III.* New York: H. Holt, 1927.

Pares, Bernard. *A History of Russia.* New York: Alfred A. Knopf, 1953.

Pears, Edwin. *The Destruction of the Greek Empire and the Story of the Capture of Constantinople by the Turks.* New York: Greenwood Press, 1968.

Peers, E. Allison. *Fool of Love: The Life of Ramon Lull.* London: S.C.M. Press Ltd., 1946.

Pennington, M. Basil. *Bernard of Clairvaux.* Kalamazoo, MI: Cistercian Publicaitons, 1977.

Pernoud, Regine. *Women in The Days of Cathedrals.* Translated by Anne Cote-Harriss. Ft. Collins, CO: Ignatius Press, 1989.

Platonov, S. F. *History of Russia.* Translated by E. Aronsberg. New York: Macmillan, 1928.

Powell, James M. *Innocent III: Vicar of Christ or Lord of the World?* Washington, DC: Catholic University of America Press, 1994.

Prawdin, Michael. *The Mongol Empire: Its Rise and Legacy.* Translated by Eden and Cedar Paul. London: G. Allen and Unwin, 1961.

Putnam, Emily James. *The Lady: Studies of Certain Significant Phases of Her History.* New York: Putnam, 1910.

Raedts, Peter. "The Children's Crusade of 1212." *Journal of Medieval History 3* (December 1977), 279–318.

Read, Jan. *The Moors in Spain and Portugal.* London: Faber, 1974.

Read, Piers Paul. *The Templars.* London: Weidenfeld & Nicholson, 1999.

Reston, James, Jr. *Warriors of God: Richard the Lionheart and Saladin in the Third Crusade.* New York: Doubleday, 2001.

Riasanovsky, Nicholas V., and Mark D. Steinberg. *A History of Russia to 1855.* Vol. 1. Oxford, UK: Oxford University Press, 2005.

Runciman, Steven. *The Sicilian Vespers: A History of the Mediterranean World in the Later Thirteenth Century.* New York: Cambridge University Press, 1958.

Runciman, Steven. *A History of the Crusades.* Volume 1, *The First Crusade and the Foundations for the Kingdom of Jerusalem.* Cambridge, UK: The University Press, 1987.

Runciman, Steven. *A History of the Crusades.* Vol. 2, *The Kingdom of Jerusalem and the Frankish East, 1100-1187.* Cambridge, UK: The University Press, 1987.

Runciman, Steven. *A History of the Crusades.* Vol. 3, *The Kingdom of Acre and the Later Crusades.* Cambridge, UK: The University Press, 1987.

Rustaveli, Shota. *The Knight in the Tiger's Skin.* Translated by Marjory Scott Wardrop. Moscow: Co-operative publishing society of foreign workers in the USSR, 1938.

Saunders, J. J. *The History of the Mongol Conquests.* London: Routledge & K. Paul, 1971.

Sayers, Dorothy L. *Creed or Chaos?* New York: Harcourt, Brace, 1949.

Sayers, Jane. *Innocent III: Leader of Europe.* New York: Longman, 1994.

Simson, Otto von. *The Gothic Cathedral: Origins of Gothic Architecture and the Medieval Concept of Order.* New York: Harper Torchbooks, 1956.

Slaughter, Gertrude. **The Amazing Frederick. New York: MacMillan, 1937.**

Southern, R. W. *Western Society and the Church in the Middle Ages.* New York: Penguin. 1970.

Stoyanov, Yuri. *The Hidden Tradition in Europe: The Secret History of Medieval Christian Heresy.* New York: Arkana, 1994.

Strayer, Joseph R. *The Reign of Philip the Fair.* Princeton, NJ: Princeton University Press, 1980.

Suger, Abbot of Saint Denis. *Abbot Suger on the Abbey Church of St.-Denis.* Translated by Erwin Panofsky. Princeton, NJ: Princeton University Press. 1946.

Sumption, Jonathan. *The Albigensian Crusade.* London: Faber & Faber, 1978.

Suny, Ronald Grigor. *The Making of the Georgian Nation.* Indiana University Press, 1988.

Tawney, R. H. *Religion and the Rise of Capitalism.* Harmondsworth, UK: Penguin, 1984.

Taylor, Gabriele. *Deadly Vices.* New York: Oxford University Press, 2006.

Taylor, Maria L. "The Election of Innocent III." In *The Church and Sovereignty, c. 590–1918,* edited by Diana Wood, 97–112. Oxford, UK: Basil Blackwell, 1991.

Tillmann, Helene. *Pope Innocent III.* New York: North Holland Publishing Co., 1980.

Torrell, Jean-Pierre. *Saint Thomas Aquinas, Volume I: The Person and His Work.* Translated by Robert Royal. Washington DC: Catholic University Press. 1993.

Urry, Thomas. *Thomas Becket: His Last Days.* Thrupp, UK: Sutton Publishing, 1999.

Villehardouin and Jean de Joinville. *Memoirs of the Crusades.* Translated by Sir Frank Marzials. Mineola, NY: Dover, 2007.

Walther, von der Vogelweide. *"I Saw the World": Sixty Poems from Walther von der Vogelweide (1170–1228).* Translated by Ian G. Colvin. Westport, CT: Hyperion Press. 1938.

Webb, Diana M. "The Pope and the Cities: Anticlericalism and Heresy in Innocent III's Italy." In *The Church and Sovereignty, c. 590–1918,* edited by Diana Wood, 135–52. Oxford, UK: Basil Blackwell, 1991.

Weir, Alison. *Eleanor of Aquitaine: By the Wrath of God, Queen of England.* London: Jonathan Cape, 1999.

Wilkinson, John, Joyce Hill, and W. F. Ryan. *Jerusalem Pilgrimage, 1099–1185.* London: Hakluyt Society, 1988.

Wood, Charles T. *Philip the Fair and Boniface VIII: State vs. Papacy.* New York: Holt, Rinehart and Winston, 1967.

Zwemer, Samuel Marimus. *Raymond Lull, First Missionary to the Moslems.* New York: Funk & Wagnalls, 1902.

PHOTOGRAPHIC CREDITS

INDEX